British Identities befo:

Inspired by debates among political scientists over the strength and depth of the pre-modern roots of nationalism, this study attempts to gauge the status of ethnic identities in an era whose dominant loyalties and modes of political argument were confessional, institutional and juridical.

Colin Kidd's point of departure is the widely shared orthodox belief that the whole world had been peopled by the offspring of Noah. In addition, Kidd probes inconsistencies in national myths of origin and ancient constitutional claims, and considers points of contact which existed in the early modern era between ethnic identities that are now viewed as antithetical, including those of Celts and Saxons. He also argues that Gothicism qualified the notorious Francophobia of eighteenth-century Britons.

A wide-ranging example of the new British history, this study draws upon evidence from England, Scotland, Ireland and America, while remaining alert to European comparisons and influences.

COLIN KIDD is Lecturer in History, University of Glasgow. His publications include *Subverting Scotland's Past* (1993).

British Identities before Nationalism

Ethnicity and Nationhood in the Atlantic World, 1600–1800

Colin Kidd

CAMBRIDGE
UNIVERSITY PRESS

CAMBRIDGE UNIVERSITY PRESS
Cambridge, New York, Melbourne, Madrid, Cape Town, Singapore, São Paulo

Cambridge University Press
The Edinburgh Building, Cambridge CB2 2RU, UK

Published in the United States of America by Cambridge University Press, New York

www.cambridge.org
Information on this title: www.cambridge.org/9780521624039

First published 1999
This digitally printed first paperback version 2006

A catalogue record for this publication is available from the British Library

Library of Congress Cataloguing in Publication data

Kidd, Colin.
British identity before nationalism: ethnicity and nationhood in the Atlantic world,
1600–1800 / Colin Kidd.
    p.   cm.
ISBN 0 521 62403 7 (hb.)
1. Great Britain – Ethnic relations – History – 17th century. 2. Great Britain – Ethnic
relations – History – 18th century. 3. National characteristics, British – History. 4. Group
identity – Great Britain – History. 5. Constitutional history – Great Britain. 6. Ethnic
groups – Great Britain – History. 7. Nationalism – Great Britain – History. 8. Ethnicity –
Great Britain – History. 9. Celts – Great Britain – History. 10. Mythology, British.   I.
Title.
DA125.A1K53   1999
309.8'00941'09032 – dc 21   98–38429   CIP

ISBN-13 978-0-521-62403-9 hardback
ISBN-10 0-521-62403-7 hardback

ISBN-13 978-0-521-02453-2 paperback
ISBN-10 0-521-02453-6 paperback

Contents

Acknowledgements

This project was begun and largely completed during the tenure of Prize and Post-doctoral Fellowships at All Souls College, Oxford: I remain conscious of an enormous debt to the Warden and Fellows. Various friends have commented on draft chapters: I should like to thank John Robertson, Ian McBride, Brian Young, Scott Mandelbrote, Peter Ghosh, Mark Elliott and Ingmar Westerman. Useful suggestions also came from two anonymous CUP readers. Krzysztof Kosela, Charles Webster and Fiona Stafford have helped in innumerable ways. John Walsh, Prys Morgan, John Durkan, Simon Dixon, Stuart Airlie and Colin Armstrong drew my attention to books I would otherwise have missed. I should also like to acknowledge the great help and kindness of Bill Davies and Karen Anderson Howes at Cambridge University Press. Dorothy Mallon helped with the final preparation of the text.

Lucy, Susan and Adam have tolerated my obsession with this project, as have my colleagues at 9 University Gardens, and I also owe a special word of thanks to Tim King for sustaining morale.

Note

Spelling and capitalisation have been modernised in quotations from English sources. In particular, I have eschewed the unfamiliar early modern rendering of Britons as 'Britains'.

Abbreviations

BJECS	*British Journal for Eighteenth-Century Studies*
Blackstone, *Commentaries*	William Blackstone, *Commentaries on the laws of England* (1765–9: 4th edn, 4 vols., Oxford, 1770)
DF	Edward Gibbon, *The history of the decline and fall of the Roman Empire* (ed. D. Womersley, 3 vols., Harmondsworth, Penguin Classics, 1995)
ECI	*Eighteenth-Century Ireland*
ECS	*Eighteenth-Century Studies*
EHR	*English Historical Review*
H+T	*History and Theory*
HJ	*Historical Journal*
IHS	*Irish Historical Studies*
JEH	*Journal of Ecclesiastical History*
JHI	*Journal of the History of Ideas*
P+P	*Past and Present*
PMLA	*Publications of the Modern Language Association of America*
SHR	*Scottish Historical Review*
SVEC	*Studies on Voltaire and the Eighteenth Century*
WMQ	*William and Mary Quarterly*

1 Introduction

This study addresses the significance of ethnic identity within the early modern British world. What was the ideological status of ethnicity in the centuries which immediately preceded the rise of nationalism and racialism? Was ethnic identity an important constituent of seventeenth- and eighteenth-century political and religious argument? Or was it largely subordinated to the claims of church, confession, kingdom and constitution? A second line of investigation attempts to unravel the orientation and nature of identity construction in this era, not least because its intellectual leaders still subscribed to the Mosaic account of the peopling of the whole world from the stock of Noah. On a more local level, how did the British, the English in particular, conceive of their ethnic relationship to the rest of Europe? Furthermore, was the familiar antithesis of Celt and Saxon part of the early modern world view?

My initial inspiration was derived not so much from the preoccupations of the new 'British' historiography,[1] though these have come to shape the eventual monograph, but from more theoretical themes which concern students of nationalism. There is a general consensus, underwritten by a variety of scholarly approaches in history and the social sciences, that nationalism is a modern invention. However, no single school of modernists monopolises the field, in large part because of the chasm of disagreement over the relative contributions of materialist and idealist factors in the rise of nationalism. Ernest Gellner and others have located nationalism within the vast social and economic upheavals of the past two centuries. Before the advent of commercialisation and industrialisation, it is argued, culture was peripheral to economic life, however

[1] See e.g. J. G. A. Pocock, 'British history: a plea for a new subject', *Journal of Modern History* 47 (1975), 601–21; Pocock, 'The limits and divisions of British history', *American Historical Review* 87 (1982), 311–36; H. Kearney, *The British isles: a history of four nations* (Cambridge, 1989); L. Colley, *Britons: forging the nation 1707–1837* (New Haven and London, 1992); A. Grant and K. Stringer (eds.), *Uniting the kingdom? The making of British history* (London, 1995); S. Ellis and S. Barber (eds.), *Conquest and union: fashioning a British state 1485–1720* (London, 1995); B. Bradshaw and J. Morrill (eds.), *The British problem, c. 1534–1707* (Houndmills, 1996).

controversial it might have been in the religious sphere. Indeed, within early modern Europe, elite and popular cultures stood at a wide remove from one another. There was often more cultural affinity between elites across borders than existed within a state between elite and indigenous folk cultures. Modernisation, according to Gellner, changed all this. The imperatives of commercial and industrial mobilisation dictated the creation of large pools of numerate and literate employees who could facilitate the requisite calculations, transactions and bureaucratic regulations. As a result, the political centres of the European state system, particularly within the great multiethnic empires, pressured peripheral communities, whether local, confessional or national, to conform to national norms. Thus culture became intensely politicised, provoking the rise of self-conscious nationalisms, a situation exacerbated by the unevenness of economic development between regions and ethnic groups.[2] Although the broad contours of the Gellner thesis are persuasive, the specifics carry less conviction. In central and eastern Europe there are problematic time lags between the advent of nationalist intelligentsias and agitations and the later appearance of the new economic structures with their attendant dislocations. Gellner's is by no means the only version of the materialist interpretation of the rise of nationalism. Eric Hobsbawm and Miroslav Hroch have advanced more straightforwardly Marxist versions of the phases of development of nationalist movements.[3] Moreover, there is another important variant of the materialist argument, associated with Karl Deutsch, Benedict Anderson and Eugen Weber, among others. This body of work stresses the role of modern communications, including developments in print media and the ever-increasing intrusion into the peripheries of fiscal-military states, in the rise and provocation of nationalisms.[4]

Even within the idealist camp scholars have staked out markedly different positions, though their basic chronologies are similar, with the late eighteenth century identified as the crucial watershed. Isaiah Berlin recognised the rise of nationalism as a by-product of the Counter-Enlightenment, a wave of particularist reaction led by Herder to the universal liberal ideals of the Enlightenment.[5] A parallel explanation was

---

[2] E. Gellner, *Thought and change* (1964: London, 1972), pp. 147–78; Gellner, *Nations and nationalism* (Oxford, 1983).

[3] E. Hobsbawm, *Nations and nationalism since 1780* (Cambridge, 1990); M. Hroch, *Social preconditions of national revival in Europe* (Cambridge, 1985); Hroch, 'From national movement to the fully-formed nation', *New Left Review* 198 (1993), 3–20.

[4] K. Deutsch, *Nationalism and social communication* (1953: 2nd edn, Cambridge, MA, 1966); B. Anderson, *Imagined communities* (London, 1983); E. Weber, *Peasants into Frenchmen: the modernisation of rural France, 1870–1914* (London, 1979).

[5] I. Berlin, *The crooked timber of humanity* (London, 1991), 'The bent twig: on the rise of nationalism'.

advanced by Elie Kedourie, who traced the emergence of nationalist doctrine specifically to late eighteenth- and early nineteenth-century German philosophy, and in particular to the evolution within Kantian and post-Kantian circles of the values of autonomy and self-determination.[6] However, other scholars, including Eugene Kamenka, have focused more predictably on the French Revolution as the spawning ground for nationalist doctrines of popular sovereignty.[7] This era has also attracted considerable attention from scholars keen to examine the transition from a classical conception of politics, focused on the institutions of the *polis*, to an obsession, both romantic and scientific, with ethnic and racial categories.[8]

The various broad churches of modernism are opposed by primordialists, led by Anthony Smith, who believe that the modernist approach has led to a neglect of important continuities in the long-term evolution of national consciousness. However, even the primordialists accept much of the basic modernist case. Smith denies the contention that nations are 'invented', but his primordialism is qualified by the concession that modern nationhood, which draws on deep ethnic roots, is nevertheless not a direct continuation of older forms of identity, but is rather 'reconstructed' out of pre-existing materials.[9]

Quite apart from this debate over the historic provenance of nationalisms, there is the related issue of whether they correspond to underlying and enduring national 'essences'. Those scholars who advance essentialist interpretations of nationhood are, in academic terms if not by the cruder criteria which reign in the public domain, an uninfluential minority.[10] Indeed, the battle between essentialists and instrumentalists has been largely won by the latter.[11] The major area of disagreement among social scientists is between varieties of instrumentalism and over the degree and type of ficticity involved in the construction of identities. At

[6] E. Kedourie, *Nationalism* (1960: new edn with afterword, London, 1985).

[7] E. Kamenka, 'Political nationalism: the evolution of the idea', in Kamenka (ed.), *Nationalism: the nature and evolution of an idea* (New York, 1976).

[8] M. Thom, *Republics, nations and tribes* (London, 1995); I. Hannaford, *Race: the history of an idea in the west* (Baltimore, 1996). Another modernist-idealist has stood on its head the central premiss that the roots of nationalism are to be found within the fabric of modern culture; rather, argues Leah Greenfeld, *Nationalism: five roads to modernity* (Cambridge, MA, 1992), the idea of nationalism is itself constitutive of modernity.

[9] A. Smith, 'The origins of nations', *Ethnic and Racial Studies* 12 (1989), 348.

[10] However, as A. Hastings, *The construction of nationhood* (Cambridge, 1997), p. 169, points out, there are some cases, such as the Jews and the Gypsies, where there are underlying biological continuities.

[11] The main challenge to the modernist consensus comes not from essentialist-primordialism, but, as A. Smith, 'Gastronomy or geology? The role of nationalism in the reconstruction of nations', *Nations and Nationalism* 1 (1995), 3–23, points out, from the 'cynical, if not playful' deconstructions of the post-modernists.

one extreme instrumentalists reduce identity to political and economic choices. For example, Paul Brass sees ethnic identity formation 'as a process created in the dynamics of elite competition within the boundaries determined by political and economic realities'.[12] Some anthropologists reduce identities to the bare binary oppositions constructed as a matter of course in the relationship of core and periphery, self and other.[13] Even primordial identities are recognised to be constructs. Smith has argued for the antiquity and longevity of ethnocentrisms founded not upon biology, but upon collective *myths* of common descent. According to Smith's formulation, the pre-modern 'ethnies' out of which many nationalisms emerged were 'constituted, not by lines of physical descent, but . . . by the lines of cultural affinity embodied in distinctive myths, memories, symbols and values retained by a given cultural unit of population'.[14]

Secondly, there is the question of ficticity. One of the major implications of the modernist consensus has been to stimulate an awareness that national and ethnic identities are unstable over the *longue durée*. Historians are becoming more vigilant in their avoidance of the fallacy inherited, as Michael Biddiss points out, from nineteenth-century nationalism itself that nations enjoy 'an entirely objective existence'.[15] Within modern historiography and the social sciences most approaches to national and ethnic identity nowadays emphasise their fictive dimensions. Historians and social scientists have become increasingly aware that ethnicity is not a straightforward reflection of common biological descent; rather, ethnic identities are now recognised as cultural fabrications, which can be imagined, appropriated or chosen, as well as transmitted directly to descendants. Many of the differences between the leading modernists, Gellner and Anderson, which lie at the heart of the current debate over identity construction revolve around their respective understandings of fiction and authenticity. Gellner imputes a degree of pejorative inauthenticity to the invention of modern nationalisms. Anderson, however, argues that all communities larger than face-to-face groups, such as tribes and villages, are in a sense imagined. Thus, according to Anderson, all ethnic and national identities are, of necessity, artificial constructs, though none the less authentic facets of the human experience. In spite of these intractable tensions, there is a keen awareness throughout the field that ethnic identities are not timeless, but provisional and pliable, with an elasticity permitting a considerable degree of invention and reinvention.[16]

---

[12] P. Brass, *Ethnicity and nationalism* (New Delhi, 1991), p. 16.

[13] See M. Chapman, *The Celts: the construction of a myth* (Houndmills, 1992).

[14] A. Smith, *National identity* (Harmondsworth, 1991), p. 29.

[15] M. Biddiss, 'Nationalism and the moulding of modern Europe', *History* 79 (1994), 413.

[16] Gellner, *Nations and nationalism*; Anderson, *Imagined communities*.

Mainstream anthropology now eschews the notion that ethnic identities reflect underlying biological, or even to a large extent cultural, truths. Ethnicity is now a question of processes and relationships rather than of ethnic and cultural essences. The Norwegian anthropologist Fredrik Barth highlighted the importance of boundary relationships and their maintenance in the construction and perpetuation of ethnic identities.[17] Yet, according to another Norwegian anthropologist, Thomas Hylland Eriksen, such boundaries are themselves unstable: ethnic identities are both 'situational' and 'negotiated', sometimes undercommunicated, sometimes overcommunicated, according to specific and changing contexts.[18]

The fluidity of identity construction discerned by anthropologists provides useful markers for students of the early modern era, the mental makeup of which was innocent of nationalism and racialism, and which was correspondingly less self-conscious about ethnocentric consistency. Indeed, it is clear that nationalist thinking was alien to the early modern era. The word 'nationalism' itself was not coined until the last decade of the eighteenth century, and thereafter enjoyed a most precarious and marginal existence, appearing in lexicographies only from the late nineteenth century.[19] Despite differences in other areas, scholars are in agreement about the basic constitution of nationalist thought. John Breuilly defines nationalist ideology as 'a political doctrine built upon three basic assertions', namely, that 'there exists a nation with an explicit and peculiar character', that 'the interests and values of this nation take priority over all other interests and values' and that the nation 'be as independent as possible', with an aspiration, 'usually', to 'political sovereignty'.[20] Peter Alter recognises a characteristic ideological feature common to nationalisms: 'In nationalism, the nation is placed upon the highest pedestal; its value resides in its capacity as the sole, binding agency of meaning and justification.'[21] In this respect, according to the primordialist J. A. Armstrong, nationalist doctrine is 'historically novel'; throughout the 'lengthy record of human association', rarely did 'group identity . . . constitute the overriding legitimization of polity formation'.[22]

Given this scholarly consensus about the recent provenance of nationalism, I found myself preoccupied with the puzzle of how one should

[17] F. Barth, 'Introduction', in Barth (ed.), *Ethnic groups and boundaries* (Oslo, 1969).
[18] T. Hylland Eriksen, *Ethnicity and nationalism: anthropological perspectives* (London, 1993).
[19] W. Connor, *Ethnonationalism* (Princeton, 1994), p. 98; R. Williams, *Keywords* (1976: London, 1988 edn), p. 213; P. Alter, *Nationalism* (1985: English transln, London, 1989), p. 7. For 'national' vocabulary in nineteenth-century Europe, see P. Cabanel, *La question nationale au XIXe siècle* (Paris, 1997), pp. 5–9.
[20] J. Breuilly, *Nationalism and the state* (1982: 2nd edn, Manchester, 1993), p. 2.
[21] Alter, *Nationalism*, p. 9.
[22] J. A. Armstrong, *Nations before nationalism* (Chapel Hill, NC, 1982), p. 4.

describe the national identities which preceded the emergence of nation-alism proper without lapsing into anachronistic usage. In a previous book on Scottish identity in the eighteenth century I borrowed the term 'eth-nocentrism' from the work of Anthony Smith to describe national con-sciousness in the early modern era, in an attempt, perhaps clumsy and over-scholastic, to avoid speaking of 'nationalism',[23] a label which I believed – and still believe – to be misleading when applied to the early modern period, which witnessed national consciousness but nothing so explicit or doctrinaire as nineteenth- and twentieth-century nationalisms. However, because I now have considerable doubts as to the role of ethnicity in early modern political culture, I have become less confident about my earlier use of 'ethnocentrism'. Hence, I arrive at my central question: what *was* the place of ethnicity in the discourses of the era preceding the rise of nationalist and racialist ideologies?

The British world between about 1600 and the 1790s provides a useful case study, an environment rich in connections and contrasts. The his-toric patriotisms of England, Scotland and Ireland did not function in isolation, but as a system of competing claims and counter-claims, dominated in the seventeenth century by tensions within the Stuart multiple monarchy, and in the eighteenth by the rise of an overarching Britishness. The eighteenth century also saw the birth of colonial patriot-isms in Protestant Ireland and America. This study aims to tease out the presence and status of ethnicity within the value systems of the intellec-tual elites – lay and clerical – who shaped and articulated the public identities of the British political nations. While a crude xenophobia was, as a number of studies have shown, a potent factor in British popular culture during the seventeenth and eighteenth centuries,[24] the pattern within the mainstream of political argument is considerably harder to discern.

[23] C. Kidd, *Subverting Scotland's past* (Cambridge, 1993).
[24] T. W. Perry, *Public opinion, propaganda and politics in eighteenth-century England: a study of the Jew bill of 1753* (Cambridge, MA, 1962); Colley, *Britons*; C. Haydon, *Anti-Catholicism in eighteenth-century England* (Manchester, 1993); D. Statt, *Foreigners and Englishmen: the controversy over immigration and population, 1660–1760* (Newark, DE, 1995), ch. 7.

Part I

Theological contexts

2   Prologue: the Mosaic foundations of early modern European identity

Historians appreciate that early modern nationhood was inextricably bound up with confessional identity. By contrast, however, the parallel connection between theology and ethnicity has largely escaped the attention of mainstream historiography. Yet this was a profound relationship whose central importance within the realm of Christian apologetic has long been recognised by students of historical theology. For the peopling of the world was a familiar part of sacred history and a topic which occupied a crucial place in the Bible. The first five verses of Genesis 10 constituted the fundamental text which associated the peopling of Europe with the Japhetan descendants of Noah, and described the basic relationships of the various tributaries of the Japhetan lineage:

Now these are the generations of the sons of Noah, Shem, Ham and Japheth; and unto them were born after the flood. The sons of Japheth: Gomer and Magog, and Madai, and Javan, and Tubal, and Meshech, and Tiras. And the sons of Gomer; Ashkenaz, and Riphath, and Togarmah. And the sons of Javan; Elishah and Tarshish, Kittim and Dodanim. By these were the isles of the Gentiles divided in their lands; every one after his tongue, after their families, in their nations.

A few other passages of Scripture also dealt with ethnological matters: the story of the confounding of languages at the Tower of Babel in chapter 11 of Genesis, and some later references to the descendants of Noah in chapter 38 of Ezekiel. These accounts of the dispersal of nations provided a recognised point of departure not only for the study of ethnicity but also for the construction of national identities.

In the seventeenth century the history of Ham, Shem, Japhet and their offspring featured prominently in vainglorious patriotic boasts about the high antiquity and noble lineage of various European nations. Writing in the late eighteenth century, Edward Gibbon noted the utility of a Japhetan genealogy to previous generations of patriotic antiquaries:

Among the nations who have adopted the Mosaic history of the world, the ark of Noah has been of the same use, as was formerly to the Greeks and Romans the siege of Troy. On a narrow basis of acknowledged truth, an immense but rude superstructure of fable has been erected; and the wild Irishman, as well as the wild Tartar, could point out the individual son of Japhet from whose loins his ancestors were lineally descended. The last century abounded with antiquarians of profound learning and easy faith, who, by the dim light of legends and traditions, of conjectures and etymologies, conducted the great-grandchildren of Noah from the Tower of Babel to the extremities of the globe.[1]

Although Mosaic history still had its defenders in the era of Gibbonian raillery, civil history was now clearly demarcated from its sacred counterpart. Yet 'the death of Adam was a slow death'.[2] Even as the human sciences were demythologised, they retained a Mosaic structure. During the seventeenth and eighteenth centuries naturalistic explanation evolved, for the most part, *within* the broad parameters of Scripture history. In the early nineteenth century, long after the bald recitation of Noachic genealogies had fallen into desuetude, many scholars still operated within the Biblical scheme of universal chronology, a matter of approximately six thousand years.[3]

The rise and fall of ethnic theology

To appreciate the discursive priorities of the clerics and literati of the early modern era who engaged with the issues of ethnicity, it is necessary to liberate the historical imagination. Otherwise the pursuit of ethnicity remains trapped within modern categories. In this particular sphere, our minds are still to a considerable degree in thrall to nineteenth-century constructions of ethnic identity. An attempt to introduce the subject of early modern ethnic constructions by way of Mosaic history sharpens the sense of ideological difference between *ancien régime* Europe and the nineteenth-century world of racialism, ethnic determinism and romantic nationalism. Though guilty in practice of prejudice, exploitation and extirpation on grounds of religion and skin pigmentation, early modern Europeans were not intellectually programmed for ethnic hatred. Within the Mosaic scheme, difference mattered less than degrees of consanguinity among a world of nations descended from Noah. Indeed, the primary value of ethnicity was not ethnological in the modern sense, but lay within the theology of 'evidences', where it functioned as a vital weapon in the defence of Christian orthodoxy and the authenticity of Scripture from heterodox assaults.

Matters of race, ethnicity and the genealogies and relationships of

---

[1] Gibbon, *DF*, I, pp. 233–4.

[2] P. Rossi, *The dark abyss of time: the history of the earth and the history of nations from Hooke to Vico* (trans. L. Cochrane, Chicago, 1984), p. 270. See also J. C. Greene, *The death of Adam: evolution and its impact on Western thought* (1959: New York, 1961).

[3] F. C. Haber, *The age of the world: Moses to Darwin* (Baltimore, 1959).

peoples and nations were, in the first instance, part of the province of theology.[4] The culture of early modern Europe – even in the sphere of what is now regarded as experimental science – was fundamentally text-driven.[5] For most of the early modern period, the foundations of human knowledge were not naturalistic. The Bible, along with the writings of the ancients which it trumped, informed the whole terrain of intellectual endeavour. The early chapters of the book of Genesis were obvious starting points for the study of several of the human and natural 'sciences'. Cosmology, geology and linguistics all had their roots in 'sacred history'. Similarly, the Mosaic history of the peopling of the world established broad parameters of Christian orthodoxy for ethnological speculation.

The early modern period fostered such a substantial literature on the Scriptural exegesis of racial, national and linguistic divisions that it seems reasonable to assume that sacred ethnology constituted an important branch of theology in its own right. For convenience this body of learning will be described as 'ethnic theology'. This choice of shorthand illuminates the substance of the argument presented below – namely, that the study of ethnic difference in the early modern period was largely harnessed to religious questions, rather than vice versa. (On the other hand, the Biblical notion of common origins, as we shall see, tended to emphasise an underlying unity – of belief, race, language – at the expense of ethnic differences.) The term 'ethnic theology' was, in fact, used in the seventeenth and eighteenth centuries to describe pagan religion, whose relationship to the patriarchal religion of the Old Testament was at the heart of this discourse.[6] Christianity would emerge all the stronger by the comparison, if heathen polytheism could be shown to be but a corrupt form of the religion of Noah. However, this issue was related to other controversies which impinged on Biblical authority, such as how the world had been peopled and how nations and languages were related. Far from being peripheral topics of antiquarian interest, these subjects intersected with the mainstream of Christian theology.

Early modern ethnography was a vital theatre of the defence of Scriptural revelation against new currents of heterodoxy and scepticism. Many of the most important intellectuals of early modern Europe grappled with the problems of ethnic theology. The voyages of discovery of the late fifteenth and sixteenth centuries, and the subsequent expansion of

---

[4] D. C. Allen, *The legend of Noah* (Urbana, 1949); M. T. Hodgen, *Early anthropology in the sixteenth and seventeenth centuries* (Philadelphia, 1964), esp. ch. 6; A. Grafton, *New worlds, ancient texts* (Cambridge, MA, 1992).

[5] A. Grafton, *Defenders of the text* (Cambridge, MA, 1991).

[6] E.g. Pierre-Daniel Huet, *Demonstratio evangelica* (Paris, 1679), propositio iv, caput tertium, p. 56, used the expression 'ethnicorum theologia' to describe the religion of pagans.

European knowledge about the histories, religions and customs of the civilisations of Asia and America, posed a number of problems for the Christian intelligentsia of early modern Europe, threatening both to subvert the unquestioned authority of European standards and to undermine the intellectual and theological coherence of the Christian world view and the credibility of the Bible as a historical document.[7] One of the most successful responses to the former threat was the natural jurisprudence of Hugo Grotius and his successors – a resort to a skeletal conjectural anthropology of natural man and a few uncontentious ethical axioms, as a way of bypassing the ingrained prejudices of the European cultural inheritance without running into the sands of an unmitigated scepticism.[8] However, while Grotian natural jurisprudence might suffice in the fields of ethics, laws and manners, the threat to the authority of Biblical revelation posed by knowledge of the extra-European world could not be defused without recourse to 'ethnic theology'.

Ethnic theology never developed as a discrete body of learning; it existed rather in the interstices of other nascent disciplines, most notably the comparative study of religion and mythology. In the first instance scholars began to collect the flood of information on the pagan religions of Asia and America in compendia of the world's religions, a new genre of the sixteenth and seventeenth centuries,[9] and then to construct systems of historical theology which accommodated the seemingly bizarre world of paganism to the traditional framework of Christian knowledge and belief.[10] If all mankind was, as the Bible proclaimed, descended from Noah to whom God had revealed himself, then one could not explain polytheistic pagan cultures as distant societies which had strayed into error and superstition inadvertently through lack of exposure to the Christian message. According to the logic of Mosaic history the distant ancestors of pagan peoples must at some stage have been the bearers of the patriarchal revelation. Of necessity, theologians constructed a history of gentile corruption as a central aspect of the history of the peopling of the world. Various presiding figures in the pantheons of gentile nations were identified by defenders of Christian orthodoxy as corrupt relics of an

[7] R. Popkin, 'Polytheism, deism and Newton', in J. Force and Popkin, *Essays on the context, nature and influence of Isaac Newton's theology* (Dordrecht, 1990), p. 27; M. Ryan, 'Assimilating new worlds in the sixteenth and seventeenth centuries', *Comparative Studies in Society and History* 23 (1981), 519–38.

[8] R. Tuck, 'The modern theory of natural law', in A. Pagden (ed.), *The languages of political theory in early modern Europe* (Cambridge, 1987).

[9] Hodgen, *Early anthropology*, pp. 168–72, 203; Grafton, *New worlds, ancient texts*, ch. 3; F. Manuel, *The eighteenth century confronts the gods* (Cambridge, MA, 1959), pp. 6–7; R. Popkin, 'The crisis of polytheism and the answers of Vossius, Cudworth and Newton', in Force and Popkin, *Essays on Newton's theology*, p. 9. See e.g. Alexander Ross, *Pansebeia: or, a view of all religions in the world* (London, 1653).

[10] Hodgen, *Early anthropology*, pp. 262, 266–8; Popkin, 'Crisis of polytheism', p. 9.

original memory of the patriarch Noah.[11] The embryonic science of comparative mythology – whose 'comparative' method was predicated upon diffusionist assumptions – had as its central task the unmasking of the traces of Biblical history which lay beneath the legends and cults of pagan cultures.[12] The practice of deciphering the Noachic survivals that lay beneath the surface of pagan cultures was often yoked to euhemerism, a critical method of deconstructing alien theogonies. Euhemerism was a reductive technique which enabled Christian scholars to expose as mere historical figures the deities of the pagan world. By conjecturing that heathen gods originated in the posthumous deification of founding fathers, statesmen and generals, scholars undermined the numinous authority of non-Christian religions. Although itself a product of pagan philosophy, the brainchild of the ancient philosopher Euhemerus of Messina in the fourth century BC, euhemerism was eagerly adopted by theologians shouldering the burden of a sceptical crisis.[13] Alternatively, Christian Platonists, who believed that humanity's inner reason partook of the divine logos, sought traces in other religions of a universal ancient monotheism, a *consensus gentium* largely concealed by the corrupting accretions of various local cultural forms.[14] There were, of course, limits to the scope for genuine comparative study. Scripture was fenced off from direct comparison; the histories of other cultures could be compared to expose falsehood and drive out myths, whereas comparisons with Hebraic history were designed only to reinforce the validity of the Old Testament.

As scholars attempted to reconcile the religious diversity of the pagan world with the truths of Christianity, comparative religion became hopelessly entangled with Biblical ethnology. The study of ethnicity, or 'gentilism',[15] was, in large part, a matter of accounting for the existence of pagan

[11] Rossi, *Dark abyss*, p. 153; P. Burke, *Vico* (Oxford, 1985), p. 44.
[12] L. Poliakov, *Le mythe aryen* (1971: new edn, Brussels, 1987), p. 162; Rossi, *Dark abyss*, p. 153.
[13] There are useful discussions of euhemerism in A. B. Ferguson, *Utter antiquity: perceptions of prehistory in renaissance England* (Durham, NC, 1993); Burke, *Vico*, p. 43; Manuel, *Eighteenth century confronts the gods*, esp. ch. 3.
[14] D. P. Walker, *The ancient theology* (London, 1972); P. Harrison, *'Religion' and the religions in the English Enlightenment* (Cambridge, 1990), ch. 2.
[15] Ethnicity was connected by etymology and usage to discussions of paganism. Note the link between gens and gentile. Not only did the Jesuit ethnographer, Joseph François Lafitau, *Moeurs des sauvages amériquains, comparées aux moeurs des premiers temps* (2 vols., Paris, 1724), use the term 'la Gentilité', I, p. 117, to describe the pagan world, but his usage of expressions for nation and people carried the same freight, as in his argument, I, p. 109, for 'le témoignage des peuples et des nations' to the truths of Christianity, where the silent epithet 'pagan' is understood; Ryan, 'Assimilating new worlds'; Herbert of Cherbury, *The antient religion of the gentiles* (London, 1705 edn); John Aubrey, *Remaines of Gentilisme and Judaisme* (ed. J. Britten, London, 1881); Theophilus Gale, *The court of the Gentiles* (2 vols., Oxford, 1669–70). For the centrality of the gentile–*gentes* relationship in the work of Vico, see M. Lilla, *G. B. Vico: the making of an anti-modern* (Cambridge, MA, 1993), pp. 93 n., 167–8.

peoples in a world populated by nations whose founding patriarchs had been exposed, prior to the dispersal, to the truths of the religion of Noah. Paganism could not simply be explained away by the fact that the peoples of Asia and America had not been known to medieval Christendom. Rather, why had these peoples forgotten the truths of the Noachic mono-theism of the immediate post-Diluvian period? Ethnology involved the study of the non-Hebraic peoples who had succumbed to false gods. Unlike nineteenth-century anthropology, it was not confined to the study of the 'other'. For the European lineage of Japhet was prominent among the gentile nations, and the theogonies of Greece and Rome were among the pagan deviations from monotheism which had to be explained.

The European encounter with the indigenous peoples of America engaged the attention of the foremost scholars in Christendom, Grotius included. So long as geographers were under the misapprehension that America was a part of Asia, or at least close to its shores, there was no theological problem about the ethnic origins of the inhabitants of the New World. However, as it became clear that America was a distinct conti-nent, the existence of a populated New World propagated doubts about the universality of the Noachian Deluge.[16] Scholars began to tackle the thorny problem of explaining the post-Diluvian origins of the American peoples, and the relationship of these nations to the stock of Noah. The early modern literature of Americana embraced a wide variety of disci-plines, and evolved as it digressed from the critical theme of Noachic origins; however, throughout the period 'extra-theological considerations – geography, ethnology, and faunal distribution – operated within limits imposed by theology'.[17] A wide variety of imaginative solutions emerged in answer to the riddle of American origins. The notion that Noah had developed the arts of navigation while on the Ark enabled some scholars to posit maritime interpretations of the peopling of America by trans-atlantic routes. The seafaring Carthaginians were a common feature of this line of thinking, as were references to Plato's Atlantis. Alternative strategies included the identification with America of Scriptural refer-ences to voyages to the land of Ophir mentioned in I Kings and II Chronicles, and, eventually, the development of the notion that the Indians were the ten lost tribes of Israel mentioned in the apocryphal book of Esdras.[18] A minority tradition attributed the peopling of America to a legendary twelfth-century Welsh prince named Madoc, whose claim was still capable of inspiring patriotic Welsh exploration and ethno-

[16] L. E. Huddleston, *Origins of the American Indians: European concepts, 1492–1729* (Austin, TX, 1967), p. 9; Rossi, *Dark abyss*, p. 30.   [17] Huddleston, *American Indians*, p. 12.
[18] *Ibid.*, pp. 17, 20, 25, 28, 30, 40–3, 65–7.

graphic speculation in the later eighteenth century.[19] However, in northern Europe the most widely accepted version of the peopling of America was based on the notion of a land bridge or short crossing from the icy wastes of northern Eurasia undertaken by post-Diluvian Scythians. The Spanish Jesuit José de Acosta (1540–1600) was perhaps the most celebrated champion of this thesis.[20]

The principal alternative to the Acostan thesis was the argument by Grotius in *De origine gentium Americanarum* (1643) that America had been colonised by the Viking seafarers of northern Europe. As a servant, by this stage of his career, of the Swedish monarchy, Grotius defended not only the legitimacy of Scripture history, but also the claim of Sweden to establish colonies in the New World. Philological researches appeared to reinforce these conjectures, with Grotius comparing the suffixes of Norse toponyms, such as Iceland and Greenland, with those of Amerindian placenames, such as Tenochtitlan and Cuatlan. The Grotian thesis did not displace the Acostan version of the peopling of America as the standard defence of sacred history; indeed, it was in fact immediately challenged by Jan De Laet, a fellow Dutchman, whose argument against the Norse thesis was continued by Georg Horn (1620–70), a German based at the University of Leiden, who in *Arca Noae* (1666) argued for the mixed origins of the indigenous American population in various waves of Phoenician, Chinese and Scythian migration. The Grotius–De Laet controversy was an argument about the relative plausibility of the Grotian and Acostan accounts of American ethnology, not about the unitarian origins of mankind. However, this dispute was a sideshow compared to the fundamental challenge posed to the authority of the Bible by the French theologian Isaac La Peyrère (1596–1676), whose work Grotius had read in manuscript and to which his treatise was, in part, a proleptic response.[21]

The debate over the theological consequences of the New World became much more fraught from the middle of the seventeenth century when La Peyrère in *Prae-Adamitae* (1655) launched one of the most controversial exegetical revisions of the early modern era,[22] which appeared to find a Scriptural basis for mankind's plural origins and a limited

---

[19] G. A. Williams, *Madoc: the legend of the Welsh discovery of America* (Oxford, 1987); Huddleston, *American Indians*, p. 57.

[20] A. Pagden, *The fall of natural man* (1982: Cambridge revised pbk edn, 1986), pp. 193–5.

[21] Grafton, *New worlds, ancient texts*, pp. 210–12, 234–5; Grafton, *Defenders of the text*, p. 206.

[22] R. Popkin, *Isaac La Peyrère (1596–1676)* (Leiden, 1987); Popkin, *The history of scepticism* (1960: Berkeley and Los Angeles, 1979 edn), ch. 11; Grafton, *Defenders of the text*, ch. 8. La Peyrère made an immediate impact in England: see the translations *A theological system upon that presupposition that men were before Adam* (London, 1655) and *Men before Adam* (London, 1656).

Deluge. La Peyrère built his revolutionary thesis for polygenesis from a difficult passage of Scripture – Romans 5, verses 12–14:

> As by one man sin entered into the world, and by sin, death: so likewise death had power over all men, because in him all men sinned. For till the time of the law sin was in the world, but sin was not imputed, when the law was not. But death reigned from Adam into Moses, even upon those who had not sinned according to the similitude of the transgression of Adam, who is the type of the future.

La Peyrère argued that the law had come into the world with Adam, and that at this stage sin, which was already in existence, took on moral significance. By contrast, if the law had come into force only with Moses, then there would be no fall of man with Adam. From this chink in the logical and theological cohesiveness of revelation La Peyrère constructed the argument that there had been men before Adam. In order to account for the continued existence of these peoples, he also rejected the universality of the Flood. Consequently, Genesis, which appeared to provide a history of the Jewish nation and its neighbours only, was too narrow a platform upon which to construct the universal history of mankind.[23]

The matter of ethnic theology ignited one of the largest heresy hunts of the age. Within eleven years of the first edition of *Prae-Adamitae* at least seventeen works had been published with the specific aim of demolishing La Peyrère's thesis.[24] The great heresiarch himself abjured the Preadamite heresy, but with some reluctance; he conceded the authority of the papacy in such matters, but did not acknowledge any intellectual deficiencies in his own scholarship.[25] Despite this renunciation, the critique of Pre-adamitism had brought into being a scholarly industry which continued to operate until at least the 1730s.[26] In part this may have been because of the wider influence of La Peyrère's ideas, which contributed to a related tradition of scepticism about the scope of the Bible as a handbook of knowledge, whether of metaphysics or of universal history. This sceptical line was continued by La Peyrère's friend and biographer, the Oratorian priest, Father Richard Simon (1638–1712) and by the renegade Jewish philosopher Baruch Spinoza (1632–77). Simon's *Histoire critique du Vieux Testament* (1678) analysed the formation of the text of the Bible, and argued, in an idiom which foreshadowed the higher criticism of the nineteenth century, that one could not construct an accurate chronology or genealogy from the Bible. Spinoza argued in his *Tractatus theologico-politicus* (1670) that the Bible was essentially the history of the

---

[23] Rossi, *Dark abyss*, pp. 133–6; Popkin, *La Peyrère*, p. 43.
[24] Rossi, *Dark abyss*, p. 138; Popkin, *La Peyrère*, pp. 80–1. According to Ephraim Chambers (d. 1740), *Cyclopedia* (4 vols., 1786 edn), III, 'Preadamite', the most effective rebuttal of La Peyrère was by Samuel Desmarets of Groningen.
[25] Popkin, *La Peyrère*, pp. 82–3.   [26] *Ibid.*, pp. 80–1.

Jewish nation, and should not be read for deeper significances. These works, which insinuated that the Bible, including the Pentateuch, was a human creation which had emerged over a long timespan, and contained its fair share of errors, developed the sort of logical inconsistencies spotted by La Peyrère into a wider assault on the validity of Scripture.[27]

The other major development that threatened the authenticity of the Mosaic world picture was the awareness that there were civilisations in the gentile world whose antiquity was difficult to reconcile with Genesis. Pre-adamitism exploited the explosive potential of this notion, but its origins predated the insights of La Peyrère. The plausible claims of the gentile civilisations of Egypt, Babylon and China to histories which stretched back into antiquity beyond the recognised limits of Mosaic chronology posed a potent challenge to the validity of the Bible as sacred history. The study of universal chronology became one of the foremost disciplines of the early modern period. It tackled questions of fundamental importance to the identity of Christendom, and it attracted some of Europe's foremost minds from the Renaissance to the Enlightenment, including Scaliger, Ussher and Newton. Astronomy, textual scholarship and mathematical calculations formed important planks in the support for Mosaic chronology. However, there were also several crucial points of contact between universal chronology and ethnic theology, since the defence of sacred history involved relating the founding of the various ancient gentile civilisations to the peopling of the world by Noah's offspring.[28] With the renaissance of classical learning it became imperative to reconcile with Judaeo-Christian accounts of the history of the world the ethnography and chronology of pagan antiquity. The development of Near Eastern studies in the work of such scholars as Guillaume Postel expanded the scope of this field of investigation to include Persian and Babylonian histories.[29] The brilliant Protestant humanist Joseph Justus Scaliger (1540–1609) transformed the whole science of chronology with his *De emendatione temporum* (1583). Scaliger invented the device of the Julian Period – an era of 7,980 years – which enabled the construction of a

[27] Popkin, *Scepticism*, pp. 224–37; P. Hazard, *The European mind 1680–1715* (1935: trans. J. L. May, Harmondsworth, 1964), pp. 213–31; Rossi, *Dark abyss*, p. 212. For the challenge of Simon's hermeneutic method to the authority of traditional chronology and 'ethnic theology', see Richard Simon, *A critical history of the Old Testament* (1678: transln, London, 1682), p. 5: 'As these books are but the abridgements of much more large records, one cannot establish upon the Scripture an exact and certain chronology, because the genealogies are not always immediate.' For the connection between Spinoza's treatment of the Old Testament and the rise of secular nationalism, see C. Cruise O'Brien, 'Nationalism and the French Revolution', in G. Best (ed.), *The permanent revolution: the French revolution and its legacy 1789–1989* (London, 1988).
[28] A. T. Grafton, 'Joseph Scaliger and historical chronology: the rise and fall of a discipline', *H+T* 14 (1975), 156–85.   [29] *Ibid.*, 159.

chronology embracing different calendrical systems, consolidated the expansion of the discipline, discussing more than fifty calendars, and employed the best standards of critical philology alongside the necessary mathematics and astronomy. However, his principal achievement was in replacing a method whereby total reliance was placed on Scripture, and pagan histories were merely complementary rather than authoritative sources, with an approach which recognised that gentile chronologies provided a useful litmus test for ascertaining the validity of rival interpretations of those places in Scripture which were vague, ambiguous or obscure. With the work of Scaliger the antiquities of the various recorded gentile civilisations of the ancient world were accorded a status alongside Mosaic history as valid chronologies. This created a problem. Scholars had long been acquainted with the claims of the Egyptians to a history which stretched back beyond the limits of Old Testament chronology. Scaliger, in effect, forced his contemporaries to admit the irreconcilability of Egyptian and sacred history. He attempted to negotiate a route through this particular chronological jungle in a further treatise *Thesaurus temporum* (1606), but scholarly integrity impeded his progress. Scaliger came to the conclusion that the earliest Egyptian dynasties did indeed predate the era not only of the Flood and Dispersal, but also the Biblical Creation, the latter by some 1,336 years. Instead of distorting historical truth in the interests of Christian orthodoxy, the virtuous humanist acknowledged the impasse which he faced: he divided the phases of universal chronology into a pre-Mosaic 'proleptic time' (the question of whose reality he chose not to discuss) and 'historic time' which accorded with the Bible.[30]

Chronology remained impaled on this paradox until the Dutch scholar Gerard Vossius achieved a plausible subordination of truth to orthodoxy by means of the argument in his *De theologia gentili* (1641) that several of the early lists of Egyptian dynasties had been collateral rather than successive. This allowed Vossius to bring Egyptian history back from an embarrassing prehistoric limbo to an acceptable location within the Mosaic timeframe.[31] However, anxious chronologists continued to gnaw at the bone of Egyptian antiquity, and the question continued to bedevil theological scholarship until the establishment of the discipline of Egypytology on independent secular foundations in the nineteenth century.[32]

---

[30] *Ibid.*; P. Burke, *The Renaissance sense of the past* (London, 1969), p. 47; H. Trevor-Roper, 'James Ussher, Archbishop of Armagh', in Trevor-Roper, *Catholics, Anglicans and Puritans* (London, 1987), pp. 156–7.

[31] Popkin, 'Crisis of polytheism', p. 10; Grafton, 'Scaliger', 175.

[32] Grafton, 'Scaliger'.

However, the antiquity of Egypt was only one of the several Achilles heels in Mosaic history which came to the attention of chronologists. Overseas exploration also brought to the attention of theologians a number of unfamiliar civilisations in Asia and America whose roots appeared to lie deep in antiquity. In particular, the vast extent of Chinese history posed a serious threat to the credibility of the Bible.[33] Paolo Rossi has identified two basic strategies which were deployed in response to the perceived irreconcilability of gentile histories with the Mosaic chronology. First, there was the attempt 'to reduce all different human histories, in more or less complicated ways, to sacred history'; the alternative method was to deny the authenticity of gentile histories which appeared to subvert the Biblical chronology.[34] The first approach included the massaging of sacred history to accommodate gentile chronology. The availability of different texts of the Pentateuch allowed a certain freedom of manoeuvre. Archbishop James Ussher (1581–1656), the leading Anglican contributor to the science of chronology, deployed the Hebrew Bible as the basis of his calendrical system. As a result, Ussher calculated that the Creation had occurred in 4004 BC and the Flood in 2349 BC.[35] Yet Jesuit accounts of China, and in particular the *Sinicae historiae decas prima res* (1658), the history of ancient China by Martino Martini (1614–61), suggested that Chinese history went back almost to 3000 BC. Martini dated the beginnings of the Chinese empire in 2952 BC.[36] However, by using the Greek Septuagint Bible rather than the Masoretic Hebrew version, Isaac Vossius, the son of the celebrated Gerard Vossius, was able to absorb the new sinology. His *Dissertatio de vera aetate mundi* (1659) added about 1,400 years on to Biblical chronology, relocating the Creation in 5400 BC.[37] This feat of creative exegesis broadened the permitted bands in which the great antiquity of gentile civilisations such as the Chinese could be accommodated to the ultimate standards of Mosaic chronology. Even by pushing the Mosaic chronology to its limits it was a tight squeeze fitting in the full history of Chinese civilisation. In the chronological paradigm provided by the Septuagint, the date of the Flood was pushed back only to around 3000 BC. It was necessary to locate the origins of China in the immediate post-Diluvial era. This meant relating Chinese chronology to the peopling of the world. If it could be demonstrated that the cultures of the Chinese and other ancient gentile civilisations still bore the Noachic hallmarks of their origin in the

[33] Rossi, *Dark abyss*, p. 140.   [34] *Ibid.*, p. 152.
[35] Trevor-Roper, 'Ussher', pp. 158–61.
[36] D. E. Mungello, *Curious land: Jesuit accommodation and the origins of sinology* (Studia Leibnitiana supplementa 25, Stuttgart, 1985), pp. 124–7.
[37] Rossi, *Dark abyss*, pp. 145–6.

dispersal of nations described in Genesis, then this would tend to reinforce sacred history. In the case of Chinese antiquity the chronological limitations on explaining its ethnic origins were so pressing that it became common to attribute the foundation of China to the earliest post-Diluvian era. Indeed, many scholars identified the Chinese founding emperor-deity Fohi as a remembrance either of Noah or of his immediate descendants.[38] The pioneering sinologists of early modern Europe transformed Chinese civilisation from a disquieting puzzle into a confirmation of Mosaic history. The visible contours of Noachic history and patriarchal religion evident beneath the patina of several millennia of cultural variation were striking proof of the testimony of Scripture.

The seventeenth century witnessed the emergence of ethnic theology as a lively branch of Christian apologetic, but the eighteenth saw something of a decline. The arguments of the orthodox tended to stagnate, while originality and ingenuity belonged to the *philosophes* who approached the study of the pagan world in a new light. They used pagan religion either as a foil for the follies and priestly tyrannies of Christendom, or to construct new naturalistic disciplines, such as mythography and the history and psychology of religious belief and organisation.[39] Nevertheless, although the names of Lafitau, Pluche, Banier and Fourmont are obviously less familiar than those of their new breed of opponents – Bernard de Fontenelle (1657–1757), Voltaire, Hume and Charles de Brosses (1709–77), who inaugurated the study of pagan fetishism in his classic *Du culte des dieux fétiches* (1760) – it would be wrong to suggest that ethnic theology had dwindled to an antiquarian bywater, the preserve only of cranks and bigots. It remained, after all, high on the agenda of the *philosophes*. Voltaire, for example, questioned the Noachic peopling of the American continent and, on the subject of universal chronology, came down on the side of the high pre-Biblical antiquity of China and India. In Voltaire's deistic brand of anti-Semitism – with attacks on the Jews used *strategically* to undermine the foundations of Christianity – the Hebrews were parvenus, their Abraham a corruption of the Hindu Brahma and Adam an obvious derivation from Adimo, the first Indian.[40] Philosophical

---

[38] For the standard Jesuit interpretation of Chinese history by Jean-Baptiste Du Halde (1674–1743) for the settlement of China by the 'sons of Noah', see P. J. Marshall and G. Williams, *The great map of mankind: British perceptions of the world in the age of Enlightenment* (London, 1982), p. 108. See also J. G. A. Pocock, 'Gibbon and the idol Fo: Chinese and Christian history in the Enlightenment', in D. S. Katz and J. I. Israel (eds.), *Sceptics, millenarians and Jews* (Leiden, 1990), esp. p. 26.

[39] Manuel, *Eighteenth century confronts the gods*; B. Feldman and R. D. Richardson, *The rise of modern mythology 1680–1860* (Bloomington, IN, 1972).

[40] P. J. Marshall, 'Introduction', in Marshall (ed.), *The British discovery of Hinduism in the eighteenth century* (Cambridge, 1970), p. 33; Voltaire, *Dictionnaire philosophique* (1764: Paris, 1964), 'Abraham', 'Adam', 'Chine (De la)', pp. 22–6, 111–14; T. F. Gossett, *Race: The history of an idea in America* (Dallas, 1963), p. 44.

irreligion often took the form of an inverted parody of ethnic theology. Instead of recounting the degeneration of patriarchal monotheism into unrecognisable heathen rites, sceptics demonstrated how, on the contrary, some pagan deities had been transfigured into Christian saints. One such sceptic, the geologist Nicolas-Antoine Boulanger (1722–59), also appropriated the Flood as a tool of anti-Christian subversion. Boulanger invoked a universal post-Diluvian trauma to deliver a psychological interpretation of the origins of religion. Some men, for example, had felt so keenly the shame of their survival and continued procreative careers that they castrated themselves, a vestigial survival of which was the ritual of circumcision.[41]

The defence of Mosaic orthodoxy was generally conducted along lines established in the seventeenth century by the French Protestant Samuel Bochart (1599–1667) and by Pierre-Daniel Huet (1630–1721), Bishop of Avranches. Where Bochart detected the figure of Noah and his sons under the central classical myth of Saturn and his children, Huet, taking in a wider sweep of heathen cultures, identified the prototype of Moses under the guise of various pagan deities, including the classical gods Apollo and Janus, the Phoenician god Taautus and even the Aztec god Teutl.[42] During the early Enlightenment, a mixture of dubious etymology, euhemerist conjectures and diffusionism – along with some interest in the psychological roots of idolatry and a willingness to debate fiercely within the parameters of Mosaic orthodoxy – remained the standard formula of writers such as Etienne Fourmont (1683–1745), Antoine Banier (1673–1741) and Noel-Antoine Pluche (1688–1761) who struggled to reconcile the world's pagan diversity with the Biblical story of mankind's primeval patriarchal monotheism.[43]

Nevertheless, the old guard was not without its innovators. The French Jesuit missionary Joseph-François Lafitau (1681–1746) drew upon his experiences among the Hurons and Iroquois to construct a strikingly original symbolic anthropology in *Moeurs des sauvages amériquains comparées aux moeurs des premiers temps* (1724). Although his methods prefigured certain aspects of modern social anthropology, Lafitau was

---

[41] Manuel, *Eighteenth century confronts the gods*, pp. 210–27.

[42] Samuel Bochart, *Geographiae sacrae pars prior Phaleg seu de dispersione gentium* (Caen, 1646), lib. I, cap. i, pp. 1–11; Huet, *Demonstratio evangelica*, propositio iv, pp. 56–131.

[43] See Etienne Fourmont, *Réflexions sur l'origine, l'histoire et la succession des anciens peuples* (new edn, 2 vols., Paris, 1747), esp. I, pp. 230–3, for psychological roots of idolatry. Antoine Banier, *The mythology and fables of the ancients, explain'd from history* (1738–40: 4 vols., London, 1739–40), while critical of the old guard – Bochart, Huet, Fourmont – esp. I, pp. 50–6, remains conventional, tracing the origins of idolatry in the line of Ham, esp. I, pp. 174–6, with the worship of stars, from I, p. 182. Note that, like Banier's treatise, Pluche's *Histoire du ciel* (Paris, 1739–41) was immediately published in English translation, with a second edition of *The history of the heavens* appearing in 1741: Manuel, *Eighteenth century confronts the gods*, pp. 5, 106–7, 115.

concerned to probe the rituals and symbols of Amerindian religion – including the emblematic meanings of solar worship and 'pyrolatrie' – for traces of the ancient patriarchal religion. The common worship of a supreme creator which lurked beneath the colourful and exotic cladding of all pagan cultures, whether in America or in ancient Greece, proved the higher truths of Christianity, from which, through the workings of providence, heathens were never totally alienated: 'dans quelques erreurs ou l'idolatrie ait plongé les Gentils, ils ne se sont pas tellement abandonnez a leurs idoles, qu'ils en ayent perdu la connoissance d'un Dieu vrai et unique, qui est l'Auteur de toutes choses'. The universality of certain core beliefs undermined the notions advanced by the likes of Pierre Bayle (whom contemporaries classed as an atheist) that men did not require religious institutions and that pagan religions were the human inventions and impostures of the cultures in which they were found: according to Lafitau, 'la religion n'a eu qu'une même origine pour tous les peuples'.[44]

Nor should we forget the theological underpinnings of Giambattista Vico's *Scienza nuova*. Vico's science of human cultural development entailed the separation of the sacred history of the Hebrew line of Shem, which was recorded in the Bible, from the civil history of the gentile races. Within this new science of society, a 'rational civil theology of divine providence' which explored how fallen bestial gentiles had gradually recovered their divine faculties and sociability after the post-Diluvial renunciation of the religion of Noah, the extraordinary providences of sacred history were clearly fenced off from the rest of human history. Designed as a Catholic rival to the anachronisms of Protestant natural jurisprudence, the sociological investigations of the new science were confined to the cultures of the Japhetans, Hamites and non-Hebraic descendants of Shem.[45]

Furthermore, scholars are now rediscovering the centrality of race as a concern of the European Enlightenment. The disengagement of race and ethnicity from theology was one of the achievements of the Enlightenment, and in part explains why abstruse matters of human geography captured the interest of the likes of Immanuel Kant, a critic of vulgar environmentalism, who stopped short of polygenesis. Kant's voluminous writings on geography and anthropology are now being reintegrated

[44] Lafitau, *Moeurs des sauvages amériquains*, I, ch. 4, pp. 108–455, esp. pp. 108–10, 113, 119, 121, 454; Pagden, *Fall of natural man*, ch. 8; Marshall and Williams, *Great map of mankind*, pp. 204–5; B. Trigger, *Natives and newcomers: Canada's 'heroic age' reconsidered* (1985: Manchester, 1986), pp. 22–3.
[45] Vico, *The new science of Giambattista Vico* (3rd edn, 1744, trans. T. Bergin and M. Frisch, Ithaca, 1984), pp. 9, 37–8, 89, 92, 112–13, 117; L. Pompa, *Vico: a study of the 'New science'* (1975: 2nd edn, Cambridge, 1990), chs. 3, 5; Lilla, *Vico*, ch. 4.

within his wider philosophical project.[46] In human racial classification as in other fields, the Enlightenment fostered a more naturalistic approach to knowledge. There were already signs of this in the late seventeenth century in a brief essay by François Bernier (1620–88) in the *Journal des sçavans* (1684), which divided the world into four or five racial divisions on the basis of physical appearance, without any reference to established Biblical categories.[47] Despite the disappearance of Noachic categories, an underlying monogenetic orthodoxy would still set limits to the scope of the new racial science.

Classification began in earnest during the eighteenth century in the work of Carl Linnaeus (1707–78) and Georges de Buffon (1707–88). These naturalists did not endorse the existing view that all the peoples of the world derived from the three branches – Semitic, Hamidian and Japhetan – of a single human stem. Linnaeus divided the races of men into four types – Americanus, Europeus, Asiaticus and Afer – with an additional category for wild men. Buffon, on the other hand, criticised the disservice done to nature by the categories of the taxonomist. In addition, Buffon's crafted mixture of subversive arguments, obscured by smoke-screen declarations of Biblical orthodoxy, and hypocritical willingness to retract particular statements which gave offence to the Sorbonne (while conserving his overall position), made his theological position difficult to parse with any confidence. Nevertheless, by the late 1770s it was clear that he had broken with traditional schemes of chronology with his estimate of about 75,000 years for the age of the cooling earth. Within the sphere of man's history, Buffon was more circumspect. Although they both treated racial difference in a naturalistic mode, neither Linnaeus nor Buffon – unlike Voltaire, who espoused a heterodox variant of stable creationism – made any attempt to displace the sacred unity of mankind with an alternative model of polygenesis. Buffon was quite insistent that environmental factors alone could explain the variety of humankind:

Tout concourt donc à prouver que le genre humain n'est pas composé d'espèces essentiellement différentes entre elles, qu'au contraire il n'y a eu originairement qu'une seule espèce d'hommes, qui s'étant multipliée et répandue sur toute la surface de la terre, a subi différents changements par l'influence du climat, par la différence de la nourriture, par celle de la manière de vivre, par les maladies épidémiques, et aussi par le mélange varié à l'infini des individus plus ou moins ressemblants.[48]

[46] E. C. Eze, *Race and the Enlightenment: a reader* (Oxford, 1997), pp. 2–4, 38–64; Greene, *Death of Adam*, pp. 232–3.
[47] François Bernier, 'Nouvelle division de la Terre, par les différentes espèces ou races d'hommes qui l'habitent, envoyée par un fameux voyageur', *Journal des sçavans* (1684), no. 12, 133–40.
[48] Jean Buffon, 'Variétés dans l'espèce humaine' (1749), in Buffon, *Histoire naturelle*

Eighteenth-century racial discourse remained transitional, a hodge-podge of biological, climatic and stadialist interpretations of racial and cultural difference. There was a basic consensus that the human race shared a common origin, though a variety of environmental factors were proposed as explanations for subsequent biological variations, including skin pigmentation.[49] For example, the influential anthropological system of Johann Friedrich Blumenbach (1752–1840), who developed the science of comparative human anatomy, has been described as a fusion of 'Christian and enlightened' approaches. Although Blumenbach divided humanity into five racial varieties, he stressed that the four variant races, the Mongolian, Ethiopian, Malay and American, were degenerations of an original Caucasian stock.[50]

The question of race (and its theological implications) was felt most acutely in North America. There European settlers directly confronted both the various indigenous peoples of the New World and an imported population of black African 'slave' labour. White colonists faced peculiarly intractable problems when explaining racial diversity. On the one hand, there was the need to justify European expropriation of Amerindian territory, the legitimacy of an – evolving – unfree labour system, the discouragement of miscegenation and, from the revolution of 1776, the exclusion of 'inferior' black slaves (whose human political value for electoral purposes was later precisely calibrated in the Constitution at three-fifths of a white American) from the full benefits of the United States' democratic creed.[51] On the other hand, the assertion of difference

(selection ed. J. Varloot, Paris, 1984), pp. 142–3; J. Roger, *Buffon* (1989: trans. S. Bonnefoi, Ithaca, 1997), pp. 42–3, 73, 84, 92, 100–5, 110, 171, 174–83, 186–9, 237, 298, 322, 339, 346, 379, 404–12, 417–18, 422, 426, 431; Greene, *Death of Adam*, pp. 226–9, 362; S. J. Gould, *The mismeasure of man* (2nd edn, Harmondsworth, 1997), p. 404; S. Toulmin and J. Goodfield, *The discovery of time* (1965: Harmondsworth, 1967), pp. 175–82; J. Burchfield, *Lord Kelvin and the age of the earth* (1975: Chicago, 1990), p. 4; I. Hannaford, *Race: the history of an idea in the west* (Baltimore, 1996), pp. 204–5.

[49] C. A. Bayly, *Imperial meridian: the British Empire and the world 1780–1830* (London and New York, 1989), p. 147; K. Thomas, *Man and the natural world* (1983: Harmondsworth, 1984), pp. 135–6. For the emergence of the race concept at varying rates in different spheres of discourse, see N. Hudson, 'From "nation" to "race": the origin of racial classification in eighteenth-century thought', *ECS* 29 (1996), 247–64.

[50] H. F. Augstein, 'Introduction', in Augstein (ed.), *Race: the origins of an idea, 1760–1850* (Bristol, 1996), p. xvii; Greene, *Death of Adam*, pp. 223–6; Gould, *Mismeasure of man*, pp. 401–12. For the development of Blumenbach's theories – including the appearance of the term 'Caucasian' in 1781 and the displacement of 'varietas' by 'gens' – between the first edition in 1775 and the third in 1795, see Hannaford, *Race*, pp. 205–13.

[51] Race slavery emerged gradually in the American colonies over the course of the seventeenth and eighteenth centuries in a complex hierarchy of labour with various subtle gradations of status and freedom, including punitive white English servitude, contractually indentured white English service and, at first, black servants. The justification at first for African-American bondage was confessional rather than racial. A Virginia law of 1670 defined slaves as 'all servants not being Christians' brought in by sea. However, from the 1660s colonial legislatures began to close the option whereby a Negro could

could not be pushed too far, for there was also a pressing need to confirm the narrative authority of the white man's Bible. While the relationship of white, red and black was clearly conceptualised in racial terms, suggestions by heterodox thinkers such as Thomas Jefferson (1743–1826) that the races of mankind might have plural origins were deeply offensive. As T. F. Gossett has emphasised, Jefferson's flirtation with the atheistic and blasphemous notion that blacks might constitute a distinct race, dabbled with 'a much more explosive issue than the question of Negro equality'.[52] The magisterial strain of the Enlightenment in America remained within safe monogenetic parameters, despite the countervailing pressures to account for substantial ethnic variation. America's leading racial theorists such as the Reverend Samuel Stanhope Smith (1750–1819), professor of moral philosophy at the College of New Jersey, and the Philadelphia physician Benjamin Rush (1745–1813), defended the unity of the human species against the heresy of separate creations. Both rejoiced in the celebrated case of Henry Moss, a black man who, within three years of spots appearing on his body in 1792, had become almost 'white'. A visit to Moss confirmed Rush in his explanation that blackness was a symptom of a mild form of leprosy which afflicted Africans, darkening their pigment. Rush had produced a remarkable solution to the American racial quandary. The diagnosis of this racially specific leprosy simultaneously bolstered the veracity of Genesis, justified a philanthropic white paternalism over the unfortunate African-American invalids and, on medical grounds, reinforced the prohibition on interracial marriage.[53]

The American experience serves to reinforce Richard Popkin's

extricate himself from slavery through baptism. Henceforth, the basis of slavery became progressively more racialist; although in 1753 the Virginia code still used anachronistic religious definitions. See e.g. O. Handlin and M. Handlin, 'Origins of the Southern labor system', *WMQ* 3rd ser. 7 (1950), 199–222; D. B. Davis, *The problem of slavery in western culture* (Ithaca, 1966), esp. pp. 210, 446; W. Billings, 'The cases of Fernando and Elisabeth Key', *WMQ* 3rd ser. 30 (1973), 467–74; W. Wiecek, 'The statutory law of slavery and race in the thirteen mainland colonies of British America', *WMQ* 3rd ser. 34 (1977), esp. 263–4; E. Morgan, *American slavery, American freedom* (New York, 1975); D. MacLeod, 'Towards caste: blacks in eighteenth-century America', in A. C. Hepburn (ed.), *Minorities in history* (Historical studies 12, Belfast, 1978); T. H. Breen, 'A changing labor force and race relations in Virginia', in Breen, *Puritans and adventurers* (New York, 1980). However, for an alternative view which emphasises the racist origins of slavery, though not without an awareness of attitudes to the 'heathen', see W. Jordan, *White over black: American attitudes towards the Negro, 1550–1812* (Chapel Hill, 1968), pp. 91–8. Nevertheless, recent scholarship reemphasises that racism was a consequence rather than a cause of slavery; see D. B. Davis, 'Constructing race: a reflection', *WMQ* 3rd ser. 54 (1997), 7–18, which introduces a special issue on this theme. Cf. T. Michals, '"That sole and despotic dominion": slaves, wives, and game in Blackstone's *Commentaries*', *ECS* 27 (1993–4), 196–7.   [52] Gossett, *Race*, p. 44.

[53] W. Stanton, *The leopard's spots: scientific attitudes toward race in America 1815–1859* (Chicago, 1960), pp. 3–13. See also M. A. Noll, *Princeton and the Republic, 1768–1822: the search for a Christian Enlightenment in the era of Samuel Stanhope Smith* (Princeton, 1989), pp. 115–21.

argument that the emergence of modern racialist ideas was predicated, in the first instance, upon deviant Scriptural exegesis and, secondly, upon enlightened assaults on the value of Scripture itself.[54] However, it would be a mistake to assume premature emancipation of ethnological discourse from theological categories. Johann Gottfried Herder (1744–1803), the philosophical father of modern nationalism, constructed his theory of the *Volk* on theological foundations. Although Herder rejected notions of the divine inspiration of language, his alternative thesis, which traced the growth of language in organic folk communities, was no less theological. Ethnic diversity was a vital part of the providential patterning of the universal moral order. Men related to God not as individuals but within communities, which were themselves in their very incommensurability expressions of the divine will. Indeed, reversing Vico's stance on the Semitic line, Herder included the Hebrews within his hybrid socio-theological vision as the most ancient and admirable example of an authentic *Volk*.[55] Philosophically, the parallel ascents of racism and nationalism were inextricably bound up with the fate of ethnic theology.

Into the nineteenth century, even the pathbreaking – and paradigm-shattering – science of geology held out the possibility of a recent catastrophe similar to the Noachian Deluge. The Swiss–French palaeontologist Georges Cuvier (1769–1832), who was no supernaturalist though a member of the French Protestant community, was able to conserve a notional Deluge as the most recent of a longer chronology of geological catastrophes. Similarly, the new sciences of ethnology, though drawing on naturalistic evidence and argument, continued to conform to the pattern of monogenesis. Even the craniologist Anders Retzius (1796–

---

[54] R. Popkin, 'The philosophical bases of modern racism' and 'Hume's Racism', in Popkin, *The high road to Pyrrhonism* (ed. R. A. Watson and J. E. Force, 1980: Indianapolis, 1993). See Pocock, 'Gibbon and the idol Fo', p. 31: 'It was a tactic of Enlightenment historiography to destroy the unity of the human race and human history, because both of these unities were founded upon the authority of the Bible.' Harrison, *'Religion' and the religions*, pp. 128–9, shows that, by undermining the universal genetic transmission of Adam's original sin, polygenesis 'called into question the whole drama of Fall and Redemption and the uniqueness of Jesus Christ'. See also D. McKee, 'Isaac de La Peyrère, a precursor of eighteenth-century critical deists', *PMLA* 59 (1944), esp. 479–80; Poliakov, *Le mythe aryen*, esp. pt 2, ch. 2.

[55] F. M. Barnard, 'The Hebrews and Herder's political creed', *Modern Language Review* 54 (1959), 533–46; Barnard, *Herder's social and political thought* (Oxford, 1965), esp. pp. 55–63; Manuel, *Eighteenth century confronts the gods*, pp. 291–301; G. Stocking, *Victorian anthropology* (1987: New York pbk, 1991), p. 20. See N. Hope, 'Johann Gottfried Herder: the Lutheran clergyman', in K. Robbins (ed.), *Protestant evangelicalism: Britain, Ireland, Germany and America c. 1750–c. 1950* (Ecclesiastical History Society, Oxford, 1990), pp. 109–34. For an alternative Francophone line of descent for ethnic nationalism (which includes, among various other factors and personalities, the place of an orthodox scheme of universal chronology in Chateaubriand's reactionary nationalist project), see M. Thom, *Republics, nations and tribes* (London, 1995), esp. pp. 130–1.

1860), who concocted the notion of the cephalic index to distinguish skull types, maintained a monogenist position.[56] An explicitly anti-Biblical theory of polygenetic racial origins would flourish only in the middle of the nineteenth century and, in France especially, in the work of scientists such as Paul Broca (1824–80). Broca's British counterparts generally kept abreast of anthropological developments without departing from the monogenist paradigm, though a polygenist subculture did flourish in the Anthropological Society.[57]

Sacred genealogies

The defence of Scripture was the primary concern of ethnic theology. However, antiquarians also hitched their own particular national and ethnic identities to the larger truths of universal history. In this way, the Mosaic account of the dispersal of peoples laid the groundwork for the construction of early modern European patriotisms. A seminal text was Isidore of Seville's seventh-century history, which told the story of the peopling of Europe by the stock of Japhet.[58] By the late medieval period, this extension of the ethnology adumbrated in Genesis had contributed to the myths of origin which accompanied the rise of regnal solidarity in many kingdoms of Europe.[59] Nevertheless, many of the myths of ethnic origin which had satisfied medieval chroniclers came unstuck in the Renaissance. The growing sophistication of Renaissance historiography, and the gestation of allied auxiliary disciplines, including chronology and a rudimentary diplomatic, would eventually put an end to many medieval myths of national origins.[60] Origin myths were purged of classical vanities and monkish inventions, especially in Protestant realms, but less obviously fabricated myths of ethnic origin, ancient constitutions and the like proliferated. Yet adherence to the Mosaic account of the peopling of the world did not immediately become a sign of reactionary orthodoxy or of

---

[56] G. Stocking, 'Race', in W. F. Bynum, E. J. Browne and R. Porter (eds.), *Dictionary of the history of science* (London, 1981), p. 357.

[57] Stocking, *Victorian anthropology*, pp. 67, 247–52; J. W. Burrow, 'Evolution and anthropology in the 1860s: the Anthropological Society of London, 1863–1871', *Victorian Studies* 7 (1963), 145. However, Count Joseph-Arthur Gobineau, whose extreme racialism coexisted with the traditional shibboleths of ethnic theology, provides an important, but idiosyncratic, counterexample to the overall argument presented in this chapter: see Hannaford, *Race*, pp. 269, 272, 351.   [58] Hodgen, *Early anthropology*, p. 55.

[59] S. Reynolds, 'Medieval *origines gentium* and the community of the realm', *History* 68 (1983), 375–90.

[60] Burke, *Renaissance sense of the past*, pp. 73–5. E.g. Jean Bodin, *Method for the easy comprehension of history* (trans. B. Reynolds, New York, 1945), ch. 9, 'Criteria by which to test the origins of peoples'.

gullibility. The cultures of humanistic philology and of the Reformation encouraged the study of the most authentic uncorrupted sources. Renewed emphasis on Mosaic ethnology at the expense of pagan origin myths was part of this scholarly drive towards original sources – *ad fontes*. In this respect national *mythistoires* were much more vulnerable than Mosaic pretensions. The early modern era witnessed a striking preference for Scripture over the origin myths propagated by vainglorious gentile nations, or unscrupulous monks. A distaste for previous origin myths often coexisted with an untroubled acceptance of Mosaic ethnology. F. L. Borchardt has demonstrated from the case of German origin myths that one of the most consistent features of patriotic historiography in the Renaissance was the displacement of one set of incredible myths by a version more acceptable to the critical standards of the age (though not necessarily any less fantastic to modern eyes).[61]

Instead of the adoption of a sceptical approach to ethnic origins, there was an accession of new myths. For instance, much of early sixteenth-century Europe was taken in by the Noachic genealogies of the peopling of Europe found in the spurious ancient annals forged by Annius of Viterbo and published in 1498, which foisted on the world the pseudo-histories of the Chaldaean chronicler Berosus and of the Egyptian Manetho. These histories from the perspective of antiquity interwove Noachic history with the history of nations. For instance, in the Celtic line it identified a great king Samothes.[62] Although Annius's forgery was soon found out, his work continued to be influential, and some of his critics were even taken in by elements of the deception.[63] Above all, it is important to note that those scholars who rejected the myths of the Pseudo-Berosus did not reject what they regarded as its substratum of truth in Mosaic history.[64] Despite the exposure of the Pseudo-Berosus, it seemed clear that the basic Scriptural accounts of the Noachids were not human forgeries; indeed, they remained central to ethnic enquiry into the eighteenth century. The critical antennae of early modern scholars were scarcely attuned to the possibility of error in sacred history. Indeed, reliance on Scriptural accounts of the peopling of the world helped to

[61] F. L. Borchardt, *German antiquity in Renaissance myth* (Baltimore and London, 1971), pp. 44–5; Borchardt, 'The topos of critical rejection in the Renaissance', *Modern Language Notes* 81 (1966), 476–88.

[62] J. H. Franklin, *Jean Bodin and the sixteenth-century revolution in the methodology of law and history* (New York and London, 1963), pp. 122–4; Grafton, *Defenders of the text*, ch. 3; Grafton, 'Scaliger', 165; T. D. Kendrick, *British antiquity* (London, 1950), pp. 70–2; S. Piggott, *Celts, Saxons, and the early antiquaries* (O'Donnell Lecture, 1966: Edinburgh, 1967), pp. 6–7. For the text of the Pseudo-Berosus, see R. E. Asher, *National myths in Renaissance France* (Edinburgh, 1993), pp. 196–227.

[63] Grafton, *Defenders of the text*, pp. 98–9.

[64] *Ibid.*, pp. 99–101, for the case of Goropius Becanus.

cleanse many cultures in early modern Europe of the most fantastical of their Graeco-Trojan origin myths, often substituting in their stead Noachic lineages which carried the reliable warranty of Scriptural veracity.[65]

The critical assault on the vanity of nations had, according to Rossi, become a familiar 'literary topos' by the middle of the seventeenth century.[66] Nevertheless, pride in a nation's Japhetan original was a much more sensitive issue. Sacred history was not only much less vulnerable than secular mythology, but was indeed a common substitute for it. For example, Vico criticised the 'conceit of nations' – not least in the matter of their boasts to high antiquity – without abandoning the Genesis story of the division of mankind. Indeed, the preposterous vainglory of national myths was an intellectual consequence of the gentile Fall from divine knowledge.[67]

The Mosaic history of the peopling of Europe – 'the isles of the Gentiles' – was incorporated into the different discursive contexts of several early modern patriotisms. The Poles, in particular, drew sustenance from the identification of Europe with the descendants of Japhet. Polish nationhood was firmly bound up with the identity of its *szlachta* or gentry caste. The *szlachta* were identified as Sarmatians descended from Japhet. By contrast, the mass of serfs over whom they ruled were identified as the cursed progeny of Ham. For example, an early seventeenth-century critique of spurious nouveaux entrants into the rank of the gentry, Trepka's *Liber Chamorum* – 'The Book of Hamites' – applied Noachic categories to Poland's ethnic and social composition.[68] Similar uses of sacred history in the construction of ethnic caste identities can be found in early modern France.[69] A very different deployment of Noachic genealogy occurred in early modern Sweden. Seventeenth-century Swedish imperialism was fuelled by powerful myths of the nation's ethnic origins and of an ancient golden age of Gothic expansionism. A central component of the myth was the identification of the noble Swedes as

---

[65] J. W. Johnson, 'Chronological writing: its concepts and development', *H+T* 2 (1962), 143; Ryan, 'Assimilating new worlds', 534.   [66] Rossi, *Dark abyss*, p. 168.
[67] Vico, *New science*, pp. 61, 68; Rossi, *Dark abyss*, p. 168; Lilla, *Vico*, pp. 119–20, 141, 165.
[68] J. Tazbir, *La république nobiliaire et le monde: études sur l'histoire de la culture polonaise a l'époque du baroque* (Wroclaw, 1986), pp. 17, 68; Tazbir, 'Poland and the concept of Europe in the sixteenth–eighteenth centuries', *European Studies Review* 7 (1977), 34; P. Burke, 'The language of orders in early modern Europe', in M. L. Bush (ed.), *Social orders and social classes in Europe since 1500* (London, 1992), p. 4; N. Davies, *God's playground* (1981: 2 vols., Oxford pbk, 1982), I, p. 234. For elsewhere in eastern Europe, see E. Niederhauser, 'Problèmes de la conscience historique dans les mouvements de renaissance nationale en Europe orientale', *Acta Historica* (Budapest) 18 (1972), 61–2.
[69] A. Jouanna, *L'idée de race en France au XVIe siècle et au début du XVIIe siècle (1498–1614)* (2 vols., Paris, 1976), II, p. 623 n.; A. Devyver, *Le sang épuré: les préjugés de race chez les gentilshommes français de l'ancien régime (1560–1720)* (Brussels, 1973), p. 177.

descendants of Noah's eldest son, Japhet, through the line of Magog, and his son Gotar, the father of the Goths. The tradition culminated in the identification of Sweden with the lost Atlantis in the Gothicist classic, the *Atlantica sive Manheim* (1679–1702) of the polymath Olaus Rudbeck (1630–1702). Rudbeck embroidered the traditional notion that Scandinavia was the womb of nations into an argument that Sweden was the birthplace of the European Japhetan nations, including the classical civilisations.[70] German Gothicism was also characterised by pride in a direct noble decent from Noah and the patriarchs.[71]

However, it is important to stress that the Mosaic paradigm emphasised affiliation and relationships within the Noachic family tree rather than the notions of difference and otherness which we associate with modern nationalism. The German Jesuit polymath Athanasius Kircher (1602–80) set his undoubted patriotism in the context of the wider peopling of Europe. Following in the footsteps of his fellow German geographer Philip Cluverius, Kircher also noted the close connection between the Germans and (Celtic) Gauls through descent from Gomer.[72]

The linguistic aspect of early modern ethnic identity was particularly affected by religious considerations. This occurred on a variety of levels. In the first place, the language of Adam and the events associated with the Tower of Babel were of greater import than ethnic vernaculars. Which was the original Adamic language? How many languages were created at the confounding of speech at Babel, and which modern vernaculars had originated as the first post-Babelian mother-languages?[73] Daniel Droixhe

[70] M. Roberts, *The Swedish imperial experience 1560–1718* (Cambridge, 1979), pp. 70–5; K. Johannesson, *The renaissance of the Goths in sixteenth-century Sweden* (1982: trans. J. Larson, Berkeley and Los Angeles, 1991); S. Brough, *The Goths and the concept of Gothic in Germany from 1500 to 1750* (Frankfurt, 1985), p. 133; K. Johannisson, *A life of learning: Uppsala University during five centuries* (Uppsala, 1989), pp. 33–5; T. Frängsmyr, 'The Enlightenment in Sweden', in R. Porter and M. Teich (eds.), *The Enlightenment in national context* (Cambridge, 1981), p. 171; Gibbon, *DF*, I, p. 234; P. Hall, 'Nationalism and historicity', *Nations and Nationalism* 3 (1997), 8–12.

[71] Brough, *Goths*, pp. 34–7, 87, 149, 202–3.

[72] Athanasius Kircher, *Arca Noe* (Amsterdam, 1675), 'Tabula geographica divisionis gentium et populorum per tres filios Noe, Sem, Cham, Japhet, posterosque eorum', at pp. 222–3.

[73] See e.g. the speculations of Robert Baillie in 1627 on the primeval language, in J. Durkan, 'King Aristotle and Old "Butterdish": the making of a graduate in seventeenth-century Glasgow', *College Courant*, no. 63 (September 1979), 19. John Lightfoot, Master of Catherine Hall, Cambridge, was keen to nail the notion that because the offspring of Noah were divided into seventy nations there were as many as seventy languages created at Babel: see Lightfoot, *A chronicle of the times, and the order of the texts in the Old Testament*, in Lightfoot, *Works* (2 vols., London, 1684), I, p. 9; *A few, and new observations, upon the book of Genesis, ibid.*, I, p. 694; *Erubhin, ibid.*, I, pp. 1009–11. These were still live issues in the eighteenth century: see the treatment of 'Language' in the classic Biblical dictionary of the Benedictine scholar Augustin Calmet, *An historical, critical, geographical, chronological and etymological dictionary of the Holy Bible* (trans. S. D'Oyly and J. Colson, 3 vols., London, 1732), II, pp. 26–30; Benjamin Holloway, *The primaevity and preeminence of the sacred Hebrew, above all other languages, vindicated* (Oxford, 1754).

has demonstrated the central importance of the Book of Genesis to the study of linguistics in seventeenth- and eighteenth-century Europe.[74] For example, the influential work of the Huguenot pastor and doyen of ethnic theologians, Samuel Bochart, stressed connections via the Phoenicians between Hebrew and the languages of western Europe.[75] However, it was the rival Scytho-Celtic paradigm which prevailed in European linguistics before the advent of the Indo-European philology developed by Sir William Jones and Franz Bopp. Scytho-Celticists tended to operate on the notion that the peoples of Europe were descended from Japhet, though historians of linguistics now recognise sophisticated comparativist and Eurasianist 'anticipations' of Jones in the notion of a lost Scythian parent language.[76] As late as the 1750s, scholars such as the prominent Celticist Jean-Baptiste Bullet continued to advance this Japhetan scheme.[77]

When patriotic humanists did attempt to advance the glory of their native languages they did so most often within a theological rather than an exclusively ethnocentric context. It was a common refrain of patriotic scholars that their own national tongue was the authentic remnant of the pre-Babelian primitive universal language. In his *Origines Antwerpianae* (1569), Goropius Becanus (1518–72) claimed that the Cimbri, direct descendants of Japhet and ancestors of the Flemish, had not been present at Babel. Hence, the Flemish dialect spoken in Antwerp was identified as the original Adamic language.[78] The claims made by Becanus were qualified and refined in the *Lingua Belgica* (1612) of Abraham Mylius, who argued that Belgian had been one of the ancient languages of the post-Noachic era.[79] Scandinavia spawned its own extravagant claims. Georg Stiernhielm (1598–1672) in *Babel destructa, seu runa suethica* (1669) and Rudbeck's *Atlantica* argued that the Scythian tongue of the ancient Swedes was the universal language, while Andreas Kempe in *Die Sprachen des Paradises* (1688) concocted a Gothic Eden where God spoke Swedish, Adam conversed in Danish and the Fall was brought about, naturally, by a smooth-talking Francophone serpent.[80]

---

[74] D. Droixhe, *La linguistique et l'appel de l'histoire (1600–1800)* (Geneva, 1978).

[75] *Ibid.*, pp. 38–9; Rossi, *Dark abyss*, p. 153; G. Parry, *The trophies of time* (Oxford, 1995), pp. 310–13.

[76] J.-C. Muller, 'Early stages of language comparison from Sassetti to Sir William Jones (1786)', *Kratylos* 31 (1986), 1–31; D. Droixhe, *De l'origine du langage aux langues du monde: études sur les XVIIe et XVIIIe siècles* (Tübingen, 1987), pp. 65–8; J. T. Leerssen, *Mere Irish and Fíor-Ghael* (1986: 2nd edn, Cork, 1996), pp. 288–9.

[77] Jean-Baptiste Bullet, *Mémoires sur la langue celtique* (3 vols., Besançon, 1754–60), I, p. 9.

[78] A. Grafton, *Forgers and critics* (London, 1990), pp. 116–17; Rossi, *Dark abyss*, p. 198.

[79] G. J. Metcalf, 'Abraham Mylius on historical linguistics', *PMLA* 68 (1953), 535–54.

[80] E. Seaton, *Literary relations of England and Scandinavia in the seventeenth century* (Oxford, 1935), p. 189; U. Eco, *The search for the perfect language* (trans. J. Fentress, Oxford, 1995), p. 97; G. Bonfante, 'Ideas on the kinship of the European languages from 1200 to 1800', *Journal of World History* 1 (1953–4), 685.

Not all linguistic patriots were quite so blatant in identifying a particular modern vernacular as the single Adamic language. Some advanced the argument that at Babel the speech of mankind had been divided into seventy (or seventy-two) core languages – *linguae matrices* – and championed their vernaculars with more plausibility as one of the un-derivative matrix languages created at Babel.[81] Thomas Fuller, for instance, an Anglican champion of his church's non-papal origins among the ancient Britons, the ancestors of the modern Welsh, took pride in the 'British' tongue as 'one of those which departed from Babel; and herein it relates to God, as the more immediate author thereof: whereas most tongues in Europe owe their beginning to human depraving of some original language'.[82] Kircher challenged the patriotic boasting of Goropius Becanus that Flemish was the original pre-Babelian speech: the *lingua Belgica* was clearly a *filia* of the German mother-tongue. However, instead of puffing German in the place of Flemish, Kircher was content to champion Hebrew as the original divine language, claiming for German only the title of being the language of the distinguished Noachids Ashkenaz and Tuiscon.[83] Breton linguistic patriotism would continue to be couched in this idiom throughout the Enlightenment, in works such as Le Brigant's *Eléments de la langue des Celto-gomérites* (1779), which alludes in its title to Gomer, son of Japhet and reputed father of the Celts.

Many of the leading minds of Europe saw the potential of language not as a way of exciting patriotic differences, but as a means of binding confessional divisions. The wars of religion which disfigured early modern Christendom kindled aspirations among linguists to recreate a universal language which might restore its unity, or at least promote a degree of ecumenical understanding.[84] According to Vivian Salmon, John Wilkins, author of the monumental linguistic treatise, *An essay towards a real character and a philosophical language* (1668), aimed to unite the divided Protestant churches of Europe 'by attempting to remove the verbal ambiguity which he considered to lie at the heart of theological disputes'.[85] It was not uncommon for early modern literati to be more obsessed with devising schemes for universal languages or with defending the sacred status of Hebrew than with mouthing the glories of their own national tongues and literatures.[86]

---

[81] Hodgen, *Early anthropology*, p. 304.
[82] Thomas Fuller, *Church history of Britain* (1655: 3 vols., London, 1842), I, p. 96.
[83] Athanasius Kircher, *Turris Babel* (Amsterdam, 1679), pp. 194, 212.
[84] J. Knowlson, *Universal language schemes in England and France 1600–1800* (Toronto, 1975), p. 10.
[85] V. Salmon, 'Language-planning in seventeenth-century England: its context and aims', in Salmon, *The study of language in seventeenth-century England* (Amsterdam, 1979), p. 130.

The connection between ethnology and theology was two-way. As Gibbon noted, the Mosaic account of the peopling of the world affected the ways in which the particular ethnic identities of the European peoples were elaborated and related one to another. Nevertheless, the fact that the Genesis account of the peopling of the world played some part during the seventeenth and into the eighteenth century in the formation of ethnic identities should not cloud the primacy of religious truth over matters of national honour. Pride in a distinguished national lineage which might be traced back to Japhet was of secondary importance to the maintenance of Christianity as an intellectual system of unimpeachable integrity.

[86] A vivid example is provided by seventeenth-century Scotland where there was little evidence of any vernacular patriotism; on the other hand two Scots produced remarkable attempts to undo the linguistic Fall at Babel: the polymathic cavalier Sir Thomas Urquhart of Cromarty (1611–60) in his *Logopandecteision* and the Oxford-based George Dalgarno (1626?–87) in his *Ars signorum* (Salmon, 'The evolution of Dalgarno's *Ars signorum*', in Salmon, *Study of language*, pp. 157–75).

3   Ethnic theology and British identities

The clerisies of the British Isles were keenly aware that questions of ethnic origin bore heavily not only upon national status and identity, but also upon the standing of Christian truth. As we saw in the last chapter British writers, such as James Ussher, the formidable Anglo-Irish chronologist, were actively involved in the great ethnological debates which enthralled the clerisies of early modern Europe. The same themes which pre-occupied theologians on the Continent – the peopling of America, men before Adam and gentile chronology – were standard features of British theology throughout the seventeenth and eighteenth centuries.

Ethnic matters pertained by definition to the province of religion. The entry for 'Ethnick' in the *Glossographia* (1656) compiled by Thomas Blount (1618–79) ran as follows: 'heathenish, ungodly, irreligious: And may be used substantively for a heathen or gentile'. A century later, Johnson's *Dictionary* (1755) defined 'Ethnick' in broadly similar fashion: 'heathen; pagan; not Jewish; not Christian'.[1] As we saw in chapter 2, the term 'ethnic theology' was in fact used in this era to refer to pagan religion;[2] however, the scope of the discussion here will be somewhat broader. As well as engaging with the unfamiliar early modern construc-

---

[1] Thomas Blount, *Glossographia* (1656: reprint, Menston, 1969), and Samuel Johnson, *A dictionary of the English language* (1755: facsimile edn, London, 1979), under 'Ethnick' and 'Ethnicks'. See also the sixth edition of Nathaniel Bailey's *Universal etymological dictionary* (London, 1733), which defined 'Ethnick' as 'heathenish, of or belonging to heathens'; T. Hylland Eriksen, *Ethnicity and nationalism: anthropological perspectives* (London, 1993), pp. 3–4; R. Williams, *Keywords* (1976: London, 1988 edn), p. 119; A. Hastings, *The construction of nationhood* (Cambridge, 1997), p. 213.

[2] E.g. Edward, Lord Herbert of Cherbury, *The antient religion of the gentiles with the causes of their errors* (1663: trans. from Latin, London, 1705), p. 3, 'ethnical superstitions', and p. 185, 'ethnick theology'. See also F. Manuel, *The eighteenth century confronts the gods* (Cambridge, MA, 1959), p. 118, for Newton's notes on 'Religio ethnica'. Charles O'Conor, *Dissertations on the antient history of Ireland* (Dublin, 1753), p. x, described the pre-Christian Irish as 'a kind of ethnic Hebrews . . . who kept the laws of nature in some force, where those of revelation found no entrance'; similarly, Sylvester O'Halloran, *A general history of Ireland* (2 vols., London, 1778), II, p. 113, referred to their rites as 'our national ethnic worship'.

tion of ethnic otherness, this chapter will also embrace our own rather different twentieth-century awareness of the 'ethnic'.

Chronological foundations

The link between ethnicity – in its modern sense – and religion was deeper than an accidental semantic connection. Historiography was shaped by theology. Not only was the civil history of mankind an offshoot of the story begun in Genesis, but, with varying degrees of sophistication, early modern historians were able to trace the hand of providence at work, either directly or through chains of secondary causes, in the course of events. British Protestants did more than genuflect to the idol of sacred history. The Bible set chronological limits to human history, and the quest for the origins of the British peoples was naturally framed by the universal history of mankind from the Noachic dispersal. Universal history told in traditional Mosaic fashion was a 'lively' staple of British historical culture well into the eighteenth century, most notably in Sir Walter Raleigh's *History of the world* (1614) which went through numerous editions and abridgements. The science of chronology existed as a branch of theology. Ussher and various successors such as John Lightfoot (1602–75), master of St Catharine's Hall, Cambridge, obsessed over the precise chronology of the Creation. Although not everybody was confident that the Creation could be pinpointed to Sunday, 23 October, 4004 BC (the machinery having been set in motion at about 6 p.m. the previous evening) or even to some other date in the autumn of 4004 BC, the parameters of chronological speculation were broadly Mosaic, ranging between 6984 BC and 3616 BC. As a result, the peopling of the world by the 'Arkite ogdoad' – Noah, his three sons and their wives – remained 'inescapable facts' of ancient history well into the first half of the eighteenth century. A vogue for chronological tabulations reinforced this outlook. Francis Tallents (1619–1708), for example, produced *A view of universal history* (1685). In Scotland the Reverend Alexander Cooper of Traquair argued for the superiority of Scripture evidence over unreliable 'profane' sources in *An essay upon the chronology of the world* (1722). Although by the start of the eighteenth century the sheer weight of antiquarian knowledge and the critical acumen of 'modern' classical scholarship had made it almost impossible to plot a convincing and certain scheme of universal history, scriptural chronology remained an integral and unembarrassing feature of the British Enlightenment. The findings of the new astronomy were fused with sacred history in such works as Isaac Newton's *The chronology of ancient kingdoms amended*

(1728) and in John Kennedy's *New method of stating and explaining the scripture chronology, upon Mosaic astronomical principles* (1751). Chronology was socially as well as intellectually respectable. The Anglo-Scottish cleric John Blair (d. 1782), who was appointed chaplain to the Dowager Princess of Wales in 1757 and who also served as mathematics tutor to the Duke of York, constructed a popular *Chronology and history of the world, from the Creation, to the year of Christ 1753* (1754: reprinted 1756, 1768, 1814).[3]

The discourse of chronologists was far from insular. Indeed, from the late seventeenth century, the upholders of both Protestant and Catholic confessions became aware of a general threat to the standards of Christian orthodoxy. French chronology, though deployed to meet different confessional objectives, exerted considerable influence on British historical thought throughout the seventeenth and eighteenth centuries. *A history of the world; or, an account of time* by Denis Petau (Dionysius Petavius) appeared in English in 1659, and *Ductor historicus: or, a short system of universal history*, which was published anonymously in London in 1698 (and later in Thomas Hearne's enlarged edition of 1704–5), was compiled in good part from *Les élémens de l'histoire* (1696) by Pierre Le Lorrain, Abbé de Vallemont. Bossuet's providentialist scheme of universal history, *Discours sur l'histoire universelle* (1681), also found its way into English. Moreover, the works of the French Jansenist and classical scholar Charles Rollin (1661–1741) were immensely popular throughout the English-speaking world, including his similarly providentialist survey of *Antient history*, in which the 'origin of profane history' was defined as

---

[3] S. Piggott, *William Stukeley* (1950: London, 1985), p. 100; J. W. Johnson, 'Chronological writing: its concepts and development', *H+T* 2 (1962), 124–5, 137; H. Trevor-Roper, 'James Ussher, Archbishop of Armagh', in Trevor-Roper, *Catholics, Anglicans and Puritans* (London, 1987), pp. 159, 291 n.; G. Parry, *The trophies of time* (Oxford, 1995), pp. 147–8; G. Daniel, *Man discovers his past* (London, 1966), p. 20, for October 4004 BC; John Lightfoot, *Works* (2 vols., London, 1684), I, pp. 707, 1020–1, for September 4004 BC; J. Levine, *The battle of the books* (Ithaca, 1991), pp. 92–3; R. Porter, *Gibbon* (London, 1988), ch. 1, 'The uses of history in Georgian England', esp. pp. 22–5; N. Rupke, *The great chain of history: William Buckland and the English school of geology (1814–1849)* (Oxford, 1983), pp. 52–6; F. Manuel, *Isaac Newton, historian* (Cambridge, MA, 1963). For the parameters of medieval and early modern speculation on the Creation, see William Hales, *A new analysis of chronology and geography* (1809–12: 2nd edn, 4 vols., London, 1830), I, pp. 211–14. Although criticised by contemporaries such as the Reverend Arthur Bedford (1668–1745), in *Animadversions upon Sir Isaac Newton's book, intitled 'The chronology of ancient kingdoms amended'* (London, 1728), for undermining the established contours of Protestant chronology, Newton's chronology was hardly paradigm-breaking, deviating from traditional datings by only a few hundred years in an attempt, indeed, to bolster the authority of the Old Testament by showing its superior accuracy over the pagan histories of Greece and Egypt; M. T. Hodgen, *Early anthropology in the sixteenth and seventeenth centuries* (Philadelphia, 1964), p. 319.

'the dispersion of the posterity of Noah into the several countries of the earth where they settled'.[4]

Although British Protestantism did not generate a classic to rival Bossuet's, Georgian England produced its own monumental *Universal history* published in twenty-three volumes between 1736 and 1765. The *Universal history* was a collaborative venture pooling the talents of various Grub Street hacks, including the prolific Scot John Campbell (1708–75), his countryman Archibald Bower (1686–1766) and the notorious quondam-'Formosan'-turned-Anglican George Psalmanazar (1679?–1763). Despite some heterodox articles on oriental topics contributed to the first edition by George Sale (1697?–1736), the *Universal history* was a massive pillar of orthodoxy, beginning with the Creation, rebutting the errors of the Pre-adamite heresy and tracing the origins of civil government and nations from the Noachic dispersal.[5]

Eighteenth-century Irish Catholics, of course, imbibed a traditional universal history through Bossuet, and also from the work of Cornelius Nary (1660–1738), author of *A new history of the world, containing an historical and chronological account of the times and transactions from the Creation to the birth of Christ, according to the computation of the Septuagint* (Dublin, 1720). The paradigm established by Ussher continued to be a feature of Irish Protestantism, upheld in the early nineteenth century by the Reverend William Hales (1747–1831), professor of oriental languages at Dublin, in his *New analysis of chronology* (1809–12) whose novelty was limited to a Creation of 5411 BC.

It was only in the 1780s that the old chronological certainties began to dissolve. George Toulmin, an eternalist, challenged the Mosaic timeframe of both natural and human history in *The antiquity and duration of the world* (1780). In a similar mechanistic vein, but with more precision, the Scottish scientist James Hutton (1726–97) unveiled in lectures to the Royal Society of Edinburgh delivered in 1785 a theory of the earth and its profound antiquity which he had begun to formulate twenty years before. Hutton's earth was a beneficently designed perpetual motion machine which created through erosion the soil required for the sustenance of life, remaking continents through the consolidation of sediments. Hutton detected a continuous tripartite cycle of erosion, consolidation and

---

[4] Jacques-Bénigne Bossuet, *A discourse on the history of the whole world* (1686: 2nd edn, London, 1703), p. 4, for the Japhetan peopling of Europe; Charles Rollin, *Antient history* (1730–8: 1st transln, 11 vols., London, 1735?–7), 'Preface', I, p. v; Levine, *Battle of the books*, p. 271; Porter, *Gibbon*, p. 25.

[5] *An universal history, from the earliest account of time to the present* (7 vols., London, 1736–44), I, pp. 47–8, 97, 171. For the background and religious slant of this project, see G. Abbattista, 'The business of Paternoster Row: towards a publishing history of the *Universal history* (1736–1765)', *Publishing History* 17 (1985), 5–50, esp. 8, 13–14, 27.

elevation in geological processes whose necessary longevity not only undermined Mosaic chronology, but obliterated the primeval contours of the world. 'The result, therefore, of our present enquiry', he concluded, 'is, that we find no vestige of a beginning, – no prospect of an end.' Yet, despite Hutton's obvious heterodoxy (which attracted an orthodox rebuttal from the Anglo-Irish scholar Richard Kirwan (1733–1812)), a benign Newtonian deity stood beyond the vastness of deep time as the prime mover of the terraqueous globe. Nor did the appearance of uniformitarian ideas in late Enlightenment Scotland immediately displace the Deluge. In early nineteenth-century England there was a distinctive non-uniformitarian school of geology championed at Oxford by William Buckland (1784–1856) which, while non-literalist and admitting a much vaster ante-Diluvian timeframe than Genesis allowed, remained committed until the 1830s to a Diluvialist interpretation of earth history which saw the Flood as the culmination of a series of catastrophes which had shaped the planet. Only in 1836 did Buckland break with the notion of the Mosaic Deluge, though not with the notion of ancient cataclysms which he now argued had preceded the appearance of man.[6] Given the persistence of sacred geochronology into the late eighteenth century, and the longer survival of elements of the Mosaic history of the world into the early nineteenth century, it is hardly surprising that Genesis should have remained throughout the seventeenth and eighteenth centuries a valid point of departure – albeit by no means the exclusive starting point – for British accounts of the history of mankind.

The resilience of orthodoxy

English exploration of the New World provoked the first stirrings of the new ethnic theology, and, appropriately, an early classic of the genre, Sir Walter Raleigh's *History of the world*. The scholar-explorer included within his *History* what passed for a major defence of Christian revelation (or at least its 'bibliolatry' cleared Raleigh from ill-founded charges of athe-

---

[6] George Toulmin, *The antiquity and duration of the world* (1780: London, 1824), see esp. pp. 5, 9, 11, 32, 47, 54; James Hutton, 'Theory of the Earth; or an investigation of the laws observable in the composition, dissolution and restoration of land upon the globe', *Transactions of the Royal Society of Edinburgh* 1 (1788), 304; Rupke, *Great chain of history*, pp. 5, 9, 16–18, 39–41, 57–60, 89–92. Consider too the complementary influences of Jean André Deluc (1727–1817) and George Cuvier on British geology: see F. C. Haber, *The age of the world: Moses to Darwin* (Baltimore, 1959), pp. 194–7, 210–21. The preface by the Scot Robert Jameson to his translation of Cuvier brought out the Mosaic orthodoxy which was only implicitly suggested in the more hesitant formulation of the original: Jameson, 'Preface' (1817), in George Cuvier, *Essay on the theory of the earth* (1817: 4th edn, Edinburgh, 1822), pp. ix, xi. See also N. Cohn, *Noah's flood* (New Haven, 1996), p. 113; J. Burchfield, *Lord Kelvin and the age of the earth* (1975: Chicago, 1990), pp. 6–8.

ism).[7] English accounts of how North America had been peopled were largely influenced by Acosta's *Historia natural y moral de las Indias* (1590) which was published in an English translation by Edward Grimston in 1604: for instance, Edward Brerewood, professor of astronomy at Gresham College, argued that America had been peopled by the progeny of the Tartars, a line also taken by Samuel Purchas (1575?–1626) and, later, by John Ogilby (1600–76) in his *America* (1671).[8] In the 1650s there was a debate over the supposed Jewish origins of the native Americans. In *Iewes in America, or probabilities that the Americans are of that race* (1650), Thomas Thorowgood drew parallels between the customs, religion and languages of these peoples, a position rejected by Hamon L'Estrange (1605–60) in *Americans no Iewes* (1652).[9] Scholars such as Alexander Ross, author of *Pansebeia* (1653), also began to compile encyclopaedic compendia of ethnographic information on the various religions of the newly discovered world which lay beyond the traditional boundaries of Christendom.[10] A characteristic account of seventeenth-century English ethnology and racial prejudice can be found in Sir Thomas Browne's intellectual miscellany *Pseudodoxia epidemica* (1646) where chapters on the blackness of Negroes and the characteristics of Jews, Gypsies and pygmies nestle alongside treatments of the relationship of Ham, Shem and Japhet and the reasons for building the tower of Babel.[11]

The expansion of Europe also encouraged philosophical voyages into the uncharted waters of religious heterodoxy, though it was by no means the sole factor. In response to the provocations of Descartes, Hobbes, Spinoza and La Peyrère, the Restoration era proved to be one of the golden ages of English theology, crowned by the achievements of the latitude-men and the Cambridge Platonists. Theologians became keenly aware that the defence of Mosaic history required the elaboration of

[7] Walter Raleigh, *A historie of the world* (1614: London, 1617), esp. bk 1, ch. 8, 'Of the first planting of nations after the floud: and of the sonnes of Noah; Sem, Ham and Iaphet, by whom the earth was repeopled'. For Raleigh's reputation as a freethinker and the orthodox limits of his scepticism, see F. S. Fussner, *The historical revolution: English historical writing and thought 1580–1640* (London, 1962), pp. 192–3, 201; C. Hill, *Intellectual origins of the English revolution* (Oxford, 1965), p. 191; D. Woolf, *The idea of history in early Stuart England* (Toronto, 1990), p. 46.

[8] Edward Brerewood, *Enquiries touching the diversity of languages and religions throughout the chiefe parts of the world* (London, 1614), pp. 96–7; L. E. Huddleston, *Origins of the American Indians: European concepts, 1492–1729* (Austin, TX, 1967), pp. 48, 114–16, 135.

[9] D. C. Allen, *The legend of Noah* (Urbana, 1949), pp. 126–7.

[10] Alexander Ross, *Pansebeia: or, a view of all religions in the world* (London, 1653).

[11] Thomas Browne, *Pseudodoxia epidemica* (1646), in Brown, *Works* (ed. G. Keynes, 4 vols., London, 1964), II, bk 4, chs. 10–11; bk 6, chs. 10–13; bk 7, chs. 5–6.

sophisticated counter-measures,[12] not least in the field of ethnic theology. La Peyrère's Pre-adamite heresy was one of the principal targets of Edward Stillingfleet's sophisticated defence of Christian orthodoxy, *Origines sacrae* (1662). Stillingfleet (1635–99) explained to educated Englishmen that more than patriotic pride was at stake in the study of ethnic origins:

> the peopling of the world from Adam . . . is of great consequence for us to understand, not only for the satisfaction of our curiosity as to the true origin of nations, but also in order to our believing the truth of the scriptures, and of the universal effects of the Fall of man. Neither of which can be sufficiently cleared without this. For as it is hard to conceive how the effects of man's Fall should extend to all mankind, unless all mankind were propagated from Adam, so it is inconceivable how the account of things given in scripture should be true, if there were persons existent in the world long before Adam was.[13]

Contradicting La Peyrère's devastating exegesis of Romans, Stillingfleet offered the unequivocal message of Acts 17:26: 'God hath made of one blood all nations of men.'[14] Moreover, he questioned whether the Flood could have been a local event confined to the Middle East, when there were Flood stories in so many other cultures.[15] Lord Chief Justice Sir Mathew Hale's *The primitive origination of mankind* (1677) was a classic text of ethnic theology, though its larger purpose lay in opposing Cartesian heterodoxy.[16] Hale supported the Acostan thesis, conjecturing the existence of a land-bridge between Asia and America. However, in his enthusiasm to bury the Pre-adamite threat to Christian doctrine, Hale (1609–76) also deployed the Norse, Carthaginian and other extant theses about the peopling of America, many of which Acosta had explicitly repudiated. These various colonies had degenerated from their early civility and religion, a process which explained the marked difference in culture between the primitive peoples of America and the civilisations of the Old World. This account of degeneration was the stark opposite of Acosta's account of primitive hunters crossing from northern Eurasia to North America where they developed their own distinct cultures.[17]

An important contribution to the sinological branch of Christian apologetics came from John Webb, who argued that 'in all probability,

---

[12] G. Reedy, *The Bible and reason: Anglicans and Scripture in late seventeenth-century England* (Philadelphia, 1985).

[13] Edward Stillingfleet, *Origines sacrae* (London, 1662), p. 534. R. Popkin, 'The philosophy of Bishop Stillingfleet', *Journal of the History of Philosophy* 9 (1971), 305, notes that *Origines sacrae* had been reissued eight times by 1709.

[14] Stillingfleet, *Origines sacrae*, p. 534.   [15] *Ibid.*, pp. 538–53.

[16] A. Cromartie, *Sir Mathew Hale 1609–1676* (Cambridge, 1995), pp. 199–203.

[17] Mathew Hale, *The primitive origination of mankind* (London, 1677), bk II, pp. 182–3, 190, 195–7; P. Rossi, *The dark abyss of time: the history of the earth and the history of nations from Hooke to Vico* (trans. L. Cochrane, Chicago, 1984), p. 30.

China was after the Flood first planted either by Noah himself, or some of the sons of Sem, before the remove to Shinaar'. Webb uncovered evidence to support this claim. Of all nations, the Chinese had 'least erred in the rules of their religion', and, 'from immemorable times', they had 'acknowledged only one God, whom they name the monarch of heaven'. Webb also detected traces of the Christian ethic within Confucianism.[18]

The type of comparative religion practised by Webb was a staple of English theological method during the Restoration era, heavily influenced by the researches of the Huguenot pastor Samuel Bochart, who discerned remembrances of Noah in various classical myths.[19] Bochart's *Geographiae sacrae* (1646) was lauded by one of its author's foremost English disciples, Theophilus Gale (1628–78), as 'a book worth its weight in purest gold'.[20] Stillingfleet, who aimed to show 'what footsteps there are of the truth of scripture-history amidst all the corruptions of heathen mythology', argued that the story of Noah 'disguised under other names' – such as Saturn, Prometheus and Janus – could be found in various non-Christian civilisations. For example, he found the twin aspects of the Roman god Janus an easy clue to decipher: this was 'not so fit an emblem of anything as of Noah's seeing those two ages before and after the Flood'.[21] Following a similar approach, Simon Patrick (1625–1707), Bishop of Ely, was but one among several scholars who identified Ham as both the Jupiter of classical paganism and the Hammon of ancient Egyptian religion.[22] The Cambridge Platonists defended orthodoxy by way of a different measure of 'comparison' between religions. As well as tracing the diffusion of the ancient patriarchal theology, they argued that man's

[18] John Webb, *An historical essay endeavoring a probability that the language of the Empire of China is the primitive language* (London, 1669), pp. 31–2, 43, 86–9, 92. See also *Universal history*, I, p. 116; *Ductor historicus: or, a short system of universal history* (London, 1698), p. 292. For a more sceptical approach to the problem of reconciling Chinese antiquity with sacred chronology, see John Beaumont, *Gleanings of antiquities* (London, 1724), pp. 2, 45–8.   [19] P. Burke, *Vico* (Oxford, 1985), p. 44.
[20] Theophilus Gale, *The court of the Gentiles* (2 vols., Oxford, 1669–70), I, 'Advertisements to the reader'.   [21] Stillingfleet, *Origines sacrae*, pp. 593, 598.
[22] Simon Patrick, *A commentary upon the first book of Moses, called Genesis* (London, 1695). See also Thomas Browne, *Pseudodoxia epidemica*, bk 8, ch. 5 (*Works*, II, pp. 497–8), who had claimed that the myth of Jupiter cutting off the genitals of his father Saturn was a corrupted memory derived of how Ham had beheld the nakedness of his father Noah in his cups. For Ham as Jupiter Ammon, see also Robert Clayton (1695–1758), Bishop of Clogher, *A journal from Grand Cairo to Mount Sinai* (London, 1753), pp. 72–3. Clayton was a heterodox Trinitarian (see J. C. D. Clark, *English society 1688–1832* (Cambridge, 1985), pp. 287–8; B. W. Young, *Religion and Enlightenment in eighteenth-century England* (Oxford, 1998), p. 39); but, like Isaac Newton, he combined this with an orthodox view of the Mosaic past. Gale, *Court of the Gentiles*, I, pp. 187–9, also identified Neptune as Japhet and Pluto as Shem. *Ductor historicus*, p. 292, argued that 'several nations look upon Noah as their head and founder', describing Saturn and his sons Jupiter, Neptune and Pluto in classical mythology as a remembrance of Noah, and his progeny Shem, Ham and Japhet. See also Bedford, *Animadversions*, pp. 98–102.

God-given faculty of reason inclined him towards the core tenets of Christian belief. Ralph Cudworth (1617–88), for example, argued that monotheism and Trinitarianism were part of the common sense of mankind. Of course, such doctrines had been disguised beneath the particular cladding of various heathen cultures; however, the proliferation of polytheism was more apparent than real: within pagan theologies there tended to be one supreme sovereign god from whom all minor deities and demons were generated or created.[23]

In the age of Enlightenment the ethnic origins of nations would remain an important rampart of the citadel of Christian orthodoxy. The broad construction put upon the Toleration of 1689 and the lapsing of the Licensing Act in 1695 let slip new forces of anticlerical raillery against the errors propagated by self-interested priestcraft.[24] Heterodox deviation from the mainstream of revealed Christianity ranged from deeply felt and scripturally based unease at the Athanasian formulation of the Trinity to outright abandonment of revealed Christianity and its replacement with forms of natural religion and deism. However, the very methods deployed by radical critics of Christian revelation and ecclesiastical authority were appropriated from those used by Christian apologists to explain away the history of the gentile world and the diversity of pagan religions, with an original natural religion substituted for the Judaeo-Christian Ur-religion. Traditional accounts of paganism as corruptions of an original patriarchal monotheism were turned upside-down by the heterodox, who argued instead that all religions, including Christianity, were superstitious and priest-ridden corruptions of a primitive natural religion. In this way ethnic theology inadvertently ignited one of the brightest fires of the

---

[23] Ralph Cudworth, *The true intellectual system of the universe* (1678: 3 vols., London, 1845), I, pp. 412–36, 453–63, 470–82, 509–10, 518, 523, 593–9, 600–1; R. Popkin, 'The crisis of polytheism and the answers of Vossius, Cudworth and Newton', in J. Force and Popkin (eds.), *Essays on the context, nature and influence of Isaac Newton's theology* (Dordrecht, 1990), pp. 13–15; P. Harrison, *'Religion' and the religions in the English Enlightenment* (Cambridge, 1990), pp. 31–4, 44–5, 131–5; A. Grafton, *Defenders of the text* (Cambridge, MA, 1991), pp. 17–18. See also Thomas Hyde (1636–1703), *Historia religionis veterum Persarum* (1700), which uncovered an inner core of monotheism within the fire worship and supposed dualism of the Zoroastrian tradition: see P. J. Marshall and G. Williams, *The great map of mankind: British perceptions of the world in the age of Enlightenment* (London, 1982), p. 102.

[24] M. Jacob, *The Newtonians and the English Revolution 1689–1720* (Hassocks, 1976), pp. 201–2; J. Israel, 'William III and toleration', in O. Grell, Israel and N. Tyacke (eds.), *From persecution to toleration: the Glorious Revolution and religion in England* (Oxford, 1991), pp. 161–2; R. Lund, 'Irony as subversion: Thomas Woolston and the crime of wit', in Lund (ed.), *The margins of orthodoxy* (Cambridge, 1995), p. 172; M. Goldie, 'Priestcraft and the birth of whiggism', in N. Phillipson and Q. Skinner (eds.), *Political discourse in early modern Britain* (Cambridge, 1993).

deistic Enlightenment;[25] yet, on the other hand, Christian ethnology remained one of the most common antidotes to the spread of philosophical irreligion.

Ethnic theology was not immediately displaced from the scholarly mainstream by the early stirrings of the Enlightenment. There were still clear limits to naturalistic explanation.[26] For example, John Locke, whatever his private views, did not refute the patriarchalist royalism of Sir Robert Filmer (1588–1653) by pulling the scaffolding of Mosaic history out from underneath the latter's superstructure of political theory. Instead Locke accepted the Biblical field of combat, though he contested Filmer's use of equivocal Scripture proofs from Genesis, moved in the direction of a critical hermeneutic and heterodox theology, and attempted to turn discussion as far as possible on to the sort of anthropological terrain associated with the Grotian tradition of natural jurisprudence.[27] Nor did the rise of Newtonian science to an intellectual ascendancy over the culture of early eighteenth-century Britain do anything to undermine the discourse of ethnic theology.

The Newtonian project did not rest on naturalistic presuppositions, but was deeply rooted in Biblical exegesis. The axis of scientific debate was, in fact, theological. While Newtonians were deeply interested in framing a concordance of Scripture, experiment and mathematics, their opponents, the Hutchinsonians, adhered to an uncompromising Hebraism and a theology of divine analogies between the spiritual and the natural world, as presented in the treatise *Moses's principia* (1724) by John Hutchinson (1674–1737).[28] Isaac Newton (1642–1727) was himself deeply absorbed in theology, and his theological speculations ran to well over a million words. Given that the truths of God's book of nature

[25] R. Popkin, 'The deist challenge', in Grell *et al.*, *From persecution to toleration*; J. Champion, *The pillars of priestcraft shaken* (Cambridge, 1992); J. Redwood, *Reason, ridicule and religion* (London, 1976); F. E. Manuel, *The changing of the gods* (Hanover, NH, and London, 1983).

[26] For an over-optimistic account of the rise of naturalistic thinking, see C. J. Sommerville, *The secularization of early modern England* (Oxford, 1992).

[27] Robert Filmer, *Patriarcha and other writings* (ed. J. P. Sommerville, Cambridge, 1991), esp. ch. 1, sect. 5, pp. 7–8, on the dispersal of nations after the Flood; John Locke, *Two treatises of government* (ed. P. Laslett, Cambridge, 1960), *First treatise*, esp. pp. 260–8, on the dispersal and the confusion of tongues; J. Marshall, *John Locke: resistance, religion and responsibility* (Cambridge, 1994), pp. 114–16, 145–6. See also Algernon Sidney, *Discourses concerning government* (ed. T. West, Indianapolis, 1990), pp. 5, 24–46. For the continuing force into the eighteenth century of a patriarchalism connected to the Genesis account of the origins of mankind, see Clark, *English society*, p. 223; R. Hole, *Pulpits, politics and public order in England 1760–1832* (Cambridge, 1989), p. 61.

[28] A. Kuhn, 'Glory or gravity: Hutchinson vs. Newton', *JHI* 22 (1961), 303–22. For the high church–tory associations of Hutchinsonianism, see L. Colley, *In defiance of oligarchy: the tory party 1714–1760* (Cambridge, 1982), p. 105. However, for a less political reading, see Young, *Religion and Enlightenment*, pp. 136–51.

complemented those found in Scripture, Newton did not separate science and mathematics from his theological obsessions. Indeed, although Newton's unconventional achievements in theology reflected the originality of his genius, his religious beliefs remained firmly grounded in Scripture. Ironically, it was his very immersion in Biblical hermeneutics – rather than any of his scientific pursuits – which were to lead Newton astray from Anglican orthodoxy. An irenicist and latitudinarian concern to scrape away the layers of metaphysical corruption which had accreted to the basic truths of the Christian tradition during the fourth and fifth centuries lured Newton into the radical heterodoxy of Arian Christology, a politically dangerous deviation which he prudently confined to his unpublished writings. Nevertheless, while rejecting the Athanasian doctrine of the Trinity, Newton did not reject Scripture, deity or a divine Christ; rather he emphasised the sovereignty of Almighty God, the 'pantocrator'. Nor did his heterodoxy pose a direct threat to Mosaic history; indeed Newton located the few plain fundamentals of uncorrupted belief in the 'religion of Noah', and in his manuscript treatise *Theologiae gentilis origines philosophicae* he traced the origins of idolatry to the Egyptian deification of Noah and his progeny. Other parts of Newton's theology seem more like a hangover from the early Reformed obsession with the apocalyptic; his interest in universal chronology, for example, was part of a project to interpret the deeper significances encoded within the prophetic books of the Bible, not least as they related to the history of the real Beast, the Athanasian Trinity. A staunch opponent of Catholicism, moreover, Newton came to associate the rise of popery with the institutionalisation of the Athanasian abomination. Stripped of its Trinitarian obsessions, Newton's religion appears more traditional, especially in the sphere of ethnic theology where it was heavily indebted to Bochart.[29]

Newtonianism involved an undoubted, but extremely circumscribed,

[29] F. Manuel, *The religion of Isaac Newton* (Oxford, 1974), esp. pp. 3, 39, 84–6, 92–4; Manuel, *Isaac Newton, historian*; R. Westfall, *Never at rest: a biography of Isaac Newton* (Cambridge, 1980), pp. 311–30, 344–5, 350–61, 812–15; A. R. Hall, *Isaac Newton, adventurer in thought* (1992: Cambridge, 1996), pp. 237–42, 339–43, 370–4; Popkin, 'Crisis of polytheism', pp. 11, 20–1; S. Mandelbrote, '"A duty of the greatest moment": Isaac Newton and the writing of biblical criticism', *British Journal of the History of Science* 26 (1993), 281–302; Mandelbrote, 'Isaac Newton and Thomas Burnet: Biblical criticism and the crisis of late seventeenth-century England', in J. Force and R. Popkin (eds.), *The books of nature and scripture* (Dordrecht, 1994), esp. pp. 158, 173 n. 45; D. Kubrin, 'Newton and the cyclical cosmos: providence and the mechanical philosophy', *JHI* 28 (1967), 325–46; J. H. Brooke, *Science and religion: some historical perspectives* (Cambridge, 1991), pp. 144–51. See Isaac Newton, 'General scholium', Newton, 'An early theological manuscript', c. 1672–5, Newton, 'A short schem of the true religion', Newton, 'Introduction to a treatise on Revelation', and R. Westfall, 'Newton and Christianity', all in I. B. Cohen and R. Westfall (eds.), *Newton: texts, backgrounds, commentaries* (New York, 1995), pp. 340, 342–56, 366–9.

radicalism. William Whiston (1667–1752), a protégé of Newton, whose heterodox ideas on the Trinity were to have him ejected from the Lucasian chair of mathematics at Cambridge, nevertheless outlined a hermeneutic scheme which qualified an unsophisticated literalism but did not deviate widely from it: 'The obvious or literal sense of scripture is the true and real one, where no evident reason can be given to the contrary . . . What ancient tradition asserts of the original constitution of nature, or of the origin and primitive state of the world, is to be allowed for true, where it is fully agreeable to scripture, reason and philosophy.'[30] Newtonianism was only the most prominent of a variety of approaches to sacred history emerging from the Anglican method of scriptural interpretation.[31] Late seventeenth-century Anglicans favoured a rational approach to Scripture, and were prepared to combine reason, including natural religion and tradition, in the quest for truth. Thomas Burnet (1635?–1715) and John Woodward (1665–1728), neither of whom was a Newtonian, also adopted strategies aimed at the reconciliation of Scripture with natural philosophy.[32] Allegorical readings of Genesis, or the placing of sacred history within a scientific framework, or the testing of canons of exegesis against observation of the natural world did little in themselves to undermine Scripture, despite the fears of the more narrowly orthodox. There was no wholesale assault on Genesis, merely the establishment of a more nuanced canon of accommodationist exegesis. The new science had accomplished 'a half-way revolution which left sacred history intact'.[33]

English ethnic theology proved responsive to the rise of scientific methods. Richard Cumberland, Bishop of Peterborough (1631–1718), employed a set of demographic calculations to refute the notion that there was not 'a sufficient increase of men from the three sons of Noah, to a number large enough to found all the nations mentioned in the earliest credible histories; and that in the times assigned to their foundation, agreeably with the Hebrew accounts'. Elaborating upon on an idea already aired by Richard Kidder (1633–1703), Bishop of Bath and Wells, in his *Commentary on the five books of Moses* (1694), Cumberland argued that the patriarchs had lived much longer lives than modern men, because of the propitious environment of the pre-Diluvial era. However, the Flood had transformed the earth for the worse, and gradually over a period of eight hundred years the human lifespan had been reduced to

---

[30] William Whiston, *A new theory of the earth* (London, 1696), p. 95. See also E. Duffy, '"Whiston's affair": the trials of a primitive Christian, 1709–1714', *JEH* 27 (1976), 129–50.   [31] Reedy, *Bible and reason*.
[32] J. Levine, *Dr Woodward's shield* (1977: Ithaca and London, 1991).
[33] Haber, *Age of the world*, pp. 3, 96–7.

about three score years and ten. In the immediate centuries after the Flood the physiology of the patriarchs was only beginning its gradual decline. Thus their longevity and stronger constitutions meant that they had been 'more able and fit to propagate mankind to great numbers than men can now do'. Adopting a system of multiplication by twenty-year cohorts Cumberland argued that the post-Diluvial world had been peopled at much quicker rates than would have been possible by degenerate modern man. Hence, the existence in the earliest centuries of post-Diluvial antiquity of civilisations far from the area where the Ark had come to rest was not an argument against the credibility of Scripture chronology. In addition, Cumberland was able to account for the extravagant ages of such Biblical patriarchs as Noah and Methuselah by synthesising the history of mankind with the sacred science of geology.[34]

Science and orthodoxy meshed in the emergent science of racial classification. John Harris (1667?–1719), a supporter of Woodward, countered critics of Scripture ethnology with his account of the Hamidian origins of the black African peoples, and his argument that the 'colour of the Negroes is not ingenite; but proceeds from accidental natural causes, and such as are peculiar to the countries they inhabit'.[35] The influence of Buffon led only to more discreet naturalistic statements of this orthodox monogenetic position. Starting from the proposition that both 'reason and religion' indicated the origins of the races from 'one common parent', Oliver Goldsmith (1730?–74) argued that the white European was the norm 'whence other varieties have sprung' through processes of degeneration brought on by climatic factors, poor nutrition or savage customs. As evidence, Goldsmith claimed that, while 'we have frequently seen white children produced from black parents', the union of two whites had never produced any black offspring: 'From hence we may conclude that whiteness is the colour to which mankind naturally tends.'[36]

The problem of accounting for the diversity of human languages within the short timespan of Mosaic chronology meant that linguistics became one of the most important bastions for the defence of revelation against deists armed with polygenism. William Wotton (1666–1727) claimed

[34] Richard Cumberland, *Origines gentium antiquissimae; or, attempts for discovering the times of the first planting of nations* (London, 1724), tract IV, esp. pp. 142–51. See also Richard Kidder, *A commentary on the five books of Moses* (2 vols., London, 1694), I, p. 54. For the seventeenth-century background, see F. Egerton, 'The longevity of the patriarchs: a topic in the history of demography', *JHI* 27 (1966), 575–84. This argument was still being made by Richard Kirwan at the end of the eighteenth century: see Cohn, *Noah's flood*, p. 107.
[35] John Harris, *Remarks on some late papers, relating to the universal Deluge* (London, 1697), p. 66.
[36] Oliver Goldsmith, *A history of the earth, and animated nature* (8 vols., London, 1774), II, ch. xi, 'Of the varieties in the human race', pp. 239–40.

that divine intervention at Babel alone explained the richness of human linguistic variation: 'the variety now actually existing of idioms spoken by the several inhabitants of this our earth, can I think be no way possible for, without supposing such a miraculous formation of languages as we find recorded in the eleventh chapter of Genesis'. Thus Wotton overturned the problem of reconciling diversity with chronology: he accepted the validity of the polygenist critique, but only to defend the authority of Scripture and the historicity of divine miracles.[37] A Scots presbyterian minister, David Malcolme (d. 1748), used perceived similarities in the languages of the Scottish Gaels, the natives of the Darien Isthmus in Panama and the Chinese to mount a refutation of those deists who 'pretend that the languages of America have no affinity to any of the languages in Europe, Asia or Africa; and then infer, that therefore they must be a quite distinct race of mortals, and not sprung from Adam and Eve'.[38]

One of the more prominent theological genres in the first half of the eighteenth century was the 'connection', an attempt to reconcile the histories and chronologies of the various gentile nations and civilisations of antiquity with the Bible.[39] Celebrated examples of this genre include Humphrey Prideaux's *The Old and New Testament connected in the history of the Jews and neighbouring nations* (1716–18), which went through at least fifteen editions by the middle of the eighteenth century, and Samuel Shuckford's *The sacred and prophane history of the world connected* (1728–37). Such works carried on the discourses of ethnic theology. Prideaux (1648–1724) argued that it was the very fact of the intimation within the ancient and universal patriarchal religion of Christ the mediator, who had not yet been revealed, which began the decline into polytheism. Noah had taught his posterity 'the worshipping of one God, the supreme governor and creator of all things, with hopes in his mercy through a mediator. For the necessity of a mediator between God and man was a general notion, which obtained among all mankind from the beginning.' However, the lack of an immediate mediator induced men to search for substitutes for the unrevealed Christ in the celestial bodies as 'intelligences . . . of a middle nature between God and them'. Hence, according to Prideaux, the true religion began to sink into a polytheism in the first rank of whose pantheon were the planetary deities such as Saturn, Jupiter, Mars,

---

[37] William Wotton, *A discourse concerning the confusion of languages at Babel* (London, 1713), p. 36.

[38] David Malcolme, *Letters, essays and other tracts illustrating the antiquities of Great Britain and Ireland* (1738: London, 1744), 'Collection of papers', no. ix, p. 22.

[39] A. Grafton, 'Joseph Scaliger and historical chronology', *H+T* 14 (1975), 156; B. Feldman and R. D. Richardson, *The rise of modern mythology 1680–1860* (Bloomington, IN, 1972), pp. 71–2.

Mercury and Venus. Shuckford (d. 1754) aimed to 'be of some service towards forming a judgment of the truth and exactness of the ancient Scripture history, by showing how far the old fragments of the heathen writers agree with it, and how much better and more authentic the account is, which it gives of things where they differ from it'. For instance, he believed the Chinese idol Fohi to be a concealed memory of Noah. On the other hand Shuckford was alert to the errors, myths and euhemeristic additions to gentile traditions: 'This, I think, is a just account of what has been the fate of the ancient heathen remains; they were clear and true, when left by their authors, but after-writers corrupted them by the addition of fable and false philosophy.'[40]

Another prominent genre of the eighteenth-century literary scene focused on the 'double doctrine' held to be a common feature of pagan religions. Beneath those superstitious outer trappings of heathenism which bore not the slightest resemblance to Christian truth, ran this argument appropriated from deistic critics of priestcraft, there often lay an inner core of esoteric truth known only as a mystery cult to an exclusive body of initiates. Thus, in explaining away the religious diversity of the world, theologians had resort to the claim that pagan exteriors often concealed a residue of the patriarchal religion of the Old Testament.[41] The classic analysis of the double doctrine was William Warburton's *The divine legation of Moses* (1738–41). Warburton (1698–1779) argued that belief in future rewards and punishments had been universal, present throughout the world's religions, albeit often only within a secret inner shell. The only exception to this universal sociological need for the divine sanction of futurity was found in the religion of the Hebrews, a people ruled directly by a special divine providence.

By the era of the high Enlightenment, ethnic theology was in decline, but far from exhausted as an integral part of British culture. Only at the sceptical extreme of the British Enlightenment were there outright criticisms of Mosaic history. In his *Letters on the study and use of history*, Henry St John, Viscount Bolingbroke (1678–1751), rejected the notion that the genealogies of the Old Testament provided a 'sufficient' basis for a universal history of the peopling of the world, and proceeded to criticise

---

[40] Humphrey Prideaux, *The Old and New Testament connected in the history of the Jews and neighbouring nations* (1716–18: 3rd edn, 2 vols., London, 1717–18), I, pp. 139–40; Samuel Shuckford, *The sacred and prophane history of the world connected* (3 vols., London, 1728–37), I, pp. ii, xx, 29, 102; A. Ross, 'Introduction', in Ross (ed.), *Selections from the Tatler and the Spectator* (Harmondsworth, 1982), p. 51. See also Richard Cumberland, 'A discourse endeavouring to connect the Greek and Roman antiquities, with those of the eldest eastern monarchies in Asia and Egypt; and consequently with the dispersion from Babel which came near the great Flood', in Cumberland, *Origines gentium antiquissimae*.

[41] Manuel, *Eighteenth century confronts the gods*, ch. 2, pt 2; Manuel, *Changing of the gods*, p. 37; P. Harrison, *'Religion' and the religions*, pp. 85, 95; Feldman and Richardson, *Rise of modern mythology*, p. 4.

those scholars who relied on the 'bare names, naked of circumstances' found in the tenth chapter of Genesis to construct erroneous 'extensions' of a dubious Mosaic history.[42] David Hume challenged the orthodox tradition of ethnic theology that pagan beliefs had developed from the progressive degeneration of the ancient patriarchal religion of Noah. There was, according to Hume, no primeval monotheism; instead, he conjectured, there had existed in the earliest ages of humankind a universal polytheism which had evolved with the help of a nascent philosophical culture into monotheism.[43] Such full-blown challenges to the Noachic system were rare. Even Henry Home, Lord Kames (1696–1782), a leading pioneer of Scottish Enlightenment sociology, was half-hearted in his deviation from Biblical orthodoxy. Kames found the environmentalist arguments for racial diversity implausible. Why did Britons in India remain white? Why were Amerindians uniformly coppertoned across the dramatically different climates of the Americas? While Co-adamitism – the thesis that God had created many different pairs of humans – seemed more likely, it was, declared Kames, an 'opinion . . . we are not permitted to adopt; being taught a different lesson by revelation'. Here Kames backtracked very unconvincingly: a miracle at the Tower of Babel had wrought 'an immediate change of bodily constitution' which fitted the dispersing peoples of the world for the various climes they were destined to inhabit.[44]

This was not simply a matter of a reluctance on the part of Kames to flaunt his heterodoxy. It also indicates the resilience of the basic contours of the Mosaic paradigm within the Scottish Enlightenment. Eighteenth-century Scotland produced a major mythographer in Principal Thomas Blackwell, of Marischal College, Aberdeen (1701–57), and, indirectly, in the converted Ayrshire protégé of Fénelon, the 'Chevalier' Andrew Ramsay (1686–1743), who detected the pattern of Biblical monotheism in the myths of heathenish cultures.[45] The mainstream rational religion of enlightened Scotland involved a reappraisal – rather than a jettisoning – of

[42] Bolingbroke, *Letters on the study and use of history*, in Bolingbroke, *Works* (5 vols., London, 1754), II, pp. 308, 313.

[43] David Hume, *The natural history of religion* (1757: ed. J. Gaskin, with *Dialogues concerning natural religion*, Oxford, 1993).

[44] Henry Home, Lord Kames, *Sketches of the history of man* (1774: 2nd edn, 1778: reprinted, 4 vols., Bristol, 1993), I, pp. 22–30, 50, 64, 73–9. See R. Wokler, 'Apes and races in the Scottish Enlightenment: Monboddo and Kames on the nature of man', in P. Jones (ed.), *Philosophy and science in the Scottish Enlightenment* (Edinburgh, 1988), pp. 155–6.

[45] Thomas Blackwell, *Lectures concerning mythology* (London, 1748); Andrew Ramsay, *The travels of Cyrus* (1727: 2 vols., Dublin, 1728), II, 'A discourse upon the theology and mythology of the ancients', esp. pp. 1–2, 7–9, 68–9; G. D. Henderson, *Chevalier Ramsay* (Edinburgh and London, 1952), pp. 113–14, 118–19, 127–8, 169, 218–19; D. P. Walker, *The ancient theology* (London, 1972), ch. 7; J. Mee, *Dangerous enthusiasm: William Blake and the culture of radicalism in the 1790s* (Oxford, 1992), pp. 124, 127, 138–9; Feldman and Richardson, *Rise of modern mythology*, pp. 5, 62.

the Genesis story, without any direct assault on its historicity. In his careful marriage of reason and revelation, Archibald Campbell (d. 1756), professor of divinity and ecclesiastical history at St Andrews, confessed: 'I do not here appeal to the books of Moses as a divine revelation. I only now regard them as a history that deserves at least as much credit as any other book of antiquity.'[46] Indeed, in tracing the rise of the economic and material arts from an Adamic fruit-gathering state through the agrarian and pastoral experiments of Cain and Abel to the hubris of Babel, Genesis seemed to complement the insights of stadial history. *De l'origine des loix, des arts et des sciences, et de leurs progrès chez les anciens peuples* (1758) by the French jurist Antoine-Yves Goguet (1716–58), translated into an Edinburgh edition in 1761 and well received in late eighteenth-century Scottish circles, explicitly acknowledged the Mosaic account as the only sure guide to the early history of man.[47] The Bible was even plundered for raw anthropological and sociological data by Scotland's historically minded moral philosophers and jurists. The Hebrew patriarchs, for example, were held to be representative of the pastoral phase of human development.[48] Indeed, J. G. A. Pocock points out that the Japhetan framework remained consistent even with the four-stage accounts of the progress of human society which were such a characteristic feature of the new historical sociology pioneered in the Enlightenment.[49] Although the conjectural histories of the Scottish Enlightenment began, according to Roger Emerson, 'at some unspecified date, which ignored the Bible or used it only as one among many sources', this sidestepping of Genesis was evidence merely that theology was increasingly 'compartmentalised' from the rest of human knowledge, and should not be assumed to indicate a secularisation of the world picture.[50] For example, on the clerical wing of the Scottish Enlightenment, William Robertson (1721–93), principal of Edinburgh University, combined stadialism, a naturalistic Humean account of the origins of pagan superstition and a providentialist account of mankind's intellectual and religious progress in a new version of ethnic theology which broke significantly with traditional euhemerist-diffusion-

---

[46] Quoted in J. K. Cameron, 'Theological controversy: a factor in the origins of the Scottish Enlightenment', in R. Campbell and A. Skinner (eds.), *The origins and nature of the Scottish Enlightenment* (Edinburgh, 1982), p. 127.

[47] P. Stein, *Legal evolution* (Cambridge, 1980), pp. 19–22; J. G. A. Pocock, 'Gibbon and the idol Fo: Chinese and Christian history in the Enlightenment', in D. S. Katz and J. I. Israel (eds.), *Sceptics, millenarians and Jews* (Leiden, 1990), p. 21 n.; Hodgen, *Early anthropology*, pp. 262–3.   [48] Stein, *Legal evolution*, p. 25.

[49] Pocock, 'Gibbon and the idol Fo', pp. 20–1. See also R. Emerson, 'Conjectural history and Scottish philosophers', *Historical Papers/Communications Historiques* (1984), 66–8.

[50] R. Emerson, 'The religious, the secular and the worldly: Scotland 1660–1800', in J. Crimmens (ed.), *Religion, secularization and political thought* (London and New York, 1989), pp. 76, 84.

ist analyses. Robertson explained the underlying similarities of the world's religions not in terms of the post-Diluvial spread of the patriarchal religion of Noah, but by way of the 'regular' and predictable operations of 'superstition' upon the 'weakness of the human mind', given the similar fears – 'dread of invisible beings', 'solicitude to penetrate into the effects of futurity' – experienced by savage peoples across the globe, which created the illusion of 'consanguinity'. Monotheism, 'the idea of one superintending mind', was 'an attainment far beyond the powers of man in the more early stages of his progress'.[51] However, in his treatment of Incan and Hindu civilisations, Robertson showed how more elevated ideas of a supreme power could arise out of 'false religion', in the solar cult of the Incas and in the learning of the Brahmin philosophers. The natural progress of mankind tended – providentially – towards the truths of Christianity.[52] Despite his distaste for the old shibboleths of ethnic theology, Robertson remained committed to the historicity of the Old Testament: 'the books of Moses' constituted 'the most ancient and only genuine record of what passed in the early ages of the world'.[53] Thus, while questioning the outlandish interpretations of ethnic theologians as to how America had been peopled, Robertson held to an 'infallible certainty, that all the human race spring from the same source, and that the descendants of one man, under the protection, as well as in obedience to the command of heaven, multiplied and replenished the earth'. Although it was now impossible 'to trace the branches of this first family' as they spread over the earth in a distant age which lay beyond the region of attested history, he advanced the probability of a Siberian migration to America, which avoided any suggestion of polygenesis.[54] Despite the challenge of the Enlightenment, the Scots intelligentsia of the late eighteenth century remained unembarrassed by sacred history: Robert Heron (1764–1807) produced *A philosophical view of universal history from the Creation* (1796) which conflated the history of Genesis with the natural history of society, economy and arts; the third edition of the *Encyclopaedia Britannica* (1797) listed the Celts as the descendants of Gomer, the eldest son of Japhet; and *Caledonia* (1807–24) by George Chalmers (1742–

[51] William Robertson, *The history of America* (1777), in Robertson, *Works* (London, 1831 edn), p. 785; Robertson, *An historical disquisition concerning the knowledge which the ancients had of India* (1791), 'Appendix', in Robertson, *Works*, p. 1094.
[52] Robertson, *America*, p. 916; Robertson, *India*, pp. 1093–9; N. Phillipson, 'Providence and progress: an introduction to the historical thought of William Robertson', in S. J. Brown (ed.), *William Robertson and the expansion of empire* (Cambridge, 1997); K. O'Brien, *Narratives of Enlightenment: cosmopolitan history from Voltaire to Gibbon* (Cambridge, 1997), p. 165; Marshall and Williams, *Great map of mankind*, pp. 119–20.
[53] Robertson, *India*, p. 1035.
[54] Robertson, *America*, pp. 784–9; E. A. Hoebel, 'William Robertson: an eighteenth-century anthropologist-historian', *American Anthropologist* 62 (1960), 653–4.

1825), the major history of early Scotland in the first half of the nineteenth century, still held fast to a Mosaic account of the peopling of Europe in the Japhetan line.[55]

The confrontation of ethnic theologians with the gods of the pagan world continued throughout the second half of the eighteenth century, but no longer occupied the central place in English religious thought which it had been accorded in the age of the Cambridge Platonists and the latitude-men. The challenge to orthodoxy had taken on new forms, and the most innovative theologians had abandoned the Noachic landscape for other terrains of apologetic. Foremost in sophistication was the Scottish Common Sense philosophy of mind, devised by Thomas Reid as an antidote to Hume's devastating metaphysical scepticism.[56] From the late 1770s a pressing need to answer Gibbon led a number of scholars, foremost among them Richard Watson (1737–1816), into defences of early church history. By the turn of the nineteenth century the field of apologetics was dominated by the 'evidences' of William Paley (1743–1805), who, conscious of Voltaire's strategy of 'attacking Christianity through the sides of Judaism', shifted his principal line of defence forward to the New Testament. Although he conceded the importance of prophecy to the credibility of Christianity, Paley was unwilling 'to make Christianity answerable with its life, for the circumstantial truth of each separate passage of the Old Testament'.[57] Nevertheless, gentilism continued to intrigue a number of figures in the second rank of English theology and in the related disciplines of ethnography and mythology.[58] As George Eliot (1819–80) indicated in *Middlemarch* (1871–2), it was the rise of the higher criticism in Germany in the early nineteenth century which made Casaubon with his 'Key to all mythologies' an intellectual anachronism by about 1830; in the high Enlightenment of the middle of the eighteenth century an ethnic theologian in the mould of Casaubon, while no longer at the cutting edge of intellectual life, was still representative of the concerns of the wider clerical intelligentsia.[59]

During the second half of the eighteenth century Anglican circles enjoyed a minor boom in 'speculative mythography',[60] and quite a vigorous debate ensued over the origins of idolatry. John Jackson (1686–

[55] H. Weinbrot, *Britannia's issue* (Cambridge, 1993), p. 485 n.; Chalmers, *Caledonia* (3 vols., London, 1807–24), I, pp. 2–9.

[56] However, Hume's heterodox ideas on racial inferiority also attracted a rebuttal from the Common Sense philosopher James Beattie, *An essay on the nature and immutability of truth in opposition to sophistry and scepticism* (1771: reprint, London, 1996), pp. 507–12.

[57] William Paley, *A view of the evidences of Christianity* (1794: 11th edn, 2 vols., London, 1805), II, pt 3, ch. 3, 'The connection of Christianity with the Jewish history', pp. 290–5.

[58] Feldman and Richardson, *Rise of modern mythology*, pp. 397–9.

[59] George Eliot, *Middlemarch* (ed. W. J. Harvey, Harmondsworth, 1965), pp. 240, 254.

[60] Mee, *Dangerous enthusiasm*, p. 121; Feldman and Richardson, *Rise of modern mythology*.

1763), although an adherent of Samuel Clarke's Arian formulation of the Trinity, remained an orthodox defender of sacred history, attributing the origins of paganism among the Japhetan peoples of Europe to ancestor-worship imported from the lineage of Ham which corrupted the ancient patriarchal religion. When the Japhetans first came to Europe in the seventh century after the Deluge, they brought with them their ancient monotheism, 'and hero-gods were not known amongst them, till the Phoenician Pelasgi, about the ninth century after the Flood, carried the Cabiric gods amongst them, and introduced their worship and mysteries'.[61] Similarly, Jacob Bryant (1715–1804), the doyen of late eighteenth-century British mythographers, argued in his influential treatise, *A new system, or, an analysis of ancient mythology* (1774–6), that pagan cults had arisen from the ethnic stock of Chus, son of Ham, a people known as the Cuthites or Amonians. The founders of the arts and sciences necessary for civilisation as well as the fathers of idolatry, the Cuthites alone had been responsible for the enormity of the events at Babel. The degenerate religion of this lineage, which involved the worship of the sun and fire but also included a vague ancestral memory of the universal Deluge, had been diffused throughout the ancient world.[62] However, the diffusionist theories of Jackson and Bryant were attacked by John Richardson (1741?–1811) and the antiquary Francis Wise (1695–1767) as deviations from Scripture.[63]

There was a continuing need to defend the truths of revealed religion against its heterodox critics. Ethnic theology provided a response to the threat posed by anti-Trinitarians. In *The remains of Japhet* (1767), James Parsons (1705–70) harnessed ethnic theology to the defence of orthodox Trinitarianism against the heterodox charge that the doctrine of the Trinity was a metaphysical corruption of true Christianity. Parsons argued that 'a plurality in the deity, was always believed by the patriarchs'; in other words, far from Trinitarianism being a corruption of Christian doctrine, it was of Noachic antiquity. He bolstered his case by arguing that the worship of the triune deity was universal, and could be found as

---

[61] John Jackson, *Chronological antiquities* (3 vols., London, 1752), III, p. 218.
[62] Jacob Bryant, *A new system, or an analysis of ancient mythology* (3 vols., London, 1774–6); Mee, *Dangerous enthusiasm*, p. 132; Harrison, *'Religion' and the religions*, pp. 142–3; T. Trautmann, *Aryans and British India* (Berkeley and Los Angeles, 1997), pp. 43–4.
[63] John Richardson, *A dissertation on the languages, literature, and manners of eastern nations* (1777: 2nd edn, Oxford, 1778); Francis Wise, *The history and chronology of the fabulous ages considered* (Oxford, 1764); Wise, *Some enquiries concerning the first inhabitants, language, religion, learning and letters of Europe* (Oxford, 1758). For Wise and his intellectual debt to Malcolme, see S. Piggott, 'Antiquarian studies', in L. S. Sutherland and L. G. Mitchell (eds.), *The history of the University of Oxford*, vol. V, *The eighteenth century* (Oxford, 1986), pp. 766–7.

far away as Tibet and Peru.[64] This was taken to be evidence that the Trinity had been disseminated throughout the world on the dispersal of nations.

The pioneers of the intellectual disciplines which were eventually to demolish the credibility of the Pentateuch as an accurate record of universal history continued to engage positively with ethnic theology. Sir William Jones's classification of Sanskrit with Greek, Latin, Gothic and Celtic in 1786 undermined the idea of a primal Hebrew language from which the post-Babelian languages of Europe were descended, yet it did not initially disturb the scheme of sacred history. Indeed, though Jones (1746–94) was a scrupulous orientalist, his philological breakthrough emerged from a wider project to preserve Mosaic orthodoxy and Biblical chronology. It was, for instance, rumoured that he had assisted Richardson in his repudiation of Bryant's Cuthite follies.[65] More openly, Jones's essay 'On the gods of Greece, Italy and India' applied some of the old arguments of ethnic theology to Indian material, highlighting religious similarities between Christianity and Hinduism, including, for example, affinities between Noah and the Indian deity Manu II (to be distinguished from an earlier Manu I whom Jones associated with Adam).[66] In his essay on 'The origin and families of men', Jones used the laws of geometrical progression to demonstrate that the whole world could have been peopled from one couple, and laid out a philological basis for the Noachic dispersion. Not only was the Deluge 'an historical fact admitted as true by every nation, to whose literature we have access', but it seemed clear from his classification of the language groups of Asia – the original seat of mankind – that the whole world 'sprang from three branches of one stem'. The composition of the ancient Vedas Jones located safely in the chronological wake of the Noachic Flood. Indeed, he could find 'no certain monument, or even probable tradition' of the rise of civilisation 'above twelve or at most fifteen or sixteen centuries before the birth of Christ'.

---

[64] James Parsons, *Remains of Japhet: being historical enquiries into the affinity and origin of the European languages* (London, 1767), ch. 7, esp. p. 218; see also ch. 8 for the universality of the triune deity. In the second half of the seventeenth century, Ross, *Pansebeia*, pp. 558–9, had noticed the trinity of powers found in Gentilism. Cudworth, *True intellectual system*, I, pp. 482, 509–10, 600–1, had drawn attention to the Trinitarian features of various pagan religions and Hyde had detected traces of Trinitarianism in Chinese idolatry: see Marshall and Williams, *Great map of mankind*, p. 115. See also Ramsay, *Cyrus*, II, 'Discourse', pp. 8–9; Henderson, *Chevalier Ramsay*, p. 218.

[65] Feldman and Richardson, *Rise of modern mythology*, p. 241; Trautmann, *Aryans and British India*, pp. 41–6; G. Cannon, *The life and mind of Oriental Jones* (Cambridge, 1990), pp. 42, 197, 239, 242.

[66] William Jones, 'On the gods of Greece, Italy, and India', in P. J. Marshall (ed.), *The British discovery of Hinduism in the eighteenth century* (Cambridge, 1970), p. 212; Feldman and Richardson, *Rise of modern mythology*, p. 268; Trautmann, *Aryans and British India*, p. 58; Cannon, *Oriental Jones*, pp. 296–7, 310, 318.

The father of modern linguistics and keen student of comparative religion explicitly confirmed 'by antecedent reasoning, and by evidence in part highly probable, and in part certain' the truth of the first eleven books of Genesis. Sad to relate, a decisive passage in the *Padma Purāna*, which dealt with Satyavarman (another Noah-figure, according to Jones) and his three sons S arma, Kharma and Jyāpati, was the recent – and all too tidy – interpolation by an unscrupulous pandit whom Jones's over-eager Asiatic Society colleague Francis Wilford (1760/1–1822) had indoctrinated into Mosaic history.[67]

Given the growing scale of British interests in India, it is unsurprising that the accommodation of Hinduism to sacred history became the hallmark of ethnic theology in its twilight phase.[68] Most notably, the credulous Thomas Maurice (1754–1824), concerned to sustain 'the truth of the ten first chapters of Genesis', read the history of India and its religion as a case study in the degeneration of the original patriarchal religion of Noah's descendants. Following in the footsteps of both Jones and Parsons, Maurice detected a distinct residue of the Trinity in the 'Indian triad of deity, Brahma, Veeshnu, and Seeva'. Within this triune godhead, Brahma represented Creation, Veeshnu the mediation associated with Christ and Seeva a spirit of regeneration. Unfortunately, Indian religion also provided a sad story of pagan corruption. The degraded cult of *lingam*, or phallus-worship, Maurice was quick to trace 'to its true source, the turpitude of Ham, whose Cuthite progeny introduced it to Hindostan, together with other depravities, destructive of the pure primeval religion of Shem'. As it transpired, the Indians were not alone in preserving the patriarchal legacy of the Trinity. Maurice saw remnants of the Trinity everywhere – in the 'triplasios mithra' of Persian religion, in the representation of a triune god depicted on a medal found in Siberia and kept in St Petersburg, in the 'tanga-tanga' of South America, in the symbolic globe–wing–serpent pattern of the ancient Egyptians. All of these were corrupt memories of a single 'grand primeval doctrine'. But could the Noachids have transmitted throughout the world a Christian doctrine not found among the Jews of the Old Testament? Thankfully, the plural term 'Elohim' for the godhead and the triadic splendours of the Sephiroth were enough to convince Maurice of the trinitarian nature of primeval Judaism (which a later rabbinical tradition had expunged, out of disappointment with the meek and far-from-militant Messiah of the

---

[67] William Jones, *Discourses delivered at the Asiatick Society 1785–1792* (reprint with intro. by R. Harris, London, 1993), 'Discourse the ninth on the origin and families of nations. Delivered 23rd February, 1792', pp. 191, 193, 196; Trautmann, *Aryans and British India*, pp. 90–2; Cannon, *Oriental Jones*, pp. 283, 317, 330–1, 338–9, 341.

[68] See e.g. Hales, *New analysis of chronology*.

Christians). The example of Maurice, like that of Jones, shows how the Mosaic paradigm shaped the response of Britons to the peoples of their Empire in the East. Subscribing to the idea of Christian monogenesis, these early orientalists sought not to establish Indian otherness, but its degenerate affiliation with the British within the universal Noachic family of nations. Maurice, indeed, identified the Druids of the ancient Britons as a caste of Brahmins who had become incorporated within the Asiatic Japhetan stock which would eventually people Europe.[69]

Although the disciplines of ethnology and philology were in the process of abandoning the overt Biblical content of ethnic theology, the underlying theological structures of these evolving disciplines would survive well into the nineteenth century, not least in a commitment to the idea of a unitary Creation.[70] By the same token, the idea of polygenesis remained until the middle of the nineteenth century on the radical fringes of British intellectual life.[71] It appeared on the heterodox frontier of the Scottish Enlightenment in a footnote to one of Hume's essays, half-heartedly in the work of Kames (though both authors were social theorists otherwise committed to assumptions of a uniform human nature) and, more prominently, in the work of the late Enlightenment racialist John Pinkerton (1758–1826), which combined a critique of the Old Testament, a Voltairean anti-Judaism, polygenesis and a virulent Celtophobia.[72] Wherever the heresy of polygenesis surfaced, its racialist implications were quickly apparent, as in the case of Edward Long (1734–1813) whose *History of Jamaica* (1774) was a self-interested justification of the white plantocracy.[73]

Racialism was but a step removed from polygenist heterodoxy. Consider the dissident scriptural exegesis of Edward King FRS (1735?–1807) who contended that 'the express words and history of Holy Writ, teach

[69] Thomas Maurice, *Indian antiquities* (6 vols., London, 1800–1), esp. I, pp. 22, 33, 112, 119–21, 126; II, pp. 16, 26–9; III, p. ix; IV, pp. 18, 21, 34–8, 41–7, 68, 74, 146, 152, 162; IV and V, 'A dissertation on the pagan triads of deity'; VI, 'A dissertation on the Indian origin of the Druids'.

[70] G. Stocking, *Victorian anthropology* (1987: New York pbk, 1991), pp. 17, 44–5, 48–52, 69, 75.

[71] *Ibid.*, pp. 49, 64, 67; J. C. Greene, *The death of Adam: evolution and its impact on Western thought* (1959: New York, 1961), p. 222. See e.g. L. Poliakov, *Le mythe aryen* (1971: new edn, Brussels, 1987), p. 199, for the English medic John Atkins (1685–1757).

[72] David Hume, 'Of national characters', in Hume, *Essays moral, political and literary* (ed. E. F. Miller, Indianapolis, 1987), p. 208 n.; John Pinkerton, 'An essay on the origin of Scotish poetry', in Pinkerton (ed.), *Ancient Scotish poems* (2 vols., London, 1786), I, pp. xxiv–xxvi; Pinkerton, *A dissertation on the origin and progress of the Scythians or Goths* (1787), included in Pinkerton, *An enquiry into the history of Scotland* (1789: 2 vols., Edinburgh, 1814).

[73] D. B. Davis, *The problem of slavery in western culture* (Ithaca, 1966), pp. 460–4; Marshall and Williams, *Great map of mankind*, pp. 248–9.

us, that there were several distinct species of men, from the Creation to the Flood', and that Adamic monogenesis was 'directly contrary' to the sense of the Old Testament. If God had created only one pair of humans, there were, for instance, major inconsistencies in the story of Cain and Abel. When Cain wandered afraid after the murder of Abel, which people did he fear and whence came Cain's wife? According to King, Genesis 1:27 revealed how God had created the 'genus' man, including not only Adam, 'the progenitor of the class or species of men, endowed with the greatest and most useful abilities', but also a variety of inferior races, whose real anatomical differences could not be explained away in environmentalist terms. Cain, King concluded, had 'debased his descent from Adam' by marrying into 'an inferior caste, or species of mankind'. But had the Flood not destroyed every living creature, barring those in the Ark? King argued that the Flood had been universal in its extent, but had not resulted in total destruction. Had there, for example, been any kangaroos on the Ark? Whereas the Adamic Noachids and the animals under their protection had survived by God's special providence, some denizens of far-flung continents had survived by 'fortunate accidents'. After the Flood, the 'sacred race' of Noah had disseminated the 'divine' Adamic knowledge of the arts, sciences and skills of cultivation in the regions of the Old World where they settled, but these had only recently been transmitted to the inferior non-Adamic races discovered in the 'savage, uncultivated countries' of America and New Holland.[74]

Where orthodox theologians emphasised the relationships between the kindred peoples found in Genesis 10 (though not forgetting the curse which had befallen the stock of Ham), polygenist heretics stressed only difference. It is salutary to contrast King's heretical racialism with the work of the orthodox mythographer George Stanley Faber (1773–1854). Revising the ideas of Bryant, to whom he dedicated his prestigious Bampton lectures, published as *Horae Mosaicae*, Faber argued that all the world's pagan religions – classical, Celtic, Gothic, Persian, Chinese, Hindu, Aztec and Incan – were built upon 'mutilated traditions of the Deluge'. Polytheistic idolatry originated in 'helio-arkite superstition', an excessive reverence for Noachic ancestors combining with the worship of celestial bodies. The sun was a symbol of Noah, while the moon represented the Ark. Remembrances of the 'Arkite ogdoad' surfaced throughout the world, for instance, in the eight primeval gods of Egypt and in the Phoenician tale of the 'just man' Sydyk and the seven Cabiri. Moreover,

[74] Edward King, *Morsels of criticism: tending to illustrate some few passages in the Holy Scriptures, upon philosophical principles and an enlarged view of things* (2nd edn, 3 vols., London, 1800), III, 'A dissertation concerning the creation of man', pp. 70–1, 74, 76–8, 85–6, 89–91, 93, 101, 103, 109, 113–14, 120, 167–9.

Faber also detected fainter traces within the pagan world of other elements of the patriarchal religion, including traditions of a Paradise, a
Fall, a serpent and a mediatorial Messiah. The ethnological implications
of this underlying uniformity were made explicit:

> The singular phenomenon of a general agreement among a vast variety of nations,
> widely separated from each other, and effectually prevented by mutual distance
> from having had any recent intercourse, can only be accounted for upon the
> supposition, that they all sprang originally from one common ancestor.[75]

Ethnic theology involved the investigation of a deeper unity concealed
beneath the world's apparent diversity.

Polygenesis would remain marginal, even as the science of race developed. The work of James Cowles Prichard (1786–1848), which
dominated British ethnology in the first half of the nineteenth century,
was conceived on the new principles of racial and philological analysis.
Yet Prichard remained keen to defend the contours of Biblical orthodoxy
against the advocates of polygenesis. At the outset of his career he
eschewed environmentalist arguments, but found that, while his thesis of
a (non-evolutionary) developmental process from black to white conser-
ved the Biblical notion of common human origins, the implicit suggestion
of a black Adam, while not strictly heretical, proved as unpalatable as
polygenesis. Over time, Prichard moved on to the safer well-trodden
ground of environmentalist monogenesis.[76] The continuation, well into
the nineteenth century, of the battle to prove the unity of mankind is a
testament to the tenacity of sacred history in the sphere of ethnology.
Even as ethnic theology was eclipsed by a range of new sciences, theology
remained intimately linked to developments in the study of ethnicity.
Indeed one of the functions of the new racialist discourse which emerged
in the middle of the nineteenth century was to provide a plausible starting
point and aboriginal identity for a deracinated intelligentsia. No longer
did the Bible and the system of universal history which it purveyed suffice
as a set of bearings by which educated Englishmen might locate themselves in some overarching plan.

---

[75] George Stanley Faber, *Horae Mosaicae: or a dissertation on the credibility and theology of the Pentateuch* (Bampton lectures, 1801: 2nd edn, 2 vols., London, 1818), I, pp. 9–10, 41–146; Faber, *A dissertation on the mysteries of the Cabiri* (2 vols., Oxford, 1803), I, pp. vii, x, 9–10, 15–19, for the origins of 'helio-arkite' worship; Feldman and Richardson, *Rise of modern mythology*, pp. 397–9.

[76] Stocking, *Victorian anthropology*, pp. 48–53, 58; Stocking, 'From chronology to ethnol-ogy: James Cowles Prichard and British anthropology 1800–1850', in J. C. Prichard, *Researches into the physical history of man* (1813: ed. Stocking, Chicago and London, 1973); Greene, *Death of Adam*, pp. 237–43; J. W. Burrow, 'The uses of philology in Victorian England', in R. Robson (ed.), *Ideas and institutions of Victorian Britain* (London, 1967), pp. 189–90; H. F. Augstein, 'Introduction', in Augstein (ed.), *Race: the origins of an idea, 1760–1850* (Bristol, 1996), p. xxiv.

British beginnings

It is clear that the discourse of ethnic theology occupied an important place in the concerns of the clerical intelligentsias of early modern Britain. However, given that the primary concern of theologians was the defence of Christian orthodoxy, did ethnic theology in its heyday have any substantial impact upon the ways in which patriotic antiquarians constructed national identities? As elsewhere in Europe, sacred history was considered a more reliable indicator of ethnic provenance than national origin myths inherited from the middle ages. The Reformation may have exacerbated this process for British scholars. Scholars subjected secular myths and sacred history to different degrees of sceptical rigour. The unreliable features of medieval origin myths, such as the legend of the Trojan origins of the Britons concocted by Geoffrey of Monmouth, were attributed to monkcraft; but Scripture was unassailable. Peter Heylin, the antiquarian of the middle of the seventeenth century, argued that there was 'express text' in Scripture for the 'division of the world by the sons of Noah'. On the other hand, Heylin had no time for the Galfridian myth; the legend of Geoffrey of Monmouth dated from an era 'when almost all nations pretended to be of Trojan race'.[77] The legends propagated by Annius of Viterbo which interwove Noachic history with the origins of nations presented more of a problem. The story retailed in Annius concerning the great Celtic king Samothes had influenced sixteenth-century English antiquarians, including John Bale and John Caius.[78] However, Stillingfleet was prepared to disentangle legend from Scripture, denouncing the ethnic lineages found in Annius as 'aery phantasms, covered over with the cowl of the monk of Viterbo'. Stillingfleet was aware of the 'darkness and obscurity' which had covered northern European history in the long centuries before the arrival of the Romans whose literacy enabled history to be transmitted reliably from one generation to the next. Between Scripture and authentic civil history was a chasm which tended to be filled by legends. On these grounds Stillingfleet was quite prepared to jettison the whole myth of British origins from 'Gomer to Brute' as 'fabulous'.[79] The leading Biblical commentator Matthew Poole (1624–79) demonstrated how a responsible scholar should approach the genealogies of nations found in Genesis. For a start, Genesis showed 'the

[77] Peter Heylin, *Cosmographie* (London, 1652), 'General introduction', p. 7; bk 1, p. 257.
[78] T. D. Kendrick, *British antiquity* (London, 1950), pp. 70–2. For the influence of the Samothes legend in Welsh antiquarianism, see R. G. Gruffydd, 'The Renaissance and Welsh literature', in G. Williams and R. O. Jones (eds.), *The Celts and the Renaissance* (Cardiff, 1990), p. 19. For seventeenth-century English versions of the Pseudo-Berosus, see Allen, *Legend of Noah*, p. 115.
[79] Stillingfleet, *Origines sacrae*, pp. 96, 99; Prideaux, *Old and New Testament connected*, I, p. 445. Nevertheless, for a partial defence of Annius, see Robert Clayton, *A vindication of the histories of the Old and New Testaments* (Dublin, 1752), pp. 185–6.

true original of the several nations, about which all other authors write idly, fabulously or falsely'. Yet, it was also important for the sacred genealogist to

avoid both carelessness . . . and excessive curiosity about every particular person here named, and the people sprung from him, which is neither necessary, nor profitable, nor indeed possible now to find out, by reason of the great changes of names through length of time, loss of ancient records, differences of languages, extinction of families, conquest and destruction of nations, and other causes.

Despite his reticence on much of the detail, Poole remained confident about the tripartite division of the world among the sons of Noah, and even some of the particular lineages found in Europe.[80] Others shared this curious combination of scepticism and confidence. The credulous Henry Rowlands (1655–1723), an Anglesey vicar who championed his island as the home of the Druid heirs of the pre-Noachic religion of the patriarchs, pretended to a critical outlook on man-made sources: 'As to the origin of nations . . . it is very presumptive that the ancientest memoirs of things, the sacred excepted, were at first but what was built on this foundation, viz. on inferences and conjectures; yet when recorded and transmitted to posterity, their credit advanced as they grew in age.' Where Scripture was unclear or ran out, then the orthodox were perfectly free to voice their scepticism about the precise course of a nation's family tree. Yet, as Rowlands discovered, Scripture went a long way. In the 'remote perplexities and deepest obscurities' of antiquity, he found 'glimmerings of light': 'the divine testimony assures us, that our first stock of people travelled hither from the coast of Armenia and Babylon, and that they were of the race of Japhet, who planted the western isles, and consequently the isles of Britain and Ireland'.[81]

Who dared take a sceptical axe to the Noachic trunk of the English family tree? The attempts by some English antiquarians to seek firmer

[80] Matthew Poole, *Annotations upon the Holy Bible*, vol. I (London, 1688 edn), introductory commentary to Genesis 10 and remarks on Genesis 10, vv. 2–3. See B. Shapiro, *Probability and certainty in seventeenth-century England* (Princeton, 1983), pp. 157–9. *Ductor historicus*, p. 17, argued that 'in point of chronology, we must depend upon the accounts we find in holy scripture, since we can expect nothing concerning the first times from profane historians'.

[81] Henry Rowlands, *Mona antiqua restaurata* (Dublin, 1723), 'Preface', p. 205. See also Levine, *Dr Woodward's shield*, ch. 4, esp. pp. 64, 67; Clayton, *Journal from Grand Cairo*, p. 131: 'The books of Moses, with regard to early antiquity, are a light that shineth in a dark place.' James Anderson, *Royal genealogies, or the genealogical tables of emperors, kings and princes from Adam to these times* (London, 1732), esp. pp. 727, 775, acknowledged the gloom of ancient history and questioned the precision with which antiquaries retailed the later histories of the descendants of Noah; nevertheless Anderson continued to privilege Mosaic history over the vanity of national origin legends. This position still had some supporters in the late eighteenth century: see e.g. Philip Howard, *The scripture history of the earth and of mankind* (London, 1797), pp. 76–8, 582–3.

foundations for myths of nationhood than those proffered by Geoffrey of Monmouth did not inhibit the capacity, or quench the desire, to trace one's ethnic origins into the Noachic past. Hale clearly distinguished the identity of the state from ethnic identity, and pointed out the importance of the Mosaic history of the dispersal of peoples to a proper understanding of the latter. He argued that profane histories were of no use in tracing the natural roots of peoples, but only of the civil histories of states: 'though they afford us the inception of new governors or governments, the *capita regiminum*, yet they give us not the *capita familiarum*'.[82] Nations and states tended to be artificial mongrel bodies, the compounds of many different lineages held together under notional founding monarchs who were not the biological forefathers of the peoples involved. Only a recourse to scriptural exegesis could trace the natural ethnic origins of a people.

Attempts at ethnic classification resulted in considerable confusion, though certain rival patterns emerged. The Celts were commonly identified with the posterity of Gomer, son of Japhet. The British Celts of Wales were almost exclusively linked to Gomer,[83] but the Gaels of Ireland and the Scottish Highlands, while sometimes located within the Gomerian family tree, were often associated instead with the Scythian lineage of Magog, another of Japhet's sons.[84] The Germanic and Gothic peoples tended to be traced either to Ashkenaz, son of Gomer, or to Magog.[85] Despite the fluidity and indeterminacy in the taxonomies generated by ethnic theology, it is possible to probe networks of ethnic affinity which were dramatically different from the categories forged later in the nineteenth century by the secularising disciplines of philology and racialist ethnology. Two paradigms existed in which the Celt was kindred to the Teuton, rather than the 'other'. Either the Gomerians and Ashkenazian Germans were yoked together in one system, or in the other the Gaels and the Magogian Goths shared the same ethnic roots. The German scholar, Philip Cluverius (1580–1622), one of the most prominent geographers and ethnographers of the seventeenth century, acknowledged the close relationship within the Japhetan line of the German and Celtic peoples.[86]

[82] Hale, *Primitive origination of mankind*, p. 175.

[83] E.g. Rowland Jones, *The circles of Gomer* (London, 1771); James Parsons, *Remains of Japhet*, pp. x, 43, 48, 179. See also R. Heppenstall, 'The children of Gomer', *Times Literary Supplement*, 17 October 1958, 600.

[84] E.g. 'Dissertation concerning the antiquity of the Caiel or Gaiel', National Library of Scotland, Adv. MS 31.6.20, f. 1; James Parsons, *Remains of Japhet*, pp. x, xvi, 25, 39, 43–4, 48, 50, 67–71, 100, 180; Parry, *Trophies of time*, p. 155; Francis Hutchinson, *A defence of the antient historians: with a particular application of it to the history of Ireland* (1733: Dublin, 1734 edn), pp. 49, 58.

[85] E.g. Richard Verstegan, *A restitution of decayed intelligence* (1605: London, 1634), p. 9; George Saltern, *Of the antient lawes of Great Britaine* (London, 1605), p. 16.

George Saltern, an early seventeenth-century antiquary, argued that the various nations of Britain were all derived from 'branches of the same stock, namely the Cimbri of Gomer, and likewise the Saxons and Danes of Ashkenaz, and the Scots, if Iberi, of Tubal, and all of Japhet'.[87] There was less scope within the parameters afforded by early modern ethnic theology to generate hard and fast distinctions between Celts and Teutons. Nor did ethnic theology provide unambiguous material for the construction of a pan-Celticist identity. It is, perhaps, unsurprising that full-blown Teutonic racialism and pan-Celticism were both ideological children of post-Biblical nineteenth-century approaches to the study of ethnicity.[88]

Scholars recognise the importance of Gothicism in the formation of English national identity during the seventeenth and eighteenth centuries, but, while Gothicist discourse was predominantly concerned with secular matters, such as the libertarian manners and democratic institutions of the Saxons, it is easy to forget that Gothicism did intersect in certain places with the concerns of ethnic theology. Antiquarians wondered how the Goths fitted in to the dispersal of peoples, debated the status enjoyed by the Germanic language at the Tower of Babel and applied euhemeristic techniques to the Teutonic pantheon as a way of bringing German antiquity into alignment with the history of Noah's offspring. Ethnic theology featured prominently in the seminal work of English Gothicism, *A restitution of decayed intelligence* (1605), by Richard Verstegan (originally Richard Rowlands, fl. 1565–1620). This was the first major antiquarian monograph devoted explicitly to the task of establishing English identity on an exclusively Germanic basis. However, it was not narrowly ethnocentric in focus. Verstegan's assertion of the German origins of the English was built on Mosaic foundations, and touched on a number of salient issues in ethnic theology: euhemerism, the origins of language and the pagan idolatry of the Germans. Verstegan argued that there was before the events at Babel 'but one language and consequently but one nation in the whole world'. The German nation had been one of the core peoples which emerged from the dispersal on the plain of Sinaar, and had been led by Tuisco, who was descended from Japhet via Gomer and Ashkenaz. In time the German peoples came to

[86] Philip Cluverius, *An introduction into geography both ancient and modern* (Oxford, 1657), p. 127.   [87] Saltern, *Antient lawes*, p. 16.
[88] See e.g. R. Horsman, 'Origins of racial Anglo-Saxonism in Great Britain before 1850', *JHI* 37 (1976), 387–410; B. Melman, 'Claiming the nation's past: the invention of the Anglo-Saxon tradition', *Journal of Contemporary History* 26 (1991), 575–95; J. Hunter, 'The Gaelic connection: the Highlands, Ireland and nationalism, 1873–1922', *SHR* 54 (1975), 178–204; D. A. White, 'Changing views of the *adventus Saxonum* in nineteenth- and twentieth-century English scholarship', *JHI* 32 (1971), 585–94.

deify Tuisco, commemorating him in the name of Tuesday.[89]

The theological aspect of the Gothicist tradition was maintained by Verstegan's successors. John Hare in his radical Saxonist tract *St Edward's ghost* (1647) derived confidence from the Noachic descent of the English through Ashkenaz to launch a bitter attack on the corrupt Norman influences which disfigured English life and institutions.[90] Less contentiously, Robert Sheringham (1602–78) traced the ethnic origins of the Goths through the Noachic lineage from the immediate post-Diluvian epoch 'a confusione linguarum, et dispersione gentium, usque ad adventum eorum in Britanniam'.[91] Stillingfleet incorporated Teutonic theogony into his theories of the rise of idolatry.[92] In the eighteenth century most Gothicist discourse bypassed theological questions. Nevertheless, the application of euhemeristic analysis to the Teutonic pantheon continued into the second half of the eighteenth century. By this stage Tuisco's importance had waned, and a consensus emerged among Gothicists that Woden, who had led a migration from Scythia to northern Europe, was the deified founding father of the ancient Gothic nation (though, alternatively, some orientalists believed Woden to be the Boodh of India, 'some deified prince of the family of the Noachidae, a distinguished avatar of India').[93]

Noachic genealogies also proved useful in the construction of poly-ethnic umbrella identities which spanned the various phases of ethnic settlement and conquest in the history of England. Daniel Langhorne (d. 1681) was convinced of the Japhetan origins – via Ashkenaz, son of Gomer – of the Germanic peoples.[94] The association of Gomer with the descent of the British peoples permitted a degree of affiliation between the various Celtic and Germanic peoples of the British Isles. Both the Cymri and the Germanic Cimbri were linked via spurious but widely accepted etymologies as kindred peoples of the Gomerian stock: 'The Germans who were Cimbrians (or Gomerians) too, and therefore of kin

---

[89] Verstegan, *Restitution*, pp. 2, 9–11.

[90] John Hare, *St Edward's ghost: or, anti-Normanisme* (1647), in *Harleian miscellany VIII* (London, 1746), p. 91.

[91] Robert Sheringham, *De Anglorum gentis origine disceptatio* (Cambridge, 1670).

[92] E. Seaton, *Literary relations of England and Scandinavia in the seventeenth century* (Oxford, 1935), p. 251.

[93] James Tyrrell, *The general history of England* (3 vols., London, 1697–1704), I, bk III, pp. 121–2; William Nicolson, *English historical library* (3 vols., London, 1696–9), I, pp. 131–2, 138; Jackson, *Chronological antiquities*, II, pp. 344–6; An English Saxon, 'Letter', *Gazetteer*, 5 May 1768; Wise, *Enquiries concerning the first inhabitants of Europe*, p. 84; John Whitaker, *The history of Manchester* (2 vols., London, 1771–5), II, p. 358. For the orientalist interpretation, see Maurice, *Indian antiquities*, I, p. 118; III, p. 61 (citing William Jones); VI, 'A dissertation on the Indian origin of the Druids' (citing Reuben Burrow).

[94] Daniel Langhorne, *An introduction to the history of England* (London, 1676), p. 33.

to the Gauls, sent over some colonies into both these islands, of which extract Tacitus reports our Caledonians to have been, and the very name of Irish Causi proves them an offspring of the German Chauci.'[95] Langhorne was not alone in this common ethnic conflation. Aylette Sammes (1636?–79?), a fellow of Christ's College, Cambridge, constructed in his monumental *Britannia antiqua illustrata* a scheme of ethnic origins involving the Cimbri which embraced both the ancient Britons and the later Saxon settlers, though via Magog rather than Gomer. Sammes used Noachic ethnology to confer a degree of meaningful continuity on an otherwise erratic national history of polyethnic settlement and conquest.[96] In his *Historical geography of the Old Testament* (1711–12), Edward Wells (1667–1727) speculated about the locations of the Garden of Eden, the resting place of the Ark and the Tower of Babel, but also added a patriotic dimension to his enquiries. Using bogus etymologies to yoke together the Germanic Cimbri and the ancient British Cymri, he was able to fuse the historic nations of England as kindred peoples:

it can't reasonably be doubted, but the true old Britons, or Welsh, are descendants of Gomer. And since it has been also observed above, that the Germans were likely descendants of Gomer, particularly the Cimbri, to whom the Saxons, especially the Angles, were near neighbours: hence it follows, that our ancestors likewise, who succeeded the Old Britons in these parts of the isle, were descended of the same son of Japhet.[97]

The idea of a common descent persisting in spite of waves of superficially different ethnic settlement strengthened the notion of immemorial continuity.

A resort to Japhetan origins enabled a similar sort of comprehension to be imposed upon the polyethnic diversity of the ancient history of Ireland. The *Leabhar gabhála*, or 'Book of Invasions', was a medieval account of the reception in ancient Ireland of a series of different waves of settlement. These peoples were the followers of Partholón, the Nemedians, the Fir-Bolg, the Tuatha-Dé-Danaan and, eventually, the Milesian Scots. The Irish took great pride in their antiquity, but there was a problem of appropriating for the Gaels, who claimed to be the descendants of the Milesians, the high antiquity of the peoples who preceded them in Ireland.[98] Resorting to the Biblical history of the Noachic line, Peter Walsh

[95] *Ibid.*, p. 17.
[96] Aylette Sammes, *Britannia antiqua illustrata* (London, 1676); Parry, *Trophies of time*, ch. 11.
[97] Edward Wells, *An historical geography of the Old Testament* (3 vols., London, 1711–12), I, p. 131.
[98] See below, ch. 7.

(1618?–88) was able to link together the polyethnic saga of Irish conquest and settlement as the common heritage of various Japhetan kindred. According to Walsh, 'all the several invasions of Ireland . . . descended from Japhet, who for their common language had the Irish tongue', though he conceded that there was 'some difference in the dialect'. Only the conquered aborigines of Ireland, the followers of Ciocal, had a distinct Noachic genealogy, being 'descended from the accursed Ham, and come out of Africa'. By associating the conquered aborigines with Ham, and the various waves of peoples identified in the Book of Invasions as Japhetan kindred, Walsh was able to weave together a rather messy ancient Irish tradition with the prevailing myth of the Fir-Bolg origins of the Milesian regnum.[99] Mosaic history persisted as a fundamental constituent of the patriotic histories propagated by Ireland's Gaelic community to a greater extent than it did in ethnic discourses elsewhere in the British Isles. In particular, *Ogygia* (1685), Roderic O'Flaherty's royalist history of Ireland, traced the descent of the Milesian Scots from Fenisius or Phenius, a great-grandson of Japhet in the Magogian line. O'Flaherty also claimed that the Irish language was one of the original languages formed in the plain of Sinaar.[100] Warmed by the Ogygian tradition and the seminal influence of Bochart's sacred geography on Irish literati, eighteenth-century Gaels continued to bask in the glory of a prominent place in sacred history. In addition, Milesian antiquities attracted the English-born Church of Ireland Bishop of Down and Connor, Francis Hutchinson (1660–1739), precisely because their longevity might be used to buttress Mosaic orthodoxy in an age of rampant scepticism. Rather than questioning the authenticity of the ancient Irish past, Hutchinson thought it 'rather a wonder that all nations have not as old as Ireland pretends to'. For although he recognised that there was 'stronger evidence of the first peoplers of nations and the first builders of cities after the Flood, than we have of following times', he argued that 'in the succession of time, when we know the first beginnings of nations, and have our share in the present, we are as certain that there hath been a continuation of intermediate generations, and a moderate degree of evidence will incline us to believe the accounts of them, because we saw what was before them'. A commitment to Mosaic orthodoxy overcame

[99] Peter Walsh, *A prospect of the state of Ireland, from the year of the world 1756 to the year of Christ 1652* (London, 1682), pp. 6–9, 356–7.
[100] Roderic O'Flaherty, *Ogygia* (1685: trans. James Hely, 2 vols., Dublin, 1793), I, pp. lxix–lxx, 14–15, 92–3. For the persistence of sacred history in early nineteenth-century Irish Catholic antiquarian circles, see *Transactions of the Gaelic Society of Dublin* 1 (1808), vi–vii.

the normal English suspicion of the fantastic Milesian past claimed by the Gaels of Ireland.[101]

It is impossible to study eighteenth-century British Celticism without reference to the ethnic theology of the Breton scholar, the Abbé Paul-Yves Pezron (1639–1706), whose treatise *L'antiquité de la nation et de la langue des Celtes, autrement appellez Gaulois* (1703) was published in 1706 in an English translation as *The antiquities of nations; more particularly of the Celtae or Gauls, taken to be originally the same people as our ancient Britains.* Pezron had an enormous influence on the construction of Celtic patriotisms in Wales and Scotland, and on the attitudes of English scholars to the Celtic peoples of the British Isles.[102] His work on the Gomerian roots of the Celts was intended as a corrective to the work of Bochart, who had ignored the role of the continental Celts in the dispersal of nations; eventually Pezron displaced the Huguenot pastor as the most cited figure in British ethnic theology.

The Abbé's earlier writings had included a work of chronology, *L'antiquité des tems rétablie* (1687), in which he had argued for an extended Biblical chronology which would render redundant some of the recent doubts about the compatibility of the ancient civilisations of the world with the scheme of Mosaic history. Pezron believed that modern chronology, unlike the patristic scheme, had been misled by errors and corruptions which had crept into the Hebraic tradition since the fall of Jerusalem. At issue was the duration of the period from the creation of the world to the coming of the Messiah: 'Tous les chronologistes modernes, qui ont écrit depuis un siècle et demy, ne donnent, après les Juifs, que quatre mille ans, tout au plus; et je soutiens après les Pères de l'Eglise, et les anciens Hébreux, qu'il a dure plus de cinq mille cinq cens ans.'[103] Pezron's treatise on the Celts was an additional euhemeristic plank of his defence of orthodoxy, but also added a rich seam of Breton patriotism.

---

[101] Hutchinson, *Defence of the antient historians*, pp. 3, 12–13. See also Trautmann, *Aryans and British India*, pp. 93–4, for the Mosaic Gaelomania of the English artillery engineer and amateur orientalist Charles Vallancey. See Lawrence Parsons, *Observations on the bequest of Henry Flood, esq. to Trinity College, Dublin: with a defence of the ancient history of Ireland* (Dublin, 1795), pp. 185–92, for the Magogian pedigree of Ireland's Phoenician ancestors. However, for a more dismissive attitude towards Irish links with the Noachic past, see the remarks of the Dublin physician and antiquary Thomas Molyneux (1661–1733), quoted in G. Daniel and C. Renfrew, *The idea of prehistory* (2nd edn, Edinburgh, 1988), p. 15.

[102] P. Morgan, 'The Abbé Pezron and the Celts', *Transactions of the Honourable Society of Cymmrodorion* (1965), 286–95; J. Sole, 'Le mythe gaulois sous Louis XIV: Paul Pezron et son *Antiquité des Celtes* de 1703', in P. Viallaneix and J. Erhard (eds.), *Nos ancêtres les Gaulois* (Clermont-Ferrand, 1982); D. Droixhe, *De l'origine du langage aux langues du monde: études sur les XVIIe et XVIIIe siècles* (Tübingen, 1987), pp. 72–4.

[103] Paul Pezron, *L'antiquité des tems rétablie et défendue contre les Juifs et les nouveaux chronologistes* (Paris, 1687), 'Avertissement'.

The Abbé's principal aim was religious – 'rendre un service important a la vraie religion, qui s'établit puissamment par le dévoilement des fables, et par le renversement de l'erreur'.[104] Pezron located the origins of the 'false heathenish divinities' of classical antiquity in the terrestrial history of the Celtic monarchy. The Celts were descendants of Gomer, who had established a universal empire across ancient Europe. According to Pezron, this was the material out of which the myth of the Titans had been constructed. Moreover, he went on to argue that the central positions in the pantheon of classical paganism had been occupied by the posthumously deified universal monarchs of the Celts, who included Jupiter and Uranus. There was also a linguistic dimension to Pezron's thesis. The ancient Celts had brought with them to Europe one of the *langues matrices* of the patriarchal era, the Ur-language of the Gomerian stock.[105]

Pezron's ethnic theology magnified the significance and achievements of the Celtic nations, now a motley collection of impoverished peoples on the western periphery of Europe. Pezron was able to use the methods of ethnic theology to construct for his native Breton culture an alternative to the prevailing Frankish idiom of French patriotism. The important Celtomane tradition in eighteenth-century French discourse had its roots in theological speculation, and throughout the age of Enlightenment antiquaries continued to engage with the theological dimensions of Gaulic antiquity, including its relationship to sacred history and the nature of Druidic religion.[106] Although the defence of Breton particularism was uppermost in Pezron's Celticism, it provided material for the revitalisation of Celtic patriotism in Britain. Pezron championed the Welsh – alongside the Bretons – as the people who 'have the honour to preserve the language of the posterity of Gomer'.[107] Moreover, he also contributed to the latitudinarian embrace of Celts and Germans which was such a marked feature of pre-romantic Celticist discourse. Gomer, the founding father of the Celtic nation, was also the natural father of Ashkenaz, the founder of the German race. Hence, there was a 'likeness and conformity' between these two nations, which proceeded 'from the first origin of them'.[108]

The reception of Pezron's ideas into the mainstream of British ethnic

---

[104] Paul Pezron, *L'antiquité de la nation et de la langue des Celtes, autrement appellez Gaulois* (Paris, 1703), 'Préface'.

[105] Paul Pezron, *The antiquities of nations; more particularly of the Celtae or Gauls, taken to be originally the same people as our ancient Britains* (trans. D. Jones, London, 1706).

[106] S. Piggott, *The Druids* (1968: New York, 1985), pp. 156–8; C. Volpilhac, 'Les Gaulois à l'Académie des Inscriptions et Belles-Lettres de 1701 a 1793', in Viallaneix and Erhard, *Nos ancêtres les Gaulois*, pp. 79–81. For a more sceptical approach to the Gomerites in the late eighteenth century, see J. Balcou, 'La Tour d'Auvergne, théoricien breton du mythe Gaulois', in Viallaneix and Erhard, *Nos ancêtres les Gaulois*, p. 112.

[107] Pezron, *Antiquities of nations*, pp. xii–xiii.   [108] *Ibid.*, p. 214.

theology excited controversy, but also had considerable influence on the construction of the Celt in eighteenth-century British ethnic discourses. Bryant and Jackson proved to be hostile critics of the Pezronian account of gentile mythology. Jackson argued that the Titans were not Pezron's Gomerian Celts, but were, in fact, Hamidians.[109] Far from accepting Pezron's account of the centrality of Celtic history in the formation of classical paganism, Bryant believed that the Greeks had been profoundly ignorant of the ethnography of northern Europe and had invented convenient umbrella terms for the peoples of this area.[110] However, other English commentators proved more receptive to Pezron's scheme, including Francis Wise.[111] The prominent tory historian Thomas Carte (1686–1754) drew heavily on Pezron in his account of the Celtic origins of the ancient Britons,[112] a view which was later repeated, albeit with a degree of caution, in Tobias Smollett's *Complete history of England*.[113] Carte accepted the Biblical account of the dispersal of nations, and of the Japhetan roots of the European peoples: prior to the eastern invasion of Europe by Gomerian Celts, the continent had been settled by Phrygians descended from Javan, fourth son of Japhet. Like Pezron, Carte linked ancient Celtic history to a euhemeristic interpretation of the origins of classical paganism. Moreover, the empire of the Titans had included the Germans, whom Carte categorised as 'a Celtic nation'. The Gomerian framework suggested an identification of the common ethnic roots of Celts and Germans, of the sort which would be unthinkable in the secularised ethnology of the nineteenth century. Inspired by Pezron, Parsons, the author of *The remains of Japhet*, called on his fellow Englishmen to show due respect for the peoples of the Celtic fringe, who were after all 'the only unmixed remains of the children of Japhet upon the globe', and related through that patriarch to the Scythian Germans.[114]

Pezron's main contribution to British ethnic discourse was the provision of a glorious usable past for the neglected 'Gomerian' Celts of the British peripheries. Celtic patriots derived inspiration from the ingenious work of the Breton Cistercian. Rowlands retold the Japhetan peopling of Europe from a Cambrocentric perspective in his *Mona antiqua restaurata* (1723).[115] Theophilus Evans (1694–1767), Rowland Jones (1722–74),

[109] Jackson, *Chronological antiquities*, III, p. 76.
[110] Bryant, *New system*, III, p. 135.
[111] See e.g. Wise, *Enquiries concerning the first inhabitants of Europe*, pp. 29–33.
[112] Thomas Carte, *A general history of England* (4 vols., London, 1747–55), I, pp. 7–14. The myth of Trojan origins was, by contrast, I, p. 15, 'utterly destitute of all support'.
[113] Tobias Smollett, *A complete history of England from the descent of Julius Caesar* (1757–8: 2nd edn, 11 vols., London, 1758–60), I, pp. 6–7.
[114] James Parsons, *Remains of Japhet*, p. x.
[115] Rowlands, *Mona antiqua restaurata*; G. H. Jenkins, *The foundations of modern Wales, 1642–1780* (Oxford, 1987), p. 250.

Thomas Richards (1710?–90) and John Walters (1721–97) drew on the theory of the glorious Gomerian past to raise the profile of the Welsh language.[116] There already existed an earlier layer of Welsh Hebraism – as, for example, in Charles Edwards's *Hebraismorum Cambro-Britannicorum* (1675)[117] – upon which the superstructure of Pezronian ideology could be raised. The Welsh Gomerians argued that Celtic was a dialect of the original Hebrew language of mankind, and compiled tables of comparative vocabulary to demonstrate the proximity of Welsh to Hebrew. There were thus two principal strands to the patriotic story projected by the Welsh ethnic theologians. They took pride both in a glorious Gomerian descent, embracing the ancient Titan empire, and in the close affinity of Welsh to Hebrew. Welsh patriots claimed to speak the most uncorrupted language of Europe. According to Jones, 'Celtic received no alteration at Babel.'[118] Richards boasted that Welsh 'comes not short of any European language in point of antiquity, copiousness and independency'.[119] Pezron's account of the Celts' Titan golden age was inserted into the origin myth of the Welsh. Richards rejoiced that the modern Welsh, though a people confined to a peripheral region of the British state, were the heirs of the Titans, and spoke 'the language of those princes called Saturn and Jupiter, who posed for great deities among the ancients'.[120] Walters argued that Greek, Latin, Teutonic, Gaulish, Welsh and Irish were merely different dialects of the language of the ancient Titan race.[121] This phase of Celticist recovery was not predicated on Welsh opposition to the Germanic stock of England. Jones wrote confidently of the original familial affinities of these distinct ethnic groups: 'historians are of late generally agreed from some passages in Ezekiel and Jeremiah, Josephus, Berosus, Bochart and others, that the Cimbri, Gauls, Celtes and Germans are the descendants of Gomer and his eldest son Ashkenas'.[122]

The ideas of Pezron also played a part in the evolution of eighteenth-century Scottish patriotism. The Gomerian scheme filled the gap which resulted from the deconstruction of the secular myth of the ancient

---

[116] Jenkins, *Foundations of modern Wales*, pp. 223–4, 400–1; G. J. Williams, 'The history of Welsh scholarship', *Studia Celtica* 8–9 (1973–4), 215–18; J. Davies, *A history of Wales* (1990: Harmondsworth, 1994), p. 303; P. Morgan, *A new history of Wales: the eighteenth-century renaissance* (Llandybie, 1981), pp. 106–9.

[117] S. Piggott, *Celts, Saxons, and the early antiquaries* (O'Donnell Lecture, 1966: Edinburgh, 1967), p. 7.

[118] Rowland Jones, *The origin of language and nations, hieroglyfically, etymologically and topografically defined and fixed* (London, 1764), 'Preface'.

[119] Thomas Richards, *Antiquae linguae Britannicae thesaurus: being a British, or Welsh–English dictionary* (Bristol, 1753), p. iv.   [120] *Ibid.*, pp. ix–x.

[121] John Walters, *A dissertation on the Welsh language* (Cowbridge, 1771), pp. 20–1.

[122] Rowland Jones, *Origin of language*, 'Preface'.

Scottish royal line and constitution by the Jacobite antiquary Father Thomas Innes.[123] The Gomerian history of the Celts provided a reliable alternative to the recently overthrown medieval myth of the settlement of Scotland from Ireland by an ancient maritime people from Iberia. Whig-presbyterian antiquarians such as David Malcolme, William Maitland (1693?–1757) and Robert Henry (1718–90) hitched the ethnic theology of Pezron to theories of universal language, ancient migration patterns and comparative ethnography as a means of infusing some glory and scriptural credibility into the denuded story of Scottish origins.[124]

Outside Pezron's sphere of influence alternative versions of Scriptural ethnology continued to influence the construction of British identities. The pedigree of the Druid religion practised by the aboriginal Britons was traced to Noachic origins. Indeed, a patriotic subtradition within the Church of England recognised Druidism as a respectable Old Testament prototype of Anglicanism, a cosy native British version of the religion of Noah and Abraham. Christianity was but retrospective Druidism, a 'republication of the patriarchal religion' which looked back rather than forwards to the coming of the Messiah.[125] According to Rowlands, who championed Anglesey as the metropolitan seat of the high Druid and Welsh as the modern descendant of Hebrew, the Druids 'being so near in descent, to the fountains of true religion and worship, as to have had one of Noah's sons for grandsire or greatgrandsire, may well be imagined, to have carried and conveyed here some of the rites and usages of that true religion, pure and untainted'. These 'great moralists and adorers of one God', he considered, in spite of their 'human sacrifices and diabolical magic', to be 'almost half Christians', who prepared the way for Britain's early apostolic reception of the gospel.[126]

William Stukeley (1687–1765), whose archaeological studies *Stonehenge* (1740) and *Abury* (1743) were conceived as elements in a larger project on the patriarchal religion, was the foremost Anglican champion of Druidism. In an attempt to counter the deists and anti-Trinitarians

[123] T. I. Rae, 'Historical scepticism in Scotland before David Hume', in R. F. Brissenden (ed.), *Studies in the eighteenth century II* (Canberra, 1973).

[124] Malcolme, *Letters, essays and other tracts*; William Maitland, *The history and antiquities of Scotland* (London, 1757), pp. 32–3, 112; Jerome Stone, 'An enquiry into the original of the nation and language of the ancient Scots', Edinburgh University Library Laing MS, La.III.251, ff. 35–9; Robert Henry, *The history of Great Britain* (6 vols., London, 1771–93), I, pp. 466–70; 'Dissertation concerning the antiquity of the Caiel or Gaiel', ff. 1–2.

[125] William Stukeley, *Abury, a temple of the British Druids* (London, 1743), p. iii; Piggott, *Druids*, p. 151. Gale, *Court of the Gentiles*, II, p. 82, traced the oak religion of the Druids back to the practices of Abraham in the plain of Mamre.

[126] Rowlands, *Mona antiqua restaurata*, pp. 45, 140–1; Jenkins, *Foundations of modern Wales*, p. 250.

from an unexpected quarter, Stukeley proclaimed that England had been the seat of orthodox religious truth ever since the age of the Old Testament patriarchs. Arriving soon after the Flood, the Druids had constructed the great stone circles at Stonehenge and Avebury, 'the great cathedral, the chief metropolitical or patriarchal temple of the island'. Stukeley depicted the Druids as learned and moderate precursors of Georgian Anglicanism steering a steady via media between the follies of enthusiasm and superstition. For example, Druidism had been Trinitarian: 'the ancients knew somewhat of the mysterious nature of the deity, subsisting in distinct personalities, which is more fully revealed to us in the Christian dispensation'. Through defending the particular ethos of the Church of England as well as revelation in general, Stukeley managed to weave a vivid pageant of English patriotism out of the unpromising material of theology: 'the true religion has chiefly since the repeopling mankind after the Flood, subsisted in our island: and here we made the best reformation from the universal pollution of Christianity, Popery'. Furthermore, not only did Stukeley celebrate the central role played by the Britons in the preservation of true religion, he also sacralised the pre-Christian landscape of England. The ancient henges about which he waxed hobby-horsical were a permanent 'impress' on the land of the 'sacred character' of the patriarchal religion.[127]

In the wake of Stukeley, a lively *mythistoire* of patriotic Druidism, variously pan-British, imperialist, English, Welsh and Cornish in focus, was maintained by the likes of William Cooke, Thomas Maurice, Rowland Jones and Edward Davies (1756–1831).[128] This tradition culminated in William Blake's epics *Milton* (1810) and *Jerusalem* (1820), which were conceived at the turn of the nineteenth century under the influence of the British patriarchal tradition. However, Blake's growing disillusionment with Druidism led to a radical reworking of its history. He transformed the myth of Biblical survivals in Britain into a story of decline from the vital uncorrupted Christianity of the patriarchs, first into the staleness and oppression of organised 'state religion', later into the very antithesis of spirituality as modern Britain became the seat of the

---

[127] Stukeley, *Abury*, pp. iv, 6, 40, 101; Stukeley, *Stonehenge, a temple restored to the British Druids* (London, 1740), 'Preface'; Piggott, *Druids*, pp. 146–50; Piggott, *Stukeley*. For the Trinitarianism of the Druids, see also William Cooke, *An enquiry into the patriarchal and Druidical religion* (1754: 2nd edn, London, 1755), pp. 33, 40, 55, 57–8.

[128] Cooke, *Patriarchal and Druidical religion*; Maurice, *Indian antiquities*, VI, 'A dissertation on the Indian origin of the Druids'; Rowland Jones, *Circles of Gomer*; Edward Davies, *Celtic researches* (London, 1804), pp. 119–20, whose scheme of Druidism is substantially modified by the helio-arkite theories of Bryant and Faber in Edward Davies, *The mythology and rites of the British Druids* (London, 1809), sect. II, esp. pp. 87, 90–1, 96, 117, 180–2; S. Piggott, *Ancient Britons and the antiquarian imagination* (London, 1989), p. 147; Piggott, *Druids*, p. 164.

mechanical philosophy of Bacon, Newton and Locke: 'All things begin and end in Albion's ancient Druid rocky shore / But now the starry heavens are fled from the mighty limbs of Albion.'[129]

Ideas of Japhetan descent did not play a dominant role in the formation of British patriotisms. As subsequent chapters will show, ethnic histories were generally deployed to further temporal ends (including the *institutional* needs of churches). Nevertheless, ethnic theology did constitute a vital arena of early modern Christian apologetics, and insights derived from it did have some influence both on the construction of identities and on attitudes to other ethnic groups. Conversely, of course, it is widely acknowledged that the secularisation of knowledge played an important role in the rise of racialism: the construction of a philology which separated Indo-European languages from the Semitic both undermined a universal Biblical history and provided a 'scientific' rationale for Europe's traditional anti-Judaic bigotry. Similarly, in the British Isles, where the Celtic fringes had always had to endure the unwanted reformist attentions of the centre, such practices acquired a clear racialist rationale only in the nineteenth century with the disappearance of a Japhetan lineage which demonstrated the affiliation of Celts and Saxons. Mosaic history, in all its hermeneutic variety, is a neglected but necessary backdrop to the history of ethnic identity.

[129] Blake, *Milton*, in Blake, *Complete writings* (ed. G. Keynes, 1957: Oxford, 1966 edn), p. 486; S. Smiles, *The image of antiquity* (New Haven, 1994), pp. 91–6; P. F. Fisher, 'Blake and the Druids', *Journal of English and Germanic Philology* 58 (1959), 592; Piggott, *Druids*, p. 165; M. Butler, 'Romanticism in England', in R. Porter and M. Teich (eds.), *Romanticism in national context* (Cambridge, 1988), pp. 49–51; Mee, *Dangerous enthusiasm*, pp. 92–4, 99.

Part II

The three kingdoms

4   Whose ancient constitution? Ethnicity and
    the English past, 1600–1800

The identity of the English nation during the seventeenth and eighteenth centuries fits neatly into neither of the main categories of classification identified by political scientists, being neither indisputably ethnic nor exclusively civic-territorial.[1] Although early modern Englishness drew heavily on the inspiration of the nation's Anglo-Saxon past, it was far from straightforwardly ethnocentric. Rather, ideological imperatives shaped a troubled legacy of repeated conquests and new ethnic settlements into an irreducible 'story' of England. This myth was well adapted to the rigours of contemporary political discourse but its chameleon qualities defy modern definitions of national identity. Englishmen enjoyed both an ethnic identity as the descendants of the libertarian Anglo-Saxons and an institutional identity derived from the historic laws and mixed constitution of the realm, a long regnal history which encompassed the ancient Celtic Britons, the Gothic Saxons who displaced them from the fifth century onwards and the Normans who arrived in the eleventh century. Anglo-Saxonism predominated as the core identity of the English people, but, throughout the seventeenth and eighteenth centuries, the 'aboriginal' ancient Britons enjoyed significantly more than a walk-on part in the national pageant. The Normans too, although often cast as villains, played an integral (and sometimes positive) part in the unfolding history of English liberty.

This rich ethnic diversity was a minor ingredient of English national identity. The copious vocabulary of the English language was generally attributed to the ethnic variety of the English people, and some common lawyers celebrated a similar wealth of legal solutions drawn from different ethnic sources. Francis Bacon, for example, celebrated both these aspects, noting that our laws 'are as mixt as our language, compounded of

---

[1] See e.g. J. Plamenatz, 'Two types of nationalism', in E. Kamenka (ed.), *Nationalism: the nature and evolution of an idea* (New York, 1976), for the crude – but influential – contrast between benign western civic patriotisms and virulent eastern ethnic nationalisms; P. Cabanel, *La question nationale au XIXe siècle* (Paris, 1997), pp. 9–14, for the distinction between 'la nation-contrat' and the ethnographic conception of 'la nation-génie'.

British, Roman, Saxon, Danish, Norman customs. And as our language is so much the richer, so the laws are the more complete: neither doth this attribute less to them, than those that would have them to have stood out the same in all mutations; for no tree is so good first set, as by transplanting.'[2] Nevertheless, as we shall see, pride in England's ethnic hybridity was more than countermatched by the political argument that these various groups had made similar contributions to the English constitution, which enjoyed a history of continuity. On the other hand, political imperatives did occasionally dictate the opposite strategy. A notable example is Daniel Defoe's *The true-born Englishman* (1701) which celebrated England's mongrel nationhood as a means of answering a particular polemical need – to ward off anti-Dutch attacks from tories who accused the Williamite regime of betraying the English national interest:

> The Romans first with Julius Caesar came,
> Including all the nations of that name,
> Gauls, Greeks, and Lombards; and by computation,
> Auxiliaries or slaves of ev'ry nation.
> With Hengist, Saxons; Danes with Sueno came,
> In search of plunder, not in search of fame.
> Scots, Picts, and Irish from the Hibernian shore:
> And conquering William brought the Normans o're.
>
> All these their bar'brous offspring left behind,
> The dregs of armies, they of all Mankind;
> Blended with Britains, who before were here,
> Of whom the Welch ha' blest the character.
> From this amphibious ill-born mob began
> That vain ill-natured thing, an Englishman.[3]

There are, of course, other examples of this strain of panegyric. For example, one Philopatriae, the pseudonymous author of the poem *South Britain* (1731), declining to 'cloud [his] verse with fab'lous tales / Of Magog, Brutus, or the Root of Wales', drew instead 'the present martial breed:

> Sprung from the Roman, Saxon, Norman Seed,
> Blended with Britains, how they all unite,
> And make the English so renown'd in Fight.[4]

[2] Francis Bacon, 'A proposition to his majesty . . . touching the compiling and amendment of the laws of England' (c. 1616), quoted in G. Burgess, *The politics of the ancient constitution* (Houndmills, 1992), p. 57. A good example of pride in linguistic diversity is Nathaniel Bailey, *An universal etymological English dictionary* (6th edn, London, 1733), 'Introduction'. For the late eighteenth-century debate over the ancient British continuities of the English language, a thesis championed by John Whitaker in his influential *History of Manchester* (2 vols., London, 1771–5), see Gibbon, *DF*, II, p. 502 n.; Ephraim Chambers (d. 1740), *Cyclopedia* (4 vols., London, 1786), IV, 'Teutonic'.

[3] Daniel Defoe, *The true-born Englishman* (10th edn, London, 1701), p. 6.

[4] Philopatriae, *South Britain: a poem* (London, 1731), p. 15.

Despite such effusions, the seventeenth and eighteenth centuries scarcely bear witness to any profounder sense of England as a multicultural nation. Some commentators placed no value at all upon ethnic diversity. In *St Edward's ghost: or, anti-Normanisme* (1647), the radical Saxonist John Hare produced an extraordinarily intemperate argument for ethnic purity, not only lambasting the Normans for having befouled – 'un-Teutonised' – England's language, laws and institutions, but displaying little fondness either for the ancient Britons. Such were the glories of England's Teutonic 'mother nation' – enthusiastically celebrated by Hare – that

our progenitors that transplanted themselves from Germany hither, did not commix themselves with the ancient inhabitants of the country – the Britons – (as other colonies did with the natives in those places where they came) but totally expelling them, they took possession of the land to themselves, thereby preserving their blood, laws and language incorrupted.[5]

Later, *The queen an empress, and her three kingdoms one empire* (1706), a pamphlet in favour of British union, boasted that the sea had kept Britons 'freer from foreign mixtures than most countries upon the Continent'. England's Roman, Saxon, Danish and Norman conquerors, the pamphleteer argued, were 'never perhaps more than a tenth to the natives of the whole island among whom they settled. And the last of these invasions being now above six hundred years since, there are very few families amongst us that can derive themselves from a Norman extraction, and fewer that can make out their Saxon and Danish pedigree.'[6]

Antiquaries commonly ascribed similar manners, the same basic institutions, sometimes even a common descent, to some or all of England's 'different' constituent peoples. Most obviously, it was possible to embrace the Danes and Normans as Gothic kindred of the Saxons. Richard Verstegan acknowledged the various invasions of England but denied that the English were a mongrel people:

And whereas some do call us a mixed nation by reason of these Danes and Normans coming in among us, I answer . . . that the Danes and the Normans were once one same people with the Germans, as were also the Saxons; and we not to be accompted mixed by having only some such joined unto us again, as sometime had one same language, and one same original with us.[7]

Hare depicted the arrival of 'Danish intruders' in a similar fashion: 'a people that were our consanguineans, our ancient countrymen and brethren, whose prevailing over us would have introduced scarce strange laws

[5] John Hare, *St Edward's ghost: or, anti-Normanisme* (London, 1647), in *Harleian miscellany VIII* (London, 1746), p. 94.
[6] *The queen an empress, and her three kingdoms one empire* (London, 1706), p. 9.
[7] Richard Verstegan, *A restitution of decayed intelligence* (1605: London, 1634), p. 187.

or language; nor other blood than Teutonic'.[8] The Anglo-Irish politician and scholar Sir William Temple (1628–99) used the common Gothic heritage of Europe to bridge the central difficulty in the history of English liberty – the Norman Conquest. The Saxons and the Normans were of the same Gothic stock: so why should we expect the Normans to undermine completely the Gothic institutions whose rudiments they too cherished? 'It is most probable', wrote Temple of trial by jury, 'that neither the English received it from the Normans, nor these from the English; but that both nations, deriving their original from those ancient Goths, agreed in several customs or institutions, deduced from their common ancestors, which made this trial by juries continue uninterrupted in England, not only by the Normans, but by the Danes also, who were but another swarm of that great northern hive.' Moreover, Temple did not ascribe the introduction of feudalism into England exclusively to the Normans: 'feudal laws, were all brought into Europe by the ancient Goths, and by them settled in all the provinces which they conquered of the Roman Empire; and, among the rest, by the Saxons in England, as well as by the Franks in Gaul, and the Normans in Normandy; where the use of their states, or general assemblies, were likewise of the same original'.[9] Bolingbroke, a tory keen for tactical reasons to appear in whig clothing, maintained that the Normans 'came out of the same northern hive' as the Saxons whom they 'subdued', and 'naturally resumed the spirit of their ancestors, when they came into a country where it prevailed'.[10]

More typically, many antiquarians did recognise that the Britons, Saxons, Danes and Normans were different peoples, notwithstanding shared ethnic origins in the mists of antiquity. Although the history of the peopling of England by a diversity of overseas nations raised heated contentions among antiquarians, these disputes did not revolve around questions of ethnicity. Rather, England's patent ethnic diversity generated questions regarding the history of the English constitution. How had the incursions of different groups from abroad altered the institutions of the host country? To what extent did waves of overseas settlement erode the inherited foundations of 'English' liberty? In particular, did the arrival of the Danes or Normans amount to a conquest of the Saxons, and a

[8] Hare, *St Edward's ghost*, p. 95.
[9] William Temple, *An introduction to the history of England*, in Temple, *Works* (2 vols., 1731), II, pp. 557, 559. Temple, *Works*, II, p. 585, also believed that the Norman Conquest had brought a bonus to the English – sovereign authority over the English Channel: 'the dominion of narrow seas seems naturally to belong, like that of rivers, to those who possessed the banks or coasts on both sides'.
[10] Bolingbroke, *Remarks on the history of England* (1730–1), in Bolingbroke, *Works* (5 vols., London, 1754), I, p. 316.

consequent loss of liberty? The manner of arrival mattered more than ethnic difference.

At the heart of English national consciousness was a pride in the nation's eponymous ancestors, the Anglo-Saxons, admired for their libertarian ways. However, the aboriginal ancient Britons and the more problematic waves of Danes and Normans who followed the Saxons also had to be fitted into the story of English liberty. There were eight broad strategies for dealing with this chequered history of settlement and invasion.

(1) At one extreme was the royalist thesis, whose most uncompromising version was formulated by Dr Robert Brady (1627–1700). Through an emphasis upon conquest, change and discontinuity in the history of English institutions, royalist antiquaries denied England's unbroken history of liberty, law and parliamentary government. Not only had the Norman Conquest led to the imposition of alien feudal tenures on the English legal system, but post-Conquest kingship had been absolutist, with parliament in its modern form taking shape, by royal grace, only in the thirteenth century.[11]

The royalist position provided an ironic complement to the radical argument found at the other end of the ideological spectrum.

(2) Formulated in the 1640s, the radical interpretation of English history involved a pessimistic reading of the Conquest. After 1066 a Norman Yoke had fallen on England's free-born Saxons, which continued to blight English law and government. Therefore, the Levellers went on to argue, the common law needed to be purged of its noxious Norman–feudal elements. Nevertheless, the radicals did acknowledge some underlying continuities from the Saxon common law.[12]

Between these extremes lay the variegated mainstream of seventeenth and eighteenth-century English political argument.

(3) Most obviously, there was the argument for the unbroken backbone of English constitutional history. Some antiquaries, who emphasised the continuity of institutions and laws at the expense of new ethnic strains and new rulers, regarded the parliament of the middle ages as

---

[11] Robert Brady, *An introduction to the old English history* (London, 1684).

[12] C. Hill, 'The Norman yoke', in Hill, *Puritanism and revolution* (1958: Harmondsworth, 1986); J. H. Baker, *An introduction to English legal history* (2nd edn, London, 1979), pp. 184–5. For a corrective to the 'strong' reading of 1066, see R. B. Seaberg, 'The Norman conquest and the common law: the Levellers and the argument from continuity', *HJ* 24 (1981), 791–806; D. Wootton, 'Introduction, in Wootton (ed.), *Divine right and democracy* (Harmondsworth, 1986), pp. 33–4; Burgess, *Politics of the ancient constitution*, pp. 90–3.

the descendant of the Saxon gemot, itself the successor of the *concilium* favoured by the ancient Britons.[13]

(4) Some antiquarians conceded that the irruption of Romans, Saxons, Danes and Normans had inevitably wrought changes in England's institutions and laws; however, these alterations were superficial. Underlying a surface history of arrival, settlement and change was a deeper-laid pattern of common institutional forms, whether through limitations on monarchy, or through legal continuity within a shared framework of custom and precedent. The blending of peoples did not disturb the basic principles of English government.[14]

(5) However, it was possible to read this story the other way round: several early Stuart antiquaries already saw the common law as 'a Norman tree with a few scattered roots in the Anglo-Saxon, Danish and British earth.'[15]

(6) An alternative version involved a recognition that there had been some discontinuity in English history, whose hallmark was a story of struggle, conflict and the survival of liberty against the odds. According to R. B. Seaberg, breaches in the saga of continuity were not necessarily 'fatal', but served to emphasise the 'recurrent drama' of English constitutional history. Restoration followed innovation; temporary abrogations of liberty were followed by reconfirmations of the ancient constitution.[16] For several historians the English libertarian tradition was not simply a complacent story of survivals, it was foremost an ongoing battle against tyrannical kings and the forces of popery. Patriotic antiquaries who operated within these strains of constitutionalism rarely extrapolated beyond this story of ethnic variation to glorify England as a melting pot. What concerned them was primarily the preservation of England's ancient constitution of liberties and laws.

(7) Logically, the Gothicist interpretation of English history which gained influence during the seventeenth century ran right against the grain of these 'national' stories. For Gothicists considered Anglo-Saxon institutions and freedoms to be the common 'Germanic' inheritance of post-Roman Europe. Just as the Anglo-Saxons, who

[13] E.g. Algernon Sidney, *Discourses concerning government* (ed. T. G. West, Indianapolis, 1990), ch. 3, sect. 28.

[14] E.g. Richard Hurd, *Moral and political dialogues* (London, 1759), pp. 243–4.

[15] D. Woolf, *The idea of history in early Stuart England* (Toronto, 1990), p. 97.

[16] Seaberg, 'Norman conquest', 793, 801. For example, Thomas Rymer, *A general draught and prospect of government in Europe* (London, 1681), pp. 31–2, conceded that at the Norman Conquest 'the old laws and policy ran a dangerous risk from the inundation of arbitrary power'. However, 'the cockatrice' was 'crushed in the egg': within a century and a half, King John had signed Magna Carta which recognised the customs of Saxon England. Cf. Blackstone, *Commentaries*, IV, p. 425.

brought Germanic customs to England, had established gemots or parliaments, so the Franks, Vandals, Visigoths and Lombards had founded similar constitutions elsewhere in Europe with parliamentary diets, such as the cortes or the Champs de Mars. Whatever the logic of Gothicism, this ethnic story of Germanic transplants never, over the course of the seventeenth and eighteenth centuries, fully occluded the idea of the immemorial constitution or the relevance of the ancient Britons.[17]

(8) In the 1730s another version of English history emerged which was largely indifferent to the country's early experience of invasion and settlement. Pioneered by Walpolean whig pamphleteers, set out at length by the sceptical North Briton David Hume in his *History of England* and exploited by defensive administrations during the 1760s, the modern whig interpretation of history ran as follows. The English past was very different from the refined and commercial post-feudal, post-Revolutionary present. The civil liberties of eighteenth-century Englishmen were not the bequest of their Anglo-Saxon ancestors; rather they were part of England's benign process of modernisation, inaugurated in Henry VII's attempts to control his overmighty magnates and culminating in the whig Revolution of 1688. Nevertheless, even the modern whigs who championed this argument and noted the defectiveness of England's much-vaunted pre-modern liberties acknowledged the significance of the longer course of English constitutional development.[18]

Antiquarian writing, even where it touched on the question of ethnic origins, generally focused on an institutional agenda. This meant that precision in the discussion of ethnic categories yielded to political imperatives. Indeed, W. H. Greenleaf notes in his discussion of seventeenth-century political theory that 'often where it suited the polemical purpose in mind, the Goths came to be confused with the Britons they supplanted', though 'on the whole the specific political point was not blurred'. For most of the eighteenth century it remained common to celebrate the shared libertarian virtues of all the non-Roman septentrional peoples, Celtic as well as Gothic, as an antithesis to the corruption and luxury of imperial Rome. Nevertheless, because the ancient Britons had experienced the Roman yoke, unlike the Anglo-Saxons, the latter tended to

---

[17] R. J. Smith, *The Gothic bequest* (Cambridge, 1987), p. 41; S. Kliger, *The Goths in England* (Cambridge, MA, 1952).

[18] I. Kramnick, 'Augustan politics and English historiography: the debate on the English past, 1730–1735', *H+T* 6 (1967), 33–56; D. Forbes, *Hume's philosophical politics* (Cambridge, 1975), esp. pp. 217–18, 246–9, for modern whigs; J. Brewer, *Party ideology and popular politics at the accession of George III* (Cambridge, 1976), pp. 259–60.

feature more prominently in moralistic disquisitions upon the historic English character.[19]

Caste was another absent factor in English political culture. The way in which the Norman discontinuities of 1066 were aligned with the English *thèse royale* militated against the emergence of a political cult of Anglo-Norman *sang*. Brady, who celebrated the Norman Conquest, and noted that the Norman military caste had monopolised attendance at the *curia regis*, wrote to establish the historical fact of monarchical conquest and the subordinate place of parliament in the English constitution, not to assert the privileges of the Norman *race*.[20] The English aristocracy, despite their individual dynastic pretensions, did not advance a corporate Norman identity, even in response to those radicals who complained of an alien yoke of 'Normanism and Francism'. Despite these anti-Norman complaints, Normanism as such had no place in English political argument. In general there were no corporate identities distinct from a consensual English nationhood. However, the notion that the English nation was in part descended from the Normans proved useful. After all, even if William the Norman had indeed conquered the Saxons, surely his Norman companions-in-arms had not forfeited their liberties in conquest, nor had their Norman–English descendants? The ecclesiastical historian Humphrey Hody (1659–1707) saw a means of escape here from the illiberal consequences of a Norman Conquest. If William had indeed been a conqueror, he asked, 'what is that to us who are descended not only from those that are supposed to have been conquered but also from their conquerors; and are the heirs and inheritors of all their rights and liberties'?[21] However, it was generally agreed that from an early stage the Norman barons had decided to limit their monarchs and, through intermarriage and cultural assimilation, had blended into the English nation.[22] Thus, although the Normans had their uses, it was the Britons and – more commonly – the Anglo-Saxons who were spoken of as 'our ancestors'.

---

[19] W. H. Greenleaf, *Order, empiricism and politics: two traditions of English political thought 1500–1700* (London, 1964), pp. 188–9; Kliger, *Goths*, pp. 84–5. See below, ch. 8.

[20] Brady, *A full answer to all the particulars contained in a book, entituled 'Argumentum antinormanicum'*, in Brady, *Old English history*. Brady's Normanism was thus quite unlike the Frankish caste identity advanced by Boulainvilliers, for which see below, chs. 7, 9.

[21] Quoted in D. C. Douglas, *English scholars* (1939: London, 1943), p. 150.

[22] Cf. the perspectives of a Huguenot, an Anglo-Scot and an Irishman, all of whom contributed enormously to eighteenth-century English identity: Paul de Rapin-Thoyras, *Dissertation sur les whigs et les torys* (trans. Mr Ozell, London, 1717), pp. 4–5; James Thomson, *Complete poetical works* (ed. J. Logie Robertson, 1908: repr. London, 1961), 'Liberty', pt IV, p. 379; Edmund Burke, 'An essay towards an abridgement of the English history', in Burke, *Works* (16 vols., London, 1803–27), X, p. 526.

From immemorialism to Saxonism

During the seventeenth and eighteenth centuries English constitutional-ism became more decidedly ethnocentric and exclusively Saxonist, until by the nineteenth century there was a racialist tinge to the celebration of the nation's Teutonic origins (though, it should be stressed, institutional continuity never lost its overriding importance in English political dis-course). During this period the ancient British component of the nation's history was significantly downgraded. However, the chequered fate of the Britons – who still received lip-service even from committed Gothicists – is indicative of a major ambiguity in English conceptions of nationhood.

Seventeenth-century Englishmen inherited a myth of an immemorial constitution. The ideas of Sir John Fortescue (c. 1395–c. 1477), put forward in *De laudibus legum Angliae* (a treatise probably composed during the 1460s, and which appeared in English translation in 1567), exerted considerable influence upon the shape of early modern English history. Fortescue argued that the laws of England had remained substan-tially unaltered since the days of the ancient Britons, despite the subse-quent invasions of Romans, Saxons, Danes and Normans.[23] This thesis recurred in the doctrine of legal immemorialism put forward by Chief Justice Sir Edward Coke (1552–1634). Coke, and fellow juridically minded antiquaries such as George Saltern and Sir John Doddridge (1555–1628), traced the common law and parliamentary institutions of the English back beyond the Saxon era to the ancient British *conventus* and the laws of Dunwallo Molmutius, articulating the strong version of immemorialism which relied upon the legendary history of British origins concocted by Geoffrey of Monmouth.[24] On the other hand, this was only a mild prototype of the 'whiggish' political myth with which immemorial-ism later came to be associated. Unlike later generations of antiquaries, the immemorialist Cokeans of the early seventeenth century did not consider the continuity of British law and custom to have been violated by the conquests of Romans, Saxons, Danes or Normans.[25]

Nevertheless, even in this early seventeenth-century heyday

[23] J. P. Sommerville, *Politics and ideology in England 1603–1640* (London, 1986), p. 88.
[24] Edward Coke, *The first part of the institutes of the laws of England* (1628: London, 1670), p. 110; Coke, *The fourth part of the institutes* (1644: London, 1797), p. 2; Coke, *The third part of the reports* (London, 1738 edn), pp. vii–xii; John Doddridge, 'Of the antiquity etc. of the high court of parliament in England', in Thomas Hearne (ed.), *A collection of curious discourses* (2 vols., London, 1773 edn), I, pp. 281–9; George Saltern, *Of the antient lawes of Great Britaine* (London, 1605). See also the summary of Fortescue by Chief Justice Popham (1531?–1607), quoted in Burgess, *Politics of the ancient constitution*, p. 6.
[25] J. P. Sommerville, 'History and theory: the Norman conquest in early Stuart political thought', *Political Studies* 34 (1986), 253; C. Hill, *Intellectual origins of the English revol-ution* (Oxford, 1965), p. 257. See e.g. Doddridge, 'Of the antiquity of parliament', I, pp. 287–9.

immemorialism was already beginning to fray. Geoffrey of Monmouth's origin myth, which had made a decisive contribution to English identity since the twelfth century, had come under critical assault in the early sixteenth century in the work of the Italian humanist scholar, Polydore Vergil (1470?–1555?), whose version found ready acceptance in some quarters, but not in others.[26] The demise of the Galfridian legends did not signal a complete collapse of confidence in the ancient British past. The Britons' appeal did not depend entirely upon the fate of Galfridian history; they continued to enjoy a respectable historical standing independent of Geoffrey's fevered imagination. If anything, the rise of anti-Galfridian criticism purged the history of the ancient Britons of obvious implausibilities.

By the early seventeenth century a more sceptical breed of historian was less inclined to rehearse the Cokean line, yet such scrupulosity did not necessarily entail a total abandonment of an ancient British constitution. Few antiquaries went as far as William Hakewill (1574–1655), who repudiated the history of legal continuity: 'the laws of the Britons were utterly extinct by the Romans; their laws again by the Saxons; and lastly, theirs by the Danes and Normans much altered'.[27] Nor, on the other hand, did many scholars endorse the full-blown immemorialism of Fortescue or Coke. More commonly, Stuart commentators came to identify the Saxons as the founders of the common law.[28]

Growing antiquarian caution did not eliminate an appreciation of the pre-Saxon roots of English laws and liberties. There was, after all, the reliable authority of Caesar and Tacitus who described the libertarian manners and representative institutions of the Gauls and Germans, peoples assumed to be closely related to the Britons.[29] While Saltern's claim that King Arthur had presided over an ancient British parliament might not stand up to scholarly scrutiny, circumstantial evidence did support the likely existence of an ancient British *concilium*, or alternatively no single centralised monarchy among the Britons.[30]

British antiquity continued to cast a powerful spell, even on hardened scholars. The rich antiquarian corpus of John Selden (1584–1654), the most accomplished and cosmopolitan English jurist of the early seventeenth century, presents a curiously mixed message. Selden based his approach to historical criticism upon 'synchronism', the search for reliable primary source material from the era in question, or, where none was found, from proximate evidence. Although firmly opposed to the

[26] T. D. Kendrick, *British antiquity* (London, 1950), ch. 7.
[27] William Hakewill, 'The antiquity of the laws of this island', in Hearne, *Curious discourses*, I, p. 2.   [28] Sommerville, *Politics and ideology*, p. 91.   [29] Kliger, *Goths*, pp. 112–13.
[30] Saltern, *Antient lawes*, pp. 29–30; Kliger, *Goths*, pp. 123–4; Woolf, *Idea of history*, p. 95.

Cokean legend, the sceptical Selden discerned none the less a basic pattern of mixed government in English history which predated the Saxons, though without diminishing the mutability of laws and creative dimension of governance. Despite his strong doubts about the incredible historical specifics of the British past, Selden reckoned that over the long run 'the fundamental shape of sovereignty had lasted'. Moreover, while Selden noted the enormous changes wrought in English law by the Normans, he recognised that there was still a measure of continuity from the Saxon era, and even earlier. Indeed, Selden's *Analecton Anglo-Britannicon* consciously echoed the title and argument of François Hotman's *Franco-Gallia*: just as the lost liberties of the Gauls conquered by the Romans had been recovered and extended by the Franks, so in England the *adventus Saxonum* had restored ancient British liberties. Nowhere was Selden's ambivalence more pronounced than in the historical notes which he contributed to his friend Michael Drayton's *Poly-Olbion* (1613). Here Selden's scholarly apparatus deconstructs the legendary matter of Britain celebrated in Drayton's poetry.[31]

The significance of the British past was also under threat from another quarter. From the late sixteenth century onwards the most concrete evidence for historic English liberties appeared to come from the reign of Edward the Confessor. Consider the canonical documents of ancient constitutionalism, as listed by Janelle Greenberg. These comprised the laws of Edward the Confessor, the *Modus tenendi parliamentum*, the *Mirror of justices*, the medieval legal treatises Bracton and *Fleta*, and the work of Fortescue. In 1568 William Lambarde (1536–1601) published *Archaionomia, sive de priscis Anglorum legibus*, compiled with the help of a medieval lawbook *Leges Edwardi Confessoris*. Lambarde's collection included not only the – apocryphal – laws of the Confessor, but also later confirmations of the Confessor's laws by William I and Henry I. William's acceptance of the Confessor's laws was reported in Ingulph, the false Croyland chronicler, and even Selden did not question it. The significance of King John's signing of Magna Carta (1215) for antiquaries was primarily as a restatement of the Confessor's laws, further confirmed by the coronation oath of Edward II; indeed the solemn compacts of William I and Henry I were described as 'Magna Cartas'. The *Modus*,

[31] P. Christianson, 'Young John Selden and the ancient constitution, ca. 1610–1618', *Proceedings of the American Philosophical Society* 128 (1984), 271–315; R. Tuck, '"The ancient law of freedom": John Selden and the civil war', in J. Morrill (ed.), *Reactions to the English civil war* (Houndmills, 1982), pp. 139–40; Tuck, *Philosophy and government 1572–1651* (Cambridge, 1993), pp. 208–9; Tuck, *Natural rights theories* (1979: Cambridge, 1981, pbk edn), p. 83; Woolf, *Idea of history*, ch. 7; Burgess, *Politics of the ancient constitution*, pp. 37–8, 63–5, 233; Kendrick, *British antiquity*, p. 109; G. Parry, *The trophies of time* (Oxford, 1995), ch. 4.

which was probably composed around 1320 by a chancery clerk, purported to be a guide to Anglo-Saxon parliaments in the era of Edmund Ironside. The *Mirror*, a tract composed in the 1290s, circulated in manuscript in the second half of the sixteenth century before being published first in Latin (1642), then English (1646). The *Mirror* included a description of parliament in the reign of King Arthur, but focused on the fact that Anglo-Saxon kings had not been above the law.[32] Although there were gaps even in this spurious record – most obviously the fact that there were no extant parliament rolls from the Saxon era – these could be plausibly explained. Although these materials were used by Coke to construct his version of the ancient constitution, in the long run they would contribute to the decline of immemorialism. Henceforth, the Anglo-Saxon past had an institutional concreteness, however bogus, which was lacking in a remote ancient British past. Corinne Weston has argued that the very abundance of this medieval material is by itself 'almost enough to explain why the common law cult of the Confessor's laws became the core of the Stuart doctrine of the ancient constitution'.[33] Furthermore, the importance of the Confessor's laws would grow in the course of the seventeenth century as the main scene of antiquarian debate shifted forward to the era surrounding the Norman Conquest. Although James I's discouragement of the reviving Society of Antiquaries in 1614 epitomises the growing politicisation of constitutional history in the early seventeenth century, the Norman Conquest had not yet become a defining axis of political debate.[34] Indeed, as Daniel Woolf notes, Coke found the Roman conquest more troubling to his thesis of the immemorial continuity of England's laws than the later Norman invasion.[35]

Some historians were also beginning to distinguish carefully between the roles played the Britons and the Saxons in shaping English nationhood. Over the course of his long scholarly career, William Camden (1551–1623) came to recognise that England was essentially a Saxon creation.[36] Then, in 1605, there appeared the first authentically Saxonist

[32] J. Greenberg, 'The Confessor's laws and the radical face of the ancient constitution', *EHR* 104 (1989), 611–37; H. Butterfield, *The Englishman and his history* (Cambridge, 1944), p. 41; Smith, *Gothic bequest*, p. 3 n.; H. MacDougall, *Racial myth in English history* (Montreal and Hanover, NH, 1982), pp. 57–8; C. Brooke, *A history of Gonville and Caius College* (Woodbridge, 1985), p. 144; Burgess, *Politics of the ancient constitution*, p. 76; M. Keen, *England in the later middle ages* (London, 1973), pp. 82–4. For the continuing influence of the Confessor's laws into the late seventeenth century, see H. T. Dickinson, *Liberty and property* (London, 1977), pp. 62–4, 73.

[33] C. Weston, 'England: ancient constitution and common law', in J. H. Burns and M. Goldie (eds.), *The Cambridge history of political thought 1450–1700* (Cambridge, 1991), p. 382 n.

[34] K. Sharpe, *Sir Robert Cotton* (Oxford, 1979), pp. 23, 36; Sommerville, *Politics and ideology*, pp. 49, 67–9; Sommerville, 'History and theory', 249–61.

[35] Woolf, *Idea of history*, p. 28.   [36] Parry, *Trophies of time*, p. 37.

history, Richard Verstegan's *A restitution of decayed intelligence*, which as well as being explicitly ethnocentric, also involved a radical departure in ethnic classification. The first scholar to argue clearly against the error of associating English identity with the achievements of the ancient Britons, Verstegan saw himself as an outspoken revisionist. His point of departure was the observation that 'divers of our English writers have been as laborious, and serious in their discourses of the antiquity of the Britons as if they properly pertained unto Englishmen, which in no wise they do or can do, for that their offsprings, and descents are wholly different'. Against this careless 'lack of distinction between the two nations', Verstegan established the ancient Germanic nations as 'our own true ancestors'. Although sceptical of the notion that Verstegan's work ignited a 'Saxon craze', Daniel Woolf, a leading expert on seventeenth-century historiography, none the less describes the *Restitution*, further editions of which appeared in 1628, 1634, 1653 and 1673, as 'a significant departure from the adulation of the British and their Trojan ancestors'.[37]

Of the two major components of Verstegan's message – a glorious Saxon descent and the real differences between the Britons and the Saxons – the first made more impact than the second. As we have already noted, the loose association of Gothicism with the libertarian, democratic and martial manners of the barbarian peoples of ancient Europe made it possible for some commentators to provide shelter for the pre-Gothic Germans and freedom-loving Celts described by Tacitus under the broad Gothic umbrella. English Gothicists were torn between a strictly ethnic definition of Englishness, which implied the Saxon beginnings of the 'English' constitution in customs transplanted from the woods of Germany, and a territorial identity in which the same broad contours of the institutions of 'England' could be discerned in the British past long before the arrival of Germanic customs. These tensions remained quite marked throughout the seventeenth and eighteenth centuries, even as a dominant Gothicism supplanted immemorialism.[38]

Consider one of the most influential of seventeenth-century 'Saxonist' treatises, Nathaniel Bacon's *An historicall discourse of the uniformity of the government of England* (1647), which went through various editions, in 1672, 1682, 1689, 1739 and 1760. Bacon (1593–1660) was a Suffolk lawyer who sat in the House of Commons until Pride's Purge, gained readmission in 1649 and served the Commonwealth and Protectorate in various judicial capacities. Bacon stressed 'the antiquity and uniformity of the government of this nation'. Noting similarities between the Britons

---

[37] Verstegan, *Restitution*, 'To the most noble and renowned English nation'; Kliger, *Goths*, p. 115; Woolf, *Idea of history*, p. 202; Parry, *Trophies of time*, ch. 2.
[38] Smith, *Gothic bequest*, pp. 40–1.

and the Saxons, Bacon wondered 'how probable it is, that this island hath been no other than a sewer to empty the superfluity of the German nations; and how the influence of these old principles doth work in the fundamental government of this kingdom, to the present day'. Although Bacon did not ignore the ancient British past (not least as we shall see below its ecclesiastical aspect), he stressed that English institutions had been defined by the Saxons – 'a free people, because they are a law unto themselves, and this was a privilege belonging to all the Germans, as Tacitus observeth'. Bacon's central point, however, was that the ancient design of English institutions, inaugurated by the Britons and consolidated by the more libertarian Saxons, had persisted in spite of the Norman invasion of 1066.[39]

The importance of the ancient British past declined dramatically during the second half of the seventeenth century. A new strain of political analysis developed by James Harrington and revised by the next generation of neo-Harringtonians (who drew a more pessimistic lesson from the same reading of history) considered the crisis of Europe's Gothic polities, which served to highlight the continental provenance of the English constitution.[40] There were also changes of emphasis within 'insular' historiography. For a variety of reasons, including both the radical thesis of the Norman Yoke which surfaced in the 1640s and the complementary royalist histories which appeared during the Restoration era, the transition between the Anglo-Saxon and the Norman era came to be seen as the crucial period in the saga of the English constitution. Whatever the Saxons inherited from the aboriginal Britons – though it still had some bearings on questions of constitutional legitimacy – mattered less than what features of Saxon law and government had survived the arrival of the Normans in 1066.[41]

Whiggish antiquarians, most notably William Petyt (1637–1707), William Atwood (c. 1661–c. 1705) and James Tyrrell (1642–1718), addressed the assorted feudalist, sceptical and downright royalist arguments of those who questioned the continuity of the ancient constitution. Sir Henry Spelman had demonstrated, through careful philological analysis of legal terms, the Norman provenance of English feudal tenures. The scrupulous – and disappointed – radical William Prynne had shown from the evidence of writs of summons that the Commons had not been present in parliament until 49 Henry III. Brady's achievement was, in

---

[39] Nathaniel Bacon, *An historical and political discourse of the laws and government of England* (1647: London, 1689 edn), pp. 9–10; Tuck, *Philosophy and government*, pp. 235–40; Greenberg, 'Confessor's laws', 622; Kliger, *Goths*, p. 138.   [40] See below, ch. 9.
[41] J. G. A. Pocock, *The ancient constitution and the feudal law* (1957: reissue with retrospect, Cambridge, 1987), chs. 6–8.

good part, to synthesise these insights into a compelling royalist interpretation of English history and to make clear that William I had indeed conquered England. The free Saxon nation had been conquered; the law had been transformed by the Normans and feudal tenures imported; parliament was a post-Conquest creation, existing by grace of the monarch; and the appearance of the Commons was even more recent.[42] The whig antiquaries denied that the accession of William of Normandy constituted an interruption in the descent of England's ancient constitution or of its primeval laws and liberties. Tyrrell, for example, wove a fine, but crucial, distinction between a conquest and an acquisition by force of arms limited by compact.[43]

Despite major advances in antiquarian learning, a few serious scholars continued to treat Geoffrey of Monmouth as a reliable historian. Loyal defenders included the distinguished Cambridge orientalist Robert Sheringham and his fellow Cantabrigian Daniel Langhorne. As evidence for the fluidity of ethnic classification, Sheringham somehow managed to combine enthusiasm for both Galfridian and Saxon origins without any trace of discomfiture.[44] Geoffrey's legends also continued to be used in historical politics, though as much concerning domestic constitutional and legal debates as in constructing a British message. For example, Silas Taylor (1624–78) suggested that Geoffrey's account of the division of Britain among the sons of Brutus was the origin of partible gavelkind inheritance. Taylor maintained that the laws and customs of the 'British aborigines' had 'received no considerable mutations or alterations' in the space of 1,700 years, notwithstanding Roman, Saxon, Danish and Norman incursions and settlements.[45] In general, however, the Galfridian origin myth was considered typical of the monkish fabrications of the middle ages, which it was the duty of Protestant scholars to detect and expunge. Nevertheless, other components of the Galfridian tradition, such as the legend of King Arthur, retained a firmer foothold in English culture than the shaky foundation myth of the Trojan–British monarchy.[46] Immemorialism too had long since gone into decline, but vestiges of it qualified the Saxonism of the ancient constitutionalists.[47] As a result

[42] Douglas, *English scholars*, ch. 6; Pocock, *Ancient constitution*, ch. 8; Brooke, *Caius College*, pp. 144–5.
[43] James Tyrrell, *The general history of England* (3 vols., London, 1697–1704), I, 'Epistle dedicatory', p. iii.
[44] Robert Sheringham, *De Anglorum gentis origine disceptatio* (Cambridge, 1670); Daniel Langhorne, *An introduction to the history of England* (London, 1676); Kendrick, *British antiquity*, p. 101.
[45] Silas Taylor, *The history of gavel-kind* (London, 1663), pp. 15–16, 46, 80, 85–6.
[46] R. F. Brinkley, *Arthurian legend in the seventeenth century* (Baltimore, 1932).
[47] Tyrrell, *General history*, I, 'General introduction', p. xxx; Kliger, *Goths*, p. 169; Greenleaf, *Order, empiricism and politics*, p. 123.

even the sceptical Brady felt compelled to insure himself against the argument that the commons had been present in the councils of the Britons.[48]

Somehow the English were the biological descendants of the Saxons, but their institutions also needed to be traced back to an ancient British ancestry. Algernon Sidney (1623–83) was a pronounced Gothicist who described the Saxons, and sometimes also the Angles, as the people 'from whom we chiefly derive our original and manners'. However, he was not prepared to jettison the argument for the immemorial antiquity of English liberties. Just as the early Saxon leaders such as Hengist and Horsa had been 'temporary magistrates', so had such ancient Celtic monarchs among the Britons such as Cassivellaun, Caratacus and Arviragus.[49]

The Britons remained important to the whiggish cult of parliament. Thomas Rymer (1641–1713) claimed that Cassivellaun had ruled as king of the Britons on conciliar authority.[50] After 1688 the British past was also invoked by some whiggish antiquaries keen to find a historical vindication of Revolution principles. Pierre Allix (1641–1717) noted that 'Nennius, the most ancient English historian after Gildas, tells us, that Vortigern was deposed by St Germain and the council of the Britons, because he had married his own daughter, who placed his son Vortimer upon the throne.'[51] Nevertheless, the British past was sketchier and less reliable than the Saxon era. Temple endorsed the Fortescuean tradition, though he acknowledged that it was 'not so easily proved, as affirmed'. While it was difficult to ascertain direct continuities from the Britons and Romans, he was nevertheless satisfied that he could establish the maintenance of the Saxon heritage through the Danish and Norman eras with 'more certainty', which was 'sufficient to illuminate the antiquity of our constitutions, without recourse to strained or uncertain allegations'.[52]

Brady's devastating scholarship ought to have sunk the ancient Saxon constitution. However, matters were not quite so simple. The Glorious Revolution and the subsequent whig hegemony artificially sustained the errors of the Saxon myth as public doctrine;[53] indeed, whig antiquaries of the early eighteenth century appropriated feudalist arguments to subvert Brady's arguments for discontinuity.[54] However, as we shall see, by the

---

[48] Brady, *A full and clear answer to a book written by William Petit, esq.*, in Brady, *Old English history*, pp. 1–2.   [49] Sidney, *Discourses*, pp. 479–81.

[50] Rymer, *General draught*, p. 13.

[51] Pierre Allix, *Reflections upon the opinions of some modern divines, concerning the nature of government in general, and that of England in particular* (London, 1689), pp. 82–3.

[52] Temple, *Introduction to the history of England*, II, p. 584.

[53] Pocock, *Ancient constitution*, ch. 9.

[54] D. Earl, 'Procrustean feudalism: an interpretative dilemma in English historical narration, 1700–1725', *HJ* 19 (1976), 33–51; Smith, *Gothic bequest*, pp. 47–56.

middle of the eighteenth century a new breed of sceptical modern whig had the sensitivity to use Brady's historical insights without subscribing to his political message.

In the course of the eighteenth century Englishmen began to depend more exclusively on the Saxons as the nation's foundational ethnic core. Saxonist historiography was not primarily a celebration of ethnicity. It focused principally on institutions – political, legal and ecclesiastical. Customs, manners and culture were subordinate considerations, though the Tacitean inheritance meant that they were always a component part of the Gothicist package. Moreover, this cultural dimension of the Saxon heritage grew in importance throughout the eighteenth century, paving the way for the more overtly racialist and ethnic-determinist Saxonism which would prevail in nineteenth-century English discourse. Another obvious sign of the Britons' declining importance lies in the reluctance of patriotic antiquaries to exploit the pre-Saxon past in the cause of British integration. Instead Gothicism, as we shall see in a later chapter, was a common feature of political argument in England, North Britain, Protestant Ireland and the American colonies.[55]

However, traces of immemorialism lingered in Saxonist history, confounding the logic of Gothicism. If one subscribed to the view that English liberties and institutions were of Anglo-Saxon provenance, imported from the forests of Germany, the history of the aboriginal Britons should have mattered little. George St Amand (1686/7–1727), who maintained a Saxonist argument for the continuity of the English constitution – that the Saxons had certainly 'subverted the ancient government of the Britons' and that William I, on the other hand, 'did not subvert, or dissolve the Saxon government' – still felt it necessary to establish that the ancient inhabitants of Britain, Gaul and Germany had all been 'one people', with a similar form of government.[56]

Although the Britons were certainly being supplanted from their former pedestal, the identities of Briton and Saxon were still conceived as complementary rather than as conflicting. John Oldmixon (1673–1742) balanced a sceptical reading of the shadowy events of the pre-Saxon era with his whiggish message that England had ever enjoyed a limited and constitutional form of government:

Though we doubt not the whole story of Brute and his posterity is invented; yet, as in all good fables there is a moral, so in this the events are as much lessons as if they were true . . . We may there see what notions the ancient Britons had of the rights of the prince and people, by the actions which are attributed to them.

[55] See below, ch. 10.
[56] George St Amand, *An historical essay on the legislative power of England* (London, 1725), pp. 48–9, 114.

Oldmixon was quick to spot the Revolution principles of the ancient Britons. Take the examples of the resistance supposedly offered to Locrinus, the son of Brute, to Ferrex, forced to give way to his younger brother Porrex, and to Archigallo, deposed for 'maleadministration'. In the better-known historical era immediately before the arrival of the Saxons, Vortigern had been overthrown 'by his subjects' in favour of his son Vortimer. When Vortigern outlived his son, the former king had again been deposed by a *concilium* of the Britons to make way for Aurelius Ambrosius. Oldmixon concluded that the ancient British government was 'in a great measure democratical'. However, Oldmixon's story remained predominantly Saxonist. 'Our parliamentary constitution', he argued, 'is as old as the Saxons.' After all, in the wake of Brady's scholarship, it was becoming hard enough for whig historians to establish Saxon continuities or even the existence of a representative assembly before 49 Henry III: 'Nobody ever pretended that the form of parliaments was in old times exactly the same as it is now.' Oldmixon conceded that originally the Lords and the Commons had sat together in one chamber. Nevertheless, by concentrating on such institutional technicalities one might miss 'the main of the matter', that 'the meeting of the estates, their enquiring into grievances, their giving of money, and exercising legislative authority, [was] as old as the Gothic government'. Historians should not become obsessed with the pedantry of legal terminology. Among the Saxons Oldmixon found many other terms and loose expressions for assemblies – 'omnium senatorum meorum consensu', 'cum concilio sapientum', witenagemots, micklegemots – which approximated to the later English parliament. Moreover, 'success' had eluded the Normans in their patent attempt to invade Saxon laws. Indeed, were not elective Revolution principles observable in the succession of the Anglo-Norman kingship, not least the exclusion of Duke Robert for a younger son? Succession by primogeniture, without which the divine right principles of modern tories were a nonsense, had not taken effect until the time of Richard I.[57]

The notion of an ancient British parliament retained some appeal, not least because a conveniently whiggish message could be spun from the sources. Thornhaugh Gurdon (1663–1733) used the authority of classical commentators to construct an immemorial lineage for parliament which stretched back to the earliest Celtic inhabitants of Britain: 'Caesar and Tacitus both agree that the laws and customs of the Germans, Gauls and Britons, were much the same.' Gurdon did acknowledge some differences between British and Saxon practices, but traced conciliar fea-

[57] John Oldmixon, *The critical history of England, ecclesiastical and civil* (2 vols., London, 1724–6), I, pp. ii, 17–19, 25–7, 33–7, 42.

tures in both systems. The Britons had held councils called 'Kifrithin', a term which in their language meant a body set up 'to debate and treat upon matters to be taken into consideration for the public weal'. Etymology revealed that the council of the Saxons had been grafted on to the original institution of the ancient Britons: 'Witenagemote, a word compounded of Saxon and British, the former part of the word being Saxon and the latter British; Wita is in Saxon a wise man . . . Gemot in the British language is a council or synod.' Such ethnic hybridity was also a feature of English law, which, while founded predominantly on Saxon principles, also included several British customs and law terms.[58]

Bolingbroke maintained that in all ages the island of Britain 'hath been the temple, as it were, of liberty. Whilst her sacred fires have been extinguished in so many countries, here they have been religiously kept alive.' Although little was known of the ancient Britons 'through the gloom of antiquity', he was convinced that they had enjoyed a free government. After all, when the Romans left in the fifth century the petty kings of Britain – *reguli* – held their authority by consent of the people. The indigenous spirit of liberty found among the Britons and the Saxons proved too strong for the Danes and the Normans, who 'were seized with it themselves, instead of inspiring a spirit of slavery into the Saxons'.[59]

During the Walpolean era supporters of the government propagated a new strain of self-consciously modern whiggery. Drawing on the insights of Brady's toryism and an emergent critique of medieval feudalism, pamphleteers including John Hervey (1696–1743) and the pseudonymous 'Walsingham' and 'Osborne' argued that the civil liberties enjoyed by modern Britons were a product of modernity, dating from the Restoration era, improved in the Revolution of 1688 and consolidated under the enlightened whig supremacy of Hanoverian Britain. In a classic pamphlet, *Ancient and modern liberty stated and compared* (1734), Hervey attempted to cleanse the Augean stables of vulgar whig mythology. The history of England since the Norman Conquest, according to Hervey, was not about the vicissitudes of an unquenchable spirit of liberty so much as the 'same melancholy vicissitude in the manner of oppressing the people, without any suspension of the thing itself', whether through royal, baronial or clerical tyrannies: 'I never hear anybody harangue with enthusiastic encomiums on the liberty of Old England, that I am not either ashamed of my ancestors for deserving these encomiums so little or of my contemporaries for bestowing them so ignorantly.'[60]

---

[58] Thornhaugh Gurdon, *The history of the high court of parliament, its antiquity, preheminence and authority* (2 vols., London, 1731), I, pp. 12, 15, 21.

[59] Bolingbroke, *Remarks*, I, pp. 313–20; Bolingbroke, *Dissertation on parties*, Letter xii, in Bolingbroke, *Works*, II, pp. 160–4.

Modern whig ideas enjoyed some influence at the rarefied peak of British historical and political sophistication, most obviously in the work of Hume and Josiah Tucker (1712–99).[61] However, revisionism enjoyed much less success in the wider political culture; 'ancient constitutionalism', defined by Duncan Forbes as 'a compelling need to assert and defend the essential continuity of the English form of government', remained 'whig orthodoxy'.[62] Why did modern whig celebrations of the benign discontinuity of 1688 not displace the longer saga of English liberties? The historic roles of parliament and common law in the evolution of English liberties were hard to ignore. George, Baron Lyttelton, a modernist who argued that civil liberty was in large part a post-Revolutionary creation, acknowledged that the English whig heritage remained of some value, despite the enormous gulf between past failings and present felicities: 'even the rudest form of our government has always been animated by the spirit of freedom'.[63]

Notwithstanding the emergence of modern whig revisionism, the arrival of the Normans continued to be regarded as the major discontinuity in the history of English liberty. Richard Hurd (1720–1808) upheld an exclusively Saxonist position: 'the principles of the Saxon policy, and in some respects the form of it, have been constantly kept up in every succeeding period of the English monarchy'. However, he was unconcerned by the fate of the Saxons as an ethnic group; what mattered was not the treatment of the Saxon people by William I (who succeeded by testamentary succession from the Confessor) but the survival of Saxon institutions: 'The Saxons methinks might be injured, oppressed, enslaved; and yet the constitution, transmitted to us through his own Normans, be perfectly free.' It was Norman barons, proclaiming 'nolumus leges Angliae mutari', who would uphold their adopted ancient constitution against the despotic pretensions of their own kings.[64]

In the course of the eighteenth century it became more common to argue that feudalisation was a Europe-wide phenomenon and one far from illiberal in its origins or effects. In England it had been inaugurated by the Saxons, and only completed by the Normans. The distinction between boc-land and folc-land was interpreted by some antiquarians as evidence for the existence of both allodial tenures and feudal benefices among the Saxons. Although scholars such as Rayner Heckford and

[60] John Hervey, *Ancient and modern liberty stated and compared* (London, 1734), pp. 6–7.
[61] David Hume, *The history of England* (6 vols., Indianapolis, 1983); Josiah Tucker, *A treatise concerning civil government* (London, 1781).
[62] Forbes, *Hume's philosophical politics*, p. 249.
[63] George Lyttelton, *The history of the life of King Henry the second* (3rd edn, 5 vols., 1769–73), I, 'Preface', p. viii.
[64] Hurd, *Moral and political dialogues*, pp. 191, 194, 222, 227–8.

James Ibbetson disagreed as to the nature of boc-land and folc-land, there was a consensus about the Saxon origins of English feudal tenures.[65] Similarly, Oliver Goldsmith argued that the Saxons had introduced the feudal law; thereafter William had merely 'reformed it, according to the model practised in his native dominions'. Goldsmith, like so many other historians, was a 'soft' Gothicist with immemorialist leanings who argued against any ascription of English laws 'entirely to Saxon original'. While Goldsmith noted that the Saxons had introduced to England many laws 'long in practice among their German ancestors', he added that they had 'adopted also many more which they found among the Britons, or which the Romans left behind after their abdication'.[66]

Indeed, the ancient British past continued to offer valuable historical reinsurance against advocates of the Brady thesis (which focused not on the Britons, but on the Norman Conquest). In his mammoth and modestly mistitled *History of Manchester* (1771–5), the antiquary John Whitaker (1735–1808), a critic of such tories as Brady, Carte and Hume, invested a significant amount of whiggish capital in the history of the ancient Britons. According to Whitaker, the undoubted whiggery of the ancient Anglo-Saxon constitution could be traced further back into the primitive history of the Britons. For example, the lineal and hereditary succession to the crown had been defeasible among both the Britons and the Saxons. Moreover, the ancient British monarchy had been limited by assemblies, though these had been composed only of nobles, as the British commons were all villeins. Feudalism, of course, was the Trojan horse in English constitutional history, which appeared to admit the reality of a Norman Conquest. Whitaker opened up another theatre of whig–tory conflict by reconstructing the feudal laws of the pre-Saxon past. He argued that British tenures of the first century AD had been 'purely military in their design and absolutely feudal in their essence'. Feudal law had not come to England through conquest, for it 'formed the primitive establishment of the Britons'. Whitaker conceded that this constituted merely 'a system of feuds in miniature' which would undergo social and legal change. Nevertheless, British feudalism had been 'the same in effect with the more enlarged system of the Normans'. This was additional security against the notion of the Conquest. Given that feudal tenures were found in the British as well as in the Saxon era, Whitaker concluded: 'Doubly unjust, therefore, is the popular opinion of our

---

[65] Rayner Heckford, *A discourse on the bookland and folkland of the Saxons* (Cambridge, 1775); James Ibbetson, *A dissertation on the folclande and boclande of the Saxons* (London, 1777). See also John Dalrymple, *An essay towards a general history of feudal property in Great Britain* (London, 1757), pp. 8–22; Samuel Squire, *An enquiry into the foundation of the English constitution* (London, 1745), pp. 103–7.

[66] Oliver Goldsmith, *The history of England* (4 vols., London, 1771), I, pp. 134–5, 149.

historical and legal antiquaries, which refers the origin of the feuds to the Normans.'[67]

Whitaker's sense that the ancient British past remained of some constitutional significance was shared, albeit in a lower key, by no less a figure than William Blackstone, in whose *Commentaries* there survived a mild version of common law immemorialism:

> The great variety of nations, that successively broke in upon and destroyed both the British inhabitants and constitution . . . must necessarily have caused great uncertainty and confusion in the laws and antiquities of the kingdom; as they were very soon incorporated and blended together, and therefore, we may suppose, mutually communicated to each other their respective usages . . . So that it is morally impossible to trace out, with any degree of accuracy, when the several mutations of the common law were made, or what was the respective original of those several customs we at present use, by any chemical resolution of them to their first and component principles. We can seldom pronounce, that this custom was derived from the Britons; that was left behind by the Romans; this was a necessary precaution against the Picts; that was introduced by the Saxons, discontinued by the Danes, but afterwards restored by the Normans.

Blackstone did, however, believe that particular survivals of the ancient body of British customs could be traced, including the partibility of land by gavelkind and the division of goods of an intestate between his widow and children, or next of kin. Moreover, 'the very notion itself of an oral unwritten law, delivered down from age to age, by custom and tradition merely' seemed to Blackstone to be 'derived from the practice of the Druids'. He acknowledged the reality, extent and degree of the Conquest, but did not erect a royalist thesis on this historical foundation. The modern liberties of Englishmen were 'not to be looked upon as consisting of mere incroachments on the crown, and infringements of the prerogative, as some slavish and narrow-minded writers of the last century endeavoured to maintain; but as, in general, a gradual restoration of that ancient constitution, whereof our Saxon forefathers had been unjustly deprived, partly by the policy, and partly by the force, of the Normans'.[68]

The idea of an ancient British parliament would survive in the radical tradition of the late eighteenth century. John Cartwright (1740–1824), a champion of the Saxons whose hero was King Alfred, claimed that annual parliaments had been 'the immemorial usage of England from the earliest antiquity', noting that both Britons and Saxons had been free nations. Thomas Oldfield (1755–1822) felt a similar polemical need to go back beyond the free Anglo-Saxons to give his arguments the copper-

---

[67] Whitaker, *History of Manchester*, esp. I, pp. 251–2, 262–4, 273–4; II, pp. 148–9, 165, 169–72.   [68] Blackstone, *Commentaries*, IV, pp. 401–2, 413.

bottomed legitimacy of ancient British illustration. Oldfield began his critical history of borough representation by noting that the free Saxon parliaments which prevailed before the coming of Norman feudalism were 'only a continuance of the Kyfr-y-then or popular assemblies of the Britons, as improved by their intercourse with the Romans'.[69] However, even within the radical tradition the ancient Britons were of only marginal importance. The two major turning points in the radical interpretation of the decline of English liberties came long after the demise of the Britons. These moments were the Norman Yoke imposed after the conquest of 1066, and – less well known – the fifteenth-century century legislation known as 'the statute of disfranchisement'.[70]

Although increasingly irrelevant to debates over the temporal constitution, the matter of Britain continued to be regarded as suitable material for a national epos, albeit one fenced off from the mainstream of political argument. The lines of demarcation between origin myth and ancient constitution, already visible in Selden's apparatus for Drayton's *Poly-Olbion*, had become much clearer. Historians of literature and art have drawn attention to the ways in which the ancient British past continued throughout the seventeenth and eighteenth centuries to supply an abundance of themes for imaginative writers and, eventually, for painters. Even the Galfridian legends, though no longer fit to grace the pages of national histories, remained prized as a source for epic poetry and drama.[71]

Nineteenth-century English political culture retained a traditional primary emphasis on institutions, their historical development and the polyethnic formation of the English nation, yet the racial – and mono-ethnic – dimension of Saxonism became much more pronounced. Sharon Turner (1768–1847) was emphatic: 'Though other invaders have appeared in the island, yet the effect of the Anglo-Saxon settlements have

---

[69] John Cartwright, *Give us our rights! Or, a letter to the present electors of Middlesex and the metropolis* (London, 1782), pp. 8 n., 26 n.; Cartwright, *The people's barrier against undue influence and corruption or the commons' house of parliament according to the constitution* (London, 1780), p. 13; Thomas Oldfield, *An entire and complete history, political and personal, of the boroughs of Great Britain* (3 vols., London, 1792), I, p. 31.

[70] James Burgh, *Political disquisitions* (3 vols., London, 1774–5), I, pp. 83–4; Cartwright, *The people's barrier*, pp. 18, 31–8.

[71] Brinkley, *Arthurian legend*; E. D. Snyder, *The Celtic revival in English literature, 1760–1800* (Cambridge, MA, 1923), esp. p. 55; I. Haywood, *The making of history* (Cranbury, NJ, 1986), pp. 58–62; H. Weinbrot, *Britannia's issue* (Cambridge, 1993), pp. 493, 562–3; Weinbrot, 'Celts, Greeks, and Germans: Macpherson's Ossian and the Celtic epic', *1650–1850: Ideas, Aesthetics and Inquiries in the Early Modern Era* 1 (1994), 17 n.; C. Gerrard, *The patriot opposition to Walpole* (Oxford, 1994), p. 120; S. Smiles, *The image of antiquity* (New Haven and London, 1994), pp. 153, 159.

prevailed beyond every other. Our language, our government, and our laws, display our Gothic ancestors in every part.'[72] Indeed, scholars are agreed that by the early nineteenth century a qualitative difference had appeared between the old language of English Gothicism – whose previous significance had been predominantly constitutional – and a new Teutonism which had 'a more distinctly racial meaning'.[73]

[72] Sharon Turner, *The history of the Anglo-Saxons* (2nd edn, 2 vols., London, 1807), I, pp. 27–8.
[73] G. Stocking, *Victorian anthropology* (1987: New York pbk, 1991), p. 62. See also D. A. White, 'Changing views of the *adventus Saxonum* in nineteenth- and twentieth-century English scholarship', *JHI* 32 (1971), 586–7; R. Horsman, 'Origins of racial Anglo-Saxonism in Great Britain before 1850', *JHI* 37 (1976), 387–410; M. Banton, *The idea of race* (London, 1977), pp. 21–6; B. Melman, 'Claiming the nation's past: the invention of the Anglo-Saxon tradition', *Journal of Contemporary History* 26 (1991), 575–95.

5   Britons, Saxons and the Anglican quest for legitimacy

The ecclesiastical past was a foreign country: antiquarians conducted their arguments very differently there. Anglo-Saxon precedents in the religious sphere were easily trumped by appeals to the primitive, apostolic era of British Christianity. During the same period when English political identity was becoming predominantly Saxonist, and the legend of the parliamentary and legal institutions of the Britons was shunted to the margins of English political discourse, the ethnic associations of the Church of England remained firmly tied to a myth of ancient *British* Christianity. Indeed, despite the rise of Gothicism, the significance of the ancient British era for Anglicans would not dim until the late eighteenth century.

For most of the seventeenth and eighteenth centuries the standard Anglican interpretation of English history ran – broadly speaking – as follows. The Church of England was an apostolic foundation, though antiquaries debated the rival merits of the various 'plausible' contenders: Simon Zelotes, Philip the Apostle, James son of Zebedee, the quasi-apostolic Joseph of Arimathea, Aristobulus, Paul, some other follower of Our Lord – though definitely not St Peter.[1] Anglican scholars did not

---

[1] See e.g. essays by Robert Cotton, Arthur Agarde, William Dethick, William Camden and William Hakewill on the theme 'Of the antiquity of the Christian religion in this island', in Thomas Hearne (ed.), *A collection of curious discourses* (2 vols., London, 1773 edn), II, pp. 155–72; Francis Godwin, *A catalogue of the bishops of England* (London, 1615), 'A discourse concerning the first conversion of this island'; Thomas Fuller, *Church history of Britain* (1655: 3 vols., London, 1842), I, pp. 8–9; Edward Stillingfleet, *Origines Britannicae* (London, 1685), esp. pp. 6, 43, 45–6; Nathaniel Crouch, *England's monarchs* (London, 1685), p. 4; Jeremy Collier, *An ecclesiastical history of Great Britain* (1708–14: London, 1852), I, pp. 7–12, 23; Henry Rowlands, *Mona antiqua restaurata* (Dublin, 1723), pp. 138–9; George Smith, *The Britons and Saxons not converted to Popery* (London, 1748), pp. 268–71; Ferdinando Warner, *The ecclesiastical history of England* (2 vols., London, 1756), I, pp. 5–10; G. Williams, 'Some Protestant views of early British church history', *History* 38 (1953), 221–2; K. Sharpe, *Sir Robert Cotton* (Oxford, 1979), p. 31; J. Champion, *The pillars of priestcraft shaken* (Cambridge, 1992), pp. 55–61; J. Levine, *Dr Woodward's shield* (1977: Ithaca and London, 1991), p. 135.

conjure such ecclesiological fantasies out of nothing. To cite only the two most compelling authorities: Tertullian in his *Adversus Judaeos* (c. AD 208) claimed that the gospel had already penetrated those areas of Britain inaccessible to Roman arms, and there appeared to be a reference in Gildas to a conversion of the Britons in the reign of the emperor Tiberius.[2] Thanks to the auspicious and plausible origins of their church, Anglicans could take pride in their institution's direct personal link to Christ. Moreover, the Church of England had clearly been established independent of Roman influence, with a system of worship and organisation of primitive purity. Bede's remark that the Celtic churches had celebrated Easter according to the pattern of the Johanine Christians of Asia Minor[3] prompted the conclusion that, in the words of Foxe's *Acts and monuments*, the Britons 'were taught first by the Grecians of the east church, rather than by the Romans'.[4] Anglican historians contended that their church had always been governed by bishops, and that the ancient British Christians had soon been organised into three provinces: York, London and Caerleon-on-Usk.[5] Despite the obvious blemish of the fifth-century Pelagian heresy, there was much in which Anglicans took great pride, not least the heroic martyrdom of St Alban during Diocletian's persecution at the beginning of the fourth century,[6] and the claim that the emperor Constantine, 'who enfranchised Christianity throughout the Roman Empire', had been born in Britain, of British stock through his mother Helen.[7]

With the ravages of the pagan Saxons, the Britons had been driven westwards into the mountains of Wales, where their church was organised around seven bishops who were subordinate to the metropolitan see of Caerleon. Augustine (also referred to as Austin) had been sent by Pope Gregory the Great to win over the Kentish Saxons under their king,

---

[2] *Councils and ecclesiastical documents relating to Great Britain and Ireland* (ed. [after Spelman and Wilkins] A. Haddan and W. Stubbs, 3 vols., Oxford, 1869–78), I, p. 3; *The works of Gildas and Nennius* (trans. J. A. Giles, London, 1841), c. 8, p. 10; John Foxe, *Acts and monuments* (8 vols., London, 1853–70), I, pt II, p. 306; Fuller, *Church history*, I, p. 28 n.; William Cave, *Apostolici* (London, 1677), 'Introduction', pp. viii–ix; Rowlands, *Mona antiqua restaurata*, p. 137; Williams, 'Protestant views', 222.

[3] Bede, *A history of the English church and people* (trans. L. Sherley-Price, Harmondsworth, 1955), bk III, ch. 25, pp. 185–6. Cf. Cotton, 'Of the antiquity of Christian religion', in Hearne, *Curious discourses*, II, p. 155.

[4] Foxe, *Acts and monuments*, I, pt II, p. 307; William Cave, *A dissertation concerning the government of the ancient church, by bishops, metropolitans and patriarchs* (London, 1683), p. 250.

[5] Isaac Basire, *The ancient liberty of the Britannick church, and the legitimate exemption thereof from the Roman patriarchate* (London, 1661 edn), pp. 24–5.

[6] Foxe, *Acts and monuments*, I, pt II, p. 327; Fuller, *Church history*, I, pp. 30–1.

[7] Fuller, *Church history*, I, pp. 37, 40; F. Levy, *Tudor historical thought* (San Marino, CA, 1967), p. 83.

Ethelbert. In this he was successful, establishing a base at Canterbury. The British bishops would not submit to Augustine or his Romish master – quite properly, given the autonomous status of their church. In a celebrated debate with Augustine, Abbot Dinoth of Bangor rejected the overtures of Rome, declaiming that the British Christians owed no other obedience to the pope of Rome than they did to every godly Christian.[8] Subsequently, the British Christians survived for several centuries in their Welsh fastness where they perpetuated their primitive worship independent of Rome.[9] However, eventually, in the reign of Henry I, the Welsh church – the original Church of England, albeit no longer enjoying its proper territorial sway – was to be incorporated within the Anglo-Norman *ecclesia anglicana*.[10] However, after this dark interlude, Henry VIII – a Tudor monarch of Welsh descent – was able to restore the church of his ancestors to its former autonomy and primitive purity.[11] During the Tudor period, of course, the British identity of the reformed church complemented the boasted Galfridian pedigree of the dynasty.

   The discrepancy between political and ecclesiastical identities emerged only in the course of the seventeenth century with the rise of Gothicism. During the early seventeenth century, the apostolic British origins of the *ecclesia anglicana* matched the Cokean legend of legal immemorialism and parliament's distant origins in the British *conventus*. Indeed, ancient constitutionalism was not confined to the temporal glories of parliament and common law. As Glenn Burgess has noted, 'many works about the ancient constitution of England also included . . . a pedigree for the Church of England that antedated the growth of the see of Rome'.[12] Chronology dictated that this branch of patriotic antiquarianism maintain 'a strongly British focus'.[13] In the 1650s, for example, Thomas Fuller transformed his scepticism about the evidence for a direct apostolic mission to Britain into a misty ecclesiastical immemorialism: 'it matters not, if the doctrine be the same, whether the apostles preached it by themselves, or by their successors. We see little certainty can be extracted,

---

[8] Foxe, *Acts and monuments*, I, pt II, pp. 337–8; John Inett, *Origines Anglicanae* (2 vols., London and Oxford, 1704–10), I, p. 4; Joseph Bingham, *Origines ecclesiasticae* (1708–22: 2 vols., London, 1878), I, p. 75; Thomas Carte, *A general history of England* (4 vols., London, 1747–55), I, p. 224; Rowlands, *Mona antiqua restaurata*, pp. 149–51.

[9] Inett, *Origines Anglicanae*, I, pp. 10–11; II, p. 135; George Smith, *Britons and Saxons not converted to Popery*, pp. 428–9.

[10] Edward Brerewood, 'The patriarchall government of the ancient church', in *Certaine briefe treatises written by diverse learned men, concerning the ancient and modern government of the church* (Oxford, 1641), p. 113; Cave, *Dissertation concerning the government of the ancient church*, p. 247; Inett, *Origines Anglicanae*, II, pp. 135–6, 489.

[11] Basire, *Ancient liberty of the Britannick church*, p. 15.

[12] G. Burgess, *The politics of the ancient constitution* (Houndmills, 1992), p. 102.

[13] *Ibid.*, p. 103.

who first brought the gospel hither; it is so long since, the British church hath forgotten her own infancy, who were her first godfathers.'[14] In fact, the displacement of the immemorialist idiom in the political and legal spheres by a more ethnocentric Saxonism did nothing to subvert the authority of the ancient British church.

The ancient British church remained an important dimension of Anglican identity throughout the seventeenth and most of the eighteenth centuries, though some of the hoarier myths associated with it were quietly shed, such as the Glastonbury legend.[15] In Stillingfleet's definitive *Origines Britannicae* (1685), the legend of Joseph of Arimathea was dropped.[16] Nevertheless, the desire for the prestige conferred by an apostolic foundation remained. Stillingfleet merely substituted the plausibly peripatetic St Paul for Joseph at the heart of the Church's origin myth.[17] In the second half of the eighteenth century Ferdinando Warner (1703–68) diluted the origin myth, but retained an apostolic connection with British Christianity as a central pillar of Anglican history and identity. Warner thought it likely that the gospel had been brought to Britain 'either by some of Christ's apostles, or their immediate followers; and from that time the Britons had always observed the customs and rules prescribed to them by those teachers'.[18] The pruned-down version of the church's British origins even received the sanction of Blackstone's *Commentaries*:

The ancient British church, by whomsoever planted, was a stranger to the bishop of Rome, and all his pretended authority. But, the pagan Saxon invaders having driven the professors of Christianity to the remotest corners of our island, their own conversion was afterwards effected by Augustine the monk, and other missionaries from the court of Rome. This naturally introduced some few of the papal corruptions in point of faith and doctrine; but we read of no civil authority claimed by the Pope in these kingdoms, till the era of the Norman conquest.[19]

What makes the historiography of the British church fascinating for the student of ethnic identity lies not only in the disparity between civil and ecclesiastical identities, but also in the consequent attitude to the Anglo-Saxon church. Not only was Saxonist identification more muted in this branch of constitutional argument, pride in the ancient British church was often accompanied by a measure of anti-Saxon sentiment. Corruptions introduced during the Saxon era constituted the thin end of the Roman Catholic wedge. The legitimacy of the reformed Church of Eng-

---

[14] Fuller, *Church history*, I, pp. 10–11.   [15] Champion, *Pillars of priestcraft*, pp. 56–60.
[16] Stillingfleet, *Origines Britannicae*, pp. 6, 28.   [17] *Ibid.*, pp. 37–48.
[18] Warner, *Ecclesiastical history*, I, pp. 5, 9–10, 52. For the persistence of the Pauline origin legend, see William Stukeley, *Palaeographia Britannica: or, discourses on antiquities that relate to the history of Britain no. iii* (London, 1752).
[19] Blackstone, *Commentaries*, IV, p. 104.

land, which was threatened by the claims of Roman Catholic apologists, rested in part on a critique of the Anglo-Saxon era as a period when the pure, proto-Protestant and autonomous church established among the Britons began to fall under the sway of Rome and its corrupting innovations. In particular, Augustine's mission to the Saxons of Kent in the late sixth century enjoyed some notoriety as the moment when Rome gained a foothold in a land which under the Britons had enjoyed several centuries of apostolic Christianity. John Jewel was merely rehearsing a commonplace of Tudor historiography when he blamed Augustine for defiling the purity of British Christianity.[20] In the opinion of Glanmor Williams the Anglican 'prejudice against Augustine' was slow to disappear.[21] There were even references to a 'Saxon yoke'.[22]

Somehow, the English clerisy squared contradictory accounts of a predominantly Saxon nationhood with a British pedigree for the *ecclesia anglicana*. William Somner (1598–1669), compiler of the first Saxon dictionary, recognised that his beloved Saxons constituted a potential Achilles heel for the Church of England. Even in his *Antiquities of Canterbury* (1640) where he dealt with the Augustinian conversion of Ethelbert's Kent of Saxon idolaters, Somner contrasted the Saxons unfavourably with the Britons who had been 'Christian almost from the time of our Saviour's death, and so they continued, though at this time living with their bishops in the remote parts of this island'.[23]

Early modern scholars were adept at furnishing contemporary power centres with illustrious pedigrees and glorious histories of achievement. In the case of Canterbury no fakery was required. Augustine's well-attested mission to the Saxons of Kent conferred legitimacy upon the Canterburian primacy within England. Yet Anglicans scholars were wary of investing too much pride in the Augustinian foundations of the Saxon church, which appeared to rest on the treacherous sands of papal usurpation. Antiquaries such as William Dugdale (1605–86) were on safer ground when they celebrated the primacy of Glastonbury as the citadel of the apostolic British church.[24]

Nathaniel Bacon, one of the principal Gothicist antiquarians of the seventeenth century, eschewed this Gothic commitment in his account of

[20] John Jewel, *The defence of the apology of the Church of England*, in Jewel, *Works* (4 vols., Parker Society, 1845–50), IV, p. 778; R. T. Vann, 'The free Anglo-Saxons: an historical myth', *JHI* 19 (1958), 261–2; Levy, *Tudor historical thought*, pp. 91, 97, 101.
[21] Williams, 'Protestant views', 230. See also A. Milton, *Catholic and Reformed: the Roman and Protestant churches in English Protestant thought 1600–1640* (Cambridge, 1995), p. 276; P. White, 'The via media in the early Stuart church', in K. Fincham (ed.), *The early Stuart church 1603–1642* (Houndmills, 1993), p. 214.
[22] Crouch, *England's monarchs*, p. 11; Williams, 'Protestant views', 224–7.
[23] Quoted in G. Parry, *The trophies of time* (Oxford, 1995), p. 185.   [24] *Ibid.*, p. 231.

the Church of England. Bacon's providential history of England was marked by a pronounced disparity between the political liberty resolutely maintained by the Saxons and their neglect of the corruptions which would progressively disfigure the church. Whereas the Welsh Britons maintained the practices of primitive Christianity for five hundred years after the coming of Augustine, the Saxons drank up 'at one draught . . . a potion of the whole hierarchy of Rome'. Bacon recognised the difficulty in reconciling the contrasting temporal and ecclesiastical portrayals of the Anglo-Saxon era. He argued, for example, that papal corruption had been slow to take effect: 'For the Saxons had a commonwealth founded in the liberty of the people; and it was a masterpiece for Austin and the clergy, so to work, as to remain members of this commonwealth, and yet retain their hearts for Rome, which was now grown almost to the pitch of that Antichrist.'[25]

According to R. J. Smith, John Inett's *Origines Anglicanae*, a continuation of Stillingfleet's history of the British church, *Origines Britannicae* (1685), into the Saxon and Norman eras, amounted to 'the Gothic history in a surplice'.[26] However, despite its remit, the *Origines Anglicanae* displayed a qualified identification with the Saxons, and evinced much warmer feelings for the ancient British era in the history of the Church of England. Inett (1647–1717) calculated that only 'one part of the English nation owed its conversion to the see of Rome'.[27] He blamed the Gothic nations, including the Saxons, for the first major wave of corruption in the western church. Papal tactics were to blame: Pope Gregory the Great had shown tolerance and comprehension towards the rites of pagan peoples as a way of winning them over to Christianity.[28]

Michael Geddes (1650?–1713), an Anglican divine of Scottish birth, advanced a similar argument. Whereas in the temporal sphere Geddes celebrated the glorious heritage of Gothic constitutionalism, in the spiritual realm, by contrast, he lamented the arrival of the pagan Saxons as clearing a way for the intrusion of Rome into the British church:

the Roman supremacy was first brought into Britain by the Saxons, who having been converted from paganism to Christianity, near the end of the sixth century, by some of the bishop of Rome's disciples; they had been taught by them, that the papal supremacy was an authority of the church of Christ's own immediate institution; which was a trick they could not have put on the Britons.[29]

The case of England bore striking affinities with the experience of Spain,

[25] Nathaniel Bacon, *An historical and political discourse of the laws and government of England* (1647: London, 1689 edn), p. 14.

[26] R. J. Smith, *The Gothic bequest* (Cambridge, 1987), p. 30.

[27] Inett, *Origines Anglicanae*, I, p. 25.   [28] *Ibid.*, I, pp. 23–5.

[29] Michael Geddes, 'A dissertation on the papal supremacy, chiefly with relation to the ancient Spanish church', in Geddes, *Miscellaneous tracts*, vol. II (London, 1705), p. 11.

whose early history was Geddes's scholarly hobbyhorse. The Moorish conquest had unsettled the organisation of the autocephalous church in Spain just as the Saxon invasion had in England: 'the Papal supremacy was never known in the ancient Spanish church, no more than it was in the ancient British; and that, had not the civil governments those two ancient churches were under, been dissolved by their being both conquered by infidels, it is most probable that the supremacy might never have been able to have crept into either'.[30]

Consider too the example of Bolingbroke, a non-doctrinal, indeed heterodox and dubiously tory, 'pillar' of the Church of England who was far from representative of eighteenth-century opinion on ecclesiastical matters. Nevertheless, even he reliably conveyed a traditional unease on the subject of Saxon churchmanship. Bolingbroke claimed to admire equally the libertarian manners of both the ancient Britons and Saxons, but he contrasted their strikingly different records when it came to the maintenance of ecclesiastical liberty. Of the Britons, he wrote: 'Their long resistance against the Saxons shows their love of civil liberty. Their long resistance against the usurpation of the Church of Rome, begun by Gregory . . . under pretence of converting the Saxons, shows their love of ecclesiastical liberty.' The same could not be said of the Saxons, who, while preserving 'their Gothic institutions of government', had 'submitted to the yoke of Rome, in matters of religion'.[31] Unambiguous pride in the Saxon church was far from being an established feature of Augustan historiography: 'The Britons received Christianity very early, and, as is reported, from some of the disciples themselves: So that when the Romans left Britain, the Britons were generally Christians. But the Saxons were heathens, till Pope Gregory the Great sent over hither Austin the monk, by whom Ethelbert King of the South-Saxons, and his subjects, were converted to Christianity.'[32]

Even where antiquarians celebrated the whole pre-Norman history of the *ecclesia anglicana* they drew some distinction between the status of the British and Saxon churches, sometimes regarding the latter with a cool politeness. Roger Twysden (1597–1672) waxed lukewarm on the Saxon phase of English church history: 'I no way doubt but the religion exercised by the Britons before Augustine came, to have been very pure and holy: nor that planted after from St Gregory, though perhaps with more ceremonies and commands, *iuris positivi*, which this church embraced,

[30] *Ibid.*, pp. 26–7.
[31] Bolingbroke, *Remarks on the history of England* (1730–1), in Bolingbroke, *Works* (5 vols., London, 1754), I, pp. 314–15; B. Cottret, *Bolingbroke's political writings: the conservative Enlightenment* (Houndmills, 1997), pp. 2–3.
[32] Jonathan Swift, 'An abstract and fragment of the history of England', in Swift, *Miscellaneous and autobiographical pieces, fragments and marginalia* (Oxford, 1969), p. 4.

rejected or varied from, as occasion served to be other, but in the foundation most sound, most orthodox.'[33] Similarly, George Smith (1693–1756), the non-juring bishop, in his treatise *The Britons and Saxons not converted to Popery* (1748), conceded that 'the Saxons converted by St Augustine were incorporated into the Catholic church, and were united by communion as well as by faith with the greatest part of that visible body'; however, this did not mean that 'the present English papists hold the same faith, and consequently are of the same communion with their ancestors'.[34] Ferdinando Warner proceeded with caution when delineating the ambivalent character of the Saxon church: 'extremely fond of the rites and usages of the Romans, yet it owned no subjection to that see, but what was founded on gratitude and civility, and consistent with the power which the canons of the first general councils allowed to every national church in Christendom'.[35] Nevertheless, Warner recalled that Peter's Pence had first been agreed to by King Offa at the Synod of Calcuith.[36]

There was also the vexing matter of the pall which Gregory had gifted to Augustine on the successful completion of his mission. The pall, or *pallium*, is a circular band of white wool granted to archbishops by the pope which they wear over their shoulders as a sign of their communion with Rome. However, in the early modern era, there was a major debate, spilling over from the Gallican writings of Pierre de Marca (1594–1662), who ended his controversial career as Archbishop of Paris, as to whether the pall constituted a mark of subjection or merely a token of esteem.[37] According to Smith, 'the Bishop of Rome never sent a pall to the British archbishops, and the first who wore that badge of subjection was St Augustine the first Archbishop of Canterbury'.[38]

However, one should not exaggerate the degree of anti-Saxonism. Hostility to the Saxons was never vociferous or universal. It is widely acknowledged among scholars that the study of Old English was 'begun for purposes of religious polemic'. Richard Vann has stressed that Saxon history remained, in spite of its blemishes, a crucial arena for ecclesiastical debate. Although the Augustinian conversion of the Kentish Jutes was 'commonly held to have commenced the subversion of the English church', England's Protestant antiquarians could not simply ignore their Anglo-Saxon heritage. The history of the ancient Britons may not have been contaminated by Romish influences, but as a storehouse of reliable

[33] Roger Twysden, *Historical vindication of the Church of England in point of schism as it stands separated from the Roman and was reformed I Elizabeth* (London, 1657), pp. 4–5.
[34] George Smith, *Britons and Saxons not converted to Popery*, pp. 442–3.
[35] Warner, *Ecclesiastical history*, I, p. 149.   [36] *Ibid.*, I, p. 157.
[37] Collier, *Ecclesiastical history*, I, pp. 159–64.
[38] George Smith, *Britons and Saxons not converted to Popery*, pp. 295–6; Inett, *Origines Anglicanae*, I, p. 26; Carte, *General history*, I, p. 223.

sources and concrete examples to supply the detail necessary for ecclesiastical polemic it was deficient. The ancient British past was vague and sketchy. On the other hand, according to Vann, 'there were too many Anglo-Saxon precedents handy in a situation where good precedents were uncommon'. Thus the Saxon phase of English church history came to play a more significant role in its identity than was warranted by confessional correctness. In spite of its deficiencies, the Anglo-Saxon past came to act as 'a witness for Protestantism'.[39]

From before about 1540 the Anglo-Saxon past had been plundered by apologists of the reformed Church of England. However, ecclesiastical Saxonism had come into its own under the research project directed by Archbishop Matthew Parker in the first half of Elizabeth's reign. Parker's team, which included his secretary John Joscelyn (1529–1603), showed that the Church of England of the Saxon era had yet to succumb to several of the major anti-Christian corruptions which had disfigured the unreformed church. The Scriptures and services remained in the vernacular, and the clergy had not been bound to celibacy. Parker also argued that transubstantiation was a relatively novel doctrine unknown in Anglo-Saxon England. For example, Parker's acolytes promoted Aelfric, an eleventh-century Anglo-Saxon abbot, as a proto-Protestant, publishing his writings in 1566, as evidence for the Protestant doctrine of the historic *ecclesia anglicana* under the title *A testimonie of antiquitie, shewing the auncient fayth in the church of England touching the sacrament of the body and bloude of the Lord here publickley preached, and also receaued in the Saxons tyme, above 600 yeares agoe.*[40]

In the seventeenth century Anglican scholars continued to hold up the Saxon church as a standard against which to measure the anti-Christian corruptions and ecclesiastical tyranny which had followed the Norman Conquest. William L'Isle (1579?–1637) argued in *A Saxon treatise concerning the Old and New Testament* (1623) that in the Saxon era the Scriptures had been in the vernacular.[41] The leaders of the reformed Church of England were keenly aware of the ecclesiastical utility of Saxonist scholarship. Sir Henry Spelman established the first Anglo-Saxon lectureship at Cambridge in 1638 for the study of 'domestic

[39] R. Tuve, 'Ancients, moderns, and Saxons', *Journal of English Literary History* 6 (1939), 165, 167–8; Vann, 'Free Anglo-Saxons', 262; E. N. Adams, *Old English scholarship in England from 1566 to 1800* (New Haven, 1917), p. 11; J. A. W. Bennett, 'The history of Old English, and Old Norse studies in England from the time of Francis Junius till the end of the eighteenth century' (University of Oxford DPhil. thesis, 1938), pp. 3–4; J. Levine, *Humanism and history* (Ithaca and London, 1987), p. 177; J. P. Kenyon, *The history men* (1983: 2nd edn, London, 1993), p. 15.

[40] T. D. Kendrick, *British antiquity* (London, 1950), p. 115; Tuve, 'Ancients, moderns, and Saxons', 166; Adams, *Old English scholarship*, ch. 1.

[41] Tuve, 'Ancients, moderns, and Saxons', 169–70.

antiquities touching our church and reviving the Saxon tongue'.[42] At Oxford, the Queen's College circle of Saxonists which flourished in the later seventeenth century included some rising clerics: Edmund Gibson, later Bishop of London, who produced an edition of the Anglo-Saxon chronicle in 1692, Edward Thwaites and William Nicolson, later Bishop of Carlisle.[43] The anti-Catholic fears provoked by the reign of James II generated such works as *No antiquity for transubstantiation, plainly proved from the judgment of the most learned men that lived in time of the Saxons* (1688). Writing in 1697, Gibson encouraged Thwaites to forage for 'undeniable evidence to all posterity, that the belief of our Papists at this day is a very different thing from that of our Saxon ancestors'.[44] Jeremy Collier (1650–1726) contended that, because the eleventh-century Saxon clergy appeared to know no grammar (that is, Latin), the church service must have been in the English vernacular, conformable, of course, to later Protestant practice.[45] George Hickes, another of the Oxford Saxonists, contended that research into the Saxon past would 'show the faith and other chief doctrines of the Anglo-Saxon church to be the same with ours and perfectly answer that never ending question: what was your church before Luther?'[46]

Nevertheless, in spite of this high profile, a question mark hovered over the character of the Anglo-Saxon church. The Saxon phase of church history lacked the unimpeachably non-Roman and 'Protestant' qualities of the previous epoch. Even the Saxonist *No antiquity for transubstantiation* equivocated:

But what was the condition and state of the church, when Aelfric himself lived? Indeed, to confess the truth it was in divers points of religion full of blindness and ignorance: full of childish servitude to ceremonies, as it was long before and after: and too much given to the love of monkery, which now at this time took root, and grew excessively.[47]

Thus, although the Saxon past remained a vital theatre in the war of words with the forces of Catholicism, it had less strategic importance than

[42] Quoted Kenyon, *History men*, p. 15; Parry, *Trophies of time*, ch. 6.
[43] D. Fairer, 'Anglo-Saxon studies', in L. S. Sutherland and L. G. Mitchell (eds.), *The history of the University of Oxford*, vol. V, *The eighteenth century* (Oxford, 1986), pp. 807–29; F. G. James, *North country bishop: a biography of William Nicolson* (New Haven and London, 1956), ch. 4.   [44] Quoted in Fairer, 'Anglo-Saxon studies', p. 808.
[45] Collier, *Ecclesiastical history*, I, p. xvi.
[46] George Hickes to the Bishop of Bristol, May 22, 1714, quoted in Levine, *Humanism and history*, p. 95. See Fairer, 'Anglo-Saxon studies', pp. 821–2, for the value of the Saxonist Anglicanism of Elizabeth Elstob.
[47] *No antiquity for transubstantiation, plainly proved from the judgment of the most learned men that lived in time of the Saxons* (London, 1688), 'Preface', p. xii.

the ancient British era. According to the champions of the Church of England, in Hugh Trevor-Roper's telling depiction of the scholarly consensus as it stood in the early seventeenth century, 'it was this sound native British Christianity, not the imported Roman kickshaws of St Augustine of Canterbury, which had supplied the real substance of the Anglo-Saxon church'.[48]

The significance of the British church

Why were the ethnic and historical associations of the Church of England so incongruent with the Gothic identity of the English political nation? Why was the English clerisy so committed to the history of the ancient British church, to a phase of church history which was out of step with the political history of English liberty? How could historians reconcile split ethnic loyalties with such remarkable equanimity?

There were a number of compelling reasons for Anglicans to retain, even to embellish, their connection with the ancient Britons. Most pressing of all was the need to meet the challenge of Roman Catholic criticism. The legitimacy of the Church of England was threatened by Roman charges of novelty and schism, and by the argument that the *ecclesia anglicana* was part of the proper jurisdiction of the pope. The debate between Rome and the Church of England was as much historical as theological. Most famously, Cardinal Baronius (1538–1607), author of the *Annales ecclesiastici* (1588–1607) which traced the history of the church universal from its beginnings to 1198, put historical research at the forefront of Counter-Reformation apologetic.

Baronius touched upon the experience of England, but there was already an emergent Catholic interpretation of English history which would flower throughout the seventeenth century in the works of Robert Parsons (1546–1610), the Jesuit author of *A treatise of three conversions* (1603); Richard Broughton (d. 1634), who wrote various works of ecclesiastical history; the Jesuit historian Michael Alford (1587–1652); and Hugh 'Serenus' Cressy (1605–74), an Anglican convert to Catholicism who took the monastic name of Serenus on his admission into the Benedictine order. In 1662 the *Historia anglicana ecclesiastica* of the sixteenth-century Catholic Nicholas Harpsfield (1519?–75) at last found its way into print. Among non-English scholars, Emanuel Schelstrate (1648/9–92), one of the successors of Baronius as prefect of the Vatican Library, devoted a particular treatise to refuting the autonomy of the Church of England. Into the eighteenth century Anglicans faced the

[48] H. Trevor-Roper, 'James Ussher, Archbishop of Armagh', in Trevor-Roper, *Catholics, Anglicans and Puritans* (London, 1987), p. 128.

continuing challenge of Hugh Tootel (1672–1743), who wrote *The church history of England* (1737) under both a false Brussels imprint and the pseudonym of Charles Dodd.[49]

The whole history of England, including the British era, was of service to Catholic antiquaries keen to elaborate an anti-Protestant interpretation of the origins and nature of the Church of England. Catholics argued from history that Catholicism or at least subjection to the papacy had been an essential part of the spiritual pillar of England's historic constitution since its first conversion, which had been accomplished by agents of the papacy. Parsons's *Treatise of three conversions* provided threefold insurance for a Roman interpretation of the origins of the Church of England. First, there had been a direct apostolic conversion of the Britons by St Peter; then King Lucius's correspondence with Pope Eleutherius had gained the Catholic church the benefits of establishment within Britain; and thirdly there was the Augustinian mission to the Saxons under the authority of Pope Gregory. Broughton also exploited the British past, arguing that St Peter had 'ordered, and settled one British church with such perfection'; in addition, he deployed the Glastonbury legend to support his claim that there had been a pre-Benedictine primitive monasticism in England. Continental polemicists saw the value of the British period to the Roman case. Schelstrate contended that the British church, being subordinate to Rome, had received papal legates.[50]

Despite the importance to Romanists of the primitive era, their awareness that the Anglo-Saxons constituted the historic core of the English nation suggested the Augustinian mission to the Saxons of Kent – Parsons's third conversion – as the likely location for the establishment of an invasive bridgehead into Anglican apologetic. In 1565 the Catholic controversialist Thomas Stapleton had produced an edition of Bede's *History of the English church and people* (731) which denied any affinity between the Anglo-Saxon church and the innovations of modern Protestantism. Stapleton claimed that the Augustinian conversion sponsored by Rome

[49] Robert Parsons, *A treatise of three conversions* (n.p., 1603); Richard Broughton, *The ecclesiastical historie of Great Britaine* (Douai, 1633); Broughton, *A true memorial of the ancient, most holy, and religious state of Great Britain* (n.p., 1650); Hugh Cressy, *The church history of Britanny from the beginnings of Christianity to the Norman Conquest* (Rouen, 1688); Emanuel a Schelstrate, *A dissertation concerning the patriarchal and metropolitical authority* (1687: transln, London, 1688); Charles Dodd [Hugh Tootel], *The church history of England, from the year 1500, to the year 1688 . . . To which is prefixed, a general history of ecclesiastical affairs under the British, Saxon, and Norman periods*, vol. I (Brussels [Sherborne], 1737); J. H. Preston, 'English ecclesiastical histories and the problem of bias: 1559–1742', *JHI* 32 (1971), 214–15; D. Woolf, *The idea of history in early Stuart England* (Toronto, 1990), pp. 38–44.

[50] Parsons, *Three conversions*; Champion, *Pillars of priestcraft*, p. 57; Broughton, *True memorial*, p. 9, and ch. 2 for monasticism; Schelstrate, *Dissertation*, chs. 1 and 6, esp. p. 101; P. Milward, *Religious controversies of the Jacobean age* (London, 1978), pp. 76–82, 201–3.

constituted the establishment of the Church of England.[51] Published in further Jesuit editions of 1622 and 1626, Bede seems to have been strongly 'tarred with the papist brush'.[52] John Bossy has also identified another possible link between Saxonism and Catholicism, arguing, with some plausibility, that Verstegan's attempts to show Englishmen that the Britons were not their real ancestors may have been founded on the need to dissociate Englishness from the legendary Protestantism of the ancient British church.[53]

The British church was emotively bound up with the identity of the Church of England from the very start. The scheme of apocalyptic reasoning inherited from the sixteenth century offered good grounds for identifying the *ecclesia anglicana* more closely with the ancient Britons than with the English proper. Major reservations have been expressed about the notion of England as the 'elect nation'. Recently scholars have argued that Foxe's interpretation of history involved 'a struggle of the elect everywhere – and not just in England – against the Popish Antichrist'.[54] Nevertheless, the ancient British church was an important element of sixteenth-century English religious polemic (and not only because of the need to establish a pre-Augustinian non-Roman pedigree for English Protestantism). The contours of the church's history of corruption and reformation, a story of primitive purity, of gradual decay and of the eventual reign of the full-blown popish Antichrist, broadly coincided with the main ethnic phases and political vicissitudes in the history of England – the era of the Britons, the establishment of the Saxons and the Norman Conquest. The Normans were linked to the introduction of the worst betrayals of the primitive Christian ideal, but the seeds of the authoritarian Hildebrandine papacy which flourished to the detriment of true religion in the high middle ages had been sown with the pretensions of the Gregorian papacy. The apocalyptic historians who emerged during the English Reformation divided the history of the Christian church into five phases of roughly three hundred years each. The first three hundred constituted a time of struggle for the primitive church, while the second

[51] F. Brownlow, 'George Herbert's "The British Church" and the idea of a national church', in V. Newey and A. Thompson (eds.), *Literature and nationalism* (Liverpool, 1991), p. 115; K. Thomas, *Religion and the decline of magic* (1971: Harmondsworth, 1978), p. 508; Kenyon, *History men*, p. 6; Levy, *Tudor historical thought*, pp. 110–11.
[52] Kenyon, *History men*, p. 6.
[53] J. Bossy, 'Catholicity and nationality in the northern Counter-Reformation', in S. Mews (ed.), *Religion and national identity* (Studies in church history 18, Oxford, 1982), pp. 291–3.
[54] Levy, *Tudor historical thought*, p. 98; J. P. Sommerville, *Politics and ideology in England 1603–1640* (London, 1986), p. 78; A. Fletcher, 'The first century of English Protestantism and the growth of national identity', in Mews, *Religion and national identity*, pp. 309–10.

saw the church in a flourishing condition. From around 600 the corruption began, an era which coincided with the coming of Augustine to Saxon England (though Foxe was much more sympathetic to Saxons such as King Alfred than he was to the Normans who followed). Although AD 1000 was the year of the Antichrist, a date sufficiently close to 1066 to permit some identification of ecclesiastical corruption with the Norman Conquest, the process had nevertheless begun long before.[55] Much as the reformers stimulated the development of Anglo-Saxon studies, the ancient British church alone had an untarnished record. The Anglo-Saxon church, though certainly lauded by comparison with the clear degeneration of the church under the Normans, was not without blemish. Bale located the origins of an English priestcraft with the mission of Augustine introduction of noxious practices.[56] Foxe's *Acts and monuments* told the history of two churches, the true church and a false church which had appropriated the institutional structures of the former to mount a plausible facade of veracity. The British church was indisputably a national manifestation of the true church universal: the Saxon church, by contrast, upheld the truth, but had also, from the time of Augustine's mission, carried the virus of falsehood. In addition, Foxe convicted the idolatrous Saxons of responsibility for some of the worst persecutions inflicted upon the noble British Christians, including that which followed the coming of Hengist and the pogrom which had prompted the flight of the Britons to Wales.[57]

From the early seventeenth century the intellectual and political leaders of Anglicanism – Bancroft, Andrewes, Overall and Laud – entered into a deep love affair with the pristine church of the early Fathers and Councils. The Huguenot scholar Isaac Casaubon was brought to England under the auspices of James I to construct a patristic alternative to Baronius.[58] After Casaubon's death in 1614 Ussher carried the torch of Anglican apologetic. According to John Spurr, the achievements of the

---

[55] Levy, *Tudor historical thought*, pp. 99–102; Vann, 'Free Anglo-Saxons', 261–2; J. Facey, 'John Foxe and the defence of the English church', in P. Lake and M. Dowling (eds.), *Protestantism and the national church in sixteenth-century England* (London, 1987), pp. 162, 164–5, 180–1 (as Facey points out, the phases were not exact; see e.g. the ambivalent place of the orthodox but declining Anglo-Saxon church of the third phase, though the key era of corruption was the eleventh century; see A. Milton, 'The Church of England, Rome and the true church: the demise of a Jacobean consensus', in Fincham, *The early Stuart church*, p. 195; Milton, *Catholic and Reformed*, p. 286).

[56] Levy, *Tudor historical thought*, p. 91.

[57] Foxe, *Acts and monuments*, I, pt II, pp. 313, 321–3, 327–8; Levy, *Tudor historical thought*, p. 94.

[58] B. Wormald, *Clarendon* (1951: Cambridge, 1989), p. 246; Trevor-Roper, 'Ussher', p. 134; G. V. Bennett, 'Patristic tradition in Anglican thought, 1660–1900', in *Oecumenica* (Gòtersloh, 1972); Sharpe, *Cotton*, pp. 87–8; Milton, *Catholic and Reformed*, p. 273.

seventeenth-century patristic tradition 'count among the great jewels of English scholarship'.[59] However, its reliance on patristic support opened the Church of England to further attack from Rome since the papacy derived much of its polemical ammunition and self-confidence from the early history and traditions of the church. In his *Concilia* (1639), which dwelt largely on the institutional history of the Saxon church before 1066, Spelman nevertheless chose to emphasise the British origins of English Christianity and to downplay the foundational role of Augustine's mission to the Saxons of Kent.[60] As the *Concilia* was part of a Laudian project which appeared suspiciously soft on popery, it was vital for Spelman to emphasise the non-Roman origins of the church. The history of ancient Britain in the first four centuries lent powerful local support for the Anglican patristic case. Indeed, they were mutually reinforcing. The universal patristic case and the special 'patristic' evidence drawn from the ancient British church provided a dual legitimation for Anglican practice. Furthermore, the history of the British church assumed the status of England's ancient ecclesiastical constitution.

In his sensitive study of seventeenth-century English antiquarianism, Graham Parry notes that an unbalanced emphasis upon the ancient British Christians to the exclusion of the Augustinian mission was 'the standard, indeed, the necessary, Anglican position'.[61] Ancient British origins proved necessary to sustain any argument for the institution of the Church of England as an apostolic and primitive church. An ancient ecclesiastical constitution which dated only from the post-patristic era of the Anglo-Saxons conferred much less prestige on the Church of England, and might possibly have conceded too much ground to Roman Catholic scholars who questioned the claim of a historic autocephalous church in England. Anglicans justified their doctrine and worship in terms of a balance of Scripture, right reason and the best and purest tradition of the church. The construction of the last pillar rested not only upon patristic scholarship, but was also founded on indigenous ecclesiastical history. For the history of the ancient British church embodied the best and purest traditions of Christianity. As Frank Brownlow has argued, when seventeenth-century Anglicans spoke of adhering to the standards of the primitive church of the first four centuries 'they had in mind a real historical entity, once actually represented in Britain'.[62]

Whereas it seemed folly to concentrate one's resources on the marshy

---

[59] J. Spurr, *The Restoration Church of England, 1646–1689* (New Haven and London, 1991), p. 158; E. Duffy, 'Primitive Christianity revived: religious renewal in Augustan England', in D. Baker (ed.), *Renaissance and renewal in Christian history* (Studies in church history 14, Oxford, 1977).

[60] Henry Spelman, *Concilia* (London, 1639); Parry, *Trophies of time*, pp. 169–71.

[61] Parry, *Trophies of time*, p. 185.   [62] Brownlow, 'Herbert's "British Church"', p. 115.

debatable lands of the Saxon era, the ancient British past provided promising terrain upon which to construct a Protestant apologetic. First of all, however, Anglicans needed to contest Catholic attempts to appropriate the British era for Rome. There were, after all, some stains on the Protestant character of the ancient British church. The champions of the Church of England easily disposed of the legend of a direct Petrine conversion of the Britons, noting its unreliable source in the work of Simeon Metaphrastes.[63] As far as Anglicans were concerned, the only major problem with the British era – barring embarrassment over Pelagianism – was the legend of King Lucius, a second-century king of the Britons, who had supposedly sent to Pope Eleutherius for religious instruction.[64] Easier to rebut was the charge that monasticism, according to Romanist polemic, enjoyed a quasi-apostolic foundation in Britain through Joseph of Arimathea's establishment at Glastonbury.[65] Stillingfleet argued that the Arimathea legend was 'an invention of the monks of Glastonbury to serve their interests, by advancing the reputation of their monastery'.[66] The evidences of the Glastonbury legend, concluded Collier, 'look untowardly when brought to the test, and do not shine at all upon the touchstone', and even his usual whiggish opponent, John Oldmixon, agreed, adding that monasticism was 'a way of life unknown to the apostles and primitive Christians'.[67]

Evidence of continuity from the first centuries of primitive Christianity constituted one of the most compelling *notae ecclesiae*, a canon of distinguishing marks carried by the 'true church'. The leading Counter-Reformation ecclesiologist Cardinal Robert Bellarmine set out fifteen evidences, or *notae*, which proved the Roman Catholic Church to be the true church. The first lay in universality and the use of the very term 'Catholic'. However, the second distinguishing feature was antiquity: the true church precedes the false as God had preceded the Devil. Uninterrupted duration was the third of the fifteen *notae*.[68] The Church of Rome, of course, had a formidable claim to such an ancient, apostolic and uninterrupted pedigree. It was therefore necessary for Protestant churches such as the Church of England both to question the authenticity of the Roman

[63] Champion, *Pillars of priestcraft*, p. 56; Stillingfleet, *Origines Britannicae*, p. 45.

[64] Bede, *English church and people*, bk I, ch. 4, p. 42; Kendrick, *British antiquity*, pp. 110, 112–13; Levy, *Tudor historical thought*, pp. 90–1; Milton, *Catholic and Reformed*, p. 277 n.; Williams, 'Protestant views', 229–30; Woolf, *Idea of history*, pp. 42, 44; Champion, *Pillars of priestcraft*, pp. 58–61. See e.g. Stillingfleet, *Origines Britannicae*, pp. 58–69; George Smith, *Britons and Saxons not converted to Popery*, pp. 274–5, 280–1.

[65] Kendrick, *British antiquity*, p. 112.   [66] Stillingfleet, *Origines Britannicae*, p. 6.

[67] Collier, *Ecclesiastical history*, I, p. 23; John Oldmixon, *The critical history of England, ecclesiastical and civil* (2 vols., London, 1724–6), I, pp. 61, 80–1.

[68] W. Rex, *Essays on Pierre Bayle and religious controversy* (The Hague, 1965), ch. 1, 'Antiquity', p. 8; Milton, *Catholic and Reformed*, p. 131; Spurr, *Restoration Church of England*, p. 91.

claim to continuity – did it, for instance, take account of corruptions and innovations in Roman practice? – and to concoct such a provenance for their own brand of Christianity which superficially appeared to be only a sixteenth-century innovation. Antiquity constituted a compelling benchmark of legitimacy. 'I cannot but hold truth more ancient than error', wrote Twysden, 'everything to be firmest upon its own bottom, and all novelties to be best confuted by showing how far they cause it to deviate from the first original.'[69] Thomas Fuller (1608–61), who would later produce a *Church history of Britain*, published an illuminating essay in 1642 on the subject of 'The true church-antiquary'. This set out contemporary expectations of the role of the Anglican scholar and reveals the ways in which the study of primitive antiquities in the ancient British era underpinned the wider enterprise of the reformed Church of England. The true church-antiquary, wrote Fuller, 'baits at middle antiquity, but lodges not till he comes at that which is ancient indeed'. If one scratched the surface of antiquity, one might plausibly become convinced of popery, but deeper probing into the primitive era confirmed the truths of Protestantism. Roman Catholic errors arose from 'adoring the reverend brow and gray hairs of some ancient ceremonies, perchance, but of some seven or eight hundred years standing in the church, and mistake these for their fathers, of far greater age in the primitive times'.[70]

There was a continuing need to answer Catholic scholars whose aim, in the words of the Anglican scholar Joseph Bingham (1668–1723), was 'to varnish over the novel practices of the Romish church, and put a face of antiquity upon them'.[71] In answer to Rome's assumption of priority over the Church of England, Inett claimed a historic precedence over Rome: 'The Britons had been converted in all probability before Christianity was settled in Rome.'[72] Proclaimed Gregory Hascard (d. 1708), Dean of Windsor: 'Our religion is the same with that of the early Christians, martyrs and confessors believed in the first three hundred years, and defended by all Councils truly general.'[73] Henry Rowlands argued that the apostolic British church 'in its first rudiments was senior to that of Rome by so many years'.[74] In 1724 John Oldmixon reiterated the message that the ancient British church had been founded 'upon a primitive scripture bottom'.[75]

[69] Twysden, *Historical vindication*, p. 4.
[70] Thomas Fuller, 'The true church-antiquary', in Fuller, *The holy state* (Cambridge, 1642), bk 2, ch. 6, p. 69. See also Milton, *Catholic and Reformed*, pp. 272–6.
[71] Bingham, *Origines ecclesiasticae*, I, 'Preface', pp. viii–ix.
[72] Inett, *Origines Anglicanae*, II, p. 488.
[73] Gregory Hascard, *A discourse upon the charge of novelty upon the reformed church of England, made by the papists asking of us the question, where was your church before Luther?*, in Edmund Gibson (ed.), *A preservative against Popery, in several select discourses* (3 vols., London, 1738), I, p. 216.   [74] Rowlands, *Mona antiqua restaurata*, p. 138.
[75] Oldmixon, *Critical history*, I, p. 78.

The defence of the Church of England from charges of schism advanced by Roman Catholic polemicists determined the strategic necessity of retaining an ancient British dimension to English identity. Twysden's *Historical vindication of the Church of England in point of schism as it stands separated from the Roman and was reformed I Elizabeth* (1657) drew on ancient British precedents.[76] Isaac Basire's *The ancient liberty of the Britannick Church, and the legitimate exemption thereof from the Roman patriarchate* (1661), a translation of an earlier version published at Bruges during the Anglican diaspora of the 1650s, developed a systematic refutation of Romish claims to jurisdiction over England. Basire defended the English Reformation on the grounds that Henry VIII had only been 'restoring the same Britannic diocese unto the ancient liberty it enjoyed in the primitive times of the ancient oecumenic councils'. A legalistic conciliarism played a crucial role in Basire's argument. The Church of England's primitive exemption from Roman jurisdiction could be demonstrated using evidence drawn from within the tradition of the Catholic church itself. The sixth canon of the Council of Nicaea had established that metropolitans were independent within their respective provinces, and that by the same token the jurisdiction of the Bishop of Rome was limited to his province, despite the concession that, in point of dignity, Rome, Antioch and Alexandria were pre-eminent within the wider church. The eighth canon of Ephesus denied any bishop the authority to exercise his jurisdiction in a foreign province and, thus, guarded against the sort of interprovincial innovations which marked the rise of Rome. These canons provided a powerful jurisdictionalist arsenal for the Church of England. In particular, Basire's reliance on the general councils suggested that British opposition to Augustine was 'grounded on very irrefragable, very Catholic reason'.[77]

Basire's conciliarist position became even more central to Restoration Anglicanism when it found reinforcement within the world of Roman Catholic scholarship. In 1662 a French divine, Jean de Launoy (1603–78), perhaps best known as the 'dénicheur des saints' for his sceptical martyrology, produced a subversively Gallican interpretation of the sixth canon of the council of Nicaea (325) – *De recta Nicaeni canonis sexti . . . intelligentia, dissertatio* – to the effect that it did not treat of patriarchs and their rights, but only the authority of metropolitans within their provinces. William Beveridge (1637–1708) saw the possibilities in Launoy's argument for the Church of England to cast off the slur of schism, and defended the Gallican against his foremost critic, Adrien de Valois, or

[76] Twysden, *Historical vindication*, esp. pp. 4–8; F. Jessup, *Sir Roger Twysden 1597–1672* (London, 1965), pp. 193–5.
[77] Basire, *Ancient liberty of the Britannick church*, pp. 15, 26, 35–8, 43.

Valesius (1607–92).[78] This argument became a fundamental pillar of Anglican constitutionalism, which, in turn, maintained the historic significance of the primitive British church of England.[79] The celebrated patristic case for Anglicanism made by William Cave synthesised a careful reading of the Councils, especially the sixth canon of Nicaea, the history of the ancient British church and the parallel – and reinforcing – claims for the ancient liberties of the Gallican church.[80]

The conciliarist thesis found an echo in Stillingfleet's *Origines Britannicae* (1685): the eighth canon of the Council of Ephesus (431) sanctioned the efforts made by the British bishops to preserve their own rights against foreign jurisdiction.[81] Bingham, in his monumental patristic survey *Origines ecclesiasticae* (1708–22), pointed out 'that the authority of the bishop of Rome in those days extended over the whole western empire, is not so much as hinted at in the Nicene canon'. In an earlier chapter on the autocephaloi, Bingham argued not only for the existence of independent metropolitans before the rise of the patriarchal sees, but also for the perpetuation of various autocephalous churches thereafter, including the seven British bishops under the jurisdiction of Caerleon at the time of Augustine's mission to England.[82]

The Councils of the early church (which dated, of course, from the centuries preceding the conversion of the Saxons and the establishment of the Saxon Church of England) constituted a vital component of the Anglican brief. Three bishops had represented the British church at the Council of Arles (314), a matter of some pride to Anglicans. In Collier's view their presence gave a reliable indication of the British church's attitude to Rome: 'the form of saluting that see is very different from that of later ages; here are no signs of submission, no acknowledgement of supreme pastorship, or universal supremacy'. The participants 'looked upon the authority of the council to be perfect in its legislative capacity, without the concurrence, or after-consent, of the bishop of Rome'.[83] At Arles, according to Warner, the supremacy of the pope was still 'a thing unknown'.[84] Another line of Anglican legalism dated the appellate authority of the papacy only to the Council of Sardica (343–4). Not only had the Bishop of Rome 'enjoyed no pretence for receiving appeals, beyond the suburbicary provinces, prior to the council of Sardica', argued

[78] Schelstrate, *Dissertation*, pp. iii–v, xx–xxi; William Nicolson, *English historical library* (3 vols., London, 1696–9), II, p. 20.
[79] See e.g. Isaac Barrow (1630–77), *A treatise of the Pope's supremacy* (1680), in Barrow, *Theological works* (9 vols., Cambridge, 1859), VIII, p. 391.
[80] Cave, *Dissertation concerning the government of the ancient church*, esp. pp. 49–52, 219, 244–55.   [81] Stillingfleet, *Origines Britannicae*, p. 364.
[82] Bingham, *Origines ecclesiasticae*, I, pp. 75, 347.
[83] Collier, *Ecclesiastical history*, I, p. 63.   [84] Warner, *Ecclesiastical history*, I, p. 16.

Collier, but even the evidence drawn from the stance taken at Sardica on appeals was not sufficient to vindicate claims to a universal Roman supremacy.[85] Geddes went a step further in his *Essay on the canons of the Council of Sardica* (1706), with his contention that the relevant canons were retrospective forgeries.[86] More judicious, despite his provocative title – *Roman forgeries in the Councils during the first four centuries* – was Thomas Comber: the Sardican changes had been 'prodigiously magnified' by Romanists, though the Council had merely 'put a new compliment on the Pope, [which] did not take away the ancient method of appealing from a lesser synod to a greater'.[87]

Anglicans defended their historic autonomy on the grounds that the authority of the Roman patriarchate had been limited in its geographical scope. Contrary to Roman claims, it had not extended over the whole of western Europe. The local argument for the primitive independence of the British churches from Roman jurisdiction was allied here to a broader investigation of the scope of the papacy's authority in the first centuries. Anglican historians argued that the patriarchal authority of the papacy had been confined to the 'suburbicary' churches in the Italian peninsula. The British era was important to the case that the English church lay outside the patriarchal jurisdiction of the papacy. Cave and others argued that the institution of patriarchal authority was a post-Nicene invention: there had been no authority superior to a metropolitan in the ecclesiastical hierarchy of the Christian church during its first three centuries.[88] According to the non-juring Smith, 'no churches were within the Roman patriarchate, which were not in the provinces under the Roman vicarius'. The British church was 'comprehended under those other independent churches, whose privileges were secured' by the sixth canon of the Council of Nicaea. In other words, these churches were 'subject to none but their own metropolitans and their provincial synods'.[89] As late as the 1750s Ferdinando Warner would restate the full historic constitutional position with forceful clarity.[90]

[85] Collier, *Ecclesiastical history*, I, p. 77. See also Stillingfleet, *Origines Britannicae*, pp. 136, 142.

[86] Geddes, *An essay on the canons of the Council of Sardica, particularly on that which relates to appeals to Rome* (London, 1706), in Geddes, *Miscellaneous tracts*, vol. III.

[87] Thomas Comber, *Roman forgeries in the councils during the first four centuries*, in Gibson, *A preservative against Popery*, III, pp. 81–2. See also Thomas Traherne, *Roman forgeries or a true account of false records discovering the impostures and counterfeit antiquities of the Church of Rome* (London, 1673).

[88] Cave, *Dissertation concerning the government of the ancient church*, esp. ch. 4; Brerewood, 'Patriarchall government of the ancient church'; Bingham, *Origines ecclesiasticae*, I, p. 347.

[89] George Smith, *Britons and Saxons not converted to Popery*, pp. 285–6. See also Inett, *Origines Anglicanae*, I, pp. 27–8, 33–4, 128.

[90] Warner, *Ecclesiastical history*, I, pp. 19–20.

The threat of Rome was not the only problem to which the British past offered a solution. In the second half of the seventeenth century the ancient British past was to become even more important to Anglicans. For now they were confronted with a powerful presbyterian challenge to the legitimacy of episcopal government whose evidence was culled from Scotland's early church history. Because the primitive era in the past of the Scottish church appeared to yield not only proto-Protestant but proto-presbyterian precedents, the early centuries of Christianity in the British Isles assumed new importance as a principal theatre of debate between presbyterians and Anglicans. Of the various arguments against episcopacy, declared William Lloyd (1627–1717), the English-born Bishop of St Asaph, there was none that had 'made more noise in the world, or that hath given more colour to the cause of our adversaries, than that which they have drawn from the example of the ancient Scottish church'.[91]

Scots presbyterians claimed that there had been an ancient non-episcopal Christian church in Scotland from around AD 200. However, English, Welsh and Irish scholars argued that the history of the Scots in Scotland before AD 500 was a figment of chauvinistic imagination. For centuries after the conversion of the shadowy King Donald I, so the Scots presbyterians claimed, the church in Scotland had been governed without bishops; instead there had been government by colleges of monks or Culdees without any episcopal supervision.[92] Anglican commentators were keenly aware that the propagation of this antiquarian thesis had been attended by dangerous practical consequences; for, when the Scots had 'covenanted against episcopacy they had only used their own right; and thrown out that which was a confessed innovation, in order to the restoring of that which was their primitive government'.[93] Furthermore, this ancient presbyterian constitution of the Scottish church had been seized upon with relish by the French Huguenot scholar David Blondel (1590–1655) as a vital example from the primitive era of a non-episcopal church.[94] Closer to home, this argument also offered succour to English Dissenters such as Richard Baxter (1615–91), who desired a non-prelatical Church of England.[95] The appearance in England of the dangerous

---

[91] William Lloyd, *An historical account of church-government as it was in Great-Britain and Ireland when they first received the christian religion* (London, 1684), 'Preface'.

[92] C. Kidd, *Subverting Scotland's past* (Cambridge, 1993), pp. 22–4.

[93] Lloyd, *Historical account*, 'Preface'.

[94] David Blondel, *Apologia pro sententia Hieronymi de episcopis et presbyteris* (Amsterdam, 1646), p. 315.

[95] Richard Baxter, *A treatise of episcopacy* (London, 1681), p. 224. See the anti-Baxterian Henry Maurice, *A vindication of the primitive church, and diocesan episcopacy* (London, 1682), pp. 563–5.

Scots presbyterian precedent of rule by Culdees seemed to undermine the patristic case for primitive episcopacy. The argument was met by Lloyd, who challenged the authenticity not only of anti-episcopal interpretations of Scotland's past, but also of the whole ludicrous farrago of legends which composed Scottish antiquity.[96] This provoked in turn a response from Sir George Mackenzie of Rosehaugh, who, while sympathetic to the bishop's ecclesiological position, argued that he had undermined the monarchy whose glorious genealogy stretched back to King Fergus Mac-Ferquhard in 330 BC.[97] During the heated debates which preceded the Anglo-Scottish Union of 1707, the history of the ancient British church provided arguments for the Church of England's metropolitan authority over Scotland.[98]

We can now see why Anglicans felt the need to resort to British precedent. More intractable, however, is the question of how Anglicans squared the ethnological contradictions of a hybrid British–Saxon 'ancestry'. Indeed, to read Anglican historical polemic is to encounter very little soul-searching about the extent and propriety of the modern – and, otherwise, proudly Saxon – English nation claiming an ecclesiastical descent from the Britons, except for some evasive tetchiness on the part of Fuller: 'Sure, Helen [mother of Constantine] was as properly an English-woman as Alban an Englishman, being both British in the rigid letter of history; and yet may be interpreted English in the equity thereof.'[99] Yet, by what right did Anglicans think that they could lay claim to the mantle of the primitive church of the Britons which their very own Saxon ancestors had expelled from England into Wales? A possible solution is hinted at in Inett's *Origines Anglicanae*. Inett narrates that 'the conquest of Wales by King Henry I united the British to the English church'.[100] This conquest, or the subsequent formal union of the Welsh principality to the kingdom of England in 1536, may have provided justification for the appropriation of what was, in effect, the ancient church history of the Welsh. There had been a similar argument in the work of Basire.[101] A vaguer suggestion appears in George Smith's history to the effect that the Britons maintained their religious 'freedom and independency, until a change in the affairs of the British nation did, in after ages, bring both their church and state to submit to the English establishment'.[102] Warner

[96] Lloyd, *Historical account*; A. Tindal Hart, *William Lloyd 1627–1717* (London, 1952), pp. 92–3.
[97] Sir George Mackenzie, *A defence of the antiquity of the royal line of Scotland* (1685) and *The antiquity of the royal line of Scotland further cleared and defended* (1686), both in Mackenzie, *Works* (2 vols., Edinburgh, 1716–22), II.
[98] C. Kidd, 'Religious realignment between the Restoration and the Union', in J. Robertson (ed.), *A union for empire* (Cambridge, 1995), p. 164.
[99] Fuller, *Church history*, I, p. 40.   [100] Inett, *Origines Anglicanae*, II, p. 489.
[101] Basire, *Ancient liberty of the Britannick church*, p. 25.
[102] George Smith, *Britons and Saxons not converted to Popery*, p. 429.

linked the British church to the incorporation of the British state within the English nation: 'In all probability the changes in the British church followed those of the state; and that at the same time, and by the same steps, by which that nation became obedient to the Kings of England, their church submitted to, and became a member of the English church.'[103] Nevertheless, the mechanism of appropriation is never spelt out. In all probability, there may have been an assumption that any ecclesiastical establishment on English soil would have merited inclusion within the history of the *ecclesia anglicana*. Complete continuity was not imperative, especially if there had only been a brief hiatus of a few centuries in the long history of the uncorrupted church. According to Nathaniel Bacon, the Britons 'were the last of all the churches of Europe that gave their power to the Roman beast; and Henry the Eighth, that came of that blood by Teuther, the first that took away that power again'.[104]

By the second half of the eighteenth century, the British identity of the Church of England was in decline. With the rise of Enlightenment and the end of outright confessional warfare, Rome no longer posed the same sort of aggressive challenge to Anglican legitimacy. Nevertheless, Anglicans continued to pay some lip-service to the traditional ecclesiastical histories formulated in the sixteenth and seventeenth centuries.[105] Indeed, the matter of the ancient British church featured prominently in the rhetoric of Welsh Anglican opposition to Catholic Emancipation. Thomas Burgess (d. 1837), Bishop of St David's (and, later, of Salisbury), gloried in the knowledge that 'the Church of Britain was a Protestant church nine centuries before the days of Luther'. Not only had the primitive church of the Britons been 'apostolical and independent', but from the arrival of Augustine 'a truly Protestant church', not only by 'protesting against the corruptions of superstition, images and idolatry', but also by rejecting the authority of the pope and 'all communion with the Church of Rome'.[106]

Although displaced from the forefront of Anglican apologetic, the

---

[103] Warner, *Ecclesiastical history*, I, p. 308.

[104] Bacon, *Historical and political discourse*, p. 13.

[105] J. Walsh and S. Taylor, 'Introduction: the church and Anglicanism in the "long" eighteenth century', in J. Walsh, C. Haydon and S. Taylor (eds.), *The Church of England c. 1689–c. 1833: from toleration to Tractarianism* (Cambridge, 1993), pp. 58–9.

[106] Thomas Burgess, 'A sermon on the first seven epochs of the ancient British church', p. 143, and 'A second letter from the Bishop of St David's to the clergy of his diocese; on the independence of the ancient British church on any foreign jurisdiction', p. 106, both in Thomas Burgess, *Tracts on the origin and independence of the ancient British church* (2nd edn, London, 1815). See also Thomas Burgess, *Christ and not Saint Peter, the rock of the Christian church; and St Paul the founder of the church in Britain* (Carmarthen, 1812), esp. pp. 42–3, 45–6.

ancient British church had in the course of the eighteenth century become part of the broader cultural identity of the English people. In particular, the revival of historical painting in the middle of the eighteenth century led certain English artists to explore the visual possibilities inherent in the story of British Christian origins. Francis Hayman inaugurated this minor patriotic genre with *The Druids; or, the conversion of the Britons to Christianity* (1752), and in 1764 John Hamilton Mortimer won the one hundred guineas top prize offered by the Society of Arts for the best historical painting for *St Paul preaching to the ancient Britons*. By the middle of the nineteenth century the heroism of the ancient British church had become an established and popular theme, in works such as J. R. Herbert's *The first preaching of Christianity in Britain* (1842), E. T. Parris's 'Joseph of Arimathea converting the Britons' (1843) and, most famously, William Holman Hunt's *A converted British family sheltering a Christian priest from the persecution of the Druids* (1850).[107]

[107] I. Haywood, *The making of history* (Cranbury, NJ, 1986), p. 59; S. Smiles, *The image of antiquity* (New Haven and London, 1994), pp. 97–100, 105–7.

6   The Gaelic dilemma in early modern Scottish political culture

In early modern Scotland Gaeldom defined the historic essence of nationhood, yet also represented an alien otherness. The history, much of it mythical, of the Gaelic Scots of the ancient west Highland kingdom of Dalriada stood proxy for the early history of the whole Scottish nation. This matter of Dalriada provided precedents for Scotland's ancient constitutions in church and state, and formed the basis of Scotland's claims to independence from English suzerainty. However, the early modern period also witnessed a conscious design on the part of Lowland elites to extirpate contemporary Gaeldom, and to assimilate the Gaelic Highlanders to Lowland standards and values in every sphere of life: culture, public order, law, religion and language. This intolerance of Gaelic 'difference' transcended political and ecclesiastical divisions, which rested, ironically, on arguments drawn from the Dalriadic past.

The making of early modern Scottish identity

The origins of this situation lie deep in the medieval Scottish past. The nation of Scotland had its origins in the incorporation of the Scotic and Pictish *gentes* in the eighth and ninth centuries. The kingdom of Alba which united Scots and Picts had its centre of gravity in the Pictish kingdom of Fortriu, but the importance of the Gaelic Columban church in the Christianising of Scotland may have contributed to the ascendancy of Gaelic language and culture in the new nation and to the complete disappearance of Pictish. During the tenth, eleventh and twelfth centuries the kingdom of Alba grew to incorporate the Lothians, which had previously constituted the northern part of Anglian Bernicia, and the southwestern British kingdom of Strathclyde. The various peoples who composed the emerging kingdom, including the Dalriadic Scots, Picts, Strathclyde and Galwegian Britons, and Northumbrians, as well as Anglo-Norman and Flemish immigrants, were gradually amalgamated under a Scotic umbrella identity as the *regnum Scottorum*. Although the Scottish regnal line included some Pictish as well as Dalriadic–Scottish kings, the monarchy which was to form the core of Scottish identity was clearly linked to the early history of Dalriada. The Scottish War of Independence firmly established the Scotic identity of the nation. In particular, the Anglo-Scottish propaganda warfare of the late thirteenth and early fourteenth centuries linked Scottish independence to the ancient autonomy of the Dalriadic Scots as a means of rebutting the claim derived from the Brut legend that the Plantagenet monarchy enjoyed suzerainty over the whole island of Britain. The history of the Gaelic Scots had become the national history of all-Scotland; indeed this particular ethnic past justified the sovereignty of the whole.[1]

However, the idea of the Highland–Lowland divide also originated in the fourteenth century just as the various ethnic origin myths of the Scottish peoples were giving way to a widely accepted Dalriadic version. The irony of this situation is apparent in the influential chronicle by John of Fordun (c. 1320–c. 1384) which in response to English claims asserted a long history of Scottish independence on the basis of an imagined and extended Dalriadic history. Yet Fordun also launched a critique of the savage and uncouth Highlanders, whom he contrasted with the trusty, decent people of the Lowland seaboard. Fordun represents an emerging and undefined Lowland consciousness which included a strong antipathy to the Highlands, yet was nevertheless too vague and tentative to displace the national myth of the Scots as the heirs of Dalriada.[2]

The values of the Lowlands exercised a growing monopoly of Scottish policy and values. This process continued apace throughout the fifteenth and sixteenth centuries. James IV's forfeiture of the MacDonald Lordship of the Isles in 1493 was aimed at integrating the Highlands more tightly within the Scottish kingdom. However, the policy backfired. The destruction of the Lordship of the Isles created a power vacuum which a remote central government could not fill, and, as a result, the Highlands became if anything more anarchic. From the late medieval era the Highlander became a stock figure of Scottish satire, the oddity of his plaid garb attracting ridicule, his poverty winning only contempt and his achievements presumed to be limited to thieving and disorder.[3]

---

[1] G. Barrow, *Robert Bruce and the community of the realm of Scotland* (1965: 3rd edn, Edinburgh, 1988). For the early history of Scotland, see W. Ferguson, *Scotland's relations with England* (Edinburgh, 1977), chs. 1–2; M. Lynch, *Scotland: a new history* (London, 1991), chs. 2–8.

[2] John of Fordun, *Chronica gentis Scotorum* (ed. W. F. Skene, Edinburgh, 1871, with companion transln, 1872), ch. 9; C. Withers, *Gaelic Scotland: the transformation of a culture region* (London, 1988), pp. 3–4; Lynch, *Scotland*, pp. 67–8.

[3] T. C. Smout, *A history of the Scottish people 1530–1830* (1969: London, 1972), p. 40.

The ever-intensifying association of the political nation with the Lowlands was reflected in the names given to Scotland's languages. The Lowland vernacular was known throughout the later medieval period as *Inglis*; the first extant reference to it as *Scottis* dates from 1494. Gaelic had been the *lingua Scotica* or *Scotorum*. Now 'Scots' began to be appropriated by Lowlanders as a description of their language. There was an exchange of terminology and with it the ethnic affiliation of language. By the sixteenth century, Gaelic was increasingly described in alien terms as the Irish tongue – *lingua Hibernica* or Erse.[4]

Yet, a growing distance from the culture, language and values of the Highlanders was not matched by the emergence of an identity which reflected the anti-Gaelic antipathies of the Lowland nation. Indeed, the identification of the Scottish nation and its institutions with the Dalriadic Scots made by the late medieval chroniclers was consolidated and reinforced by two gifted humanist mythmakers, Hector Boece (c. 1465–1536) and George Buchanan (1506–82). The humanist Boece celebrated the civic virtue of the ancient Scots and grafted on to the history of the Dalriadic monarchy a 'mirror of princes' theme. On the other hand, although Buchanan, a supremely gifted Latinist and pioneering philologist whose history of Scotland remained the standard version until the Enlightenment, rejected the Gathelus–Scota legend, he saw great ideological potential in the Fergusian myth of the settlement and early political establishment of the Dalriadic Scots in Britain, which he glossed with a Calvinist theory of resistance. Buchanan claimed that the monarchy was anciently elective, and that the earliest Gaelic kings had been held accountable by the notables of the political nation for any deviations into tyranny, and deposed. He argued that in 330 BC the *phylarchi*, or clan chiefs, had elected the first king of the Scots on mainland Britain, Fergus MacFerquhard. Buchanan's theory of an ancient elective monarchy was also built on the Gaelic practice of tanistry, under whose inheritance rules a successor was appointed from within the kinship unit or derbfine, a system quite unlike personal hereditary succession by primogeniture. In this way, a historical memory of this Gaelic practice was embellished as a prescriptive ancient elective constitution of the Scottish kingdom, or *ius regni*. The very first transfer of the monarchy, the succession to Fergus MacFerquhard by his brother Feritharis rather than by either of his sons, Mainus or Ferlegus, Buchanan interpreted as an example of election. No longer simply a national origin legend legitimating Scottish sovereignty

---

[4] D. Murison, 'The historical background', in A. J. Aitken and T. McArthur (eds.), *Languages of Scotland* (Association for Scottish Literary Studies, Edinburgh, 1979), p. 8. However, for the continuing importance of Gaelic into the early seventeenth century (despite its *relative* decline), see Ferguson, *Scotland's relations*, p. 98.

and independence, the history of the Gaels had evolved into a political myth validating a radical interpretation of the Scottish constitution.[5]

The familiar contours of the Gaelic past were also to be exploited by royalist historians and commentators who disagreed with Buchanan's politics. Adam Blackwood (1539–1613) reversed one of Buchanan's central arguments for an elective monarchy. Buchanan had claimed in *De iure regni apud Scotos* that the clan chiefs who had first elected Fergus to be king of the Scots had themselves been elected by their followers. According to Blackwood, these clan chiefs constituted a model of unconstrained patriarchal authority, whose hereditary powers had been transferred intact to Fergus I. Blackwood invested great significance in the ancient Dalriadic phase of Scotland's history. He argued that not until the accession of King Gregory in AD 875, 1,200 years after the foundation of the monarchy, were Scottish kings to be bound by a coronation oath: 'ante Gregorii tempora Scotiae reges sacramento non erant obnoxii'.[6]

The Reformation exacerbated the division between Gaeldom and the rest of Scotland. Indeed, according to Victor Durkacz, 'linguistic repression sprang from the Reformation'.[7] Given that the church had been a genuinely national institution bridging the divisions of Highlands and Lowlands, the Reformation removed a vital point of contact. Henceforth the Highlands – perceived as a lost world of Catholicism and superstition – became a prime target of the Lowland Protestant mission. The Union of the Crowns also brought the opportunity to co-ordinate action against the Gaelic societies of Ireland and the Highlands. The Union of the Crowns led to the pacification of the Borders; from a tense frontier zone they became the Middle Shires of the British dual monarchy. This led to a greater focus on the Highlands as the source of disorder in Scotland. Moreover, the transformation of the Lowland economy, which involved the conversion of its feudal tenures into a system of emphyteusis based on commercial feu-ferm holdings, stood in stark contrast to the stagnant militarised Celtic feudalism and subsistence farming of the Highlands.[8]

From the late sixteenth century a stronger antipathy to the Highlands had manifested itself in public policy. James VI abandoned the traditional reliance on loyal clans to preserve order in the Highlands, sponsoring a

[5] A. Duncan, 'Hector Boece and the medieval tradition', in *Scots antiquaries and historians* (Abertay Historical Society, Dundee, 1972); R. Mason, 'Kingship and commonweal: political thought and ideology in Reformation Scotland' (University of Edinburgh Ph.D thesis, 1983); I. D. McFarlane, *Buchanan* (London, 1981), pp. 392–440; A. Williamson, *Scottish national consciousness in the age of James VI* (Edinburgh, 1979); J. H. Burns, *The true law of kingship: concepts of monarchy in early modern Scotland* (Oxford, 1996), chs. 2, 6.

[6] Adam Blackwood, *Apologia*, ch. 26, in Blackwood, *Opera omnia* (Paris, 1644), p. 134.

[7] V. Durkacz, *The decline of the Celtic languages* (Edinburgh, 1983), p. 1.

[8] Smout, *Scottish people*, pp. 43, 103–4, 127.

'concerted programme' of legislation in 1597 whose centrepiece was a scheme of plantation. The Highlands were to be colonised by Lowlanders, with royal burghs established in Lewis, Lochaber and Kintyre. In addition, Highland landholders would be required to produce their title deeds, to pledge security for crown rents and to ensure the maintenance of good behaviour among their kin and retainers. Between 1597 and 1609 there was a substantial change of strategy, though not of policy objectives. Colonisation was abandoned as impractical, and in its stead there emerged a more realistic approach to the extirpation of the Gaelic way of life. In 1608 Bishop Andrew Knox and Lord Ochiltree led a state-sponsored raid in which several refractory Highland chiefs were captured and then released on a bond which stipulated their co-operation with the authorities. These conditions became the basis of the Statutes of Iona of 1609, a body of legislation which outlawed the carrying of arms, forced chiefs to establish kirks and made illegal the patronage of bards. The Statutes involved an assault on Gaelic cultural difference as well as upon disorder. For example, the sixth article enjoined the education of the eldest son of Highland gentry and yeomen in the Lowlands, and in 1616 a further measure promoted the establishment of schools, in large part to assist the cause of Gaelic's extirpation.[9] Yet, the hammer of the Highlanders, James VI and I (1566–1625), showed no reluctance to base his political theories on the ancient Scots of Dalriada (though, reacting against the historical lessons of Buchanan, his boyhood tutor, he described Dalriadic government as an absolute, rather than elective, monarchy).[10]

This Gaelic dilemma intensified in the course of the seventeenth century when the ancient Fergusian constitution adumbrated by Buchanan dominated political culture, whether as a model for radical presbyterian aspirations, or target of royalist reinterpretation. On the other hand, the century also witnessed the enactment and implementation of anti-Gaelic legislation and policies in kirk and state. Yet the region which in practice constituted the periphery of the Scottish nation, and was treated accordingly in the public policy of an anti-pluralist centre, continued – as its recognised aboriginal heartland – to define Scotland's identity and the historical legitimacy of its institutions.

[9] Durkacz, *Decline*, p. 5; D. Stevenson, *Alasdair MacColla and the Highland problem in the seventeenth century* (Edinburgh, 1980), p. 6; G. Donaldson (ed.), *Scottish historical documents* (Edinburgh, 1970), pp. 171–5, 178–9; Withers, *Gaelic Scotland*, pp. 112–14; J. L. Campbell, *Gaelic in Scottish education and life* (Saltire Society, 2nd edn, Edinburgh, 1950), p. 115.

[10] King James VI and I, *The trew law of free monarchies* (1598), p. 73, and *Basilicon doron* (1599), p. 24, both in King James VI and I, *Political writings* (ed. J. P. Sommerville, Cambridge, 1994).

The politics of the Kirk

From the Reformation until the middle of the seventeenth century Scottish religious identity was not based on the same Dalriadic past which increasingly defined the temporal nationhood. It is not easy to explain the ideological disjunction between church and nation. Certainly, it would have been possible to construct a powerful ecclesiastical identity centred on the Dalriadic ethnie. The resources available included most obviously the legacy of Columba and Iona. Nevertheless the Reformation directed Scots towards a British rather than an ethnocentric identity. The fact that the English Reformation had taken place some thirty years before Scotland's break with Rome encouraged Scottish Reformers to address the idea of Britain. The influence of the English Bible in Scotland reinforced this tendency, as did the Union of the Crowns (1603) which stimulated a Scoto-British strain of apocalyptic discourse. The Covenanting idea, so central to the Scottish Reformed tradition, also hindered the expression of an indigenous religious identity, for it led Scottish theologians and religious propagandists away from a historical presentation of the vicissitudes of true Christianity in Scotland. Covenanting focused rather on contemporary Scotland as an antitype of Old Testament Israel, a nation forging a compact with God to reform and renew its church and the whole moral aspect of its commonweal.[11]

Nevertheless, the history of the ancient Dalriadic church was to be useful in fending off a perceived Anglican imperialism. Following the Union of the Crowns of 1603 the Stuarts attempted to impose a measure of religious conformity throughout the realms of their multiple monarchy.[12] This threatened Scots of both an episcopalian and a presbyterian bent. Those Scots committed to a presbyterian form of discipline had obvious reasons for emphasising the freedom of the Kirk, while the episcopal leadership of the Scottish church was equally concerned to preserve the autonomy of a national Scots episcopalian church from the metropolitan claims of York and Canterbury. Together presbyterians and episcopalians produced different but analogous defences of an unassimilable Scottish ecclesiastical tradition. In religious as in civil affairs, the best ideological guarantor of Scottish independence was prescription from history. In particular, Scottish churchmen needed to refute the ecclesiastical counterpart of the Galfridian legend, namely the mythical conversion of the whole island, the imperium of Lucius, king of the Britons, during the second century AD.[13] Although there had been vague intima-

---

[11] Williamson, *Scottish national consciousness*; R. Mason (ed.), *Scots and Britons* (Cambridge, 1994).   [12] C. Russell, *The causes of the English civil war* (Oxford, 1990), ch. 2.
[13] See above, ch. 5.

tions since the fourteenth century of a possible ecclesiastical subplot to
the history of the Dalriadic Scots,[14] only in the early seventeenth century
did Scots begin systematically to exploit the ecclesiological potential of
their history. Archbishop John Spottiswoode (1565–1639) drew in part
on the Buchananite story of Dalriadic Christianity, describing a non-
papal non-presbyterian conversion of the ancient Scottish nation by
disciples of John driven to Scotland by Domitian's persecution. Spottiswoode constructed a history of the Dalriadic church which complemented his own vision of a moderate episcopacy: he noted Boece's claim that
the first bishops had been elected by the common suffrage of priests, and
argued that there had been no diocesan episcopacy in Scotland until the
ecclesiastical corruptions of the eleventh century. Spottiswoode, just as
much as any presbyterian, was also concerned to emphasise Scottish
autonomy from Canterburian jurisdiction.[15] However, it was the radical
presbyterian wing of the Scottish reformed tradition which mined Dalriadic antiquity to the full. David Calderwood (1575–1651) described the
existence of a primitive Christianity in Scotland without the government
of bishops. David Buchanan (c. 1595–c. 1652) proved more expansive in
the preface to his edition of Knox's *History*, adding a significant extension
to Knox's own account of the Scottish presbyterian past. According to
David Buchanan King Cratilinth had established the order of Culdees in
the third century. The Culdees had chosen overseers from within their
own ranks, but these superintendents had not formed a different order in
the church. Overseers had enjoyed 'no preeminence or rank of dignity
above the rest' of the clergy, their position being more akin to that of the
modern presbyterian 'moderator' than to the episcopacy. Diocesan episcopacy, Buchanan argued, had appeared only in the eleventh century,
and only some period thereafter had colleges of Culdees lost their rights
to elect bishops.[16] Above all, the differences between Celtic and Roman

[14] Fordun, *Chronica*, pp. 64, 93–4; Hector Boece, *Scotorum historiae a prima gentis origine* (1527: Paris, 1574), pp. 86, 99, 128; Buchanan, *Rerum Scoticarum historia* (1582), in Buchanan, *Opera omnia* (2 vols., Edinburgh, 1715), lib. iv, R. 27, R. 35; lib. v, R. 42; lib. vi, R. 69.

[15] John Spottiswoode, *History of the Church of Scotland* (1655: 3 vols., Spottiswoode Society, Edinburgh, 1851), I, pp. 2–7. See also Alexander Mudie, *Scotiae indiculum* (London, 1682), pp. 9–11; George Mackenzie, MD, *The lives and characters of the most eminent writers of the Scots nation* (3 vols., Edinburgh, 1708–22), I, pp. 18, 26, 237–8, 358; II, p. 30.

[16] David Calderwood, *The history of the Kirk of Scotland* (ed. T. Thomson, Wodrow Society, 8 vols., Edinburgh, 1842–9), I, pp. 34–43; David Buchanan, 'Preface', in John Knox, *The history of the Reformation of the Church of Scotland* (1644: Edinburgh, 1731), pp. lvii–lxxxiv. For the continuation of this tradition, see John Brown, *An apologetical narration* (1665: Edinburgh, 1845), pp. 17–18; S. A. Burrell, 'The apocalyptic ideas of the early Covenanters', *SHR* 43 (1964), 1–24; Alexander Petrie, *A compendious history of the Catholick church* (The Hague, 1662), pp. 55–6; Robert Wodrow to George Ridpath,

Christianity over paschal observance and the tonsure were interpreted by presbyterian historians as evidence of a profound gulf between Petrine and a purer Asiatic Christianity derived from the Johannine tradition which extended even to church government. The Synod of Whitby (664), which met to resolve these differences, was built up into an ethnoreligious clash of the corrupt Romanism of the Saxons and a pure non-hierarchical Celtic Christianity.[17] In the second half of the seventeenth century, as presbyterians moved on to the defensive, the moderates amongst them abandoned the disturbing Covenanting ideal of a new British reformation, in its stead fashioning an apology for an ancient and strictly indigenous presbyterian polity.[18]

Although Scotland's ecclesiastical identity assumed Dalriadic hues in the course of the seventeenth century, this development did not prompt a revision of the Kirk's basic opposition to Gaeldom. In principle, Gaelic, universally referred to as 'Irish' or the 'Erse' tongue, remained pigeonholed with popery in the Kirk's taxonomy of the alien. The extirpation of 'Irish' culture remained one of the ultimate goal of the Kirk's missionary activities in the Highlands. The other aim of policy, however, was the winning of souls from the anti-Christian clutches of Counter-Reformation Catholicism. The threat posed by Catholic missions meant that, in practice, there were limits to anti-Gaelicist policy. When it came to a choice between linguistic purity and Protestantism, the Kirk chose the latter. Evangelism in Erse was more than a shade better than a harvest of souls lost to popery. Durkacz has advanced a plausible explanation for the linguistic bifurcation which characterised religious policy in the Highlands from the 1640s: 'English in education, serving the long-term aim of civilising and reforming the Highlands; Gaelic in preaching and religious instruction, serving the immediate end of saving souls and holding back the Counter-Reformation'.[19] Already in 1567 Carswell had translated Knox's liturgy into Gaelic, and a Gaelic version of Calvin's Catechism appeared in 1631. Gaeldom was viewed largely as a hindrance to evan-

---

23 September 1717, in T. McCrie (ed.), *The Wodrow correspondence* (3 vols., Wodrow Society, Edinburgh, 1842–3), II, p. 313; Robert Wodrow, *Analecta* (4 vols., Maitland Club, Glasgow, 1842–3), II, p. 326; III, p. 383; Andrew Stevenson, *The history of the church and state in Scotland, from the accession of King Charles I* (3 vols., 1753–7), I, 'Introduction', pp. 3–26. Cf. William Nicolson, *The Scottish historical library* (London, 1702), p. 203.

[17] Calderwood, *History of the Kirk*, I, pp. 42–3; James Kirkton, *The secret and true history of the Church of Scotland* (ed. C. K. Sharpe, Edinburgh, 1817), pp. 2–3; James Dalrymple, *Collections concerning the Scottish history preceding the death of King David the first* (Edinburgh, 1705), pp. 45–7; Stevenson, *History of church and state*, I, 'Introduction', p. 15.

[18] C. Kidd, 'Religious realignment between the Restoration and Union', in J. Robertson (ed.), *A union for empire* (Cambridge, 1995), esp. pp. 157–61.

[19] Durkacz, *Decline*, p. 10.

gelisation, given a lack of Gaelic-speaking clergy and of religious texts in Gaelic, whether Bibles, psalters or Catechisms. On the other hand, Gaelic was recognised as a necessary missionary medium. Expedients included schemes for training Gaelic-speaking boys in divinity. Bursaries were awarded to Gaelic speakers during the 1640s that they might further the work of godly reformation in the Highlands. In 1649 the Synod of Argyll authorised the translation of the Shorter Catechism into 'the Irish language', and in 1651 approved the version of Dugald Campbell and Ewen Cameron. In 1659 the same synod produced a Gaelic translation of the first fifty psalms, and in 1684 the first Gaelic Psalter was published.[20] However, the Kirk's promotion of Gaelic was largely a matter of expediency. Although the Scottish Kirk was 'ambivalent' about the methods to be used in evangelising the Highlands, the long-term goal was Anglicisation. The Synod of Argyll which promoted so much of this evangelical activity in Gaelic contended that 'the knowledge of English [was] so necessary for the weall of the Gospel', and referred constantly to Gaelic as the Irish language.[21]

The identity of the Kirk appears to have been riddled with anomalies. Increasingly it drew sustenance from Celtic Christianity, yet it was also bound up with attempts to remould and eventually to extirpate Gaeldom; and these anti-Gaelic policies were in turn qualified by the exigencies of the missionary situation. As with the state, the Kirk had an ethnic policy, one directed against Gaelic culture, but, in general, treated ethnicity as a second-order dimension of its institutional life, deploying the Dalriadic past in an indifferent and instrumentalist fashion.

Whigs, Jacobites and the ancient Gaelic constitution

The Revolution of 1689 heightened the significance of Gaeldom, but did nothing to reduce the tensions inherent in its ambivalent status at the core of Scottish political culture. Revolution principles in Scotland were essentially Buchananite, and inextricably linked to the ancient Fergusian constitution of 330 BC. In addition, the re-established, but unconfident, presbyterian kirk of 1690 increasingly came to rely on the legend of Culdeeism to legitimise presbyterian government as Scotland's historic ecclesiastical polity. For the next fifty years whigs and Jacobites, presbyterians and episcopalians, waged ideological warfare over the familiar prescriptive ground of the legendary ancient Dalriadic past. Nevertheless,

---

[20] D. MacTavish (ed.), *Minutes of the synod of Argyll 1639–1651* (Scottish History Society 3rd ser. 37, Edinburgh, 1943), pp. 127, 222; Durkacz, *Decline*, pp. 10, 15–16; Withers, *Gaelic Scotland*, p. 115; C. Withers, *Gaelic in Scotland 1698–1981: the geographical history of a language* (Edinburgh, 1984), p. 33.   [21] MacTavish, *Minutes*, p. 193.

the Highlands had become even more of a thorn in the side of the Lowland political nation. The Jacobite war in the Highlands from 1688 to 1691 firmly established the military importance of the region in European grand strategy. In particular, the Scottish Highlands were envisaged as a potential beachhead for a diversionary campaign on the British mainland by enemies of the post-Revolutionary regime such as France.[22]

The new whig–presbyterian establishment was keenly aware of the threat posed by a contumacious Highlands to the new order of things. The presbyterian Synod of Glasgow and Ayr noted in 1703: 'while they continue in their present neglected state strangers to the gospel, and bound up to a separate language and interest of their own, they are most dangerous to this church and nation'.[23] However, the argument that by the end of the seventeenth century there was no longer an association of the Gaelic language with Scottish nationality has to be weighed against the continuing significance of Dalriada in political culture, and the growing importance of the Culdees. Anti-Gaelicism, though powerful, continued to lack any association with an alternative historical identity which might loosen the reliance of whig–presbyterian ideology on the matter of Dalriada.

Whig political culture was far from oblivious of its debt to Gaelic institutions. Clanship was far from being the model exclusively for Jacobite–tory patriarchal politics. In Scotland patriarchalism enjoyed a whiggish significance far removed from English Filmerism because of the place of the phylarchs in the ancient Buchananite constitution. George Ridpath (d. 1726) argued that Scotland's original parliamentary constitution had been a confederation of clans ruled over in times of war by a captain-general or chief of chiefs whose rudimentary monarchy was limited by the suffrages of the various tribal heads or phylarchi, who had assembled prior to the election of the first king, Fergus I.[24] William Jameson (fl. 1689–1720), a staunch whig–presbyterian who lectured in history at Glasgow University, recognised the Gaelic dimension of his political creed. Jameson acknowledged that it had been the phylarchs or clan chiefs who had elected Fergus MacFerquhard as captain-general of the Scottish people in the west Highlands in their conflict with the Picts. Drawing on the ideas of Buchanan, he argued that the clan chiefs had themselves been elected by their followers. Indeed, Jameson conjectured that the election of Fergus had taken place because none of the chiefs would yield to any of their peers lest they concede the superiority of one

[22] D. Szechi, *The Jacobites: Britain and Europe 1688–1788* (Manchester, 1994).
[23] Quoted in Durkacz, *Decline*, p. 49.
[24] George Ridpath, *An historical account of the antient rights and power of the parliament of Scotland* (n.p., 1703), pp. 118, 120, 144, 148.

clan over another. Jameson did attempt to weave together Dalriadic whiggery together with anti-Gaelicism into a consistent body of historical interpretation: he acknowledged the corruption of the Highlands, and the decline into barbarity of Highlanders as the court, institutions and centre of gravity of Scottish kingdom had moved southwards during the middle ages. In this way Jameson was able to rationalise the disparity between attitudes to the historic and the contemporary Gael. However, he was atypical in his attempt to reconcile the Dalriadic and the anti-Gaelic in his historical politics: Scots were generally oblivious of the Gaelic anomaly at the heart of their political culture.[25]

As the Scottish political nation drew its last breath of independent statehood before the incorporating union of 1707, it remained wedded to its traditional confusion over the Gaelic dimension of national identity. At the Union the many petitions and pamphlets submitted and published in support of Scottish independence were committed to the 2,000-year Fergusian history of the kingdom; one celebrated pamphlet denoted Scotland by the name 'Fergusia'.[26] The traditional landmarks of Scottish identity were not immediately obliterated by the advent of British 'nationhood'. The Union of 1707 transformed but did not settle the traditional dispute over Scotland's historic sovereign independence: Scots needed more than ever to convince their fellow Britons that the Union had been a treaty between sovereign equals, and not the reabsorption within an English pan-Britannic imperium of a wayward vassal-nation.[27]

The patriotic exegesis of ancient geography continued to be a staple of Scottish polemic, whig as well as Jacobite. The Antonine Wall featured in a patriotic archaeology as the ultimate frontier of the Roman province of Britannia, north of which lay the unconquered and historically independent Scottish heartland.[28] Within Scottish political culture contemporary issues and institutions continued to be filtered through the lens of Dalriadic legitimacy. The Peerage Bill (1719), which proposed the limitation of Scottish aristocratic representation at Westminster to a permanent group of twenty-five selected peers, elicited the Scottish whig argument that the Scottish nobility – a body descended from the phylarchs – was the most ancient and treasured part of the Scottish constitution, being older than the Fergusian monarchy itself.[29] Despite the Union of 1707, whig

---

[25] William Jameson, 'The history, of the wisdom, valour and liberty of the ancient Albion-Scottish nation', National Library of Scotland Wodrow MS 97 (ii), ff. 141–53.

[26] [William Wright?], *The comical history of the marriage betwixt Fergusia and Heptarchus* (1706).

[27] W. Ferguson, 'Imperial crowns: a neglected facet of the background to the Treaty of Union of 1707', *SHR* 53 (1974), 22–44.

[28] Alexander Gordon, *Itinerarium septentrionale* (London, 1726), pp. 135–9.

[29] *The dignity of the Scottish peerage vindicated* (Edinburgh, 1719), p. 8.

and Jacobite polemic would resound for the next forty years to the old debates over the *ius regni*.[30]

The same whig establishment in Scotland which was legitimised by reference to the authority of phylarchical elections 2,000 years previously was committed to the extirpation of clanship. The Highlands were viewed as an alien drag on Scottish society. Not only did Jacobite disloyalty threaten Scotland's Revolution settlement, Highlanders also fell foul of the new secular ideal of economic improvement. Whig policy, though since the Revolution clearly British in scope and formulated in conjunction with politicians in London, was heavily influenced by the Scottish whig elite, and given an important non-governmental kick-start by Scottish voluntary initiatives. The pacification of the region and the defeat of Jacobitism were but the initial goals of Highland policy. Scottish whigs intended to transform the people of the Highlands from a nuisance into a national resource, that is, economically productive as well as loyal and law-abiding. Assimilation remained the long-term aspiration. The state papers contain a wealth of schemes for reforming the Highlands.[31] Certain of these Scottish projects would become reality in legislation. The martial aspects of clanship were abolished in the aftermath of the Jacobite rebellion of 1715, while the '45 was followed by a spate of initiatives, including the abolition of Scottish wardholding vassalage and feudal courts (which tended to be at their most arbitrary and oppressive in the Highlands) a new bout of reforms on forfeited estates, and the proscription of tartan.[32]

The tensions found in whiggery were also present in the political culture of Scottish Jacobites, who drew upon the same Dalriadic past as their whig–presbyterian rivals. Some Jacobite historians did exploit Gaelic history for royalist ends. Patrick Abercromby (1656–1716?) drew on the researches of Sir James Ware on Irish Gaelic manners and institutions to give a backbone of comparative sociology to his absolutist – and prelapsarian – interpretation of the history of Scotland's ancient government from the era of Fergus MacFerquhard. The fall had occurred during the reign of Malcolm II who had introduced to Scotland a system of Gothic feudal tenures which were to undermine the smooth operation of the benevolent Gaelic despotism idealised by Abercromby.[33] Another Jacobite historian, James Wallace, put a royalist spin upon Gaelic

---

[30] C. Kidd, *Subverting Scotland's past* (Cambridge, 1993), ch. 5.

[31] R. Mitchison, 'The government and the Highlands, 1707–1745', in N. Phillipson and R. Mitchison (eds.), *Scotland in the age of improvement* (Edinburgh, 1970).

[32] B. F. Jewell, 'The legislation relating to Scotland after the Forty-five' (University of North Carolina Ph.D thesis, 1975).

[33] Patrick Abercromby, *The martial atchievements of the Scots nation* (2 vols., Edinburgh, 1711–15), I, pp. 210–19.

tanistry, a practice which had been used by whigs as evidence for an ancient elective *ius regni*. Instead, argued Wallace, selections from within the derbfine which bypassed lineal primogeniture should be understood as temporary expedients akin to regencies by uncles during royal minorities. These substitute rulers, according to Wallace, had been assigned the office of *rex fidei commissarius*, a term which suggested implying that they had merely been entrusted with the kingship on behalf of the real hereditary monarch. Wallace also argued that the marble chair, or stone of destiny, associated with the ancient Celtic rite of inauguration had been the symbol of the Scottish nation's ancient sovereign independence.[34]

Nevertheless, there was little Jacobite identification with the Highlands as they really were. Scottish Jacobitism was primarily dynastic, ecclesiastical and committed to indefeasible hereditary monarchy.[35] As Jacobitism was based in the first instance on notions of political and ecclesiastical legitimacy, its ethnic associations, like those of other early modern ideologies, were secondary. The notion of a culture clash between a traditionalist patriarchal Highlands and a modernising commercial Lowlands was developed in the middle of the eighteenth century during the debate over post-Forty-five reconstruction and reform, and would later crystallise in Sir Walter Scott's *Waverley* (1814).[36] Jacobitism was not a Gaelicist ideology *per se*. The intellectual citadel of Scottish Jacobitism was Aberdeen, a university city in the north-east Lowlands, and central to royalist interpretations of Scottish history were strong monarchs such as James I and James IV, who had in their reform projects attempted to tame the Highlands.[37] Despite the reasonable assumption that Jacobites would have felt a natural affinity with the Gaelic heartland of their military support, Jacobite literati were not committed exclusively to a Dalriadic idea of Scotland. Although most Jacobite historians and pamphleteers waged battle with whigs over the traditional terrain of the history of the Fergusian monarchy, there were some figures who opted for alternative ethnohistorical platforms for their political arguments. While it was generally held by Jacobites that the Stewart line was descended from the ancient line of Fergusian kings through Banquo, thane of Lochaber and contemporary of Macbeth, the Catholic Jacobite antiquary Richard Augustine Hay (1661–1736) asserted that the Stewarts were more probably of British or Norman descent.[38] Another Jacobite historian, Dr George

[34] James Wallace, *The history of the lives and reigns of the kings of Scotland from Fergus the first king* (Dublin, 1722), 'Introduction'.
[35] B. Lenman, *The Jacobite risings in Britain 1689–1746* (London, 1980); Szechi, *Jacobites*.
[36] Kidd, *Subverting*, ch. 7, esp. pp. 158–9.
[37] Abercromby, *Martial atchievements*, II, pp. 277–80, 291.
[38] Richard Augustine Hay, *An essay on the origine of the royal family of the Stewarts* (1722: Edinburgh, 1793).

Mackenzie (1669–1725) even abandoned the traditional Milesian–Celtic account of the origins of the Scottish people from Ireland. Instead he relocated the ethnic origins of the Celto-Scythian Scots in a Germanic context, among such staple features of Gothicist treatises as the Cimbri and the Gotones.[39]

Ultimately, it was the Jacobite antiquary Father Thomas Innes (1662–1744) who undermined the evidential foundations of the Fergusian argument by exposing the forged regnal lists upon which Boece had based his account of the early Scottish kings. However, Innes was also a creative polemicist who constructed an equally ancient and flimsy indefeasible hereditary Pictish monarchy to bear the freight of Jacobite conclusions. According to Innes, the modern Scottish monarchy was in fact the successor of the ancient hereditary Pictish crown, not of the Dalriadic line. Innes demonstrated, moreover, that the Scots were relative newcomers to mainland Britain; that they had been for a long time confined to a small corner of the west Highlands; and that they had not (contrary to the Fergusian tradition) extirpated the older established Pictish nation in the ninth century. As a consequence of Innes's critical breakthrough there was no reason why Scottishness ought to be defined exclusively in terms of the continuity of the Dalriadic Scots: 'the present inhabitants of Scotland', either nobility, commonalty or royal family – meaning the Stuarts – were 'not universally descended from those Scots that came from Ireland, or owe not chiefly to them what makes for their greatest lustre and honour in ancient times'.[40]

Civil religion

Celtic Christianity had also remained central to the legitimacy of the fragile presbyterian Kirk established by the Revolution settlement of 1690. The Kirk was faced by a propaganda assault from episcopalians who not only challenged the validity of presbyterian orders, but charged the Scots presbyterian tradition with a legacy of political anarchy, resistance, assassination and social levelling. Some presbyterians were also embarrassed by the Covenants, and, in particular, the pledge in the Solemn League and Covenant (1643) to presbyterianise England. To wipe away the smears of innovation and radicalism, and to distance the new establishment from the pan-Britannic presbyterian imperialism of the Solemn League and Covenant, several of the Kirk's leading defenders

---

[39] Mackenzie, *Lives of writers*, I, pp. v–viii.

[40] Thomas Innes, *A critical essay on the ancient inhabitants of the northern parts of Britain, or Scotland* (1729: Edinburgh, 1879), esp. pp. 110–13; C. Kidd, 'Antiquarianism, religion and the Scottish Enlightenment', *Innes Review* 46 (1995), 139–54.

resorted to cautious and conservative ecclesiological formulae. These included the patristic defence that the term bishop in the primitive church had been the equivalent of a modern presbyter, and quite unlike a modern diocesan bishop, and the argument for the legitimacy of presbyterianism as the original model of the Church of Scotland from Dalriadic antiquity. These approaches were part of the presentation of Scots presbyterianism as an unthreatening 'civil religion'.[41]

In particular, the notion that the proto-presbyterian government of the church of the Dalriadic Scots was Scotland's original ecclesiastical polity suggested that the Revolution of 1689–90 had, contrary to the impression of innovatory cataclysm projected in episcopalian polemic, restored the nation's ancient ecclesiastical constitution. The Culdees became a symbol of a less threatening, less radical presbyterianism, more attuned to compromise within a multiconfessional multiple monarchy; the defence of the ancient presbyterianism of Dalriada as the legitimate system of ecclesiastical discipline in Scotland neutralised some of the universalist and anti-Anglican thrust of presbyterian ecclesiological principles. Moreover, the learning associated with the Hebridean monastic community of Iona strengthened the Kirk from the episcopalian taunt that the presbyterian tradition was the sectarianism of unlettered fanatics.[42]

Ironically, this appropriation of a learned Dalriadic civil religion coincided with a renewal of the Kirk's efforts to eradicate Gaelic illiteracy, ignorance and barbarity. As Culdeeism began to play a more central role in the identity of the Scots presbyterian Kirk, so the campaign against the Gaelic language waged by the Kirk and its lay supporters became more intense. In the first half of the eighteenth century, according to John MacInnes, Highlanders were confronted with the phenomenon of 'militant presbyterian evangelicalism', an anti-Gaelicist movement, which like its predecessors bowed to the tactical necessity of using Gaelic as a missionary medium. The Kirk accepted Gaelic in worship, but became even more strongly committed to English schooling. In 1694 the revenues of the suppressed bishopric of Argyll and the Isles were used to fund English schools in the west Highlands, of which there were twenty-five by 1698. The education act of 1696 passed by the Scots parliament ignored Gaelic in its prescriptions for a national parochial school system. Under an Act of the General Assembly of 1699, ministers who knew the 'Irish' language were to be sent to Highland parishes; where Highland

[41] Kidd, *Subverting*, ch. 4.
[42] *Ibid.* E.g. William Jameson, *Nazianzeni querela et votum justum* (Glasgow, 1697), pp. 33–47. For an unusual example, see Patrick Cuming, *A sermon preached before the Society in Scotland for Promoting Christian Knowledge* (Edinburgh, 1760), pp. 78–80, who incorporated a celebration of Iona into an anti-Gaelic tract.

congregations understood any English, they were to be preached at in that tongue; and there was to be an English-speaking schoolmaster in every Highland parish. The General Assembly also legislated that 'English schoolmasters be erected in all Highland parishes, according to former acts of parliament and general assemblies'.[43]

The Society in Scotland for the Promotion of Christian Knowledge (Scottish SPCK) was established in 1709 out of the movement for the reformation of manners which had arisen in Scotland from 1699. The Scottish SPCK planned to establish charity schools in the Highlands of Scotland in order to win that area for presbyterianism, whig loyalty, industry and, of course, the English language. The schools established were to be limited to a few core subjects: 'the principles of religion, reading of English, writing, arithmetic and church music'. Gaelic literacy was not encouraged. In 1713 the Scottish SPCK prohibited Gaelic reading in its schools, a state of affairs which would continue until the 1760s. Yet, there was considerable tension between the Scottish SPCK authorities, with their anti-Gaelic purism, and their teachers in the Highland localities. Schoolmasters noted that rote learning in English did not entail comprehension in English. In 1723 the Society's General Committee responded with a restatement of the organisation's basic anti-Gaelic policy in the Overtures on the teaching of English, which enjoined the almost total exclusion of Gaelic from the Society's schools except at a very few specially designated moments in the learning process. The Society set out its achievements in stridently anti-Gaelicist terms: 'In some places where the minister had so few hearers who understood English, that he was obliged to perform all the parts of his office in the Irish language, he now officiates in English, to the full understanding of many of his hearers.' Anglicisation meshed with the aim of the Hanoverian state to assimilate Scotland's 'Jacobite' periphery to whiggish norms. From 1725 the crown made an annual donation to the Kirk 'for the reformation of the Highlands and Islands, and other places where popery and ignorance abound'. This grant was administered by the Kirk's Committee of the Royal Bounty, which used its funds for the employment of catechists, usually local men, in Highland parishes, to inculcate Protestantism, loyalty and respect for the law. The Kirk's administration of the Royal Bounty, characterised by the use of Gaelic-speaking catechists and the insistence only that part of every sermon need be in English, was, as

---

[43] J. MacInnes, *The evangelical movement in the Highlands of Scotland 1688 to 1800* (Aberdeen, 1951), p. 223; Durkacz, *Decline*, p. 17; Campbell, *Gaelic in Scottish education and life*, pp. 50–1; Withers, *Gaelic in Scotland*, pp. 29–36; *Acts of the General Assembly of the Church of Scotland, 1638–1842* (2 vols., Edinburgh, 1843), I, p. 282.

Michael Lynch has noted, less 'consistently dogmatic' than the stated Gaelophobic policies of the SSPCK.[44]

Ironically, the anti-Gaelicist policies of the Scottish SPCK began to mellow during the same period when Scots presbyterians abandoned an untenable Dalriadic identity. William Robertson, the mouthpiece of the increasingly influential Moderate party in the Kirk, constructed a historical defence of the Kirk which did not rely upon Culdaic legends.[45] Although the rules of the Scottish SPCK had become even harsher in 1750 with the insistence that children speak English to the total exclusion of Gaelic not only in school but also when playing around the school premises, there was, all of a sudden, a thaw in attitudes. In 1754 the Scottish SPCK commissioned its own Gaelic New Testament, which eventually appeared in 1767. Moreover, in 1766 there had been an important reformulation of policy. Highland schoolmasters were henceforth to 'teach their scholars to read both Erse and English', though the ultimate goal was still the attainment of reading, speaking and understanding the English language.[46]

Lowland identity and the politics of legitimacy

Why did early modern Lowlanders uphold with such vigour and commitment these apparent contradictions? Why did exploitation of a traditional ethnic identity continue when there were obvious defects in the capacity of Gaeldom to provide a suitable identity for a law-bound burgh-oriented Lowland elite? Above all, why was there no apparent awareness of the Gaelic dilemma in Scottish political culture?

The situation arose out of a unique conjunction of factors in the late medieval and early modern Scottish experience, but also bears the hallmarks of a deference to inherited custom and authority common to most early modern European societies. The subordinate status of ethnicity in early modern European political discourse suggests that the congruence of ethnic identities in different spheres of public life might well have mattered less than compatibility between other concerns which were firmly entrenched as unquestioned primary goods. Hence, when existing

[44] Durkacz, *Decline*, pp. 26, 51; W. Ferguson, 'The problems of the established church in the west Highlands and islands in the eighteenth century', *Records of the Scottish Church History Society* 17 (1969), 15–31; J. MacInnes, *Evangelical movement*, pp. 224–5; Withers, *Gaelic Scotland*, pp. 122–5; *The state of the Society in Scotland for Propagating Christian Knowledge, anno 1729* (Edinburgh, 1729), p. 34; Lynch, *Scotland*, p. 364; A. Macinnes, *Clanship, commerce and the house of Stuart* (East Linton, 1996), pp. 178–9.
[45] See C. Kidd, 'The ideological significance of Robertson's *History of Scotland*', in S. J. Brown (ed.), *William Robertson and the expansion of empire* (Cambridge, 1997).
[46] Withers, *Gaelic Scotland*, p. 125; Durkacz, *Decline*, pp. 63, 66–7; J. MacInnes, *Evangelical movement*, pp. 64, 246–7.

goods appeared to rely on distinctive ethnic identities, there was no clash of irreconcilables. For example, Scottish independence and a thriving Protestant realm free of disorder were values which loomed so large that they obliterated any perceptions of ethnological incoherence arising from the contrasting attitudes Lowlanders held towards historic Dalriada and contemporary Gaeldom. Lowland Scots inherited a usable Dalriadic past which for centuries had proved vital to the propaganda war for Scottish independence, and had since been elaborated into a past which legitimated both royalist and monarchomach interpretations of Scotland's political institutions. There was no pressure to abandon this association with Dalriada simply because of the existence of anti-Gaelic attitudes. Lowlanders inherited distinctively non-Gaelic manners and speech together with a history whose content was Gaelic. This unusual combination of inherited cultural characteristics formed the identity of Scottish Lowlanders, a people untroubled by any ethnic schizophrenia in large part because political discourse was not driven by an ethnic imperative.

Why was the Dalriadic past so important when the values of the 'old Scots' of the Highlands conflicted so sharply with Lowland standards of 'civility'? The Dalriadic past was vital to the defence of Scottish sovereignty, an imperium for which many generations of late medieval Scots had had to struggle to preserve, but which could be in danger of being surreptitiously eroded within the post-1603 regal union. The principal argument for Scottish independence was historical and prescriptive: the Scots had possessed territory in Scotland free of any overlord from the darkest antiquity of 330 BC. Scotland's claims to precedence and dignity rested on the same foundations, and were similarly threatened by the Stuarts' adoption of an English metropolitan court for their multiple monarchy. Sir George Mackenzie of Rosehaugh tried to establish the precedence of the Scottish monarchy on basic juridical principles drawn from the antiquity of the Dalriadic kingdom. According to Mackenzie British kings derived their 'precedency' over the various other monarchs of Europe through their Scottish title 'for it is an uncontroverted ground in law, that amongst those of equal dignity, he who first attained to that dignity is to be preferred'.[47]

It was obvious that the patriotic boasts of Scottish precedence and antiquity could apply only to the Dalriadic heartland of the kingdom. The Romans had, for a time, incorporated the Lowlands as far north as the

[47] George Mackenzie, *Observations upon the laws and customs of nations as to precedency*, in Mackenzie, *Works* (2 vols., Edinburgh, 1716–22), II, p. 516. See also Mudie, *Scotiae indiculum*, 'Epistle dedicatory'; W. Alexander, *Medulla historiae Scoticae* (London, 1685), 'Introduction'; Alexander Nisbet, *A system of heraldry speculative and practical* (2 vols., Edinburgh, 1722–42), II, pt iv, pp. 145–6, 173–4.

Antonine Wall within the province of Britannia. The Lothians had also been part of the Anglian kingdom of Northumbria until the tenth century. English historians claimed that medieval kings of Scotland had been accustomed to perform homage to the imperial crown of England for this part of their territory. Edinburgh, the modern capital of a Scotland whose political, ecclesiastical and economic centres of gravity were in the Lowlands, was not the historic navel of the kingdom. The north of Scotland alone had been absolutely free of foreign conquest.[48]

Gaelic identity was subordinated to a politics of prescriptive legitimacy; the fundamental commitment was to the Dalriadic past as the basis of institutional continuity – not as an ethnic history of the Scottish people *per se*. Although there was some pride in the manners of the people, particularly their martial valour, the rationale behind the Dalriadic identity was not primarily ethnic. Dalriadic ethnocentrism was, in a sense, weak. Although supplying the ideological underpinnings of Scotland's church and state, it did nothing to inhibit the destruction of a regional Gaelic particularism, nor was it so exclusive as to prevent the gradual emergence of Scottish Gothicist antiquarianism. The coexistence throughout the early modern period of a powerful critique of Highland values, manners and institutions with a starkly contradictory and yet equally powerful national adherence to ideologies grounded in Dalriadic historical myths stands testimony to an ethnocentrism qualified by an essentially legitimist purpose. Hence the possibility of a nation depending on ancient Gaeldom for its notions of political legitimacy, operating an anti-Gaelic cultural policy without apparent unease or sense of incongruity. Scots were not overwhelmed by a sense of Dalriadic ancestry, but used the imagined affiliation of the whole nation and its institutions with ancient Dalriada for specific purposes. Legitimacy was reinforced by ethnic history; yet Scots remained aware of the reality of ethnic pluralism, and indeed of a vast Highland–Lowland gulf within the nation.

The fertile humanistic and antiquarian cultures of early modern Scotland failed to encourage any significant exploration of the nation's plural origins. Arthur Williamson, for example, has noted how vague Buchanan was about the timing of the feudalisation of Scottish institutions and

---

[48] For the identification of the 'Ierne' of the ancients – and its 'Scottish' inhabitants – as Scotland north of the firths of Clyde and Forth (and for the corollary that during the Roman era the Scots had been present in mainland Scotland, rather than Ireland), see George Mackenzie, *A defence of the antiquity of the royal line of Scotland*, in Mackenzie, *Works*, II, pp. 370–8; Mackenzie, *The antiquity of the royal line of Scotland, further cleared and defended*, *ibid.*, II, pp. 404–10; Alexander Taitt, *The Roman account of Britain and Ireland in answer to Father Innes* (Edinburgh, 1741); Walter Goodall, *An introduction to the history and antiquities of Scotland* (1739: transln, Edinburgh, 1773), pp. 2–16; William Maitland, *The history and antiquities of Scotland* (London, 1757), pp. 99–105.

Lowland life.[49] There may have been a suspicion that, if the myth of a single ancient line of institutional continuity were shattered, the very idea of nationhood independent of English claims to suzerainty might be rendered perilously fragile. During the seventeenth century Scottish jurists were clearly aware of the Gothic provenance of the nation's laws and, by implication, its other feudal institutions. Nevertheless, feudal jurisprudence was woven into the seamless Dalriadic history of the Scottish nation. Most historians argued that the feudal law had arrived in Scotland in the early eleventh century in the reign of Malcolm II, and were proud that they had received the feudal tenures before their arrival in England at the Norman Conquest. Thus Scottish historians boasted of these *Leges Malcolmi* as evidence of Scotland's early reception of feudalism,[50] but did not allow this boasting to become in any way Gothicist, or allow it to dent the ethnic hegemony of political argument from supposed original Dalriadic precedent. There was no acknowledgement that feudal law had transformed the Dalriadic inheritance, or that feudal institutions provided an alternative institutional basis for a Lowland-oriented national identity. There was no apparent tension that the laws were of a different ethnic origin from the monarchy. Parliament was a puzzle. There was some recognition among royalists that it was the king's feudal court. However, both royalists and monarchomachs resorted to the Dalriadic *ius regni* for their major arguments. Ancient constitutionalists neglected the feudal parliament as the basis of a tradition of mixed government for the myth of an ancient Gaelic assembly of clan chiefs or phylarchs as the basis of institutional limitations on the Scottish monarchy. The Covenanting minister John Brown of Wamphray argued that it had been an ancient Dalriadic parliament – 'partakers and fellow-sharers of the supremacy with the king' – which had first entailed the Scottish crown out of the direct Fergusian line conferring it on Fergus MacFerquhard's brother Feritharis.[51] Mackenzie of Rosehaugh, the king's advocate and a sophisticated jurist, knew that Scottish government was a palimpsest whose most recent layer, that of feudalism, had almost completely obliterated all but a few vestiges of earlier Celtic institutions and law. Nevertheless, it was the ancient Dalriadic origins of the monarchy that remained uppermost in Mackenzie's political treatises. Although Mackenzie knew the royalist argument for the parliament as a feudal court of the kingdom's paramount feudal superior, this had to take second place in his historical ideology to an anti-Buchananite interpretation of the mythical events of 330 BC.[52]

[49] Williamson, *Scottish national consciousness*, p. 125.   [50] Kidd, *Subverting*, p. 148.
[51] Brown, *Apologetical narration*, pp. 70–6.
[52] Mackenzie, *Ius regium*, in Mackenzie, *Works*, II, pp. 442, 446–7, 451–7.

Ethnic continuity from antiquity was an important dimension of the defence of sovereign independence rather than an aspect of racial chauvinism *per se*. When Mackenzie boasted that 'we are still the same people and nation, but the English are not the old Britons, but are a mixture descending from Danes, Saxons and French',[53] he was not, I suspect, making a point about Scotland's ethnic composition. His aim was rather to establish the continuity of a sovereign Scottish *regnum* in the absence of foreign conquest: 'no historian can pretend that we obeyed any race, save that which now reigns: Whereas we can condescend, where the English and French were conquered by strangers, and had their royal line dethroned and inverted'.[54] Although the eminent antiquary Sir Robert Sibbald (1641–1722) explored the tribal diversity of ancient Scotland, he maintained a strict commitment to the Gaelic origins of Scottish institutions in church and state, and, indeed, explicitly defended the integrity of the Dalriadic myth as the basis of Scottish nationhood.[55]

Did Scotland possess an alternative myth of national origins? The Brythonic peoples of ancient Scotland, the Caledonians and Picts, who might have provided one, were accommodated to the Dalriadic mainstream of Scottish historiography. The ancient Caledonian people might have provided a possible ethnic identity for Scotland distinct from Gaeldom. After all, the rediscovery of Tacitus had exerted a profound influence on the development of early modern British historiography. And had not Tacitus made Calgacus, the ancient Caledonian general who opposed Agricola at the battle of Mons Graupius, the very model of civic virtue, a leader who combined valour with inspiring eloquence?[56] However, the Caledonians, and particularly Calgacus, were absorbed within the developing matter of the Dalriadic Scots. Boece, influenced by civic humanist ideas, presented Tacitus's Calgacus as the Scottish king Corbred Galdus: 'Galdus (Galgacum Tacitus eum vocat)'.[57] Similarly, Buchanan challenged the views of the Welsh antiquary Humphrey Lhuyd that the Caledonians had been Britons, and, like Boece, appropriated Calgacus as a Scottish king.[58] Innes would later criticise the assumption of previous Scottish historians that the various ancient inhabitants of the north of

---

[53] Mackenzie, *Observations upon precedency*, in Mackenzie, *Works*, II, p. 518.
[54] *Ibid.*, II, p. 517; Abercromby, *Martial atchievements*, I, pp. 2–3, 210–11.
[55] Robert Sibbald, 'A (defence or) vindication of the Scotish history and of the Scotish historians' (c. 1685), National Library of Scotland Adv. MS 15.1.3.
[56] Tacitus, *On Britain and Germany* (trans. H. Mattingly, Harmondsworth, 1948), pp. 78–83.
[57] Boece, *Scotorum historiae*, p. 57. Improbably, Caractacus, the heroic leader of the Catuvellauni, an ancient British tribe based around Hertfordshire, was also appropriated as a Scottish king. See Mackenzie, *Lives of writers*, II, pp. 15, 21–5.
[58] H. Trevor-Roper, *George Buchanan and the ancient Scottish constitution*, *EHR* supplement 3 (1966).

Britain, including the Caledonii, the Maeatae of the southern Lowlands and even the Brigantes of Yorkshire, 'made a part of the Scots'.[59] Nor did Boece and Buchanan champion Scotland's Pictish origins. They argued that when King Kenneth (II) MacAlpin had conquered and absorbed the Pictish kingdom, most Picts had either fled or been massacred in the triumphant Scottish victory. In other words, the history of the Picts was a dead end irrelevant to medieval and modern Scotland, a view later overturned by Innes, who made the continuity of the Pictish monarchy central to his revisionist interpretation of the Scottish past.[60]

Curiously, there was very little effort expended in the construction of a non-Gaelic Scottish identity which might recognise the dominant role played by Lowlanders in the making of early modern Scotland. From the late sixteenth and early seventeenth centuries jurists such as Thomas Craig (1538–1608) and John Skene (c. 1543–1617) began to describe Scottish laws and institutions in Gothic terms, attributing the origins of feus, for example, to the Germanic peoples of the Continent.[61] However, such insights did not resonate with Scotland's largely Gothic or Gothicised political nation, which remained trapped, by its Gaelic political imagination, in a Dalriadic fantasy. While Gothicism remained confined to juridical discourse, the Lowlands lacked a convincing or usable identity in which to construct a non-Gaelic version of Scottishness.

The fiction of a common national ancestry was a necessity given the predominance of prescriptive argument in the prevailing patterns of British political discourse, including the continuing debate over the status of the Scottish kingdom relative to the imperial crown of England. Since the late thirteenth century the argument for Scottish independence had depended on an acceptance of regnal and national solidarity as descendants of the Dalriadic Scots.[62] It would have undermined Scotland's sovereignty, independence and constitution to concede the plural origins of Scotland's Pictish, British, Saxon, Norman and Flemish peoples. In any case there were problems with these traditions. The Britons were associated in Scottish eyes with the despised imperialist myths concocted by Geoffrey of Monmouth, and the Saxons were held to have arrived in

[59] Innes, *Critical essay*, p. 4.
[60] Buchanan, *Rerum Scoticarum historia*, lib. v, R. 69; R. Mason, 'Scotching the Brut: politics, history and national myth in sixteenth-century Britain', in Mason (ed.), *Scotland and England 1286–1815* (Edinburgh, 1987), pp. 65, 77.
[61] Thomas Craig, *Ius feudale* (ed. and trans. J. A. Clyde, 2 vols., Edinburgh and London, 1934), I, pp. 49–70; J. Cairns, T. Fergus and H. MacQueen, 'Legal humanism and the history of Scots law: John Skene and Thomas Craig', in J. MacQueen (ed.), *Humanism in Renaissance Scotland* (Edinburgh, 1990); J. G. A. Pocock, *The ancient constitution and the feudal law* (1957: reissue with retrospect, Cambridge, 1987), pp. 79–90, 97.
[62] See S. Reynolds, 'Medieval *origines gentium* and the community of the realm', *History* 68 (1983), 375–90.

Scotland a defeated people seeking refuge from the Norman Conquest.[63] Moreover, the Saxons and Normans provided little in the way of a history of ethnic and national differentiation from England, which was vital to the patriotic assertion that the community of Scotland was distinctive and independent and had never been part of, or subject to, an English *imperium*. The Flemish contribution to Lowland history tended to be neglected until the work of George Chalmers at the turn of the nineteenth century.[64] There were specific drawbacks to each particular component of the Lowland mosaic. Above all, the primary good of national freedom dictated that the Scottish political nation recognise one single ethnic origin. It was necessary to trace one clear indisputable genealogy of the relevant institutions of sovereign nationhood. By the seventeenth century such had been the predominance and functional capacity of the Dalriadic defence of Scottish nationhood that the emergence of a rival identity, which might have reflected more appropriately the non-Gaelic ethnic balance of the Lowland-dominated Scottish nation, was in large part dependent either on the exposure of the ancient Dalriadic past as the fraudulent invention of late medieval chroniclers or on the decline of prescriptive argument.

The combined effect of Innes's deconstructive scholarship, the rise of the Scottish Enlightenment and the first stirrings of romanticism led to the dissolution of these tensions between Scotland and the Highlands. The watershed of the middle of the eighteenth century did not mark a straightforward transition from a negatively 'political' to a positively 'poetical' view of the Highlander. Rather one system of ambivalence succeeded another. The romantic Highlands of the Lowland imagination were not invented *ex nihilo* in the late eighteenth and nineteenth centuries; rather they were reinvented after the dissolution of an earlier and equally fantastical vision of Gaeldom. Notwithstanding the influence of romantic primitivism, there remained a strong antipathy to the real Highlands. The kitsch Gaeldom of the nineteenth century would conveniently obscure the sacrifice of the Highland peasantry on the altars of political economy.[65]

---

[63] Mason, 'Scotching the Brut', p. 74; Kidd, *Subverting*, p. 44.

[64] George Chalmers, *Caledonia* (3 vols., London, 1807–24), I, pp. 600–9.

[65] See L. Leneman, 'A new role for a lost cause: Lowland romanticisation of the Jacobite Highlander', in Leneman (ed.), *Perspectives in Scottish history* (Aberdeen, 1988); P. Womack, *Improvement and romance* (London, 1989).

The contentious role played by ethnic identity in the history of Ireland makes it easy to forget that the Irish, like other nations, have played out their conflicts in a world of imagined communities. Yet, a variety of typical early modern ideological constructions confounds the historian who expects to find a clear and unambiguous relationship between communal ancestry and identity. Indeed, 'real' and 'imagined' pedigrees were often incongruent, and numerous inconsistencies occurred in the use of overlapping ethnic and religious labels. It is one of the poignant ironies of its history that the undisputed reality of ethnic division and hostility is fuelled in Ireland as elsewhere by a large measure of invention. Ongoing and creative processes of ethnogenesis – rather than biological or cultural continuities – form the early modern backdrop to the tragedy of Ireland's story.

There is no contesting, however, the central importance of ethnicity in early modern Irish politics. The 'nation' was divided into three distinct groups defined largely by ethnic origin, though secondarily and increasingly by religious confession. The Old Irish – also known in their histories as the Milesians – were the historic inhabitants of the island whose presence long preceded the twelfth-century Anglo-Norman settlement. The Old English were largely the descendants of this latter group of medieval colonists. Over the course of subsequent centuries they had, according to their New English detractors, gone native, becoming suspiciously Hibernicised in their customs. The New English were the post-Reformation settlers of Ireland. This new breed of colonist would appropriate the Anglo-Irish identity of their medieval colonial predecessors, though without using this particular terminology: rather they defined themselves as the Protestant Irish nation.[1]

---

[1] Not all contemporaries recognised exactly these categories. Sir John Davies, the speaker of the Irish Commons, in 1613 referred to 'all the inhabitants of the kingdom, English by birth, English by blood, the new British colony, and the old Irish natives': quoted in D.G. Boyce, *Nationalism in Ireland* (1982: 2nd edn, London, 1991), p. 73. Many of the new colonists in Ulster were, of course, Scots, that is, British rather than English.

The divisions of Old Irish, Old English and New English did reflect genuine interests, political groupings and ideological positions. However, the intellectual and cultural leaders of early modern Ireland – scholars, churchmen and antiquaries – constructed categories of ethnic classification which did not correspond to historical reality. In particular, identities were often appropriated, one group stealing the ethnic clothes of another group's collective past. This tended to occur when the latter group's historical experience complemented the former's ideological needs. There were a number of examples of this phenomenon in early modern Ireland; indeed, no group eschewed the practice of appropriation. An element of ethnic borrowing figured in the identities of Old Irish, Old English and New English nations. Generally speaking, the identities of the majority core-population of the various ethnic groups in early modern Ireland were dressed to some extent in purloined historical garb. Not only did the Old English and New English, in their different ways, have colonial identities, but even the Milesian Irish claimed neither to be autochthonous (though an ancient presence on the island) nor to be the original founders of the Irish high-kingship. The arrival of the Milesians had been preceded, in succession, so legend ran, by the invasions of Partholón and his followers (who had displaced the island's aboriginal giants), the Nemedians, the Fir-Bolg and the Tuatha-Dé-Danaan. The Gaelic community identified in particular with the institutional histories of the Fir-Bolg, under whom the Irish monarchy had been established, and the Tuatha-Dé-Danaan. In the course of the seventeenth century Old English antiquarians adopted the Gaelic past as the core element in their identity. The most striking anomaly was the identity of the New English. This community, which was settled in Ireland only in the sixteenth and seventeenth centuries, claimed as its own both the constitutional history of the twelfth-century Old English colonists and the ecclesiastical history of the Celtic church. Later, a perceptible divergence between Anglo-Irish and English interests in the eighteenth century created the space for 'a growing identification with a Gaelic Ireland (which had meanwhile absorbed the remaining Catholic Old English)'.[2]

The recognised ethnic identities of the seventeenth and eighteenth centuries failed in several respects to match the ethnic constructions imposed upon the various historic 'Irelands' of the antiquarian imagination. Patriotic antiquarians were pragmatists, and did not regard the complexities and ambiguities in the ethnic composition of Irish history as an insurmountable obstacle to the achievement of their mythistorical projects. An overriding commitment to institutions and non-ethnic

[2] J. T. Leerssen, *Mere Irish and Fíor-Ghael* (1986: 2nd edn, Cork, 1996), p. 297.

values distorted Irish ethnic identities. In particular, the importance of asserting priority of settlement in contemporary legitimist debate meant that there was an in-built preference for the extension of one's lineage beyond the immediate history of one's ethnic ancestry to encompass an earlier phase of the Irish past. The litmus test for the selection of historical backdrops was not so much the plausibility of the link between a phase of the Irish past with the ethnic situation of the authors as its functional adaptability to reinforce a particular ideological position. Imagined lines of ancestry were invoked unselfconsciously. There arose instead a marked degree of incongruence between contemporary ethnic identity and its historical expression. Somehow the heirs of medieval conquerors or recent sixteenth- and seventeenth-century settlers were able to affiliate themselves with aspects of Irish institutional history which occurred in more distant eras of the nation's past, ignoring subsequent ethnic upheaval and displacement. Ethnic and historical accuracy were sacrificed on the altar of ideological utility.

The status of Ireland as a political entity and the nature of the Irish ecclesiastical tradition constituted the primary foci of early modern Irish political culture. What was the nature of Ireland's relationship with the crown and kingdom of England, and what claim – temporal as well as spiritual – did the papacy have over Ireland? Furthermore, did the primitive church in Ireland established by St Patrick in the fifth century approximate more to the modern standards of apostolic Anglican Protestantism or to Counter-Reformation Catholicism? These regnalist and confessional controversies distorted any natural and straightforward correspondence between ethnic groups and their proper pasts. A store of precedents culled from one ethnic history alone could not supply the answers to all these questions. As a result, in some cases polemical antiquarians rode two horses simultaneously, oblivious of the hazards attendant on the historical acrobatics being performed. To take the most obvious example: the recent history of the New English immigrants was of very little use in establishing the legitimacy of their institutional privileges. Instead, the constitutional history of the Old English and the ecclesiastical heritage of the Gaels were plundered to endow the Protestant nation with a usable past.[3] Why did polemical antiquarians resort to such implausible fictions and appropriations? The primary role of ethnic history was the legitimation of institutions. To invest in a variety of ethnic pasts was to take out insurance, to spread the risk of one's ideological position becoming discredited.

Being in many respects vehicles for the advancement of particular

---

[3] See not only below in this chapter, but also ch. 10.

ideological positions, such identities tended to be provisional. The Old English, in particular, lacked fixed ethnic bearings, and veered between the twin poles of their Norman colonial heritage and an assimilated Gaelicism.[4] Ethnic identities also shaded into confessionalism. Sean Connolly has argued convincingly that after the civil wars of the middle of the seventeenth century there was a 'new primacy' of religious confession in the manufacture of identity. However, he also notes a time lag in the adoption of the appropriate 'terminology' to describe the shifting proportions of ethnic descent and religion in the structure of seventeenth-century Irish society.[5] The New English of the seventeenth century did eventually become the Irish Protestant nation of the eighteenth.

Not only were ethnic categories unstable and liable to mutate, but the particularities of the individual family genealogies which lay behind these broad communal identities undermine any casual assumptions that these were rigid or totally consistent groupings. In the course of the seventeenth century there was a considerable degree of intermarriage between, on the one hand, the Gaelic and Old English communities and, on the other, between the Old English and the New English settlers.[6] Religion also complicated traditional identities, especially given the growing opportunities and penalties attached to confessional allegiance. From the Restoration, the Protestant community included the Old English Dillons and Fitzgeralds, and a few Gaelic families such as the O'Briens, O'Haras and O'Neills, the heads of whose dynasties conformed as Protestants lest they jeopardise their estates.[7] On the other hand, it was not only proud Old English families such as the Butlers who, lumped together with their

---

[4] A. Clarke, 'Colonial constitutional attitudes in Ireland, 1640–1660', *Proceedings of the Royal Irish Academy* 90 (sect. C) (1990), 357–75.

[5] S. Connolly, *Religion, law, and power: the making of Protestant Ireland 1660–1760* (1992: Oxford pbk, 1995), pp. 115–19. Note the tension between religious and ethnic perspectives in attitudes to Protestant Gaelic missions: was it more important for Protestants to spread the Word or to maintain an Anglocentric language policy? T. Barnard, 'Protestants and the Irish language, c. 1675–1725', *JEH* 44 (1993), 243–72; T. Bartlett, *The fall and rise of the Irish nation: the Catholic question 1690–1830* (Dublin, 1992), pp. 25–6; R. Eccleshall, 'Anglican political thought in the century after the Revolution of 1688', in D. G. Boyce, Eccleshall and V. Geoghegan (eds.), *Political thought in Ireland since the seventeenth century* (London, 1993), p. 45. See Leerssen, *Mere Irish*, p. 286, for the anonymous pamphlet *Preaching the gospel in Irish not contrary to law* (1713).

[6] N. Canny, 'Irish, Scottish and Welsh responses to centralisation, c. 1530–c. 1640', in A. Grant and K. Stringer (eds.), *Uniting the kingdom: the making of British history* (London, 1995), p. 160; Connolly, *Religion, law, and power*, p. 114; J. C. Beckett, *The Anglo-Irish tradition* (London, 1976), pp. 39, 52; Bartlett, *Fall and rise*, p. 3; F. G. James, *Lords of the Ascendancy* (Dublin, 1995), pp. 103–4.

[7] Beckett, *Anglo-Irish tradition*, p. 40; Connolly, *Religion, law, and power*, pp. 103, 113; T. Barnard, 'Conclusion. Settling and unsettling Ireland: the Cromwellian and Williamite revolutions', in J. Ohlmeyer (ed.), *Ireland from independence to occupation, 1641–1660* (Cambridge, 1995), p. 282.

fellow Catholic co-religionists, lost their 'Anglo-Irish' identity, but also the most Protestant of the New English: in 1728 Archbishop Boulter wrote of 'the descendants of many of Cromwell's officers and soldiers here being gone off to Popery'.[8]

Consider too the cases of prominent individuals who reshaped Irish identities, such as Archbishop James Ussher of Armagh, the primate of the New English-dominated Church of Ireland in the troubled reign of Charles I. Though a committed Protestant of Calvinist convictions, Ussher came from an Old English background. His family had been in government service in Dublin for about four centuries, and it was this loyal adherence to the establishment which provides the most likely explanation for the conversion of the Usshers to Protestantism. However, traditional Old English links remained: Ussher's mother's brother, Richard Stanihurst (1547–1618), was an eminent Roman Catholic apologist based at Louvain. To complicate matters further, on his forays into polemical church history Ussher invoked a Gaelic ancestry for the Protestant Ireland.[9] The eminent Protestant Irish patriot William Moly-neux (1656–98) came from a similarly chequered background. Borrow-ing the rhetoric of the Old English lawyer Patrick Darcy, Molyneux, whose great-grandfather had come from the English community in Calais to Ireland (via Bruges) during the reign of Elizabeth I,[10] asserted the privileges of the triumphant but beleaguered 'New English' Protestant nation of the 1690s by appropriating the history of the Old English parliament of the later middle ages. Even more unusual, perhaps, was the background of Charles Vallancey (1721–1812), who in the late eight-eenth century championed the distinguished oriental provenance – Phoe-nician via Carthage – of Milesian civilisation. Raised in England by Huguenot parents, Vallancey came to Ireland as an oppressor, a military engineer whose cartographic surveys for fortifications led him into anti-quarian investigations, and eventually to Gaelicist fantasies.[11]

[8] Quoted in Connolly, *Religion, law, and power*, p. 113 n.
[9] R. Buick Knox, *James Ussher, Archbishop of Armagh* (Cardiff, 1967), p. 7; H. Trevor-Roper, 'James Ussher, Archbishop of Armagh', in Trevor-Roper, *Catholics, Anglicans and Puritans* (London, 1987), p. 126; N. Canny, *From Reformation to Restoration: Ireland 1534–1660* (Dublin, 1987), p. 154; G. Parry, *The trophies of time* (Oxford, 1995), pp. 130–1; U. Lotz-Heumann, 'The Protestant interpretation of history in Ireland: the case of James Ussher's *Discourse*', in B. Gordon (ed.), *Protestant history and identity in sixteenth-century Europe* (2 vols., Aldershot, 1996), II, esp. pp. 110, 116.
[10] J. G. Simms, *William Molyneux of Dublin* (ed. P. H. Kelly, Dublin, 1982), pp. 11–12; J. Smyth, '"Like amphibious animals": Irish Protestants, ancient Britons, 1691–1707', *HJ* 36 (1993), 786.
[11] C. O'Halloran, 'Golden ages and barbarous nations: antiquarian debate on the Celtic past in Ireland and Scotland in the eighteenth century' (University of Cambridge Ph.D thesis, 1991), pp. 92–105. For Huguenot and other alien Protestant elements within the Protestant Ascendancy, see F. G. James, *Ireland in the empire 1688–1770* (Cambridge, MA, 1973), pp. 219–20; M. Bence-Jones, *Twilight of the Ascendancy* (London, 1987), p. 15.

There were, however, limits to the processes of self-invention. Although considerable amount of ideological ingenuity went into the fashioning of convenient identities, their fabrication was far from an arbitrary act of will. Patriotic antiquarians were bequeathed the raw material of Irish history, but were able to choose from a range of strategic options, and to exploit polemical opportunities as they presented themselves.

Moreover, Irish politics in the raw did not conform to this pronounced pluralism in historic ethnic affiliation. In the seventeenth century and the classic penal law era of the early eighteenth century, the pluralism which characterised the historical fantasies of legitimation penned by the island's literati was not matched by any real tolerance or burying of prejudices. The vivid imaginations of early modern Ireland's antiquarians produced very little diminution of ethnic or confessional hatred, though they did provide cover for individual and dynastic reinvention. The provisional and artificial dimensions of identity construction did not preclude the emergence of ideologies of ethnic intolerance, nor did they inhibit the execution of ethnically orientated policies of expropriation and persecution. The horrors of ethnic hatred and paranoia coexisted with confused ethnic classification.

Catholic ethnogenesis: the Old English, the Milesians and the pre-Milesian kingdom

Ireland's troubled seventeenth century of civil war and expropriation witnessed the coalescence of the two distinct ethnic Catholic groupings, the Old Irish and the Old English, to create an embattled Irish Catholic nation. In the course of this amalgamation, moreover, Old English antiquaries – together with a continental clerical diaspora of Gaels and Norman–Irish – contributed enormously to elaborating and propagating resilient successor-myths of 'Old Irish' Ireland, namely that an ancient Milesian civilisation in pre-Christian antiquity had been followed by early Christian Ireland's pre-eminence in dark-age Europe as an 'island of saints and scholars'.

Not that the Milesian myth which the Old English refashioned was itself a straightforward history of the Gaelic people. Milesianism also included a polyethnicist dimension embracing the histories of the pre-Milesian peoples of Ireland. The polyethnic framework provided by the medieval chronicle the *Leabhar gabhála*, or 'Book of Invasions',[12] enabled the Gaels to weave the pre-Milesian peoples of Ireland into a potent regnal myth of immemorial Irish national autonomy. This medieval

[12] R. A. S. MacAllister (ed.), *Leabhar gabhála* (5 vols., Dublin, 1938–56).

origin myth remained the standard interpretation of the peopling of Ireland throughout the early modern era. In 1631 a new edition of the Book of Invasions was completed by Micheal Ó Cleirigh, a Franciscan antiquary based at Louvain.[13]

The compound identity of the Gaelic nation embraced not only the Milesian ethnie from whom the Old Irish claimed descent, but also the pre-Milesian peoples of Ireland. The Book of Invasions recognised a series of peoples in Ireland before the coming of the Milesians – the followers of Partholón, Nemedians, Fir-Bolg and Tuatha-Dé-Danaan. Gaels did not discard the pre-Milesian aspect of their heritage. Instead the peoples described in the Book of Invasions were absorbed within Gaelic identity. By embracing the history of the earlier ethnic groups who had settled in Ireland, this greater Milesian past associated the Gaels with the whole history of the island. Pre-Milesian antiquity held the same appeal for Old English Catholics. In the course of the seventeenth century the post-Milesian Old English invaders of the middle ages, the Norman–Irish, finding themselves both marooned as Catholics from their traditional English allegiances and in the Counter-Reformation vanguard of Irish Catholic life, would come to identify with their Old Irish co-religionists, and, as fellow Catholics in adversity, to reshape – and appropriate – the ancient Milesian past. Conversely, the Old English would abandon their commitment to the ancient English constitution (and its extraterritorial embodiment in the medieval Irish legislature).

Catholic antiquaries did not locate the beginnings of the Irish kingdom or of its institutions in Milesian antiquity. Rather they outlined the establishment of political community and indeed of the pentarchical Irish *regnum* in the pre-Milesian era.[14] The origin myth and ancient prescriptive constitution of the 'indigenous' Old Irish nation was a polyethnic hybrid, bearing in some respects marked similarities to the more obviously contrived creole identities of Anglo-Irish colonists. The pre-Milesian past could not be ignored. Attempts to found immemorial rights or privileges in the Gaelic nation needed to address the pre-Milesian history of the institution under discussion if the Milesian position were to be rendered watertight (not least because the New English saw the potential of identifying the pre-Milesians with the ancient Britons).[15] Thus the pre-Milesian past tended to be tacked on to Milesian history, the para-

[13] B. Cunningham, 'Native culture and political change in Ireland, 1580–1640', in C. Brady and R. Gillespie (eds.), *Natives and newcomers* (Dublin, 1986), p. 156; M. Caball, 'A study of intellectual reaction and continuity in Irish bardic poetry during the reigns of Elizabeth I and James I' (University of Oxford DPhil. thesis, 1991), p. 8.

[14] Peter Walsh, *A prospect of the state of Ireland, from the year of the world 1756 to the year of Christ 1652* (London, 1682), 'Preface'; Roderic O'Flaherty, *Ogygia* (1685: trans. James Hely, 2 vols., Dublin, 1793), II, pp. 14–16.   [15] See below, n. 100.

digm established by the Book of Invasions framing the histories of the followers of Partholón, Nemedians, Fir-Bolg, Tuatha-Dé-Danaan and Milesians as the ancient national epos of Ireland. The pre-Milesian peoples had to be absorbed within the Milesian past to lend the weight of prescriptive antiquity and priority of settlement to Gaelic arguments. The desire to assert a regnal identity was an important influence on the construction of a polyethnic Irishness. The origins of the high-kingship were traced back to King Slangy, a Fir-Bolg. The recognised line of Irish high-kings began with eight Fir-Bolg kings and seven of the Tuatha-Dé-Danaan followed by the Milesian lineage of 171 monarchs.[16] The ancient Milesian constitution, like the immemorial common law of the early modern English nation, was conceived in terms of polyethnic continuity.

The Old English, or Norman Irish, retained until the seventeenth century a corporate identity which was ambiguously Anglo-Irish and distinct from that of the Gaelic Old Irish. After several centuries' presence on the island, the Old English were accused of having degenerated – that is, gone native – by New English detractors of the early modern era, who included the jurist Sir John Davies (c. 1570–1626).[17] Yet, however Hibernicised in customs and manners the Old English may have appeared to the new colonists, there were limits to the processes of acculturation. Stanihurst was, in his earlier writings, among the harshest critics of Gaelic barbarity, as were English Catholics, including the Jesuit Edmund Campion.[18] Although the emergence of a common Irish Catholic interest may be detected as far back as the reign of Elizabeth,[19] the religious affiliations of the Old Irish and the Old English were far from identical. Aidan Clarke has demonstrated how the sixteenth-century Anglo-Irishness of the medieval settlers mutated in the early seventeenth century into an Old Englishness whose combination of *politique* allegiance to the Stuart monarchy in the temporal sphere and self-consciously up-to-date Tridentine Catholicism distinguished this community from both New English Anglo-Irish and Old Irish Catholics.[20] The English constitutional component of Old English identity gradually disappeared. Over the course of the seventeenth century, a Catholic nation was to be forged out of the Old Irish and Old English communities, but this was to be a long process and marked by ethnic differences which were quite manifest in religion and politics.[21]

[16] Walsh, *Prospect*, 'A catalogue of the Kings of Ireland', pp. 9, 11.
[17] H. Pawlisch, *Sir John Davies and the conquest of Ireland* (Cambridge, 1985); N. Canny, *Kingdom and colony: Ireland in the Atlantic world, 1560–1800* (Baltimore, 1988), pp. 36–7.
[18] For later ambivalences in Stanihurst's views of the Gaels, see C. Lennon, 'Richard Stanihurst (1547–1618) and Old English identity', *IHS* 21 (1978), 121–43.
[19] Caball, 'Intellectual reaction'.
[20] A. Clarke, 'Colonial identity in early seventeenth-century Ireland', in T. Moody (ed.), *Nationality and the pursuit of national independence* (Historical studies 11, Belfast, 1978).

Until the interrelated crises of the British civil wars of the 1640s, the Old English community retained a proud sense of loyal Englishness, which encouraged rather than inhibited their commitment to Irish parliamentary institutions. The remonstrance compiled in 1640 under the auspices of the Irish House of Commons, a body composed of Old and New English, Catholic as well as Protestant, had proclaimed the rights of the 'loyal and dutiful people of . . . Ireland, being now for the most part derived from British ancestors' to be 'governed according to the municipal and fundamental laws of England'.[22] In a celebrated speech of 1641, Patrick Darcy, an Old English lawyer from Galway educated at the Inns of Court, who was to become a Confederate Catholic during the 1640s, vaunted the identity and concomitant liberties of the king's loyal English subjects of the Irish kingdom:

> to be governed only by the common laws of England, and statutes of force in this kingdom, in the same manner and form, as his majesty's subjects of the kingdom of England, are and ought to be governed by the said common laws, and statutes of force in that kingdom; which of right the subjects of this kingdom do challenge, and make their protestation to be their birthright and best inheritance.[23]

However, this proved to be an ideological cul-de-sac, at least for the Old English. In future this song would be sung only by the Protestant nation in Ireland. The 1640s saw Gothicist constitutionalism displaced by a more overtly Catholic pan-Irishness which did not sacrifice Stuart loyalism, an ideology whose internal tensions were captured by the Confeder-

---

[21] P. Corish, *The Catholic community in the seventeenth and eighteenth centuries* (Dublin, 1981), pp. 25, 39–46, 72; B. Fitzpatrick, *Seventeenth-century Ireland* (Dublin, 1988), pp. 68, 72, 74, 177–8; M. Mac Craith, 'The Gaelic reaction to the Reformation', in S. Ellis and S. Barber (eds.), *Conquest and union: fashioning a British state 1485–1725* (London, 1995), pp. 156–7; Connolly, *Religion, law, and power*, pp. 114–16. For divisions *within* the Old English community in the middle of the seventeenth century where Keating and Darcy deployed similar ancient constitutionalist arguments, but with reference to different ethnic-historical matter, see B. Bradshaw, 'Geoffrey Keating: apologist of Irish Ireland', in Bradshaw, A. Hadfield and W. Maley (eds.), *Representing Ireland: literature and the origins of conflict, 1534–1660* (Cambridge, 1993), pp. 186–7; Leerssen, *Mere Irish*, p. 277; Canny, 'Responses to centralisation', p. 156. However, for the absorption of 'Old English recusancy' through a 'general identification between Gaelic culture and Irish sanctity', see Leerssen, *Mere Irish*, p. 268. For the role of Stuart loyalism in the emergence – not without serious tensions until after 1691 – of Irish Catholic nationhood, see B. Ó Buachalla, 'James our true king: the ideology of Irish royalism in the seventeenth century', in Boyce, Eccleshall and Geoghegan, *Political thought in Ireland*, and Barnard, 'Settling and unsettling Ireland', pp. 289–91.

[22] Quoted in J. Hill, '"Ireland without union": Molyneux and his legacy', in J. Robertson (ed.), *A union for empire* (Cambridge, 1995), pp. 280–1.

[23] *An argument delivered by Patrick Darcy esquire, by the express order of the House of Commons in the parliament of Ireland, 9 Iunii, 1641* (Waterford, 1643), p. 4. See A. Clarke, *The Old English in Ireland 1625–1642* (London, 1966), pp. 145–6.

ate Catholic slogan: 'pro Deo, pro rege, pro patria Hibernia unanimis'.[24]

The Old English would shed their dual Anglo-Irish identity for an alternative hybrid, a Milesian *mythistoire*, refashioned by the Old English antiquary Geoffrey Keating (1570?–1644?) in his widely disseminated manuscript treatise *Foras feasa ar Éirinn* (c. 1634),[25] which celebrated the grafting of the twelfth-century Normans on to the ancient Milesian stem of the Irish nation. Though it has been described as 'a monument to a doomed civilization',[26] Keating's *Foras feasa ar Éirinn* marked a watershed in the emergence of an Irish Catholic identity capable of transcending the ethnic divisions of native Irish and Old English. As Brendan Bradshaw has shown, Keating recognised the importance of explaining the twelfth-century arrival of the Normans not as a conquest which extinguished traditional Irish rights and institutions, but as a *translatio imperii* under papal auspices by which Henry II was made responsible for safeguarding the Catholic faith and the existing privileges of Ireland. Furthermore, as Keating recognised, the Book of Invasions offered a traditional template for reconciliation, showing how the various ancient waves of settlement on the island had contributed to the development of its culture and institutions. The Old English conquest was assimilated to this existing 'multicultural' vision. In the long run Keating's polyethnicist framework allowed the Old English to appropriate the history of Gaelic Ireland as their own.[27]

As elsewhere in the early modern world, the primary domestic function of stories of ethnic origins was to lend historic legitimacy to institutions, both temporal and ecclesiastical. Externally, origin myths were deployed to found or refute claims made by neighbouring kingdoms upon their prized jurisdictions. For example, Geoffrey of Monmouth's claim that Ireland had been a tributary kingdom of a pan-Britannic English *imperium* remained a staple of English political commentary into the seventeenth century.[28] In particular, Irish Catholic scholars – Old English as well as Old Irish – rejected the charge that King Arthur had ever extracted tribute

---

[24] Boyce, *Nationalism in Ireland*, p. 15; Fitzpatrick, *Seventeenth-century Ireland*, p. 178. For divisions between Old Irish Rinuccinians and Old English loyalists which frustrated the religious solidarity of the Catholic Confederation of the 1640s, see Leerssen, *Mere Irish*, pp. 257–9.

[25] Geoffrey Keating, *Foras feasa ar Éirinn* (ed. D. Comyn and P. Dineen, 4 vols., Irish Texts Society, 1902–14).

[26] T. Dunne, 'The Gaelic response to conquest and colonisation: the evidence of the poetry', *Studia Hibernica* 20 (1980), 19.

[27] Bradshaw, 'Keating', esp. pp. 174–6; B. Cunningham, 'Seventeenth-century interpretations of the past: the case of Geoffrey Keating', *IHS* 25 (1986), 116–28.

[28] Geoffrey of Monmouth, *The history of the kings of Britain* (trans. L. Thorpe, Harmondsworth, 1966), pp. 221–2; A. Hadfield, 'Briton and Scythian: Tudor representations of Irish origins', *IHS* 28 (1993), 390–408.

as a suzerain from their Milesian forebears.[29] These antiquaries further denied that English monarchs from Henry II onwards had enjoyed regal sovereignty over Ireland. Rather, they argued, the kings of England from Henry II to Queen Elizabeth I had exercised only a 'lordship' – without any suggestion of conquest – over Ireland.[30] John Lynch (1599?–1673?) also challenged the authenticity of the supposed papal bulls transferring sovereignty to the kings of England.[31] From the reign of James VI and I, however, as Irish royalist antiquaries boasted, matters were different. For James and his descendants came of Milesian blood through the Scottish royal line. Coincidentally, it was only under the early Stuarts that Ireland had been properly subdued by the British. Fortuitously, sovereignty remained with the ancient Milesian kings and the Stuarts had justly compelled the full allegiance of their Milesian kinsmen in Ireland. The Gaelic antiquary and champion of Irish royalism, Roderic O'Flaherty (1629–1718), argued in his *Ogygia* (1685) that only in 1603 was Ireland formally subordinated to a mainland-based monarchy. Significantly, Ireland had never submitted to the English nation or legislature, 'nor ever could submit to be governed by any prince save those descended from the line of her ancient kings'.[32]

Similarly, there was a dispute between Scottish and Irish historians as to whether the Scots colony of Dalriada had acknowledged a tributary status to the Milesian kingdom of the Irish motherland. Peter Walsh denied the story found in the work of Scots historian George Buchanan that King Gregory of Scotland had conquered Ireland in 875.[33] Irish historians also asserted that the Scottish nation in Scotland – 'Scotia Minor' – had been tributary to the Hibernian parent-race.[34]

Patriotic antiquaries rejoiced that Ireland had enjoyed well over 2,000 years of regal sovereignty. O'Flaherty boasted that the Stuarts derived their greatest glory from their Milesian ancestry, and trumpeted the superior antiquity of the kingdom of Ireland to the kingdoms of England and Scotland. It was the antiquity of the Milesian throne, he claimed,

---

[29] Keating, *Foras feasa ar Éirinn*, I, pp. 13–17; John Lynch, *Cambrensis eversus* (1662: trans. M. Kelly, 3 vols., Dublin, 1848–51), II, pp. 81–5; Walsh, *Prospect*, pp. 342–4, 396. Keating also denied the claims that the Irish had been subjected to the Saxons and that the Church of Ireland had been subordinate to Canterbury since the coming of Augustine: *Foras feasa ar Éirinn*, I, pp. 25, 51–3.

[30] Lynch, *Cambrensis eversus*, II, ch. 24, esp. pp. 517, 523, 525–7.   [31] *Ibid.*, II, p. 567.

[32] Roderic O'Flaherty, *Ogygia*, 'Dedication', I, p. xiv; Lynch, *Cambrensis eversus*, III, p. 53.

[33] Walsh, *Prospect*, p. 373.

[34] Keating, *Foras feasa ar Éirinn*, I, pp. 13–15; III, pp. 95–7; Lynch, *Cambrensis eversus*, II, pp. 183, 227–9; Walsh, *Prospect*, pp. 16–18, 23–4. For the persistence of this argument, see Hugh MacCurtin, *A brief discourse in vindication of the antiquity of Ireland* (Dublin, 1717), pp. 3, 166; Charles O'Conor, *A dissertation on the first migrations, and final settlement of the Scots in North-Britain* (Dublin, 1766), p. 7; Theophilus O'Flanagan, *Deirdri* (Dublin, 1808), 'Preliminary discourse', pp. 10–11.

which gave the Stuarts precedence among the crowned heads of Europe.[35]

In Catholic Ireland the Milesian past also served another primary function. The Gaels of Ireland, and the Hibernicised Old English, needed to repudiate the charges of barbarism which had first been heaped on their culture by Giraldus Cambrensis and which were later reprised by sixteenth- and seventeenth-century New English colonisers.[36] In their efforts to recover the historical origins of the Irish nation, Catholic antiquaries, Old English as well as Old Irish, endowed Ireland with a powerful sense of identity rooted in the idea of an ancient Gaelic civilisation. Some writers answered these calumnies by projecting the legend of dark-age Ireland as an island of saints and scholars.[37] For example, the work of the Four Masters in constructing a national past for the Gaelic Irish in the seventeenth century was subordinate to the imperative for a patriotic hagiography.[38] A large part of the effort on this front involved the repatriation of many of the Irish saints and scholars appropriated for Scotland by the 'notorious hagioclept' Thomas Dempster (who had exploited confusions surrounding the geographical term Scotia).[39] Other writers, including Philip O'Sullevan Beare, Keating and, most famously, John Lynch in *Cambrensis eversus* (1662), saw that there were secular aspects of ancient Gaelic civilisation of which the nation could be proud, including law, medicine, commerce and the arts.[40]

Nevertheless, Gaeldom was neither promoted on its own terms, nor defended in its totality. Keating, for example, argued that foreign critics applied the wrong standard of judgement to Irish culture: they were oblivious of the refined life of the higher echelons of Gaelic society, and what they denigrated was in fact the culture of the common people. Keating objected fiercely to the assumption that the culture of the aristocratic elite was barbaric, but he did not insist on a wholesale rehabilitation of Gaeldom. The reputation of the lower segment of Gaelic society was a

---

[35] Roderic O'Flaherty, *Ogygia*, I, p. 56. See also Thomas Comerford, *The history of Ireland* (Dublin, 1755), 'Preface', p. vii; *A letter from Dr. Anthony Raymond, to my Lord Inchiquin, giving some account of the monarchs and ancient state of Ireland* (Dublin, 1723), p. 10; Sylvester O'Halloran, *A general history of Ireland* (2 vols., London, 1778), II, p. 68, for the Irish basis of English claims to precedence at Constance.

[36] See Leerssen, *Mere Irish*, pp. 277–8, for Stephen White's manuscript treatise *Apologia pro Hibernia adversus Cambrensis calumnias* (c. 1615: ed. M. Kelly, Dublin, 1849) and John Lynch, *Cambrensis eversus* (1662).   [37] Leerssen, *Mere Irish*, pp. 259, 265–6.

[38] *Ibid.*, p. 267; Ó Buachalla, 'James our true king', p. 21.

[39] W. Reeves, *The Culdees of the British Islands* (Dublin, 1864), p. 68; M. Mac Craith, 'Gaelic Ireland and the Renaissance', in G. Williams and R. Jones (eds.), *The Celts and the Renaissance* (Cardiff, 1990), p. 78.

[40] T. O'Donnell (ed.), *Selections from the Zoilomastix of Phillip O'Sullivan Beare* (Dublin, 1960), bk V, ret. vi–vii; Keating, *Foras feasa ar Éirinn*, I, pp. 39–41, 67–79; Lynch, *Cambrensis eversus*, II, pp. 166–93, 272–9, 363–75.

matter of some indifference to Keating.[41] His view was typical of early modern Europe, a world where a commitment to hierarchy cut across ethnic solidarity, and where an international caste of scholars had not yet begun to value popular cultures.[42]

There was a political dimension to the argument for ancient Milesian civility. Keating showed how under the lawgiving monarch Ollamh Fodhla a parliament, or *feis*, had been established at Tara in which the various learned orders of Irish society had been represented.[43] In the late seventeenth and early eighteenth centuries there was a royalist–Jacobite version of the argument for Milesian civility. Antiquaries such as O'Flaherty and Hugh MacCurtin (1680?–1755) answered the English charge of Gaelic anarchy by envisaging an ancient Irish kingdom blessed with institutional regularity and a due subordination of ranks.[44] They were especially keen to point out that the Irish pentarchy bore no resemblance to the ramshackle and anarchic Anglo-Saxon heptarchy. O'Flaherty contended that one could not 'produce an instance in all Europe of a more ancient, perfect or better established form of government than that of Ireland; where the sovereign power was concentrated in one king, and the subaltern power gradually descending to the lowest class of men, represents and exactly resembles, the hierarchy of celestial choirs'.[45]

In the middle of the eighteenth century the Gaelic past was reimagined by a new generation of 'enlightened' Catholic antiquarians. In 1756 the Catholic Committee was established by Thomas Wyse (fl. c. 1700–70), Dr John Curry (d. 1780) and the antiquarian Charles O'Conor of Belanagare (1710–90) to campaign for a relaxation of the anti-Catholic penal laws.[46] To succeed in its aims the Catholic Committee had first to challenge a well-established set of Protestant prejudices, for the penal laws had been introduced over a thirty-year period from the 1690s in response to the anxieties of Ireland's ruling Protestant minority.[47] Protestant worries about the numerical dominance of Ireland's Catholics were far from chimerical, given popular memories of the 'massacres' which had accompanied the Catholic rebellion of 1641 and the sufferings of the siege of Londonderry during the Jacobite uprising of 1689. A culture of Protestant defensiveness had grown up around these traumatic episodes, fed by bestselling works such as Sir John Temple's *The Irish rebellion* (1646), a one-sided account of the events of 1641, and Archbishop

---

[41] Keating, *Foras feasa ar Éirinn*, I, pp. 5–7, 55–9; Ó Buachalla, 'James our true king', p. 18.
[42] See P. Burke, *Popular culture in early modern Europe* (London, 1978).
[43] Keating, *Foras feasa ar Éirinn*, II, p. 133.
[44] Roderic O'Flaherty, *Ogygia*, I, p. 86; MacCurtin, *Brief discourse*, esp. pp. 61–2.
[45] Roderic O'Flaherty, *Ogygia*, I, pp. 51–2.
[46] C. Leighton, *Catholicism in a Protestant kingdom* (Houndmills, 1994), p. 69.
[47] Bartlett, *Fall and rise*, ch. 2.

William King's *The state of the Protestants of Ireland under the late king James's government* (1691), both of which went through numerous editions.[48] The 23rd of October, the anniversary of the 1641 rising, became a focal date in the Protestant calendar, a day devoted to anti-Catholic sermonising.[49] In addition to demonising seventeenth-century Catholic atrocities, Protestant propagandists also rehearsed the traditional English attack on Gaelic barbarity, which provided an additional reason to fear the Irish.[50] Indeed, appropriating the Old English past for Protestant purposes, Bishop Dopping calculated that the contumacious Gaels had launched twenty-two general and forty-four local rebellions against the English since 1172.[51]

The Catholic Committee devised a series of strategies to overcome these various prejudices. For a start, the Catholic Committee pointed out that the early modern wars of religion had run their course. In their *Observations on the Popery laws* (1771), Curry and O'Conor endorsed the *politique* tolerationist policies of post-Revolutionary Britain. Civil government might flourish free from domestic broils, eighteenth-century experience had shown, so long as all parties and confessions in a nation could unite 'in one creed of political faith'. The authors then set out to prove from pre-Reformation English history that Roman Catholics, in spite of slurs against the coincidence of popery and arbitrary rule, were capable of passing a test of 'civil fidelity' set by Hanoverian whiggery: 'Magna Carta itself, annual elections of our representatives, and the great sanctions of the British constitution, were fought for, and obtained, by our Popish ancestors.'[52]

But could Ireland's 'barbaric' Gaelic Catholics pass such a test? Would Ireland's Protestants be secure if they dismantled the protective rampart of penal legislation? Were not the superstitious and submissive Catholics of Ireland addicted to Jacobitism and absolutism? Could the Hanoverian regime trust the loyalty of their reluctant Irish Catholic subjects? Curry tackled the recent Irish past, producing a revisionist account of the rebellion of 1641 which explained away the Protestant mythology of the massacres.

However, the contested seventeenth-century past continued to smoulder as a subject of sectarian bickering. There was limited potential in the

[48] *Ibid.*, pp. 7, 13.
[49] T. Barnard, 'The uses of 23 October 1641 and Irish Protestant celebrations', *EHR* 106 (1991), 889–920.
[50] John Temple, *The Irish rebellion* (London, 1646), pp. 2–3, 5, 8–9; William King, *The state of the Protestants of Ireland* (3rd edn, London, 1692), pp. 35–7.
[51] Connolly, *Religion, law, and power*, p. 264.
[52] John Curry and Charles O'Conor, *Observations on the Popery laws* (Dublin, 1771), pp. 14–16, 22–3, 29, 33.

controversial history of the recent civil wars to build bridges between Catholic and Protestant, or to show Gaelic Catholics in a peaceable and civilised light. Hence the main prong of O'Conor's strategy lay in pressing into service the myth of ancient Milesian civilisation conjured up by Keating and Lynch in the seventeenth century, transforming it, in the words of John Hutchinson, into 'a *philosophe*'s dream'.[53] O'Conor would not champion the Milesian ancestors of the Gaelic Irish for their Celtic particularities, but for their conformity to an enlightened whiggish ideal.

O'Conor answered Protestant slurs about Gaelic Catholic politics by demonstrating the commitment of Irish Catholics to eighteenth-century whiggish values. The Catholics of Ireland were heirs of an ancient Milesian civilisation of commerce, science and sound constitutional government. O'Conor imported into the ancient Milesian constitution the shibboleths of English whig constitutionalism. He emphasised the triadic balance found in the orderly triennial meetings of the ancient Irish *feis* at Tara, where the Commons had been represented in the estate of artificers. The ancient Milesians had been governed by a regular constitutional mechanism. Moreover, O'Conor suggested that in the practices of tanistry the mixed monarchy of the ancient Milesians had been subject to processes of election akin to English Revolution principles. Far from Gaelic Ireland having been a scene of anarchy and barbarity prior to the arrival of the Old English, its ancient constitution appeared to foreshadow the English parliamentary tradition. The modern descendants of the ancient Milesians could surely be expected to conform to the mores of Hanoverian Britain.[54]

Not only were the ancient Milesians promoted as proto-whigs, but also as a maritime race of merchants. O'Conor's antiquarian efforts were complemented by those of Sylvester O'Halloran (1728–1807), a surgeon with opthalmic interests,[55] whose vision of a polite and commercial Milesian past embraced the values of Ireland's emergent Catholic middle orders.[56] Commerce was now a vital element in the case for Gaelic civility.

---

[53] J. Hutchinson, *The dynamics of cultural nationalism: the Gaelic revival and the creation of the Irish nation state* (London, 1987), p. 58.

[54] Charles O'Conor, *Dissertations on the history of Ireland* (Dublin, 1766 edn), pp. 45–65; Sylvester O'Halloran, *An introduction to the study of the history and antiquities of Ireland* (London, 1772), pp. 103, 107, 150–1; J. Hill, 'Popery and Protestantism, civil and religious liberty: the disputed lessons of Irish history, 1690–1812', *P+P* 118 (1988), 104–6; C. Kidd, 'Gaelic antiquity and national identity in Enlightenment Ireland and Scotland', *EHR* 109 (1994), 1202; Leighton, *Catholicism in a Protestant kingdom*, pp. 101, 104–5; Comerford, *History of Ireland*, p. 274.

[55] J. B. Lyons, 'Sylvester O'Halloran, 1728–1807', *ECI* 4 (1989), 65–74.

[56] M. Wall, 'The rise of a Catholic middle class in eighteenth-century Ireland' and 'The position of Catholics in mid-eighteenth-century Ireland', both in Wall, *Catholic Ireland in the eighteenth century: collected essays of Maureen Wall* (ed. G. O'Brien, Dublin, 1989).

O'Halloran proclaimed that Ireland 'was very early an extensive commercial country'.[57] Nor had Irish commerce lacked an enabling framework of suitable laws and institutions. In answer to Davies's famous charges that Gaelic Ireland had lacked an adequate framework of laws, O'Halloran claimed that Irish feudal tenures, far from being a Plantagenet import, were of Milesian origin.[58] After all, he argued, were not the key terms of feudal jurisprudence of obvious Gaelic provenance? The parliament at Tara had also been supplemented by the work of *aonachs*, auxiliary assemblies concerned with trade and commerce.[59] The maritime Irish had developed the sciences of navigation and astronomy, their learning institutionalised in great Druid universities at Tara, and at Emania, Cruachan and Carman, the royal cities of the provinces of Ulster, Connaught and Munster.[60]

O'Conor and O'Halloran also massaged the Irish religious inheritance to meet immediate ecclesiastical needs. They endowed Gaelic Christianity with a mild cisalpine hue. The Christian message had come to Ireland from Asiatic disciples of John, not directly from St Peter.[61] O'Conor argued that the establishment of the ancient Irish church 'upon the true principles and firm foundation of primitive Christianity' had involved 'no collision with the civil power'.[62] O'Halloran took a similar view. Not only had the ancient Gaels been an enlightened, tolerant people, but they had also received Christianity as a civil religion which complemented their refinement: 'Our ancestors, humane and polished, admitted of no persecution for conscience sake. The power of judging of the human heart, they left to the sole judge of it, the Almighty; and [King] Loagaire, though an idolater, as he found in the new religion no tenets dangerous to the state, did not oppose it.'[63] O'Halloran had few doubts that such an ethical religion – indeed, a brand of primitive Christianity resembling rational stoicism – had encountered little trouble in winning adherents: 'Preaching to a learned and polished people a doctrine so elevated and pure as that of Christ, a doctrine which taught its votaries to rule and govern their passions, not the passions them . . . needed neither miracles from above, nor restraining penal laws on earth to support it.'[64] Thereafter, although Milesian Christianity had exhibited a moderate Catholic temper in worship and doctrine, the Irish church had remained beyond the immediate reach of Rome. Until the middle of the twelfth century the Milesian Irish, stationed on the far western fringe of Christendom, had enjoyed an

[57] Sylvester O'Halloran, *General history*, II, p. 145.   [58] *Ibid.*, II, pp. 143–7.
[59] *Ibid.*, II, p. 34. See O'Conor, *Dissertations on the antient history of Ireland* (Dublin, 1753), p. 134.   [60] Sylvester O'Halloran, *Introduction*, p. 172.
[61] Sylvester O'Halloran, *General history*, II, pp. 7–8, 14–15, 17, 23.
[62] O'Conor, *Dissertations* (1753), p. 145.   [63] Sylvester O'Halloran, *Introduction*, p. 182.
[64] Sylvester O'Halloran, *General history*, II, p. 20.

autonomous Catholicism, a conformity in faith and discipline unsupported by any institutional connection with Rome.[65]

Protestant ethnogenesis: the New English, the Old English constitution and the Old Irish church

The bulk of the Protestant landed class were descended from the sixteenth- and seventeenth-century settlers, the expropriating colonial caste. Although in the early part of the eighteenth century numerous representatives of the Old English gentry conformed to preserve their estates, less than 40 per cent of Ascendancy families came of Gaelic or Norman–Irish stock.[66] The New English were never quite secure with their genuine Tudor and Stuart pedigree as 'Irishmen' of recent vintage. Instead, they felt a compulsion to poach the medieval colonial origins of the Old English, now dignified with age. In the ecclesiastical sphere, Irish Protestants, supported moreover in the eighteenth century by their English-born bishops such as William Nicolson of Derry and Francis Hutchinson of Down and Connor, delved back even further to appropriate for the Church of Ireland the ancient and renowned history of the early Celtic church. This quest for prescriptive legitimacy led to an undervaluing of the authentic historical identity of the recent waves of New English colonists. In its place the New English and their Anglo-Irish descendants of the eighteenth century invented alternative identities which supplied a historical legitimacy of much greater authority than could be derived from the genuine history of New English settlement. These largely bogus identities conferred on the New English community a longer and more intimate historical association with Ireland than it had in practice enjoyed. As a result the New English and Anglo-Irish nations, without dropping their distinctive Englishness – which distinguished them from the other ethnic groups and confessions in Ireland and also provided useful ideological ammunition in their relations with the motherland – came to adopt a more Hibernian identity.

Not only were the historical identities projected by the Protestant Irish nation largely spurious, New Englishness and Anglo-Irishness were Janus-faced. The intellectual leaders of the New English community painted distinct ecclesiastical and political aspects to their ethnic identity. Thus the logic and coherence of identity construction yielded to political and ecclesiastical imperatives as New English literati performed the ethnohistorical splits. Broadly speaking, the Protestant nation in Ireland

---

[65] *Ibid.*, II, pp. 28–9.
[66] Bartlett, *Fall and rise*, p. 23; Beckett, *Anglo-Irish tradition*, pp. 38–40; James, *Lords of the Ascendancy*, pp. 52, 99–100; Bence-Jones, *Twilight of the Ascendancy*, p. 14.

appropriated its constitutional identity from the history of the Old English settler community of the twelfth century, while its ecclesiastical identity drew on the history of the Celtic church established in dark-age Ireland. The ecclesiastical identity of the New English was in this vital respect congruent neither with the reality of their post-Reformation settlement and colonisation, nor with their appropriation in the constitutional sphere of the twelfth-century Norman–Irish heritage.

There was no acknowledgement of the obvious problem of ethnic discontinuity – that, although religion and ethnicity were incommensurable categories, there was very little genuine ancestry linking Gaelic Christians and modern Irish Protestants. Nevertheless, a further complicating factor – the association of the New English not only with the Gothic peoples of medieval England, but also with their more distant ancient British compatriots – offered a way of consolidating the English identity of Ireland's original Celtic Christianity. Just as early modern English identity was polyethnic, resting on both British and Saxon phases of the English past, so the New English and later the Anglo-Irish Protestant nations drew on both British and Saxon elements of their English heritage. The affiliation with the ancient Britons reinforced the otherwise absurd appropriation by the New English and Anglo-Irish of the Gaelic founding era of the Church of Ireland. Since the ancient British past was an acknowledged component of English and hence of Anglo-Irish history, it provided a bridge of sorts between Gaelic ecclesiastical history and the New English nation which appropriated it.[67] Thus the Protestant community in Ireland, whose political identity was bound up with the Gothic heritage of liberty associated with the migration of the Old English in the twelfth century, subscribed to an ecclesiastical identity with strong Celtic foundations, both in the apostolic purity of the British church as transmitted to Ireland, and in the non-papal uncorrupted religion of the ancient Milesians before the Catholicisation of the high middle ages. New English and Anglo-Irish identities were protean and fabulous, but also opportunistic and self-serving. Without these largely spurious and somewhat inconsistent extensions to their shallow roots in the Irish historical experience, the New English nation would have been disabled from waging effective ideological warfare against its political and religious competitors.

The most exotic and outrageous forms of New English ethnicist appropriation occurred initially in the ecclesiastical sphere. Protestantism was not a natural outgrowth from the native textures of sixteenth-century Irish church, society or culture. As Alan Ford points out, the Irish

[67] See above, ch. 4.

Reformation was 'conceived in England and imposed upon Ireland as an exercise in dynastic politics'.[68] The main threat to the Irish Protestant nation came from the assault of Roman Catholic polemicists both on Protestantism in general and on the particular legitimacy of the reformed Church of Ireland. How were Irish Protestants to respond to the likes of the Jesuit controversialist Henry Fitzsimon (1566–1643) who claimed Roman Catholicism as the original expression of Christianity in Ireland?[69] Obviously, the Church of Ireland required a myth of indigenous foundations.

The importation of clergy from England and the establishment in 1591 of Trinity College, Dublin, fostered an Irish Protestant intelligentsia capable of inventing and sustaining an Irish Protestant apologetic which would not only defend the general principles of the European Reformation but would also secure the Church of Ireland in particular against the various arguments put forward by Irish Catholic polemicists.[70] A lively cohort of Protestant propagandists emerged to counter Catholic charges of Protestant illegitimacy. The Church of Ireland's team of controversialists included John Rider (1562–1632), George Synge (1594–1653) and Joshua Hoyle (d. 1654).[71] However, the foremost champion of the Church of Ireland was Ussher, who would eventually become its primate.

Although the crucial theatres of ecclesiastical pamphlet warfare were Scripture and patristics, Ussher recognised that the early history of Irish Christianity in its foundational era had the potential to confer a particular aura of legitimacy on the Church of Ireland. Ussher began a public epistle to Sir Christopher Sibthorp (d. 1632), a judge and active lay supporter of the Irish Protestant cause, with a persuasive case for an Irish historical apologetic:

I confess, I somewhat incline to be of your mind, that if unto the authorities drawn out of scriptures and fathers (which are common to us with others) a true discovery were added of that religion which anciently was professed in this kingdom, it might prove a special motive to induce my poor countrymen to consider a little better of the old and true way from whence they have hitherto been misled.[72]

Why was the 'ancient' profession of Irish Christianity so important? Tradition was the watchword of both Roman Catholic and Protestant

[68] A. Ford, *The Protestant Reformation in Ireland, 1590–1641* (Frankfurt, 1985), p. 9.
[69] Henry Fitzsimon, *A Catholike confutation of M. Iohn Riders clayme of antiquitie* (Roan [Douai], 1608).   [70] Ford, *Protestant Reformation*, pp. 218–19.   [71] *Ibid.*
[72] James Ussher, *A discourse of the religion anciently professed by the Irish and British*, 'Epistle to Sir Christopher Sibthorp', in Ussher, *Whole works* (ed. C. Elrington and J. Todd, Dublin, 17 vols., 1847–64), IV, p. 237.

controversialists. Supporters of Catholicism argued that their form of Christianity had the sanction of tradition. It was necessary to refute the Catholic position 'that their religion of Popery, is of great and long continuance in the world', and to answer Catholic slurs that Protestantism was a novel heresy of the sixteenth century.[73] In an age where so much ideological energy was invested in legitimation by tradition, it is scarcely surprising that there was considerable theorising about the distinguishing characteristics of the essential core of authentic Christian tradition.[74] Synge, who privileged the doctrinal core of Christianity over Catholic tradition, maintained that genuine tradition had to be apostolic and grounded in Scripture. 'The succession of true doctrine in the church' culminated in Protestantism; on the other hand, as 'for Popish traditions we respect them not, because they were never delivered by the apostles. They are of a later invention.'[75]

Local ecclesiastical antiquities constituted a vital adjunct of the debate over Christian tradition. The importance attached to the history of the foundational eras of national churches was also linked to the crucial role played by primitive Christian antiquity within the overall scheme of Protestant apologetic. Protestants laid claim to the best and purest antiquity in their battles with Catholic apologists. This meant the history of Christian missions in the early Christian centuries. Protestant antiquarians aimed to demonstrate instead that Protestantism was a return to the first principles of a Christianity undefiled by Romanist corruptions. This in turn put the burden of apology back on to Roman propagandists who had to defend their church against the charge that Roman corruptions were the unwarranted novelties within the Christian tradition. Within every national reformed tradition there was a strong ideological impetus towards ancient ecclesiastical history which would provide particular local case studies to support the basic Protestant contention that reformed religion rather than modern Catholicism better represented the original model of Christian worship, doctrine and ecclesiastical polity.[76]

In the case of Irish Protestantism there was an additional need to appropriate the nation's ecclesiastical antiquities. The Protestant Church of Ireland was keen to downplay any sense that it was a sixteenth-century Anglican transplantation. Protestant churchmen needed to demonstrate that the established Church of Ireland was not an alien importation that owed its status to the colonial relationship that existed between England

---

[73] Christopher Sibthorp, *A friendly advertisement to the pretended Catholickes of Ireland* (Dublin, 1622), p. 35.   [74] *Ibid.*, 'Preface' and p. 35.

[75] George Synge, *A reioynder to the reply published by the Iesuites under the name of William Malone* (Dublin, 1632), pp. 10, 26.

[76] See the local historical arguments for the English and Scottish Protestant churches outlined above in chs. 5 and 6.

and Ireland. Implicit in Ussherian argument was the need to disentangle the Protestant Church of Ireland from *modern* Anglicanism (though not from the historic Celtic Christianity of the ancient Britons). Rather it was an indigenous and historic restoration of the true native tradition. In substance, if not in name, Protestantism was the historic religion of Ireland.[77]

Ussher's primary aim was to establish institutional, doctrinal and sacramental continuities, with scant regard for the ethnic implications of his ideological construct. Nevertheless, this Old English Protestant did establish a plausible case for New English appropriation of ancient Gaelic religious history. With considerable sophistication Ussher established the ancient Hibernian credentials of Irish Protestantism, yet also managed to accord a leading role in the first Irish missions to the apostolic church of the Britons, the forerunner of its modern sister, the Church of England. The connected histories of the ancient Britons and early Gaels not only provided particular local evidence to reinforce Ussher's interpretation of the church universal and its decline from primitive purity, but also conferred on the Protestant Church of Ireland a compelling foundation charter.[78]

Ussher was concerned to highlight the novelty of Roman Catholic doctrine and worship. In the particular context of Ireland's ecclesiastical polity, he was keen to demolish the assertion of the Roman Catholic Church to be the legitimate and historic institutional expression of Christianity in the island.[79] In particular, Ussher brought Ireland within the frame of his apocalyptic scheme of ecclesiastical corruption in Europe after the thousand-year binding of Satan in the first Christian millennium. The corruption of Irish Christianity was largely a twelfth-century phenomenon.[80] The 'reforms' of St Malachy had put paid to the uncorrupted primitive Christianity of the Irish, and had firmly established the Irish church's subordination to Rome.[81] Nor had there been any legatine presence in Ireland until the appointment of Gille in the twelfth century.[82] Above all, it appeared that the early Gaelic Christians had followed the Protestant pattern in worship and doctrine. Had they not received the Eucharist 'in both kinds', wine as well as wafer, and adhered to a predes-

---

[77] A. Ford, 'Dependent or independent? The Church of Ireland and its colonial context, 1536–1649', *Seventeenth Century* 10 (1995), 163–87.

[78] Parry, *Trophies of time*, pp. 136–41; J. McCafferty, 'St Patrick for the Church of Ireland: James Ussher's *Discourse*', *Bullán* 3 (1997–8), 92. For the 'British' context of Ussher's researches into ecclesiastical history, see K. Sharpe, *Sir Robert Cotton* (Oxford, 1979), pp. 33–4.   [79] Parry, *Trophies of time*, p. 131.

[80] Ford, *Protestant Reformation*, pp. 221–2.

[81] Ussher, *Discourse*, IV, pp. 274–5, 298; Knox, *Ussher*, p. 104; Ford, 'Dependent or independent?', 171.   [82] Ussher, *Discourse*, IV, p. 319.

tinarian theology?[83] On the other hand, Ussher did not deny the reality of a strong Catholic tradition in Ireland. Instead, he argued that the Celtic founders of the Irish church, whom he claimed as 'our ancestors', had been to all intents and purposes close kindred of modern Irish Protestants:

the religion professed by the ancient bishops, priests, monks and other Christians in this land, was for substance the very same with that which now by public authority is maintained therein, against the foreign doctrine brought in thither in later times by the Bishop of Rome's followers. I speak of the more substantial points of doctrine, that are in controversy betwixt the Church of Rome and us at this day; by which only we must judge, whether of both sides hath departed from the religion of our ancestors.[84]

However, there are further complications to this story. Scholars today are still divided over Ussher's attitude to the language of these 'ancestors'. William Bedell (1571–1642), Bishop of Kilmore, clearly made strenuous but unavailing efforts towards evangelising in the vernacular (to the extent that he embarked upon a Gaelic translation of the Old Testament), a mission revitalised later in the seventeenth century under the auspices of the Calvinist Narcissus Marsh (1638–1713), who would succeed to the archbishopric of Armagh in 1703; by contrast, Ussher, in other respects committed to the spirit of Protestantism and willing to assume the philological burdens imposed by Biblicism, was less enthusiastic – at best – about establishing a Gaelic Protestantism where word and worship were available in the native tongue.[85]

On the other hand, there were clear limits to Ussher's desire to preside over an Anglicising church. Although the ancient British past was important to Ussher's argument for the similar Protestant traditions indigenous to Britain and Ireland, he was far from suggesting that the Church of Ireland was subject to the Church of England. He stoutly resisted any notion that the Anglican primate enjoyed a patriarchate over the British Isles. Anglican–Hibernian conformity should not infringe the distinctive traditions and identity of the historic Church of Ireland. Witness Ussher's stance against the attempt to make the Church of Ireland adopt the

[83] *Ibid.*, IV, chs. 2–4; William Nicolson, *The Irish historical library* (Dublin, 1724), p. 68; Knox, *Ussher*, p. 159; A. Capern, 'The Caroline church: James Ussher and the Irish dimension', *HJ* 39 (1996), 80–1.   [84] Ussher, 'Epistle to Sibthorp', pp. 238–9.
[85] Parry, *Trophies of time*, p. 151; R. F. Foster, *Modern Ireland 1600–1972* (1988: Harmondsworth, 1989), p. 49 n.; Barnard, 'Protestants and the Irish language', esp. 248–9; J. Leerssen, 'Archbishop Ussher and Gaelic culture', *Studia Hibernica* 22–3 (1982–3), 50–8; Leerssen, *Mere Irish*, pp. 283–5; Ford, *Protestant Reformation*, p. 141; Connolly, *Religion, law, and power*, p. 294. Despite the imperative to make Scripture available in the vernacular, the Reformation went hand-in-hand with Anglicisation throughout the British Isles; see V. Durkacz, *The decline of the Celtic languages* (Edinburgh, 1983).

Anglican articles in 1634. Ussher was not only suspicious of Laudianism for its departure from Calvinism, but also for its strategy to enforce ecclesiastical uniformity within the Stuart realms.[86] Moreover, Ussher's protégé Sir James Ware (1594–1666) continued Ussher's antiquarian interest in the ancient Gaelic church, including the argument for the similarities and close connections of ancient British and Irish Christians. In the long run, it was through Ware, whose works appeared in English translation between 1739 and 1746, that Ussher's influence would be felt upon the hobby-horsical Gaelicism of the late eighteenth-century Ascendancy.[87]

The crisis of the Caroline regime also witnessed a vigorous assertion of New English political identity which bore marked similarities to the amphibious Old English patriotism of Darcy. In a speech of 1641 asserting the privileges of the Irish parliament, Audley Mervyn (d. 1675), a recent colonist from Hampshire, began by discussing the ancient English constitution, referring back not only to the institutions of the Anglo-Saxons – invoked as ancestors, *majores nostri* – but also to the laws of 441 BC granted by the ancient British king Dunwallo Molmutius. The privileges of the Irish parliament were indeed 'of most ancient birth and extraction', being the immemorial rights inherited from the parliaments of the Britons and Saxons (the Norman Conquest notwithstanding), and guaranteed to Ireland in the reign of King John, who in the twelfth year of his reign went to Ireland, where 'attended with the advice of grave and learned men in the laws (whom he carried with him) *de communi omnium de Hybernia consensu*, which is to be understood of parliament, ordained and established that Ireland should be governed by the laws of England'. The Irish legislature, therefore, enjoyed the 'title of coheir with the parliament of England'.[88] English history validated Irish constitutionalism.

In the aftermath of the civil wars, this 'Anglo-Irish' position, coined by the Old English, but now adopted by the New English colonists, would become the sole monopoly of the New English Protestant community. Significantly, a key figure in the appropriation of this Anglo-Irish constitutionalism was William Domville, father-in-law of the future patriot

---

[86] Ford, 'Dependent or independent?', 176–80; A. Milton, *Catholic and Reformed: the Roman and Protestant churches in English Protestant thought 1600–1640* (Cambridge, 1995), p. 339 n.

[87] Walter Harris (ed.), *The whole works of Sir James Ware concerning Ireland* (1739–46: 2 vols., Dublin, 1764); Leerssen, *Mere Irish*, pp. 56–7, 322; Parry, *Trophies of time*, pp. 153–6.

[88] *Captaine Audley Mervin's speech, delivered in the upper house to Lords in parliament, May 24, 1641 concerning the judicature of the high court of parliament* (London, 1641), pp. 4–6, 8–9.

William Molyneux.[89] The dominant Protestant elite engrossed not only the institutional fabric of Irish nationhood, such as church and parliament, but also began to claim exclusive title to be seen as the Irish political nation. Two main strategies were advanced by the New English Protestants during the eras of Restoration and Revolution. There was a political argument to the effect that in the twelfth century the indigenous inhabitants had been conquered by King Henry II of England, and that only the unconquered English settlers of Ireland could enjoy political rights as the Irish nation.[90] However, while this argument strengthened the arm of the ascendancy over the Irish peasantry, it threatened to undermine the status of the Irish parliament relative to the English crown. In 1667 Arthur Annesley (1614–86) put the case that, although Ireland was a 'conquered nation', it should 'not be so treated, for the conquerors inhabit there'.[91] This ambiguous argument from conquest coexisted with the genealogical claim that most of the people of Ireland – in defiance of the realities of demography and the uncomfortable fact that the Old English remained mostly Catholic – were of English descent.[92] 'Four parts in five of the inhabitants in Ireland are of English extraction', calculated Richard Cox (1650–1733), 'and have settled there since the conquest, and by virtue of it.'[93] Molyneux appeared oblivious of the existence of another community with a better title to an exclusive possession of Irish identity:

'tis manifest that the great body of the present people of Ireland, are the progeny of the English and Britons, that from time to time have come over into this kingdom; and there remains but a mere handful of the ancient Irish at this day; I may say, not one in a thousand.[94]

However, Molyneux was unusual in rejecting the dangerous but conventional argument that Ireland had been conquered by Henry II. Instead Molyneux believed that the chieftains of the indigenous Irish had submitted voluntarily to Henry II, which meant that the Anglo-Irish relationship was founded upon a contract.[95]

[89] Clarke, 'Colonial constitutional attitudes', 363; Boyce, *Nationalism in Ireland*, p. 103; C. Robbins, *The eighteenth-century commonwealthman* (Cambridge, MA, 1959), p. 140; N. L. York, *Neither kingdom, nor nation: the Irish quest for constitutional rights, 1698–1800* (Washington, DC, 1994), pp. 19–20, 22.
[90] P. Kelly, 'Ireland and the Glorious Revolution: from kingdom to colony', in R. Beddard (ed.), *The revolutions of 1688* (Oxford, 1991), p. 183; J. Smyth, 'Anglo-Irish unionist discourse, c. 1656–1707', *Bullán* 2 (1995), 19; Hill, '"Ireland without union"', p. 279.
[91] Smyth, 'Anglo-Irish unionist discourse', 19.
[92] Smyth, '"Like amphibious animals"', 790.
[93] Richard Cox, *Hibernia anglicana* (2 vols. London, 1689–90), I, p. 8; Smyth, '"Like amphibious animals"', 790.
[94] William Molyneux, *The case of Ireland's being bound by acts of parliament in England, stated* (1698: n.p., 1706), pp. 20–1.   [95] *Ibid.*, esp. p. 13.

There were two main reasons why the New English eagerly appropriated the political identity of the Old English who had accompanied Henry II in his Irish venture. The Old English past yielded an ancient constitution for Protestant Irish parliamentarians. In 1692 Anthony Dopping (1643–97), Bishop of Meath and Molyneux's brother-in-law, published an edition of the *Modus tenendi parliamenta in Hibernia,* a document – purporting to be a charter of Henry II's – which appeared to justify the antiquity and status of the Irish parliament.[96] More importantly, identification with the Old English obviated the argument that the English crown enjoyed a title to Ireland by conquest. If Henry II *had* indeed conquered Ireland – which Molyneux of course denied – then his Norman warrior-companions would surely have been among Ireland's aristocratic conquerors, rather than among the mass of the conquered.[97] Although Irish Protestants exploited the Norman–Irish heritage as their own, they had scant regard for the actual confessional preferences of the majority of the authentic descendants of the Old English. Cox complained that many of the Old English were 'so blinded with an ignorant zeal for Popery, that they have endeavoured to cut the bough they stand on', namely the twelfth-century English conquest.[98] The medieval Old English were useful to advance the constitutional claims of the Anglo-Irish nation, but the harsh facts of contemporary Old English culture in the raw provoked only anathemas.

The Protestant Irish nation identified not only with the twelfth-century settlers and the early Celtic Christians, but also with a couple of the recognised pre-Milesian peoples of Ireland, the Fir-Bolg and the Tuatha-Dé-Danaan. English and Protestant Irish literati exploited the potential of an early wave of Anglo-Irish colonists who preceded the Gaels to undermine the historical supports of Old Irish ideology. The link with the ancient Britons also added a further complicating strand to the political identity of the Anglo-Irish nation. Though in most ideological contexts the Anglo-Irish deployed a Gothicist self-image drawn from the twelfth-century invasion, on certain occasions they identified themselves with the settlement of the island by the ancient British Belgae and Damnonii, supposedly the parent tribes of the Fir-Bolg and the Tuatha-Dé-Danaan. The Fir-Bolg and Tuatha-Dé-Danaan were conflated with these ancient British tribes in order to establish English claims to priority of settlement in Ireland. Relying on this equation, Cox contended that it was 'certain

[96] *Modus tenendi parliamenta in Hibernia* (1692: Dublin, 1772); York, *Neither kingdom, nor nation*, pp. 19–20 n.; Robbins, *Commonwealthman*, p. 140; Boyce, *Nationalism in Ireland*, p. 101.
[97] Molyneux, *Case of Ireland*, pp. 19–20. See also the various Protestant discussions of conquest in Leighton, *Catholicism in a Protestant kingdom*, pp. 36–7, 67, 78–9.
[98] Cox, *Hibernia anglicana*, I, p. 8.

that most of the original inhabitants of Ireland came out of Britain', a claim supported by the practice of Irish gavelkind which appeared to be the relic of an ancient British custom.[99] With more precision, the English historian Nathaniel Crouch argued in 1693 that, while the Gaelic west of Ireland had first been settled by the Scythian–Milesians, the east of Ireland, the area of the Anglicised Pale, had been 'first planted by the old Britons, several of their words being still in use'.[100] Belgic priority of settlement exploded the argument for ancient Milesian possession and sovereignty, and hence provided an immemorial pedigree to justify English authority over early modern Ireland.

Protestant scholars continued throughout the eighteenth century to celebrate the long history of autonomy enjoyed by the ancient Church of Ireland. Cox argued that St Patrick 'was the person that had the good fortune to convert the body of that nation to Christianity, but he was so far from bringing them to Popery, that they owned no jurisdiction the Pope had over them, but differed from the usage at Rome both in tonsure and in celebrating the feast of Easter, and were therefore counted schismatics by the Romanists'.[101] The English clergyman and historian, Ferdinando Warner, contended that Ireland's early ecclesiastical history was a story of autocephalous privileges from its first conversion by St Patrick: 'Indeed it does not appear from any monument of antiquity . . . that the See of Rome pretended to exercise any spiritual or temporal jurisdiction at this time in Ireland; or that Patrick had any powers or ensigns of a primate conferred upon him by the Pope or by any other person. Neither was it until seven hundred years after this that Eugenius transmitted by his legate Papiron, four palls to Ireland, whither a pall had never before been brought.'[102] Mervyn Archdall (1723–91), in *Monasticon Hibernicum* (1786), claimed that the ancient Irish monastic orders had not subscribed to the Roman form of monastic rule.[103] Bishop Hutchinson of Down and Connor noted that the twelfth-century Irish church was 'in schism from the Pope. Those rugged kings would not pay him Peter-Pence, nor

---

[99] *Ibid.*, I, 'An apparatus: or introductory discourse to the history of Ireland'.
[100] Nathaniel Crouch, *The history of the kingdom of Ireland* (London, 1693), pp. 33–4. Cf. Laurence Echard quoted in Smyth, '"Like amphibious animals"', 790 n.; *The queen an empress, and her three kingdoms one empire* (London, 1706), pp. 9–10. For earlier versions of this argument, see Hadfield, 'Briton and Scythian', esp. 390, 399. For the continuation of this type of argument into the later eighteenth century, see C. O'Halloran, 'Golden ages', pp. 130–1; John Whitaker, *The history of Manchester* (2 vols., London, 1771–5), I, p. 262. For Irish Protestant identification with the more 'civilised' Belgic Fir-Bolg, see Edward Ledwich, *Antiquities of Ireland* (Dublin, 1790), pp. 9, 15, 107, 137.
[101] Cox, *Hibernia anglicana*, I, 'Apparatus'.
[102] Ferdinando Warner, *The history of Ireland* (2 vols., Dublin, 1760), II, pp. 16–17.
[103] C. O'Halloran, '"The island of saints and scholars": views of the early church and sectarian politics in late eighteenth-century Ireland', *ECI* 5 (1990), 14.

release their clergy from the power of his laws and courts. They kept not their Easter at the same time, nor in the same way that the Pope did; and by that they were known to follow the rights of the Greek church, which kept it free from his usurpation.'[104] In a similar vein, Edward Ledwich continued the argument that Ireland had first been converted to Christianity not by Rome, but by missionaries from the churches of Asia Minor.[105]

However, the twelfth century proved to be a major stress point in the Protestant interpretation of Irish history. There was the unfortunate coincidence between the arrival of the Old English (whose constitution was championed by eighteenth-century Irish patriots) under the auspices of the papal bull *Laudabiliter* (1155) and the corruption of the Irish church, which at last fell into line with the papacy. The standard Protestant response to this ambiguous episode, as Clare O'Halloran notes, was to argue that the English Reformation had 'redeemed'[106] the Catholicising Anglo-Norman conquest of the twelfth century: 'The battles, by which the Pope was beaten, and his yoke was broken in Ireland, were fought in England; for, as England had been made the instrument of enslaving us to the Pope, God's providence made it the instrument of our deliverance from his bondage. The hand that smote, healed us again.'[107]

The eighteenth-century Church of Ireland also found itself having to fend off an assault on its other flank. Gaelic ecclesiastical antiquity was used by John Toland (1670–1722), a radical Protestant convert from Gaelic Catholicism, to launch an assault on the legitimacy of a hierarchical, disciplined and landed Church of Ireland. In the Irish section of *Nazarenus* (1718), Toland questioned the historic legitimacy of Irish adherence to both papal and episcopal forms of ecclesiastical polity. Although Toland was himself an anticlerical heterodox extremist beyond the pale of mainstream Protestantism, his antiquarian arguments, which, in places, echoed the anti-episcopalian systems advanced by David Blondel and by the Scots presbyterian school of church history, provided ammunition for Ireland's penalised presbyterian community. Toland argued not only that Gaelic Christianity had been non-papal in government and free of such Catholic practices as auricular confession, but also that it had been without tithes, glebes or diocesan episcopacy. Moreover, Toland claimed that matrimony, a central area of anti-presbyterian discrimination in eighteenth-century Ireland, being a 'civil contract', had

---

[104] Francis Hutchinson, *A defence of the antient historians: with a particular application of it to the history of Ireland* (1733: Dublin, 1734), p. 123.
[105] C. O'Halloran, 'Golden ages', pp. 288–9; C. O'Halloran, '"Island of saints and scholars"', 13.   [106] C. O'Halloran, '"Island of saints and scholars"', 19.
[107] Hutchinson, *Defence of the antient historians*, pp. 130–1. See Warner, *History of Ireland*, I, p. 86.

been the province of the magistracy, and not of the clergy. The ancient Irish had enjoyed the full scope of 'Christian liberty' to differ 'among themselves' in 'discipline' and 'modes of worship'.[108] In reply, William Nicolson met Toland's challenge at its most devastating point, rejecting his arguments for an ancient presbyterian polity in the Church of Ireland. What Toland took to be an elective form of democratic government in the church, suggested Nicolson, had been more akin to the operations of an English dean and chapter than it was to modern presbytery.[109]

Churchmen had played a crucial role in fostering the Anglo-Irish discovery of Gaeldom. Ecclesiastical antiquarians sustained the traditional identity of the historic Church of St Patrick, and, by upholding the claim that early medieval Ireland was the *insula sanctorum*, nourished in embryo a more latitudinarian conception of Hibernian patriotism.[110] Then, for a few decades during the second half of the eighteenth century the literati of the Protestant nation who had traditionally derided the incivility of the Gaelic Irish began to explore the possibility of a broader *cultural* Gaelicism. A segment – and no more – of the Anglo-Irish community in the middle of the eighteenth century acknowledged the Milesian civilisation as an integral part of its own heritage.[111]

Why did this element within the Ascendancy, a body firmly attached to a Gothicist identity, begin to cultivate so keen an interest in the Milesian past? The work of Joep Leerssen provides part of the answer. During the 1720s disputes with the motherland, which appeared to disregard the

---

[108] John Toland, 'An account of an Irish manuscript of the four Gospels; with a summary of the ancient Irish Christianity, before the papal corruptions and usurpations: and the reality of the Keldees (an order of lay religious) against the two last Bishops of Worcester', in Toland, *Nazarenus* (London, 1718); J. G. Simms, 'John Toland (1670–1722), a Donegal heretic', in Simms, *War and politics in Ireland 1649–1730* (ed. D. Hayton and G. O'Brien, London, 1986), p. 44; R. Kearney, 'John Toland: an Irish philosopher?', in Kearney, *Postnationalist Ireland* (London, 1997), esp. pp. 158–9.

[109] Nicolson, *Irish historical library*, 'Preface', pp. xxix–xxx.

[110] Ecclesiastical issues were important in the emergence of a Protestant *Irish* identity. Divisions over the distribution of ecclesiastical patronage led to divisions between English- and Irish-born bishops in the Irish House of Lords: see P. McNally, '"Irish and English interests": national conflict within the Church of Ireland episcopate in the reign of George I', *IHS* 29 (1995), 295–314. For St Patrick as an icon shared by both confessions (though, in the eighteenth century, without any point of contact between the traditions except in symbolism), see J. Hill, 'National festivals, the state and "protestant ascendancy" in Ireland, 1790–1829', *IHS* 24 (1984), 30–51. Note that the claims of English whigs to the historic *imperium* of the English kingdom over Ireland (and its parliament) were reinforced by arguments for the subordination of the Church of Ireland to the jurisdiction of Canterbury: see William Atwood, *The history and reasons of the dependency of Ireland upon the imperial crown of the kingdom of England* (London, 1698), pp. 20–3.

[111] Hill, 'Popery and Protestantism', 102–4; Boyce, *Nationalism in Ireland*, p. 117. For the *political* limits of Protestant Gaelicism, see R. B. McDowell, *Irish public opinion 1750–1800* (London, 1944), pp. 23–4.

health of the Irish economy, over issues such as Wood's Halfpence led to a growing sense not only of a separate Irish economic interest, but of an interest shared by all Irishman. Not only did Swift's ironic *Modest proposal*, for example, display a Protestant patriot sympathy for the plight of the impoverished Gael, but William Philips, in his play *Hibernia freed* (1722), exploited the Gaelic past for patriot ends. The next few decades, according to Leerssen, witnessed the 'cultural osmosis of Gaelic culture into the Anglo-Irish classes', beginning with the antiquarian endeavours of the Physico-Historical Society established in 1744.[112]

Was a growing feeling of Protestant security, perhaps, the necessary obverse of this heightened Irishness? With an enduring peace, a marked Irish Catholic quiescence during the Scottish Jacobite rising of 1745–6, and the recognition of a de facto Catholic loyalism came a loosening of the straitjacket of beleaguered Protestantism. The Enlightenment was not a phenomenon external and oppositional to Catholicism, but a living and dynamic force within the church, which by the second half of the eighteenth century was no longer the formidable Counter-Reformation monolith of seventeenth-century Protestant caricature. The ultramontane claims of the papacy faced various cisalpine challenges from within the wider church. Gallicans who had wished for some time to limit the authority of the pope over the French church now received theoretical support from the influential German theologian Febronius. In his treatise *De statu ecclesiae* (1763) Febronius advocated a decentralised Catholicism of national churches run by synods of bishops. In the Italian peninsula jurisdictionalists were campaigning to curtail excessive clerical powers. The papacy itself became aware of the need to refashion the outworn identity of the militant Counter-Reformation church, and in 1773 Pope Clement XIV suppressed the Jesuit order.[113] Catholic Ireland was exposed to this wave of reformism, with Archbishop Butler of Cashel heading its cisalpine wing. Indeed, the Gallicanism of Irish Catholicism's French-educated higher clergy proved attractive to Gallican sympathisers within the Anglican establishment. By the 1760s there had been a discernible relaxation and transformation of the anti-Catholicism of the Protestant elite, both in Britain and Ireland.[114]

Not only did Ireland's Protestant elite begin to dismantle the penal laws, but religious tolerance was paralleled in some quarters by an interest in Gaelic cultural projects. In 1760 the staunchly Protestant hackwriter Henry Brooke (1703?–83), author of the anti-Jacobite *Farmer's letters*

---

[112] Leerssen, *Mere Irish*, pp. 295–329 (quotation at p. 315). See F. G. James, 'Historiography and the Irish constitutional revolution of 1782', *Eire–Ireland* 18 (1983), 13–16; Leighton, *Catholicism in a Protestant kingdom*, p. 115.   [113] Bartlett, *Fall and rise*, ch. 5.
[114] E. O'Flaherty, 'Ecclesiastical politics and the dismantling of the penal laws in Ireland 1774–1782', *IHS* 26 (1988), 33–50; C. Haydon, *Anti-Catholicism in eighteenth-century England* (Manchester, 1993), ch. 5.

(1745), was hired to write on behalf of the Catholic movement, producing *The tryal of the Roman Catholics* which challenged the black legend of 1641.[115] In addition, Brooke's *Essay on the ancient and modern state of Ireland* (1760) reiterated the arguments of O'Conor about the glories of ancient Milesian civilisation: 'remote from the storms and revolutions of the greater world, and secured by situation from its hostile incursions, there is no doubt but the cultivation of religion, philosophy, politics, poetry, and music, became the chief objects of popular study and application'.[116] However unconvincing one finds the multiple identities of Henry Brooke, who was also the author of the Gothicist play *Gustavus Vasa* (1739), his daughter Charlotte (1740–93) threw herself with tremendous vigour into the history and culture of Gaelic Ireland. Charlotte Brooke's *Reliques of Irish poetry* (1789) stood alongside the antiquarian treatises of Joseph Walker (1761–1810) celebrating bards and ancient Irish dress as the most sympathetic of the new Protestant explorations of indigenous Gaelic culture.[117] Vallancey's eccentric – but influential – philological works lent support to the notion that Gaelic was descended from Phoenician and by extension that Milesian Ireland, far from being a scene of savagery, had been a glorious western bastion of the achievements of the high civilisation of the ancient Mediterranean and Near East.[118] In 1785 the establishment of the Irish Academy (from 1786 the Royal Irish Academy) provided a further boost to Protestant Gaelicism.[119]

Revisionism, however, had its limits. The self-consciously enlightened historian Thomas Leland (1722–85), who attempted to break away from the black narratives of traditional Protestant propaganda, ran up against the intractable problem of producing a non-sectarian account of the rebellion of 1641.[120] The revived sectarianism of the 1780s encapsulated by the agrarian Rightboy movement led to new bouts of Protestant

[115] Leerssen, *Mere Irish*, p. 314; Bartlett, *Fall and rise*, p. 54.
[116] Henry Brooke, *An essay on the ancient and modern state of Ireland* (Dublin, 1760), p. 7.
[117] Joseph Walker, *Historical memoirs of the Irish bards* (Dublin, 1786); Walker, *An historical essay on the dress of the ancient and modern Irish* (Dublin, 1788). C. O'Halloran, 'Golden ages', p. 223, argues that there is no evidence for the claim – found e.g. in N. Vance, 'Celts, Carthaginians and constitutions: Anglo-Irish literary relations 1780–1820', *IHS* 22 (1981), 221 – that the Catholic Sylvester O'Halloran was the godfather of Charlotte Brooke.
[118] Charles Vallancey, *An essay on the antiquity of the Irish language* (Dublin, 1772); Vallancey, *A vindication of the ancient history of Ireland* (Dublin, 1786); Vallancey (ed.), *Collectanea de rebus Hibernicis* (5 vols., Dublin, 1770–90); Vance, 'Celts, Carthaginians and constitutions'; J. Leerssen, 'On the edge of Europe: Ireland in search of Oriental roots, 1650–1850', *Comparative Criticism* 8 (1986), 91–112.
[119] Foster, *Modern Ireland*, p. 184; R. B. McDowell, *Ireland in the age of imperialism and revolution 1760–1801* (Oxford, 1979), pp. 154–5.
[120] W. Love, 'Charles O'Conor of Belanagare and Thomas Leland's "philosophical" history of Ireland', *IHS* 13 (1962), 1–25; J. Liechty, 'Testing the depth of Catholic–Protestant conflict: the case of Thomas Leland's *History of Ireland*, 1773', *Archivium Hibernicum* 42 (1987), 13–28.

anxiety, while Richard Woodward, Bishop of Cloyne, produced another influential bestselling classic of Protestant defensiveness which went through numerous editions.[121] In the 1790s controversy also broke out over the terms of Henry Flood's will. The patriot Flood, who died in 1791, had willed the bulk of his estate to Trinity College, Dublin, for the purchase of Gaelic manuscripts and to promote the study of the Irish language. If Vallancey were still alive, he was to be the first holder of a new chair of Erse. This bizarre bequest was challenged by Flood's family, and defended by Lawrence Parsons, later second earl of Rosse, a close ally of Flood's in the Irish legislature, who, in a pamphlet published in 1795, broadened the scope of his argument to vindicate the richness, significance and high antiquity of Milesian civilisation. Parsons still felt the need to counter Protestant suspicions of Gaeldom, which were founded on 'the most unjust charges of ignorance and barbarism, at a time when it was by far more enlightened and civilized than any of the adjacent nations'.[122] These slurs reflected badly not only on the Gaels, but on the whole island. In the end, the family successfully contested the will. Some prominent Protestant historians, including Edward Ledwich (1738–1823) and Thomas Campbell (1733–95), doubted the historicity and incredible achievements of this vaunted Milesian civilisation. Nevertheless, even Ledwich and Campbell subscribed to elements of the dark-age history of saints and scholars which now composed an integral part of Irish 'Anglican' identity.[123]

By 1800 Gaelic antiquity was a palimpsest upon which could be discerned in various hands the *mythistoires* of the Old Irish, the Old English and the New English. However, this antiquarian interest in the Gaelic past barely diluted the political identification of the Anglo-Irish community with the heritage of English liberty. The rhetoric of the patriot revolution of 1780–2 dwelt on the perceived exclusion from the historic liberties of Englishmen. Not even Flood exploited the Gaelic past for political ends in his patriot oratory.[124] Eighteenth-century Protestant Gaelicism was not only of marginal political importance, it was also short-lived. The sectarian turn taken by the rebellion of 1798 checked the latitudinarian spirit of the Irish Enlightenment.[125] Nevertheless, Protes-

---

[121] Richard Woodward, *The present state of the Church of Ireland* (1787: 7th edn, Dublin, 1787).

[122] Lawrence Parsons, *Observations on the bequest of Henry Flood, esq. to Trinity College, Dublin: with a defence of the ancient history of Ireland* (Dublin, 1795), pp. 24–5; Leerssen, *Mere Irish*, pp. 361–2.

[123] Thomas Campbell, *A philosophical survey of the south of Ireland* (London, 1777); C. O'Halloran, '"Island of saints and scholars"', 12–15; C. O'Halloran, 'Golden ages', pp. 281–93.   [124] See below, ch. 10.

[125] O. MacDonagh, *States of mind: two centuries of Anglo-Irish conflict, 1780–1980* (1983: London, 1992), pp. 2–5; C. O'Halloran, 'Golden ages', pp. 222–3; Hill, 'Popery and Protestantism', 124–7.

tant Gaelicism was far from extinct, and, flourishing anew between about 1830 and 1848, and again from the 1890s, it would prove influential in the formation of modern Irish nationalism.[126]

Comparisons: ancient constitutionalism, gentry patriotism and colonial regnalism

The constructions of ethnic identity in early modern Ireland bear strong affinities both with the common run of identity formation in most early modern European kingdoms and political cultures, and with European colonial identities in the Americas. More recently, Connolly and Cadoc Leighton have questioned the colonial model of early modern Irish history, assimilating the island's experience instead to the norms of early modern Europe.[127] Neither the colonial nor the European model on its own adequately conveys a fully rounded picture of early modern Irish history, and different types of ideological constructions associated on the one hand with the colonial expansion of Europe and on the other with regnal identities of the European *ancien régime* together complicated the formation of identity in early modern Ireland. However, the colonial context was only one facet of identity construction in early modern Ireland. Historic Irish identities were shaped by ideological pressures common to other early modern European nations. The identities of early modern Irishmen were constructed out of the familiar conceptual building blocks of early modern political thought.

Political and ecclesiastical legitimacy was derived from the Milesian past; but this did not mean that Irishmen felt obliged to avoid tampering with that history. There is little sense of a taboo against trimming the Gaelic heritage to meet current ideological needs. Rather Irish antiquaries regarded their ancestral past – a remote and sketchy Milesian antiquity – as a partly completed canvas whose empty spaces could be filled with ideologically appropriate images. The hallmark of the Gaelic past was its utility. Though largely constructed out of indigenous materials, the shape of the Milesian *mythistoire* conformed to wider European patterns. The criteria and recognised procedures of political and ecclesiastical debate were of international currency. Thus early modern Milesian identity tended to be calibrated against a variety of external standards. In

[126] T. Dunne, 'Haunted by history: Irish romantic writing 1800–1850', in R. Porter and M. Teich (eds.), *Romanticism in national context* (Cambridge, 1988); J. Leerssen, *Remembrance and imagination* (Cork, 1996); Hutchinson, *Dynamics of cultural nationalism*; J. Sheehy, *The rediscovery of Ireland's past: the Celtic revival, 1830–1930* (London, 1980); R. Foster, 'History and the Irish question', *Transactions of the Royal Historical Society* 5th ser. 33 (1983), 169–92; F. S. L. Lyons, *Culture and anarchy in Ireland 1890–1939* (1979: Oxford, 1982), p. 28; S. Deane, *Celtic revivals* (London, 1985), pp. 20–1.

[127] Connolly, *Religion, law, and power*; Leighton, *Catholicism in a Protestant kingdom*.

the course of the seventeenth and eighteenth centuries, this was to entail, at various stages, mimicry of the ideological contours of English mixed constitutionalism, an assimilation of Gaelic antiquity to the civilisations of classical antiquity and the casting of the Druidic paganism of the Milesians in the mould of Enlightenment civil religion.

Early modern Gaelic ethnocentrism was shot through with humanistic values. It was driven not by a self-confident assertion of the particular characteristics of the Gaelic people, but by an aspiration to prove that ancient Milesian culture had been the equal of the civilisations of classical antiquity. Even historians from within the ranks of Gaelic nationalism eschew essentialism and acknowledge the contemporary European influences on the construction of seventeenth-century Milesian identity. Breandán Ó Buachalla and Brendan Bradshaw, for example, have described the reception of a 'new political lexicon' in seventeenth-century Irish discourse, which included Gaelic terms for kingdom, crown, sovereign, commonweal and majesty. Furthermore, Bradshaw has argued that seventeenth-century Irish discourse has to be understood in the context of Counter-Reformation humanistic antiquarianism. *Foras feasa ar Éirinn* was similar to the sort of 'project being mounted at this time by patriotic antiquarians elsewhere in Europe'.[128]

There are other European comparisons to be drawn, notably with the phenomenon of racial elitism. In the century after the Treaty of Limerick (1691) the term 'Irish' had numerous meanings, and there was no single term which did service for the Protestant community. The Protestant Irish referred to themselves on occasions as the Irish nation, which, as Connolly points out, involved 'accepting, in some vague way, an identity that overlapped with that of the native population'.[129] However, Protestant writers appeared to forget that the predominantly lower-caste Catholic population existed as a community with its own identity. Consider the Irish Protestant patriotism of the penal law era when figures such as Molyneux, Cox and Henry Maxwell – who claimed that 'the people of Ireland are naturally the offspring of England'[130] – appeared to conflate the Irish nation with the English in Ireland, to the exclusion of the wider population over whom they ruled. David Hayton argues that the use of labels such as 'wild Irish' or 'mere Irish' not only made 'the ordinary peasant appear less than human' but also made it 'easier for the Protestant gentleman to appropriate his nationality'.[131] In this respect, the

---

[128] Bradshaw, 'Keating', pp. 167–8; Ó Buachalla, 'James our true king', p. 14.
[129] Connolly, *Religion, law, and power*, p. 124. See also p. 119, where Connolly points to the terminological 'absurdities' arising from the identification of the Protestants as 'the people of Ireland' and the Catholics as 'the Irish'.
[130] Henry Maxwell, *An essay towards an union of Ireland with England* (London, 1703), p. 19.
[131] D. Hayton, 'Anglo-Irish attitudes: changing perceptions of national identity among the

Anglo-Irish identity resembled the aristocratic and gentry patriotisms of continental Europe, such as the celebrated Frankish *thèse nobiliaire* articulated by Boulainvilliers, the corporate patriotism of the Magyars and, most especially, the Sarmatic identity of the early modern Polish *szlachta*. A story of common Sarmatic origins not only united an ethnically diverse caste of Polish and Polonised gentry, but also suspended disbelief in an arrogant display of oligarchical ventriloquism. The Polish identity of the *szlachta*, like the national consciousness of the Protestant Irish elite, was quasi-republican, but only because it disregarded the subordinate peasantry as an identity-less mass with no genuine claim on nationhood.[132]

Valuable insights into the construction of early modern Anglo-Irish identity can also be gained from comparisons with the ways in which the 'otherness' of native American cultures was appropriated by Hispanic colonists in the manufacture of creole identities. Creoles acknowledged that their racial stock, or *nación*, was Hispanic, yet they differentiated themselves from Peninsular Spaniards, whom they termed *gachupines*, by fostering a local territorial identity. The cult of the colonial *patria* fulfilled a 'yearning to secure roots that sank deep into the history of the New World', and also nourished a commitment to the colonial province as a distinct political community. Putting a regnalist as well as an ethnicist spin on colonial identity, creole mythmakers forged a 'continuous, instructive and politically legitimating past' out of the local histories of 'the very peoples their ancestors had conquered'. Thus, a polyethnic patriotism could coexist with the sort of ethnic chauvinism typical of colonialism. Anthony Pagden notes that, without acknowledging contemporary Amerindians as fellow citizens, creoles could none the less appropriate a mythical Aztec past as part of their civic identity: 'The *criollos* might not constitute one race with the Indians; but they could make some claim to being the true heirs of their imperial past.' The patriotic literati of New Spain including Carlos Sigüenza y Góngora (1645–1700) and Francisco Javier Clavigero (1731–87), a colonial Jesuit consigned to exile in Italy

    Protestant Ascendancy in Ireland, ca. 1690–1750', *Studies in Eighteenth-Century Culture* 17 (1987), 150.
[132] Leighton, *Catholicism in a Protestant kingdom*, pp. 26–7, 31–2, 36–7; E. Carcassonne, *Montesquieu et le problème de la constitution française au XVIIIe siècle* (Paris, 1927), pp. 19, 43; P. Goubert, *The ancien régime: French society, 1600–1750* (1969: transln, New York, 1973), p. 160; G. Chaussinand-Nogaret, *The French nobility in the eighteenth century* (1976: trans. W. Doyle, Cambridge, 1985), pp. 16, 23; S. Cynarski, 'The shape of Sarmatian ideology in Poland', *Acta Poloniae Historica* 19 (1968), 5–17; J. Tazbir, *La république nobiliaire et le monde: études sur l'histoire de la culture polonaise a l'époque du baroque* (Wroclaw, 1986), esp. pp. 15, 22, 32–3, 51–3, 160; J. Lukowski, *Liberty's folly: the Polish–Lithuanian commonwealth in the eighteenth century* (London, 1991), pp. 3–22; N. Davies, 'Polish national mythologies', in G. Hosking and G. Schopflin (eds.), *Myths and nationhood* (London, 1997), pp. 143–4.

after the expulsion of his order from the Spanish empire, invented a Mexican identity founded on a 'syncretised past' comprehending pre-conquest Aztec history. In other words, the colonial situation of early modern Latin America spawned multiple identities. Mexico's Hispanic colonists could have satisfied themselves with responsible and accurate histories limited to their own relatively modest post-Conquistadorial roots in the New World. However, according to John Phelan, this authentic tradition 'was too brief in duration and too European in content to satisfy their need to identify with a historical tradition indigenously American'. There were further parallels with early modern Ireland. The Amerindians were like the Gaels. Their pasts were appropriated, sanitised and rendered useful to the colonial cause, but as a real contemporary people they were despised, downtrodden and excluded. Phelan has described the phenomenon of 'neo-Aztecism' as the classicising of the Aztecs. The Aztec past was glossed as an American equivalent of Europe's Graeco-Roman antiquity, a civilisation which yielded a rich vein of moral and civic exempla, a native iconography and patriotic inspiration. Although Mexican creole identity embraced a noble civic lineage stretching back to the glories of the Aztec state, only historic Aztecs were included. Modern Amerindians and even mixed bloods were not accepted as citizens of the glorious Mexican *patria*. Phelan suggests that contemporary Indians were 'considered remote and rather brutish descendants of the "classical" Indians of Aztec antiquity'. Lafaye dwells on the important role of 'spiritual hybridisation' in the formation of a creole-sponsored Mexican national consciousness. In the eighteenth century Mexican clergy argued that the indigenous deity Quetzalcoatl was a corrupted memory of the apostle Thomas; thus, according to Edwin Williamson, 'Christianity was presumed to have roots in America which were independent of the [Spanish] Peninsula.'[133]

Ireland bore witness to similar dual strategies combining both appropriation and denigration of the indigenous culture as a means of ensuring territory-specific legitimacy. Such tensions were apparent in the construction of both Old and New English versions of settler-consciousness in Ireland. In the case of the Old English, one can see how this colonial

[133] J. L. Phelan, 'Neo-Aztecism in the eighteenth century and the genesis of Mexican nationalism', in S. Diamond (ed.), *Culture in history* (New York, 1960), pp. 760–70; A. Pagden, *Spanish imperialism and the political imagination* (New Haven and London, 1990), pp. 91–104, 116; J. Lafaye, *Quetzalcoatl and Guadalupe: the formation of Mexican national consciousness 1531–1813* (1974: trans. B. Keen, Chicago, 1976), pp. 7, 44–50, 62–7, 107–12, 173, 252; E. Williamson, *The Penguin history of Latin America* (Harmondsworth, 1992), p. 154. For a similar comparison, see N. Canny, 'Identity formation in Ireland: the emergence of the Anglo-Irish', in Canny and A. Pagden (eds.), *Colonial identity in the Atlantic world, 1500–1800* (Princeton, 1987), pp. 195–6.

nation shed its sense of ethnic kinship with the motherland, and its Catholic community assimilated in the course of the seventeenth century to an indigenous Irish identity. The New English, on the other hand, remained a colonial nation with a much stronger sense – to use Pagden's terminology – of *nación* in its Anglo-Gothic stock, and a correspondingly weaker, though nevertheless important, sense of Irish *patria*. A creole pattern also prevailed in the seventeenth- and eighteenth-century Church of Ireland where Ussher and his intellectual disciples attempted to establish an indigenous and fully Hibernian pedigree for Protestantism which removed from it the taint of exclusive association with New English Anglican colonialism. There was a stark differentiation in New English attitudes to the modern Catholic Irish and their early Christian ancestors. Suitably 'sanitised', historic Gaels were used to legitimise the predominantly New English Church of Ireland at the same time as the cultural elite of the Anglo-Irish community denigrated the contemporary Gaelic nation as barbaric and benighted.

Part III

Points of contact

8   Constructing the pre-romantic Celt

Since the nineteenth century we have become accustomed to the notion of a vast historic gulf between the characters, values and achievements of the Celtic and Anglo-Saxon worlds. However, in recent decades, scholars working in a number of different fields have begun to dismantle this paradigm. Some anthropologists, using core–periphery models, have even gone as far as to suggest that Celtic is an empty category signifying 'otherness' whose fluctuating cultural definition has depended more on the vague prejudices of the centre than the actuality of the periphery.[1] Less contentiously, cultural historians have revealed the origins of the modern duality of Celt and Saxon: the twin influences of romanticism and racialism forged the modern myth of the Celt, and contributed to the emergence of related phenomena such as the ideology of pan-Celtic nationalism. The opposition of the pragmatic, freedom-loving Teuton and the mystical, sentimental, but improvident Celt was not a feature of early modern ethnic stereotyping. This romantic conception of the Celt took shape gradually, beginning with the Ossianic vogue of the late eighteenth century, and culminated in the vision of the high-minded Celt peddled by Matthew Arnold. In the interim the romantic Celt had been appropriated by Teutonic racialists as the hapless antithesis of the vigorous and prosperous Saxon.[2] Pan-Celticism has even shallower roots in ethnological thought, and flowered in the late nineteenth century when contacts were established between land leaguers and Gaelic nationalists in Ireland and the Scottish Highlands. Only in 1886–7 was the idea mooted of mounting a Celtic League to promote the common interests of the Celtic fringes of the British Isles, a venture which proved abortive, though a pan-Celtic congress was eventually held in Dublin in 1901.[3]

[1] M. Chapman, *The Celts: the construction of a myth* (Houndmills, 1992); M. McDonald, 'The invention of the Celts' (O'Donnell Lecture delivered at Oxford University, Trinity term, 1993).

[2] M. Chapman, *The Gaelic vision in Scottish culture* (London, 1978); P. Sims-Williams, 'The visionary Celt: the construction of an ethnic preoccupation', *Cambridge Medieval Celtic Studies* 11 (1986), 71–96; F. E. Faverty, *Matthew Arnold, the ethnologist* (Evanston, IL, 1951); P. Womack, *Improvement and romance* (London, 1989).

How unlike the seventeenth and eighteenth centuries, when Scottish, Irish and Welsh antiquaries advanced their own particular (and irreconcilable) patriotic shibboleths without any sense of a common 'Celtic' identity or interest. The Celts were fashioned in a complex multipolar world. The eighteenth-century literati who began to formulate many of the modern myths of the Celts were heirs to long-standing patriotic debates among English, Welsh, Irish and Scottish scholars over such issues as inconsistencies between different national origin myths, questions of imperial suzerainty and regnal autonomy within the British Isles, and matters of national honour.[4]

'Irish' culture, for example, exercised a curious attraction and repulsion on Scottish literati. Despite the hostility to Gaeldom as an extension of the barbarism of Irish culture to Scotland, patriotic Scots were keen to appropriate much of medieval Ireland's rich history of learning and holiness to lend solidity and amplitude to Scotland's comparatively impoverished pantheon. The émigré Scottish Catholic Thomas Dempster provoked an indignant Irish response when, by exploiting the ambiguities in the term 'Scotia', he hijacked for Scotland Ireland's saints and scholars.[5] Thereafter, until the Enlightenment, captured Irish icons became the mainstay of Scottish hagiography and literary patriotism.[6] In the 1760s the historical apparatus which James Macpherson deployed in support of the Ossianic epic initiated a new round of these old debates. Charles O'Conor of Belanagar, a keen defender of Irish antiquities, saw in Ossianic history an attempt to reconstruct Dempster and Sir George Mackenzie in the aftermath of Father Innes's unpatriotic demolition of Scottish antiquity.[7]

Throughout the vital period of 'Celtic' invention, national traditions of discourse persisted which cut across the centre–periphery model. The Welsh, for example, did not identify themselves with their fellow 'Celts', but saw themselves as the descendants of the ancient Britons, 'the primary people of the British Isles' and founders of the proto-Protestant church of pre-Augustinian 'England'. Indeed, in certain areas English

---

[3] J. Hunter, 'The Gaelic connection: the Highlands, Ireland and nationalism, 1873–1922', *SHR* 54 (1975), 178–204. For an early example of pan-Celticism, see the ideas of Thomas Price (Carnhuanawc; 1787–1848) outlined in J. Davies, *A history of Wales* (1990: Harmondsworth, 1994), pp. 386–7.

[4] H. Trevor-Roper, *George Buchanan and the ancient Scottish constitution, EHR* supplement 3 (1966); J. Leerssen, *Mere Irish and Fíor-Ghael* (1986: 2nd edn, Cork, 1996).

[5] M. Mac Craith, 'Gaelic Ireland and the Renaissance', in G. Williams and R. Jones (eds.), *The Celts and the Renaissance* (Cardiff, 1990), p. 78; Leerssen, *Mere Irish*, pp. 264–5.

[6] George Mackenzie, MD, *The lives and characters of the most eminent writers of the Scots nation* (3 vols., Edinburgh, 1708–22).

[7] C. O'Halloran, 'Irish re-creations of the Gaelic past: the challenge of Macpherson's Ossian', *P+P* 124 (1989), 69–95.

and Welsh identities overlapped, while the Welsh continued to champion the myths of Geoffrey of Monmouth long after most English historians had abandoned them.[8] In Scotland, as we have seen, the patriotic inspiration drawn from the ancient Irish settlers of the west Highland kingdom of Dalriada did not prevent Lowland Scots from persecuting the early modern descendants of the Dalriadans.[9] In Ireland, the Old Irish and the Hibernicised Old (Norman) English defended their Gaelic ways from English detractors not by asserting the superiority of Celtic culture, but by showing how their ancient civilisation stood comparison with the classical cultures of the ancient Mediterranean and with the humanistic standards of modern Christendom.[10]

Moreover, seventeenth-century literati did not construct the historic Celts of the British Isles as an alien 'other', however much the New English in Ireland or Scots Lowlanders might in practice treat the Old Irish or Gaelic Highlanders as inferior uncivilised peoples. In the realms of scholarship, or pseudo-scholarship, a number of factors, according to Stuart Piggott, conspired to prompt belief in some degree of 'Anglo-Celtic sanguinity', notably between the Germanic peoples and Brythonic Celts of Wales, Britanny and ancient Gaul.[11] Not until Thomas Percy (1729–1811) published his critical edition of Mallet's *Northern antiquities* in 1770 did a clear distinction between Celts and Germans begin to take hold among scholars. This would gradually become established as a permanent feature of the scholarly firmament, but in the meantime it was still common to lapse into confusion or inconsistency. The 1786 edition of Ephraim Chambers's *Cyclopedia* claimed that the 'Celtes' were northern nations, that the Druids were to be found among the 'ancient Celtae, or Gauls, Britons, and Germans' and that the Icelandic Edda were 'said to contain the Celtic mythology', while elsewhere in the same edition other contradictory articles argued that the Edda were 'Gothic' and that the Celts were to be clearly distinguished from the Goths.[12]

---

[8] P. Morgan, *A new history of Wales: the eighteenth-century renaissance* (Llandybie, 1981), pp. 17, 57, 86. See also Davies, *History of Wales*, pp. 242, 251. For the Welsh championship of Geoffrey of Monmouth's 'British' history into the eighteenth century, see G. H. Jenkins, *The foundations of modern Wales, 1642–1780* (Oxford, 1987), pp. 246–7; Davies, *History of Wales*, p. 303. Among the London Welsh the Society of Ancient Britons was established in 1715, and in 1751 the Society of Cymmrodorion (or 'aborigines', i.e. earliest natives of Britain): see Morgan, *Eighteenth-century renaissance*, pp. 57–8; Jenkins, *Foundations*, p. 390.   [9] See above, ch. 6.

[10] C. Kidd, 'Gaelic antiquity and national identity in Enlightenment Ireland and Scotland', *EHR* 109 (1994), 1202–4.

[11] S. Piggott, *Celts, Saxons, and the early antiquaries* (O'Donnell Lecture, 1966: Edinburgh, 1967), p. 11.

[12] Ephraim Chambers (d. 1740), *Cyclopedia* (4 vols., London, 1786 edn), I, 'Celtes'; II, 'Druids', 'Gothic'; IV, 'Teutonic'. See Piggott, *Celts*, p. 18, for Gibbon's confusion on this topic; Leerssen, *Mere Irish*, p. 412 n. 94.

On the other hand, throughout the early modern era, the Goidelic Celts – or Gaels – were identified as a race apart from the Brythonic Celts, the former linked – in the opinion of some antiquaries – through descent from the shadowy Scythians (not least because of a pseudo-etymological derivation of 'Scot' from Scythian). To complicate matters further, the Goths, themselves distinguished from the Germans, were also held by some scholars to descend from the Scythians. Within interpretations of sacred history, the Scythian forefathers of the Gaels were ascribed to the lineage of Magog, son of Japhet, while the 'Celts', whom we would consider Brythonic Celts, were held to be of the line of Gomer, another son of Japhet and father of Ashkenaz, from whom descended the Germans.[13]

Only with the onset of romanticism and racialism did a strong sense of a Celtic identity emerge. For most of the early modern period Saxons were barely distinguishable from Celts in the eyes of scholars working in the fields of ethnic classification and the histories of nations. A variety of factors contributed to the affiliation of Celtic (especially Brythonic) and Germanic identities. Some were intrinsic to the practices of ethnological and linguistic scholarship; others arose from broader ideological currents. The phenomenon reflected the contours of political argument. English antiquarians committed to a prescriptive ancient constitution tended to minimise the differences between the Saxons and the ancient Britons.

Classification

The 'Celts' of early modern scholarship were not the 'Celts' of nineteenth- and twentieth-century ethnology. Celtic and Germanic differences were blurred in the fog of confusing ethnic terminology which shrouded the terrain of early modern antiquarianism. Although the modern observer can peer only so far into the scholastic miasma of ethnic labelling, we can nevertheless discern some of the basic strategies, difficulties and lines of interpretation.

For a start, the term Celtic had two meanings in the early modern period, neither of which referred directly to the peoples of the peripheries of western Europe known as Celtic in the late twentieth century. Stuart

---

[13] For Ireland's Scythian–Magogian origins, see Peter Walsh, *A prospect of the state of Ireland* (London, 1682), pp. 7, 12, 356; Roderic O'Flaherty, *Ogygia* (1685: trans. James Hely, 2 vols., Dublin, 1793), I, pp. lxix–lxx, 12–15; Nathaniel Crouch, *The history of the kingdom of Ireland* (London, 1693), pp. 6, 33–4; Francis Hutchinson, *A defence of the antient historians: with a particular application of it to the history of Ireland* (1733: Dublin, 1734), pp. 49, 58; Charles Vallancey, *An essay towards illustrating the ancient history of the Britannic Isles* (London, 1786), pp. 11–13. For Scotland, see Mackenzie, *Lives of writers*, I, pp. v–viii.

Piggott warned that only in the eighteenth century did the term Celt assume its current meaning.[14] The groups we know today as Celtic peoples tended to be referred to in the early modern period as Gallic or Gaulic, stressing their affinity in manners with the tribes described by Caesar in *The Gallic war*. On the one hand, Celtic had a narrow definition, which associated it with Gaul. Thomas Blount's dictionary of 1656 defined Celt as 'one born in Gaul'.[15] The other meaning of Celtic was exceptionally broad. The vague ethnological terms 'Celtic' and 'Scythian' were used very loosely as umbrella categories to describe vast and disparate ethnic groupings.[16] From the medieval era, as J. W. Johnson points out, the Scythians had come to be regarded 'as the parent of virtually every nation in western Europe'.[17] This had the effect of linking Celtic and German peoples in the same racial supergroup. The category of Celt was almost equally wide. Percy noted that the consensus among his errant predecessors ran as follows: that from the Celts 'were uniformly descended the old inhabitants of Gaul, Germany, Scandinavia, Britain, and Spain, who were all included by the ancients under the general name of Hyperboreans, Scythians, and Celts, being all originally of one race and nation, and having all the same common language, religion, laws, customs and manners'.[18] The vagueness of the terms Celtic and Scythian, and the tendency to conflate both categories, proved a recipe for ethnological confusion. The early eighteenth-century German scholar Johannes Wachter (1663–1757) identified three distinct groups of Scythians among the peoples of Europe – the northern Scythians proper, the western Celtae and the Germanic Celto-Scythians – and described the Celtic tongue as 'the final stage of a united Germanic language before the evolution of its various dialects'.[19] Another eighteenth-century writer on the Celts, Simon Pelloutier (1694–1757), noted 'divers noms que les peuples Celtes portoient autrefois', including 'Scythes', 'Iberes', 'Gaulois' and 'Teutons'.[20]

Despite this terminological elusiveness, we can establish the sources

[14] Piggott, *Celts*, p. 11.   [15] Blount, quoted in Piggott, *Celts*, p. 6.

[16] D. Droixhe, *La linguistique et l'appel de l'histoire (1600–1800)* (Geneva, 1978); Droixhe, *De l'origine du langage aux langues du monde: études sur les XVIIe et XVIIIe siècles* (Tübingen, 1987), pp. 65–80; J.-C. Muller, 'Early stages of language comparison from Sassetti to Sir William Jones (1786)', *Kratylos* 31 (1986), 10–12.

[17] J. W. Johnson, 'The Scythian: his rise and fall', *JHI* 20 (1959), 250–7. See Edward Stillingfleet, *Origines Britannicae* (London, 1685), p. 38.

[18] Thomas Percy, 'Translator's preface', in P. Mallet, *Northern antiquities* (2 vols., London, 1770), I, pp. iii–iv.

[19] G. Bonfante, 'A contribution to the history of Celtology', *Celtica* 3 (1956), 31; S. Brough, *The Goths and the concept of Gothic in Germany from 1500 to 1750* (Frankfurt, 1985), pp. 157–8; Droixhe, *La linguistique*, p. 129.

[20] Simon Pelloutier, *Histoire des Celtes* (The Hague, 1740), p. 152.

out of which these flimsy categories were constructed and the basic contours of ethnological and philological discourse. Classical writings constituted a vital reservoir of source material and evidence for early modern ethnographers. Like other areas of intellectual endeavour in this era the study of ethnic groups was largely a text-based activity. Archaeology impinged only slightly on the construction of ethnic difference, though a new and important role was opening up for comparative philology. To the humanist intellectual elites of sixteenth- and seventeenth-century Europe the Celtae were familiar as one of the major prehistoric founder-settlers of northern Europe – the Keltoi of the ancient Greeks, and Celtae of ancient Roman authors. The Keltoi were perceived to have some affinity with the Galatae; others interpreted the Celtae to be the Gauls and other peoples related to them in Spain and Italy.[21]

The works of Tacitus and Caesar remained necessary buttresses of ethnological argument, and shaped the construction of the Celt. Caesar advanced a more restricted view of the Celtae, limiting the term to the tribes of middle Gaul. Only one thing seems clear – that classical commentators did not include the Britons among the Celtae. The literati of early modern Europe found the classical ethnographic legacy difficult to master, and varied widely in their exegeses of the vague and conflicting textual references to the Celtae, as also in their discussions of the Scythians. In particular, it appeared that the manners of the ancient Germans described by Tacitus in the *Germania* bore a marked similarity to the customs of the Gauls described in Caesar's *Gallic war*. Moreover, the noble Caledonians who appeared in Tacitus's *Agricola* appeared to have the same ferocious libertarian characteristics as the tribes of ancient Germany. The *Germania* was used as a pertinent source both in Gothicist ideology and in investigations of the Celt (and vice versa in the case of Caesar's *Gallic war*).[22] Samuel Squire, extolling the virtues of the Anglo-Saxons, warned his readers: 'I shall not scruple to illustrate this account of the ancient German customs and manners by what I find in Caesar, or any other author concerning the Gauls, and the other Celtic nations.'[23]

In addition to the efforts of classical geographers and historians, early modern scholars were also burdened with the efforts of medieval chroniclers to reconcile the Genesis account of the dispersal of peoples with classical ethnography. Such glosses further confounded the existing vagueness in classical accounts of the barbarian peoples who lived outside the expanding sphere of central and eastern Mediterranean civilisation,

---

[21] Piggott, *Celts*, pp. 4–5.

[22] See Philip Cluverius, *An introduction into geography both ancient and modern* (Oxford, 1657), p. 127.

[23] Samuel Squire, *An enquiry into the foundation of the English constitution; or, an historical essay upon the Anglo-Saxon government both in Germany and England* (London, 1745), pp. 17–18 n.

and added to the miasma of possible genealogies surrounding the origins of the Celtae. Gaps were filled where possible with (apparently) relevant scraps of information found in classical authors and medieval chronicles. Antiquarians, as we shall see, were quick to exploit superficial etymological resemblances as a means of establishing genealogical relationships between ethnic groups. It so happened that the notional descents of the Celtic and German peoples were littered with tribal nomenclature suggestive of some degree of kinship between these two ethnic stocks.[24]

The dominant figure in early modern ethnic classification was the renowned German geographer and antiquary, Philip Cluverius (1580–1622). In his influential treatise *Germania antiqua* (1616), Cluverius divided the peoples of Europe into two broad groupings, the Celts and the Sarmatians. Among the Celts Cluverius listed most of the nations of northern and western Europe: the Gauls, Germans, Britons, Saxons and Scythians. The Sarmatians, on the other hand, were basically the Slavic peoples of central and eastern Europe. The sacred genealogies of Noah's descendants found in Genesis reinforced the close link between the Celts and Germans in the Japhetan line.[25] The system of ethnic classification which Cluverius established in the early seventeenth century was maintained well into the eighteenth century by later generations of linguistic and ethnographic scholars, most prominent among whom were Justus Georg Schottel (1612–72), Johann Georg Keysler (1689/1693–1743), the Genevan antiquary Paul-Henri Mallet (1730–1807) who went on to become professor of literature at Copenhagen, the Swedish philosopher Johann Ihre (1707–80) and Simon Pelloutier, a Lyonese Huguenot born in Leipzig who ministered to the French church in Berlin and acted as librarian of the Berlin Academy. The theories of most of these figures were familiar to British scholars. Cluverius's *Introduction into geography, both ancient and modern*, which included ethnological matter, was published in English translation at Oxford in 1657, and the widely travelled Keysler, who lived in England for a while, was to be elected a Fellow of the Royal Society.[26]

[24] Johnson, 'Scythian'; Piggott, *Celts*.

[25] G. Bonfante, 'Ideas on the kinship of the European languages from 1200 to 1800', *Journal of World History* 1 (1953–4), 689; Droixhe, *La linguistique*, pp. 126–7; H. Weinbrot, 'Celts, Greeks, and Germans: Macpherson's Ossian and the Celtic epic', *1650–1850: Ideas, Aesthetics, and Inquiries in the Early Modern Era* 1 (1994), 12.

[26] *Correspondence of Thomas Gray* (ed. P. Toynbee and L. Whibley, 3 vols., Oxford, 1935), II, pp. 546, 553; Droixhe, *La linguistique*, pp. 129–32, 141; Bonfante, 'Contribution to Celtology', 33; Brough, *Goths*, p. 86; S. Piggott, *William Stukeley* (1950: London, 1985), p. 82; Piggott, *The Druids* (1968: New York, 1985), pp. 140, 162. See Antoine Banier, *The mythology and fables of the ancients, explain'd from history* (1738–40: 4 vols., London, 1739–40), III, p. 306. However, Gray believed that the (misunderstood) Keysler's 'Celtic and his septentrional antiquities [were] two things entirely distinct': see Gray to William Mason, 13 January 1758, in *Correspondence of Thomas Gray*, II, pp. 550–1.

In early seventeenth-century linguistics a Scytho-Celtic compound was hypothesised as the probable basis of the modern European languages. However, not all of the modern 'Celtic' languages were included within the Scytho-Celtic group. While many eighteenth-century philological models tended to link the Brythonic peoples with the Germanic, there was some reluctance, ironically, to embrace the Goidelic tongues within this 'Celtic' group. Ethnologically, the 'Celts' constituted a much broader grouping of peoples than the modern-day 'Celts', but excluded the Irish.[27] With the exception of Joseph Justus Scaliger (1540–1609), who grouped Welsh discretely among the seven *matrices minores* rather than the four basic groupings, or *matrices maiores*, of Latin, Greek, Teutonic and Slavonic, the mainstream of seventeenth-century European linguistic scholars identified the Brythonic as a close kin of the principal continental tongues within the broad supergroup of Celto-Scythian languages.[28] Goidelic, by contrast, was usually seen as doubly isolated: it was neither linked to the main body of European languages, nor was its affiliation to Brythonic generally established. The main exception was the pan-Germanist linguistic model of Schottel which embraced the full range of Celtic tongues, including Irish, as well as the Gothic family of languages.[29]

Abraham Mylius (1563–1637) used a bewildering series of interchangeable terms to denote the Germanic language group – *lingua Teutonica*, *lingua Germanica*, *lingua Celtica*, *lingua Cimbrica*, and *lingua Belgica*, not forgetting luxuriant hybrids such as *lingua Cimbrica-Belgica*. The Teutonic peoples, according to an excessively latitudinarian Mylius, consisted of the Belgae, Celtae, Cimbri, Cimmerii, Galatae, Galli, Germani, Getae, Goti, Langobardi, Saxones, Scytae, Teutones and Vandali.[30] Similarly, another leading philologist Marcus Boxhorn (1602–53) of Leiden, though illuminating the relationship between Welsh and ancient Gaulish, assumed a deeper Celto-Scythian connection between Welsh and the Germanic languages.[31] The philosopher and polymath Gottfried Wilhelm Leibniz (1646–1716), who had a deep interest in philology, located a shared origin for Greek, Latin, Germanic and Gallic in an archaic *langue commune*. Leibniz thought that the Brythonic, which in-

---

[27] D. Droixhe, 'Ossian, Hermann and the Jew's harp', in T. Brown (ed.), *Celticism* (Amsterdam, 1996), pp. 21–2.

[28] Scaliger also classified Irish as another minor European language quite separate from Welsh. Droixhe, 'Ossian', p. 22; Leerssen, *Mere Irish*, p. 288; Bonfante, 'Ideas on the kinship of the European languages', 687; Bonfante, 'Contribution to Celtology', 22–3.

[29] Droixhe, 'Ossian', p. 23.

[30] G. J. Metcalf, 'Abraham Mylius on historical linguistics', *PMLA* 68 (1953), 535 n.

[31] P. Morgan, 'Boxhorn, Leibniz and the Welsh', *Studia Celtica* 8–9 (1973–4), 220–8; Droixhe, *La linguistique*, pp. 334–5.

cluded ancient Gaulish and its closest surviving relatives, Welsh and Breton, was half-Teutonic: 'linguam Wallicam aut Armoricam proximam veteri Gallicae ipse credo, nec indiligenter inspexi, et semi-Germanam agnosco'. Irish Gaelic was, however, considerably more distant from the Germanic languages.[32] With his suspicion of an uncritical etymologising, belief that a distinction had to be made between cognates and loan-words and suspicion of some of the Abbé Pezron's claims for the high antiquity of Gaulic, Leibniz stood at the limits of early modern linguistic speculation. Yet, he did not challenge the basic Scytho-Celtic model, which remained influential within the eighteenth-century republic of letters.[33] According to Pelloutier, for example, the German tongue was a remnant of the Celtic Ur-language, 'un reste de l'ancienne langue des Celtes'.[34]

'British' origins

Cluverian ethnology and Scytho-Celtic linguistics – together with the Book of Genesis and the legacy of classical authorities – constituted essential points of departure for early modern treatments of British origins. An etymological-cum-diffusionist tradition flourished into the eighteenth century which combined universal Mosaic history with a very slack approach to onomastics. Names found in classical geographers and historians and unsupported by any substantial ethnographic context were used as connecting links in the genealogies of the British peoples, often to fill in the huge gaps between their present location and their Noachic origins in the Near East. The Cimbri, a Germanic tribe associated with the Cimbric Chersonesus, or Jutland, the homeland of the Jutes, happened to posses a name which resembled the vernacular Celtic term for the Welsh descendants of the ancient Britons, Cymri. The Cimbri were directly linked to the Teutons, Jutes and Germanic history, but etymology hinted at deeper connections with the Cymri, Kimmerians and ultimately at descent from Gomer. The Scythian tribe of Cimmerians were also assumed to be a branch of the Gomerian line. Such etymological connections helped forge the rudimentary structures of ethnological taxonomy. It was often easier to accommodate subversive data within the

[32] Bonfante, 'Contribution to Celtology', 26–9; Bonfante, 'Ideas on the kinship of the European languages', 693; Droixhe, *La linguistique*, p. 133. See Leibniz to the linguist Hiob Ludolf (1624–1704), July 25, 1702, in J. T. Waterman (ed.), *Leibniz and Ludolf on things linguistic: excerpts from their correspondence (1688–1703)* (University of California publications in linguistics 88, Berkeley and Los Angeles, 1978), p. 56 (and Waterman, 'Commentary', pp. 59–60).

[33] Droixhe, *De l'origine du langage*, pp. 74–5; Bonfante, 'Contribution to Celtology', 29–31; Leerssen, *Mere Irish*, pp. 291–2; Droixhe, *La linguistique*, pp. 132–3.

[34] Pelloutier, *Histoire des Celtes*, p. 165.

established parameters of Celto-German kinship than to challenge the paradigm.

In the early seventeenth century the Mosaic paradigm held sway. Various English antiquaries made the pseudo-etymological connection of Gomerites, Cimmeri and Cimbri which linked Celts and Germans.[35] Verstegan, a founding father of the English Gothicist tradition, acknowledged the kinship of the Saxon and Celtic peoples in the lineage of Noah's grandson Gomer, and noted that both the Germans and the Gauls were referred to by the ancients as Celtae.[36] John Speed believed the Cimbrians to be the ancestors of the Celts and Gauls.[37] Peter Heylin traced the descent of the Cimbri back through the Cimmerians to Gomer, the supposed grandfather of the Celts.[38] In *Pansebeia* (1653), his influential encyclopaedia of the world's religions, which went through six editions in the second half of the seventeenth century, Alexander Ross grouped together the common religious practices of the Germans, Gauls and Britons (though he dealt separately with those of the Scythians, Getes, Cimbrians and Goths).[39] The Cambridge antiquary Daniel Langhorne believed the Germans to be 'Cimbrians (or Gomerians) . . . and therefore of kin to the Gauls'. With a misplaced genealogical precision he identified the Angles as a tribe of the Suevi offspring of the Asiatic Syebi and Sasones who were 'of the same Gomerian original with the Cimbrians'. Moreover, Langhorne derived the various other peoples of the British Isles from Germanic stock. The Picts and Scots were 'Gothic nations, of the same Gomerian original with the Cimbrians, and came from Scandia, which is also called Scythia Germanica'; the Irish too could be traced to the 'German Chauci'.[40] Langhorne's fellow Cantabrigian, the orientalist Robert Sheringham, argued that the Cimbri, the ethnic stock of the Saxons, Angles and Getae, had been known to the ancients as – and confounded with – the Celts, Gauls, Germans and Galatians.[41]

The institutions, laws and manners of the Celtic Britons were woven into the ancient libertarian pattern of English history. Like the awkward 'conquering' Normans, the Celts were trimmed to fit the Procrustean bed of Anglo-Saxon constitutionalism. Within the prevailing languages of seventeenth- and eighteenth-century English political culture, such as

---

[35] J. W. Johnson, 'The Scythian: his rise and fall', *JHI* 20 (1959), 256; Kliger, *Goths*, p. 292.
[36] Richard Verstegan, *A restitution of decayed intelligence* (1605: London, 1634), pp. 9, 28; Piggott, *Celts*, p. 11.
[37] D. Woolf, *The idea of history in early Stuart England* (Toronto, 1990), p. 69.
[38] Peter Heylin, *Cosmographie* (London, 1652), 'General introduction', p. 15.
[39] Alexander Ross, *Pansebeia: or, a view of all religions in the world* (London, 1653), pp. 127–32.
[40] Daniel Langhorne, *An introduction to the history of England* (London, 1676), pp. 17, 197.
[41] Robert Sheringham, *De Anglorum gentis origine disceptatio* (Cambridge, 1670), ch. 3.

common law immemorialism and whiggish ancient constitutionalism, Celtic and Saxon characters tended not to be contrasted as timeless antitheses. The logic of these prescriptive schemes dictated otherwise. Thus Celts and Saxons were, instead, linked temporally as successive and almost indistinguishable manifestations of the libertarian spirit which had inspired the peoples of the realm of England since its earliest recorded settlement. Ethnic affinity reinforced the plausibility of immemorialism.[42]

Writing in the immediate aftermath of the Union of the Crowns of 1603, George Saltern gave voice in his antiquarian treatise *Of the antient lawes of Great Britaine* (1605) to the argument that all the peoples of Britain were descended from the same lineage.[43] Saltern inserted this notion of the ethnic consanguinity of Britain's Celtic and Germanic stocks into an overarching thesis that the common law was of ancient British origin, had been maintained by the Saxons, and also bore strong affinities to the ancient customary laws and institutions of the Scots.[44] Thus, a more perfect union of the laws would betray neither legal heritage.

In his *History of gavel-kind* (1663), Silas Taylor denied that this custom was peculiar to Kent. Rather, he argued, gavelkind tenures had been established in England by 'our British aborigines'. Underlying Taylor's excursion down this antiquarian byway was a concern to defend the shibboleth of an immemorial chain of continuity in English legal history: in spite of 'several changes and revolutions of affairs, and governments', the previous 1,700 years had witnessed 'no considerable mutations or alterations in our laws and customs'. The cause of prescriptive legitimacy entailed the neglect not only of substantial differences between the customs and institutions of the Celtic Britons – 'the first planters of our isle' – and their successors, but also the assumption of a Celtic provenance for gavelkind.[45] A century later, Smollett too traced gavelkind to an ancient British origin.[46]

An examination of the ethnological fantasies constructed by the late seventeenth-century English antiquarian Aylette Sammes reveals the twin influences of scholarly confusion and ideological motivations. Sammes captured the ancient Britons for the same Germanic lineage as the Anglo-Saxon nation. Sammes was obsessed with proving the ethnic

---

[42] See Nathaniel Bacon, *An historical and political discourse of the laws and government of England* (1647: London, 1689 edn), p. 10.

[43] George Saltern, *Of the antient lawes of Great Britaine* (London, 1605), pp. 12–16.

[44] *Ibid.*, esp. pp. 3, 5, 29–31, 58–9, 69–73.

[45] Silas Taylor, *The history of gavel-kind* (London, 1663), p. 80.

[46] Tobias Smollett, *A complete history of England from the descent of Julius Caesar* (1757–8: 2nd edn, 11 vols., London, 1758–60), I, p. 232 n. See also Thomas Carte, *A general history of England* (4 vols., London, 1747–55), I, p. 79.

unity of the peoples of England. Not only were the Saxons, Angles and Jutes 'all branches of the same stock, though called differently, agreeing exactly in language, customs, and religions', but the superficially alien Celts, the Britons, who had preceded these Gothic peoples were also of Germanic stock:

> I have been more particular in treating of these Cimbri, because from a branch of this very same nation, in after ages, our English ancestors proceeded, providence so ordering it, that although the ancient Cumri of Britain were grievously molested by the Gauls, and afterward afflicted and kept under by the Romans, yet may they be said to have recovered these seats again, although not by themselves, being but a small relic, yet by the succession of a people descended from the same original.

Apparent differences of language, and of closer affinities with the Gauls, were explained away. The 'concordance' between the Britons and the Gauls 'in point of language and other customs' did not arise from ethnic kinship, but from circumstances, notably 'their joint commerce with the Phoenicians'.[47]

Sir William Temple subscribed to the view that the ancient septentrional peoples had enjoyed similar primitive manners and institutions. Clanship was found even among the Gothic peoples. Temple noted that the government of the ancient Britons was 'like that of the ancient Gauls, of several small nations under petty princes, which seem the original governments of the world, and deduced from the natural force and right of paternal dominion: such were the hordes among the Goths, the clans in Scotland, and septs in Ireland'. The Gaels of Ireland and Scotland, Temple believed, were both peoples of northern Scythian stock.[48]

In the late seventeenth century there were strong links between Saxonist and Celticist scholarship. The pioneering Celticist Edward Lhuyd (1660–1709) took an interest in Saxon and Danish studies, and belonged to the same close-knit if quarrelsome cohort of Oxford literati as the renowned Saxonist George Hickes.[49] Lhuyd made a tremendous contribution towards undoing the terminological confusion which surrounded the notion of Celticity. Elaborating upon insights made by the humanist George Buchanan in the late sixteenth century between the Belgic and 'Celtic' languages of the ancient peoples of the British Isles,[50] and carrying out philological fieldwork in the Celtic peripheries, Lhuyd grouped

---

[47] Aylette Sammes, *Britannia antiqua illustrata* (London, 1676), 'Preface' and pp. 15, 411.
[48] William Temple, *An introduction to the history of England*, in Temple, *Works* (2 vols., London, 1731), II, pp. 531, 533–4.
[49] G. J. Williams, 'The history of Welsh scholarship', *Studia Celtica* 8–9 (1973–4), 209–11.
[50] A. Williamson, *Scottish national consciousness in the reign of James VI* (Edinburgh, 1979), p. 123.

and classified the Celtic languages.[51] Thus, by the early eighteenth century, the linguistic affinities of Welsh, Irish Gaelic, Scots Gaelic, Manx, Cornish and Breton were known, and the distinction between the P-Celtic group (Welsh, Breton and Cornish) and the Q-Celtic (the Gaelic tongues and Manx) had been established. Yet, the work of Lhuyd was far from creating a pan-Celtic identity.

Lhuyd's pioneering technical contribution to Celtic studies was less widely read and much less influential within British antiquarian circles at the turn of the eighteenth century than the vivid fantasy-picture of ancient Europe woven by his French contemporary the Abbé Pezron (whose work Lhuyd was, ironically, keen to promote).[52] As a result, the latter's Japhetan scheme remained a major building block of British Celticism well into the age of Enlightenment. According to Pezron, Celts and Germans could take pride in their kindred genealogies:

As therefore the language, which Gomer, who was the father of the Celtae, left his posterity, was an original language, made in the time of the confusion at Babel, some ages after the Deluge; we must say and think the same thing concerning that of Ashkenaz, who was the father of the Germans, which he left to his descendants: And this without doubt is the reason, why Moses took so much care to mention these two men in the tenth of Genesis; they being the father and founders of two of the most famous and potent nations that came from Japhet, Noah's eldest son. Now in viewing the origin of these two powerful nations, the conformity between their languages may easily be discovered: For the Celtae descending from Gomer, and the Germans from Ashkenaz, his eldest son, it's no difficult thing to imagine, that the language of these two nations, who had in a manner the same origin, must be in some sort like to one another.[53]

Lhuyd's comparative approach was unable to displace the established etymological-diffusionist tradition. Thomas Carte attributed the ancient peopling of Europe to the Gomerian Celts, of whom the Germans, descendants of Ashkenaz, were an important branch.[54] The *Universal history* (1736) made the classic connection between the descendants of Gomer, the Galatians – 'the Gauls of Asia Minor', the Cimmerians, Cimbri and the Welsh Cymri.[55] This was still the case in the middle of the eighteenth century. According to the revisionist *History of the Cymbri (or Brittains)* (1746):

[51] Edward Lhuyd, *Archaeologia Britannica* (Oxford, 1707); F. V. Emery, *Edward Lhuyd FRS 1660–1709* (Cardiff, 1971), esp. p. 87.

[52] P. Morgan, 'The Abbé Pezron and the Celts', *Transactions of the Honourable Society of Cymmrodorion* (1965), 286; Morgan, *Eighteenth-century renaissance*, pp. 87–9, 106; Williams, 'History of Welsh scholarship', 214–15, 218; Jenkins, *Foundations*, pp. 223–4.

[53] Paul Pezron, *The antiquities of nations; more particularly of the Celtae or Gauls, taken to be originally the same people as our ancient Britains* (1703: trans. D. Jones, London, 1706), p. 222.   [54] Carte, *General history*, I, p. 12 n.

[55] *An universal history, from the earliest account of time to the present* (7 vols., London, 1736–44), I, p. 166.

Tis very generally held that the Germans, Gauls, Britons and Irish were originally one and the same nation, only divided in process of time into so many different clans or branches. This opinion prevails among our historians, very few to be found of different sentiment. But it is a gross error.[56]

Nevertheless, this treatise also retailed the traditional line about the lack of any strong connection between the Welsh and Irish: 'the Irish Celtae and the Cymbri were two different nations, and had each their peculiar different tongue even since mankind were cantoned into several different tribes at the Tower of Babel'.[57] In *The origin of language and nations* (1764), the Welsh scholar Rowland Jones argued that the 'Cimbri, Gauls, Celtes and Germans [were] the descendants of Gomer and his eldest son Ashkenaz'.[58] Similarly, in his *History of England* the London-based Scot Tobias Smollett associated the ancient Celtae with the Cimbri and Teutons.[59]

The Celto-Scythian paradigm remained intact throughout much of the English Enlightenment. In this era antiquarians were still groping towards a hard and fast distinction between Celtic and Germanic cultures and peoples. Many of the literati of the middle of the eighteenth century took similar interests in the Celtic and Gothic pasts, and often confused them. Squire referred to 'the Celts, part of whom the Britons, as well as the Germans undoubtedly were'.[60] Bolingbroke even included the Normans within an almost meaningless Celtic supergroup. The Normans, he claimed cavalierly, 'were originally of Celtic, or Gothic extraction, call it what you please, as well as the people they subdued. They came out of the same northern hive.' Bolingbroke used Celtic and Scythian in a 'large and general sense', their original meanings. For by Celtae the ancients had comprehended not only the people of Gaul, but a much wider grouping.[61]

An ancient constitutional imperative reinforced the notional resemblances between the Celtic and Gothic peoples of the English past. If whigs claimed feudal tenures as an institution which preceded the irruption of the Normans in 1066, then would that argument not be stronger if they could establish the earlier provenance of feudalism in the customs of the indigenous ancient Britons? Unsurprisingly, some English antiquaries believed that Celtic British tenures had conformed to a basic feudal model. Henry Rowlands devoted a section of his *Mona antiqua restaurata*

---

[56] *The history of the Cymbri (or Brittains)* (n.p., 1746), p. 141.   [57] *Ibid.*, pp. 153–4.

[58] Rowland Jones, *The origin of language and nations* (London, 1764), 'Preface'.

[59] Smollett, *Complete history of England*, I, pp. 6–9. Cf. William Stukeley, *Stonehenge, a temple restored to the British Druids* (London, 1740), pp. 47–8, on the descent of the Welsh through the Germanic Belgae.

[60] Squire, *Enquiry into the foundation of the English constitution*, p. 25 n.

[61] Bolingbroke, *Remarks on the history of England* (1730–1), in Bolingbroke, *Works* (5 vols., London, 1754), I, p. 316.

(1723) to the rents, services, duties, mulcts and attendances of an ancient British feudalism.[62] In a similar vein, Squire noted the basic similarities between the *comites*, *ambacti* and *soldurii* of the Britons and the thanes and *vasses* of the Saxons.[63] Most explicit of all, John Whitaker claimed that the ancient Britons had enjoyed a system of land tenures whose guiding principle was essentially feudal.[64] Thus, not only was feudalism an integral thread in the immemorial fabric of English customs and laws, but the British Celts and their Saxon cousins had also shared similar values and institutions.

Despite the decline of immemorialism, there remained an important place for the British Celts within Gothicist ideology. Seventeenth- and eighteenth-century Gothicism was a loose 'agglutinative'[65] tradition – dominated by the controlling metaphors of the hive, or storehouse, of nations – quite different from the certainties and chauvinistic exclusivism of nineteenth-century Teutonic racialism. The terms Goth and Celt displayed a similar elasticity in their range of ethnic reference. For instance, the Gothicist rhetoric of the anti-Walpolean Patriots embraced a variety of non-Roman peoples, Celts included.[66] The contrast between the classical and septentrional worlds embodied a more vivid opposition than the differences comprehended within the latter catch-all.

In the eighteenth century the voguish appetite for libertarian primitivism was fed from both Gothic and Celtic sources. Pelloutier, in particular, made a vivid and unqualified case for the libertarian characteristics of the ancient Celtic peoples. He pointed to their love of liberty and to the popular accountability of their elective leaders. Above all, from the perspective of Germano-Celtic kinship, Pelloutier conferred on the ancient Celtic nations tribal meetings akin to rudimentary parliaments: 'il est constant que les assemblées générales où toutes les affaires de l'état se décidoient à la pluralité des voix, étoient le plus ferme rempart de la liberté des nations Celtiques'.[67]

Furthermore, the familiar stereotype of the industrious Teuton, and the economically hopeless Celt wrapped up in melancholy, mysticism, sentiment and the poetic was in large part a nineteenth-century invention.[68] According to the Gothicist antiquarian, Samuel Squire, the Anglo-Saxons 'were formerly extremely averse to trade; they looked upon it as

---

[62] Henry Rowlands, *Mona antiqua restaurata* (Dublin, 1723), pp. 116–32.

[63] Samuel Squire, *An historical essay upon the ballance of civil power in England* (London, 1748), pp. 124–5 n., 148–9.

[64] John Whitaker, *The history of Manchester* (2 vols., London, 1771–5), I, pp. 262–4.

[65] Kliger, *Goths*, pp. 26, 84–5.

[66] C. Gerrard, *The patriot opposition to Walpole* (Oxford, 1994), pp. 112, 136–7; B. Cottret, *Bolingbroke's political writings: the conservative Enlightenment* (Houndmills, 1997), p. 71.

[67] Pelloutier, *Histoire des Celtes*, p. 503.   [68] Sims-Williams, 'Visionary Celt'.

beneath the dignity of a soldier to condescend to practise the mechanic arts; none but a slave, agreeably to their notion of things, would submit to do the work of other people'.[69] James Ibbetson, another Gothicist, concurred: 'When the Saxons were introduced into the kingdom by Vortigern for its defence against the Scots and Picts, they had neither time nor inclination for the culture of the land; it is probable that this fell to the lot of the less warlike though more industrious Britons, who retained their former possessions under the powerful protection of their new allies.'[70] Gibbon, for instance, concluded of the Germans that a 'people jealous of their persons, and careless of their possessions, must have been totally destitute of industry and the arts, but animated with a high sense of honour and independence'.[71] By contrast, Tobias Smollett associated the ancient Celtae with commerce and trade.[72]

Moreover, the Irish historiographical tradition explicitly celebrated the ancient Milesian ancestors of the Gaels as a civilised, commercialised and technologically advanced nation.[73] Not only did the Milesians have parliaments, it was claimed, they were also governed by *aonachs*, special assemblies which 'had for their objects a close inspection into the state of trade, commerce and mechanic arts'.[74] Indeed Charles O'Conor boasted that ancient Ireland had once been a great trading nation, 'the prime emporium of the northern commerce'.[75] Only in eighteenth-century Scotland, where a progressive sociology of development was qualified by a nostalgic cult of primitive virtue and fine feelings, were the indigenous Celts, the Gaelic Highlanders, associated with economic backwardness and a lack of commercial ingenuity or application.[76] In time, this was to become the common image of the feckless Celt; but it did not hold sway in the eighteenth-century British world.

Ossian and the Picts

The most striking examples of ethnological confusion are found in eighteenth-century Scotland, in the Ossianic phenomenon and in the debate over the origins of the Picts. The ethnic politics of Ossian are not reducible to an exclusively Celtic interpretation. Indeed, it is not clear whether James Macpherson, though a Highlander and champion of Scotland's Celtic antiquity, distinguished between Celts and Germans, or, if he did,

---

[69] Squire, *Enquiry into the foundation of the English constitution*, p. 247.
[70] James Ibbetson, *A dissertation on the folclande and boclande of the Saxons* (London, 1777), p. 19.   [71] Gibbon, *DF*, I, p. 242. See also pp. 235–8.
[72] Smollett, *Complete history of England*, I, p. 7.   [73] Kidd, 'Gaelic antiquity'.
[74] Sylvester O'Halloran, *A general history of Ireland* (2 vols., London, 1778), II, p. 34.
[75] Charles O'Conor, *Dissertations on the antient history of Ireland* (Dublin, 1753), p. 4.
[76] Kidd, 'Gaelic antiquity'.

even considered himself a Celt.

It is possible that Macpherson may have thought of himself as Germanic rather than Celtic. He argued that the only ancient people of Caledonia of Germanic (though not Gothic) stock were the Catti, the ancestors of the Clan Chattan, a confederation of clans which included the Macphersons.[77] The Clan Chattan, according to Macpherson, were the descendants not of Celts but of the Germanic tribe of Catti who had in ancient times crossed the North Sea to Caithness:

It must be confessed, that several tribes in the north-east angle of Scotland have preserved in their traditions, and the genealogical histories of their families, pretensions to a German origin. The Clancattin, or the tribe of Catti, consisting of a great variety of branches . . . affirm, with one consent, that the famous Catti of ancient Germany were their ancestors.[78]

This was no fantastic invention of Macpherson's. This tradition was already an established feature of Scottish antiquarianism. For example, the celebrated antiquary Sir Robert Sibbald had advanced a similar thesis in the early eighteenth century: 'Germanicae autem originis ex Pictis fuere incolae Cathenesiae. Quae lingua Pictica dicta fuit Cattai-nes, seu promontorium Cattorum. Catai hi ex Cattis Germaniae orti sunt, nominis vestigium manet in Catana tribu Clanchattan dicta.'[79] Dr George Mackenzie also conjectured that Scotland had been populated from northern Europe. Noting 'the conformity that was to be observed betwixt the customs and manners of the ancient Celto-Scythae and our Highlanders', Mackenzie went on to confound the scalds of the Germans and the bards of the Gaels: 'The Celtae had their schaldres, who recited the genealogies of their great men; and our highlanders have their sanachies, who do the same.'[80] Although Macpherson conceded that there had been only a limited amount of migration from Germany to Caledonia, he suspected that it might nevertheless have been influential in the shaping of Caledonian identities: 'the German colony might, by intermixing their blood with the eastern Gael, have been the chief cause of that separation of government, which gave rise to the two national names

---

[77] See Macpherson's obituary in the *Scots Magazine* 58 (April 1796), 221, which begins: 'This gentleman was descended from one of the most ancient families in the north of Scotland, being cousin-german to the chief of the clan of the Macphersons, who deduce their origin from the ancient Catti of Germany.'

[78] James Macpherson, *Introduction to the history of Great Britain and Ireland* (3rd edn, London, 1773), p. 139.

[79] Robert Sibbald, *Introductio ad historiam rerum a Romanis gestarum, in ea borealis Britanniae parte, quae ultra murum Picticum est* (Edinburgh, 1706), p. 36, in Sibbald, *Tractatus varii ad Scotiae antiquae et modernae historiam facientes* (Edinburgh, 1711). See also Christopher Irvin, *Historiae Scoticae nomenclatura Latino-vernacula* (Edinburgh, 1682), p. 186.

[80] Mackenzie, *Lives of writers*, I, p. vi.

of Picts and Scots'.[81] Furthermore Macpherson himself managed to combine with his Ossianic interests a warm appreciation of the English Saxonist tradition. In his *Introduction to the history of Great Britain and Ireland*, Macpherson celebrated not only the glories of Scotland's ancient Celtic liberties, but also the English heritage of Anglo-Saxon liberty.[82] Moreover, although Macpherson believed that 'the great body of the people' of the Scottish nation was composed principally of the 'remains' of the ancient Caledonians, he none the less paid due acknowledgement to the 'Scoto-Saxon' blending in the south and east. The Saxons being 'in some measure addicted to commerce', they had fostered 'the arts of civil life' in medieval Scotland.[83]

However, there is a further level of confusion here. For Macpherson also distinguished Germans from Goths. The ancient Germans were assimilated to the Celts, but were classified separately from the Gothic race. According to James Macpherson, 'the Saxons, who poured into Britain in the fifth century, trod only in the steps of many more ancient migrations from the lower Germany', by which he meant those of the Cimbri and Belgae.[84] The Cimbri he described as 'Celtic Germans'.[85] Macpherson, however, distinguished the ancient Germans from later waves of Goths whom Macpherson classed as Sarmatae. The Celts were Germans, but not Goths. Macpherson believed the Celtic, 'Teutonic' and Slavonic language groups to be distinct and 'radically different from one another'.[86] By Teutonic, Macpherson appears to have meant Scandinavian, though he noticed close alliances between the Celto-German Cimbri and the Teutoni. The Anglo-Saxons were, according to Macpherson, 'the most unmixed of the posterity of the Sarmatae'.[87] Nevertheless, Macpherson admired the similar libertarian manners of both Celts and Sarmatic Saxons. Apart from a measure of Druid theocracy the 'public freedom' of the Celts had been as extensive as that of the Saxons.[88] In Macpherson's confused system of ethnic classification one can find warring and ill-digested elements of both the old Cluverian system and the new insights of Percy.

Macpherson's supporters were also latitudinarian in their ethnic affiliation. The Reverend John Macpherson (1710–65), whose son John was to be James Macpherson's protégé, noted parallels between the manners and forms of government of the Caledonians and the ancient Germans.[89]

---

[81] James Macpherson, *Introduction to the history of Great Britain and Ireland*, p. 82.
[82] *Ibid.*, pp. 315–404.   [83] *Ibid.*, pp. 91–2.   [84] *Ibid.*, p. 48.   [85] *Ibid.*, p. 55.
[86] *Ibid.*, p. 45.   [87] *Ibid.*, p. 38.   [88] *Ibid.*, pp. 289–97.
[89] John Macpherson, *Critical dissertations on the origins, antiquities, language, government, manners and religion of the ancient Caledonians* (London, 1768), pp. 151–73. Such attitudes even found their way into the law courts. See Advocates' Library (Edinburgh), Session Papers, Elphinstone 32.1, cases 1–7, Allan Maconochie, 'Information for Joseph

James Grant (1743?–1835), an advocate who wrote in defence of the glories of Ossian and took pride in Gaelic as the universal language, felt no inhibitions about including Gothicist sentiments in these Celticist treatises. He expressed admiration for the libertarian manners of the ancient Tacitean Germans, and also celebrated the roles of the 'industrious' Anglo-Saxons who had fled England in the aftermath of the Norman Conquest, as well as Normans and Flemings, in the benign Gothicising of medieval Scotland: the Anglo-Saxons had not only 'mixed with the ancient inhabitants of Scotland', but, 'being farther advanced in the knowledge of the useful arts than were the people with whom they had inmixed', had 'gradually improved the condition of the Scottish people'.[90] Among the champions of Ossian, the Reverend John Smith of Kilbrandon in Argyleshire noted that 'Tacitus ascribes to the old rude Germans all the virtues which Ossian ascribes to his heroes, who were originally the same people, and had the same customs, religion and laws.'[91]

The appeal of Ossian reached well beyond the 'Celtic' world. Given that the Caledonian epic made its appearance when the basic Cluverian categories remained operative, it should occasion little surprise that the works of Ossian made a profound impact in Germany and Scandinavia. Ossian provided for the peoples of northern Europe an ancient epic, a cast of heroes and an iconography to rival those of the classical antiquity of the Mediterranean.[92] Ossian was acknowledged as the northern Homer. In Germany, the cult of Ossian fuelled the rise of a nationalist consciousness. Not only was Herder, the intellectual father of nationalism, an Ossianic enthusiast, so was the poetic champion of ancient Germanic martial valour, Friedrich Gottlieb Klopstock (1724–1803). Klopstock's glorification of the ancient German hero Hermann, or Arminius, was accomplished between 1764 and 1774 under the spell of Ossian. Indeed, Klopstock considered Macpherson's ancient Caledonians to be a Germanic people.[93] Similarly, in Scandinavia Ossian inspired the composition of patriotic Gothic history and the rise of national romanticisms.[94]

Knight, a native of Africa, pursuer in the action at his instance; against John Wedderburn of Ballandean, Esq., defender' (1775), p. 21: 'The Celtic tribes who inhabited Scotland, probably possessed the same laws and customs which prevailed among the aborigines of Germany.'

[90] James Grant, *Essays on the origin of society* (London, 1785), pp. 126–9; Grant, *Thoughts on the origin and descent of the Gael* (Edinburgh, 1814), pp. 21–2, 336–7, 346–53.

[91] John Smith, *Galic antiquities* (Edinburgh, 1780), p. 110 n.

[92] J. L. Greenway, 'The gateway to innocence: Ossian and the Nordic bard as myth', in H. E. Pagliaro (ed.), *Studies in eighteenth-century culture*, vol. IV (Madison, WI, 1975), p. 165.

[93] P. Van Tieghem, *Ossian et l'ossianisme dans la littérature européenne au XVIIe siècle* (Groningen, 1920), pp. 33, 41; T. J. Beck, *Northern antiquities in French learning and literature (1755–1855)* (New York, 1934), pp. 10–11, 114–17; H. Gaskill, 'Herder, Ossian and the Celtic', in Brown, *Celticism*.

The Scottish antiquarian debate over the origins and identity of the Picts recapitulates some of the same confusions and cross-appropriations found in the Ossian phenomenon. In Scotland the Picts, a Brythonic people, were mistakenly adopted as a Gothic people by a great many eighteenth-century commentators, in part because of a few stray references in Tacitus and Bede.[95] The prominent English cleric and scholar Edward Stillingfleet believed that the Picts had migrated to Scotland from the Cimbric Chersonesus.[96] Sir Robert Sibbald described the Picts as 'Scano-Goths'.[97] John Macpherson was sceptical of any direct link, preferring an interpretation of Pictish origins which dwelt on their migration from Gaul via south Britain rather than on any conjectured North Sea crossing, but the weight of evidence pushed him towards agnosticism: 'It evidently appears to any one acquainted with the early history of the Germans and Caledonians, that the point of customs and national manners, is much more striking than between the Caledonians and Britons. This seems greatly to favour the opinion of Tacitus, and the tradition preserved by Bede. But it must be confessed, that nothing decisive can be said on this head.'[98] In the late eighteenth century, John Pinkerton used the Gothic associations of the Picts as the foundation for a full-blown Scottish Teutonism. Absurdly, Pinkerton celebrated the (Celtic) Picts as a libertarian and industrious Teutonic people – the ancestors of the successful Lowlanders of modern Scotland.[99] In the great Pictish debate which ensued, scholars such as George Chalmers and the Northumbrian Joseph Ritson established the case that the Picts were Brythonic Celts. Nevertheless, Pinkerton had his supporters and some influence on the emergence in nineteenth-century Scotland of a racist ideology celebrating the common Teutonic origins of Britain's core English and Lowland Scots nations.[100] By a delicious irony, this version of Teutonic racialism took its rise from a confused appropriation by Gothicists of a shadowy Celtic past.

---

[94] Van Tieghem, *Ossian et l'ossianisme*, pp. 41–2; J. Simpson, 'Some eighteenth-century intellectual contacts between Scotland and Scandinavia', in G. G. Simpson (ed.), *Scotland and Scandinavia 800–1800* (Edinburgh, 1990), p. 127.

[95] Tacitus, *Agricola*, in Tacitus, *On Britain and Germany* (trans. H. Mattingly, Harmondsworth, 1948), ch. 11; Bede, *A history of the English church and people* (trans. L. Sherley-Price, Harmondsworth, 1955), ch. 1.

[96] Stillingfleet, *Origines Britannicae*, pp. 245–8.

[97] Sibbald, *Introductio ad historiam rerum a Romanis gestarum*, pp. 37–42.

[98] John Macpherson, *Critical dissertations*, p. 168.

[99] John Pinkerton, *An enquiry into the history of Scotland* (with Pinkerton, *A dissertation on the origin and progress of the Scythians or Goths* (1787); 1789: 2 vols., Edinburgh, 1814).

[100] C. Kidd, 'Teutonist ethnology and Scottish nationalist inhibition, 1780–1880', *SHR* 74 (1995), esp. 51–5; B. H. Bronson, *Joseph Ritson, scholar-at-arms* (2 vols., Berkeley, CA, 1938), I, pp. 200–14.

The divorce

Druidism played an important role in the divorce of the Celt from the septentrional concept, but only in the long run. The Druids were valued, as we have seen in earlier chapters, as 'sacred bards' who transmitted the *prisca theologia* of the patriarchs to the ancient Britons, thus preparing the way for the easy and early reception of Christianity in England.[101] Though some antiquaries continued throughout the eighteenth century to celebrate the Druids as patriotic proto-Protestants, an alternative thesis of Druid priestcraft and tyranny emerged in the late seventeenth century. The negative stereotype of Druid priestcraft and sacrifice made an influential appearance in Aylette Sammes's *Britannia antiqua illustrata* (1676), with its vivid imagery of the sacrificial wicker man (though Theophilus Gale's *Court of the Gentiles* (1669–70) had already manifested some concern about human sacrifice and a powerful priestly hierarchy).[102] Promoters of deism and natural religion, most notably John Toland in his *History of the Druids* (1726), projected on to the Druids the evils they detected in the corrupt mystery religions upheld by the priesthoods of Rome and Canterbury.[103] At a lower level of intensity, orthodox Anglican and presbyterian clerics denounced Druidism for its resemblance to Romish corruptions and clericalist pretensions. Some antiquaries captured the ambivalence of the Druid legacy, noting both the original truths of Druid religion and the benefits of Druid wisdom in legislation, while tracing a sorry story of subsequent corruption and tyranny. Rowlands described both how the patriarchal religion had been brought to British shores in ancient times, and how 'soon after [it] became, as well here as in other countries, abominably corrupted, and perverted into the grossest heathenish fictions and barbarities'. Yet, despite the immolations, human sacrifices and 'diabolical magic' of the Druids, they remained staunch upholders of monotheism.[104]

Henceforth, the pre-Christian religion of the ancient Britons proved an arena of contention and ambiguity. Were the Druids sacred bards and philosophers or juggling magicians and power-hungry prelates? Were their sacred oak groves and stone circles the simple cathedrals of an uncorrupted patriarchal religion or the sacrificial temples of an illiberal priesthood? Should the Druids be praised for their legislative wisdom or

---

[101] See above, ch. 3.
[102] Sammes, *Britannia antiqua illustrata*; Theophilus Gale, *The court of the Gentiles* (2 vols., Oxford, 1669–70), II, pp. 79–81.
[103] R. Huddleston (ed.), *A new edition of Toland's history of the Druids* (Montrose, 1814); J. Mee, *Dangerous enthusiasm: William Blake and the culture of radicalism in the 1790s* (Oxford, 1992), p. 94.
[104] Rowlands, *Mona antiqua restaurata*, pp. 45, 140. For the persistence of such views, see S. Piggott, *Ancient Britons and the antiquarian imagination* (London, 1989), p. 149.

denounced for their gross usurpation of lay offices? To some Protestant scholars, the Druids practised the tyranny, superstition and encroachments upon the temporal sphere later perfected in the Roman Catholic Church. The tory historian Thomas Carte faced criticism for building a clericalist interpretation of English history upon the ancient precedent of Druidic involvement in the civil administration of the Britons. Squire, his whig opponent, detected suggestions of Cardinal Bellarmine's outrageous claims for the powers of the papacy in Carte's depiction of a quasi-papal Arch-Druid and of Druid involvement both as magistrates and legislators in the civil administration of the Celts.[105] The new legend of Druid priestcraft did not accord with the values of an Erastian Anglican whiggism.

Robert Henry, a Scots presbyterian minister and author of a multi-volume *History of Great Britain* (1771–93), upheld the notion that Druidism had been of patriarchal derivation. 'Knowledge of the true God, and of the most essential principles of religion', had descended to the Celts from Gomer, the eldest son of Japhet. However, the Celts had squandered this legacy. As the Druids became established as a powerful priestly caste they had resorted to the standard stratagem of priestcraft, the maintenance of a double doctrine. Initiates into the Druid order were indoctrinated into a secret esoteric religion which included truths about such matters as the immortality of the soul, while to the ignorant laity the order collectively propagated an inferior public theology composed of 'a thousand mythological fables'. Not only did the Druids engross power and privilege to their order and indulge in barbarous sacrifices, but they corrupted the beliefs of their flocks, allowing God to be worshipped by the vulgar as a plurality of different divinities, including the sun, moon and stars.[106]

Smollett produced a mixed account of Druidism. The Druids had dominated the legislature, confounded civil and religious jurisdictions and, in the person of the chief Druid, engrossed an unlimited power in religious matters. Nevertheless, they had upheld monotheism, albeit alongside Pythagorean metempsychosis, and they had contributed to the impartial administration of justice.[107] Despite some equivocation about the intellectual achievements of the Druids, there was a general consensus among historians that they had been guilty of a high-handed theocracy.[108]

[105] [Samuel Squire?], *Remarks upon Mr. Carte's specimen of his 'General history of England'* (London, 1748), pp. 13, 19–20, 31.

[106] Robert Henry, *The history of Great Britain* (6 vols., London, 1771–93), I, pp. 92, 102–4, 113. See also William Maitland, *The history and antiquities of Scotland* (London, 1757), pp. 154–5.

[107] Smollett, *Complete history of England*, I, pp. 9–17.

Besides Druid priestcraft, other untoward elements were creeping into the picture. Pelloutier, for example, drew attention to the vices of the Celts. Their famed libertarianism was but the obverse side of Celtic manners, which were strongly characterised by indolence – *la paresse* – and a susceptibility to drink – *l'yvrognerie*.[109] The Celts had also lacked a high culture, commercial ways and material civilisation. The long-term decline of immemorialism undermined the notion of the shared political customs of Briton and Saxon. Oliver Goldsmith saw no similarity between the basic customs and political institutions of the Britons – governed by 'despotic' monarchies – and the libertarian Germans.[110] However, these criticisms and contrasts did not amount to a systematic assault on the notion of Celtic–German affinities. For example, Rowlands did not attempt to disaggregate the pagan religions of Celt and Goth. He argued, for instance, that many Druids had fled to Scandinavia after the Roman invasion, which in turn explained 'the congruity' of the Runic religion with Druidism. Were not the Druids similar to 'the Schaldry of Iceland'? The Icelandic Edda had 'a very considerable coherence' with Druidism, and their altars resembled Druid cromlechs.[111]

Cluverian ethnology truly hit the intellectual buffers with Thomas Percy's *Northern antiquities* (1770), an English edition of Paul-Henri Mallet's *Introduction a l'histoire de Dannemarc* (1755–6). Percy subverted the very text he was editing. Indeed, he refined Mallet's work by replacing its ethnological scheme with the first serious attempt to break up the indiscriminate septentrional yoking of Celt and German. Percy felt obliged to puncture 'an opinion that has been a great source of mistake and confusion to many learned writers of the ancient history of Europe, viz., that of the ancient Gauls and Germans, the Britons and Saxons, to have been all originally one and the same people; thus confounding the antiquities of the Gothic and Celtic nations'.[112] Percy spelt out the fact that ancient Britain, Germany, Scandinavia and Gaul had not been 'inhabited by the descendants of one single race'.[113] Nor had the Celts and Germans been closely related peoples who shared similar ethnic characteristics. Reacting to the stubborn hold of Cluverian ethnography, Percy was obliged to hammer home the message 'that these were *ab origine* two distinct people, very unlike in their manners, customs, religion and laws'.[114] Percy had no truck with the familiar correspondence between Celtic and Gothic liberties:

---

[108] Oliver Goldsmith, *The history of England* (4 vols., London, 1771), I, pp. 6–7; Maitland, *History and antiquities of Scotland*, p. 51.

[109] Pelloutier, *Histoire des Celtes*, pp. 556–73.   [110] Goldsmith, *History*, I, p. 47.

[111] Rowlands, *Mona antiqua restaurata*, pp. 110–11.

[112] Percy, 'Translator's preface', p. ii.   [113] *Ibid.*, p. iv.   [114] *Ibid.*

They differed no less in their institutions and laws. The Celtic nations do not appear to have had that equal plan of liberty, which was the peculiar honour of all the Gothic tribes, and which they carried them, and planted wherever they formed settlements: On the contrary, in Gaul, all the freedom and power chiefly centred among the Druids and the chiefmen, whom Caesar calls equites, or knights: But the inferior people were little better than in a state of slavery; whereas the meanest German was independent and free.[115]

Percy had begun to shake the ethnological foundations upon which the polyethnicist version of English ancient constitutionalism rested. This traditional framework relied upon a basic similarity or affinity between Anglo-Saxon and ancient British manners, values and institutions.

The priestly order of Druids constituted another major difference which Percy detected between the Celts and the Germans 'that peculiar hierarchy or sacred college among the Celts . . . has nothing to resemble it among any of the Gothic or Teutonic nations'.[116] Although there had been priests among the Goths, these had been less obtrusive than the Druids who had, according to Percy, interfered in the civil as well as the religious governance of the Celts. Moreover, whereas the Celts had subscribed to bizarre doctrines of metempsychosis, Percy perceived in the Edda of the northern nations a solid unsuperstitious civil religion with a proto-Christian doctrine of future rewards and punishments, including 'a fixed Elyzium, and a Hell, where the valiant and just were rewarded; and where the cowardly and wicked suffered punishment'.[117] In Percy's work one can already see the familiar lineaments of the nineteenth-century stereotype of the superstitious mystical priest-ridden Celt.

In general, Percy criticised the practice of confounding the 'traits . . . found in every savage nation upon earth'. Instead, he stressed differences between the Celts and Germans, not the 'general resemblances' which might lead the unwary ethnographer to posit a direct connection, for example, between such disparate peoples as the ancient Britons and the North American Cherokee, both of whom happened to put war paint on their bodies.[118]

Percy was not alone in his findings. In 1754 Johann Schoepflin's treatise *Vindiciae Celticae* had demonstrated the radical differences between the Celtic and Germanic languages.[119] The correspondence of Thomas Gray with the dramatist William Mason, whose ancient British tragedy *Caractacus* would appear in 1759, is also indicative of a sea-change in attitudes to the Celtic past. Gray rebuked Mason for failing to distinguish between Celts and Germans,[120] though he conceded how

[115] *Ibid.*, pp. xii–xiii.   [116] *Ibid.*, p. xiii.   [117] *Ibid.*, p. xvi.   [118] *Ibid.*, p. x.
[119] Droixhe, *La linguistique*, p. 141.
[120] Gray to Mason, 13 January 1758, in *Correspondence of Thomas Gray*, II, pp. 550–1; E. D. Snyder, *The Celtic revival in English literature 1760–1800* (Cambridge, MA, 1923), p. 54 n.

easily one could be misled by the errors of the Cluverian school. Not only did Gray think Mallet 'but a very small scholar, except in the erudition of the Goths', he also marked Pelloutier's card: 'an idle man of some learning, that would make all the world Celts, whether they will or no'.[121]

Percy and Gray were unusual in their sensitivity to the gulf between Celtic and Gothic antiquities. In eighteenth-century Britain the Gothic and Celtic pasts constituted 'two aspects of one fashionable nostalgia'.[122] Joseph Jefferson in *The ruins of a temple* conflated deities from the Norse pantheon such as Woden and Thor with Celtic Druidism.[123] Similarly, George Monck Berkeley's *Maids of Morven* confounded Odin with Ossianic heroes.[124] Moreover, even in the late eighteenth century as Percy's attack on the traditional blurring of Celtic and German identities began to take hold, the septentrional assimilation of the two stocks received an additional boost, as we have seen, from the Nordic cult of Ossian.

Almost a century later, I. A. Blackwell's edition of Mallet's *Northern antiquities* from the middle of the nineteenth century neatly exhibits the amplification of Percy's classification into a full-blown racialism. According to Blackwell the Teutonic and Celtic races were divided both by physiological and by psychological characteristics. The former were 'indelible', while the latter were capable of being 'modified' by differing civil or religious institutions. Nevertheless, there were also 'certain psychological traits, which may be regarded as inherent, susceptible of undergoing a slight modification – of assuming a greater or lesser degree of intensity; but so long as the race remains unmixed, totally ineradicable'. How did Celts and Teutons differ physically? Celts, a people of middling stature, had dark complexions, black hair, brown eyes and narrow chests, while Teutons were broad-chested and fair, with large blue eyes. Needless to say craniology featured in Blackwell's analysis. The Teutons had larger, rounder skulls than the oval-headed Celts. Temperament was also ascribed to physiology, the Teutons categorised as sanguine, the Celts tending to a 'bilious/bilious-nervous' nature. Psychologically, the gulf was equally large between the two races. The Celts were irascible, sexually incontinent, lacking in 'caution and providence' and with 'little disposition for hard work', though also gallant, quick in perception and egalitarian. The Teutons, on the other hand, had bottom; they were slower but more acute in perception, lacking the Celtic capacities for witticism and flippancy, but with greater depth of mind and sincerity. They were, moreover, a clean and prudent people who placed more value upon

[121] Gray to Mason, [24 March] 1758, in *Correspondence of Thomas Gray*, II, p. 567; Gray to Mason, [22] January 1758, *ibid.*, II, p. 557.
[122] R. Heppenstall, 'The children of Gomer', *Times Literary Supplement*, 17 October 1958, 600.   [123] Snyder, *Celtic revival*, p. 182.   [124] *Ibid.*, p. 185.

independence than equality of condition or rank.[125] We have come a long way from the confused overlapping classifications of Cluverian ethnography.

[125] I. A. Blackwell, 'Remarks on Bishop Percy's Preface', in P. H. Mallet, *Northern antiquities* (ed. Blackwell, London, 1847), pp. 33–6. For the wider culture of nineteenth-century British Teutomania and anti-Celticism, see e.g. L. P. Curtis Jr, *Apes and angels: the Irishman in Victorian caricature* (Newton Abbot, 1971); Kidd, 'Teutonist ethnology'.

The Gothicism of seventeenth-century Englishmen and eighteenth-century Britons presents a subtle challenge to one of the most influential approaches to the study of ethnicity within history and the social sciences, the boundary thesis. Proponents of this line of analysis, most notably Fredrik Barth, argue that frontier relationships, binary oppositions and stereotypes of the alien are fundamental elements in the construction of ethnic identity.[1] The processes of group definition, it is claimed, have always depended less on self-image than on perceived contrasts with the characteristics of outsiders. Although a central component of English national identity, England's Saxon identity did not magnify the differences between England and the Continent. Paradoxically, the very matter of English ethnicity also served to diminish the sense of distance between England and the 'other'.

There was a crucial ambiguity in the commonplace contrast between England's libertarian achievement and the benighted monarchies of Catholic Europe. Against a backdrop of persistent international conflicts driven by confessional divisions, mercantilist goals and the interplay of national and dynastic interests, seventeenth- and eighteenth-century English commentators demonised many of their continental European adversaries, the French in particular; but they did not forget – and, indeed, continued to celebrate – the common descent of the various Gothic nations of Europe, Anglo-Saxons and Franks included. For the craven, despotic and Roman Catholic 'other' of the Continent was not wholly alien, but a deformed and corrupted version of the hardy libertarian Goth. Certainly, Englishmen boasted of their unique national freedoms; but, as Gothicism displaced the cult of the immemorial constitution inherited from the aboriginal Britons, so they tended to emphasise the exceptional nature of England's historical experience rather than any

---

[1] F. Barth (ed.), *Ethnic groups and boundaries* (Oslo, 1969). Cf. J. Armstrong, *Nations before nationalism* (Chapel Hill, NC, 1982). However, for a more nuanced view of 'analogic' categorisation according to degrees of ethnic difference and similarity, see T. Hylland Eriksen, *Ethnicity and nationalism: anthropological perspectives* (London, 1993), pp. 66–7.

qualitative difference between the peoples of England and Europe. National differences were real and substantial, but a result of historical processes, not of inherent and aboriginal ethnic characteristics.

Nevertheless, traditional interpretations of English Saxonism leave little scope for this reading of the phenomenon. The Teutonic racialism which dominated the nineteenth-century English ethnic self-image has distorted our understanding of early modern English conceptions of ethnicity. Although Teutonism evolved out of the preoccupation of seventeenth- and eighteenth-century English antiquarians with the Anglo-Saxon origins of England's institutions, freedoms and national characteristics, nineteenth-century racialists altered its orientation. Their revisions included a greater emphasis on ethnic determinism, the drawing of a sharper distinction between Gothic and non-Gothic peoples, a heightened awareness of English exceptionalism and the reclassification of certain European peoples, formerly thought of as Gothic, within alien categories. Altered perceptions of Europe's ethnic contours led to a redrawing of the map of Anglo-Saxondom's ethnic affinities. It became common to relate Anglo-Saxon values and manners with an exclusively Nordic cousinhood in Scandinavia and Germany. The achievements of this extended Nordic family, in which the Anglo-Saxon stood out supreme, were set against the foil of Europe's less fortunate racial stocks, among whom were the Latins, a group which included peoples formerly recognised as Gothic libertarians – the French, Spanish and Italians.[2] These nineteenth-century perspectives have been repudiated by the late twentieth-century English intelligentsia, but they still stand in the way of our attempts to reconstruct the place of Anglo-Saxonism in early modern English political culture.

Linda Colley has recently argued that British identity was forged in the course of eighteenth-century warfare as a Protestant and libertarian foil to a Roman Catholic and authoritarian French 'other'. According to Colley, a British identity was constructed not so much through 'an internal and domestic dialogue' involving the nations of England, Scotland, Ireland and Wales, but through a series of wars with France which enabled an artificial Britishness to be 'superimposed' on 'much older alignments and loyalties'. Similarly, Gerald Newman has traced the emergence of an 'English nationalism' in the middle of the eighteenth century whose cultural impetus was derived from a nativist reaction to Grand Tour cosmopolitanism.[3] While I do not wish to challenge the broad sweep of

[2] J. Urry, 'Englishmen, Celts and Iberians: the ethnographic survey of the United Kingdom, 1892–1899', in G. Stocking (ed.), *Functionalism historicized: essays on British social anthropology* (Madison, WI, 1984), p. 84.
[3] L. Colley, *Britons: forging the nation 1707–1837* (New Haven and London, 1992), pp. 5–6;

the theses championed by Colley and Newman, each requires some measure of refinement and qualification. England's patriotic intelligentsia of the late seventeenth and eighteenth centuries – Saxonist antiquaries included – do not conform to the narrowly xenophobic picture of national identity outlined above. Englishness was presented in large part as an exceptionalism, and as a Protestant jewel resplendent against a largely Roman Catholic continental backdrop of dark superstition and spiritual tyranny. Nevertheless, one should not exaggerate the crudity of the juxtaposition. The oppressed subjects of the modern European despotisms were depicted not as pathetic Calibans, but as fellow Goths, who through accident and complex chains of historical causation had had the misfortune to succumb to the new political force of absolute monarchy. Although European character was often contrasted unfavourably with the sterling qualities of the stolid John-Bullish English fibre, a number of commentators, historians especially, paid more than lip-service to the notion of a common Gothic origin. Furthermore, British anxieties about the emergence of a Bourbon 'universal monarchy', however self-centred in fact, were filtered through expressions of concern for the fate of the 'liberties of Europe' and the continental 'balance of power'.

To what extent did eighteenth-century Englishmen think of themselves as a unique ethnic group? This view was, it seems, most prevalent in the realm of popular xenophobia and within the more radical ranks of English Saxonism, where an insular chauvinism prevailed. Radical Saxonism was nourished by a critique of the feudal yoke which the Gothic Normans had imposed on the libertarian Saxons of Old England.[4] Catherine Macaulay, a celebrated purveyor of an uncompromisingly whiggish history of England, was chauvinistic in her attitudes. The English, she maintained, enjoyed privileges unknown to other nations. Indeed, Macaulay was forthright in her condemnation of the part played by a continental Grand Tour in the education of England's future leaders: 'This is the finishing stroke that renders them useless to all the good purposes of preserving the birth-right of an Englishman.'[5]

However, English historians were generally less self-centred in their approach to the history of English liberty. Within the articulate elite of clerics and gentlemen-scholars, a sense of English superiority tended to be qualified by feelings of a deep-rooted kinship with the less fortunate nations of Europe. Patriotic Gothicism was Janus-faced. How was the

Colley, 'Britishness and otherness: an argument', in M. O'Dea and K. Whelan (eds.), 'Nations and nationalisms: France, Britain, Ireland and the eighteenth-century context', *SVEC* 335 (1995), 66–7; G. Newman, *The rise of English nationalism: a cultural history 1740–1830* (London, 1987).

[4] C. Hill, 'The Norman yoke', in Hill, *Puritanism and revolution* (1958: Harmondsworth, 1986).   [5] Catherine Macaulay, *History of England* (8 vols., London, 1763–83), I, p. xv.

exceptional nature of English constitutional history to be explained? Not in terms of ethnic differences. Britishness might be providential, but it was nothing to do with any notion that God's Englishman was made of a different stuff from his European neighbours. Indeed, historians now recognise that the apocalyptic tradition was not a saga focused exclusively on the vicissitudes of the *ecclesia anglicana*, but told the story of the universal corruption and renewal of Christianity.[6] The truly providential aspect of British liberty was the fact of insularity. As an island, Britain had been protected by geographical factors from conquest and expansionist Counter-Reformation Catholicism. Furthermore, it had also obviated the need for a substantial standing army, upon whose foundations a despotism might have arisen, as it had in many of the formerly limited monarchies of continental Europe.

The widely shared view that Europe consisted of a common family of Gothic kingdoms served to dilute the 'nationalist' force of Saxonism. Although English Gothicism is typically associated with chauvinism, the mental universe of early modern antiquarian scholarship bore marked affinities with the international sophistication of the Grand Tourists. Although Newman identifies Saxonist rhetoric as a product of a more assertively nationalist culture which emerged in the middle of the eighteenth century, English Gothicism had, in fact, also flourished long before this era. Moreover, while Newman is right to suggest that late eighteenth-century Englishmen, radicals especially, *were* becoming more insular in their Gothicism, his argument becomes less surefooted when he points to Saxon identity as the nativist antithesis of the cosmopolitan perspective. The Anglo-Saxon myth not only vindicated the deeds of England's island story; it also located English history within a wider context, as but one element, albeit exemplary, of the lively mosaic of limited Gothic monarchies which arose during the medieval period to replace the monolithic uniformity of the Roman Empire. Part of its message of Gothicist historiography was that England was not as exceptional as insular common law mythographers such as Edward Coke had claimed. Eighteenth-century Saxonists were to inherit a vision of Europe which located England and its arch-rival France as part of a glorious constellation of Gothic nations. Gothicism did not open up a high road to Francophobia. Rather it introduced a leavening of some political and historical sophistication into the differences between English liberty and French slavery which were such a stock feature of late seventeenth- and eighteenth-century English rhetoric.

Instead Gothicism fostered concentric loyalties. A shared heritage of manners and institutions connected the Anglo-Saxons with the libertar-

---

[6] K. Firth, *The apocalyptic tradition in Reformation Britain 1530–1645* (Oxford, 1979); J. P. Sommerville, *Politics and ideology in England, 1603–1640* (London, 1986), p. 78.

ian barbarians who established limited monarchies throughout western Europe as they overran the later Roman Empire. Indeed, William Camden, one of the first major historians to establish the Anglo-Saxon descent of the English nation, was keenly attuned to a wider set of Gothic resemblances in language and manners.[7] The European scope of the influential Gothic concept meant that our received idea of a 'unique' Anglo-Saxon heritage was, in fact, very severely qualified among English literati of the seventeenth and eighteenth centuries. For example, the economic projector and political commentator Charles Davenant (1656–1714) associated a shared ancestry with common manners, freedoms and institutions:

these several branches springing from the same stem, it must follow, that the fruit they bore would be near of a taste; by which we mean, that in their manners, laws, and principally in their politic government, they must of consequence, as indeed they did, very much resemble one another. And whoever looks into the ancient constitutions of England, France, Spain, Denmark, and Sweden will find, that all these nations had one and the same form of government; and though they might vary in some circumstances, yet they all agreed in certain fundamentals, which were, that the people should have their rights and privileges; that the nobles, or men of chief rank, should have some participation of power, and, that the regal authority should be limited by laws.[8]

The loose association of Gothicism with the libertarian, democratic and martial manners of the barbarian peoples of ancient Europe also made it possible for some commentators to provide shelter for the pre-Gothic Germans and freedom-loving Celts described by Tacitus under the broad Gothic umbrella.[9] Identities were not exclusively determined by ethnicity, nor were ethnic identities crudely confined by national categories. Indeed, Gothic identities could be based either on descent from these peoples or, in the case of a non-Gothic nation, on the adoption of free Gothic institutions. The Poles, for instance, were often classified as Gothic, on the basis of their rigorously limited elective monarchy. Algernon Sidney, for example, described the free nations of Europe under a variety of terms, including 'the northern nations', 'all the nations that have lived under the Gothic polity' and 'the legal kingdoms of the North'.[10] There was a vagueness in Sidney's Gothicism, characteristic of the idiom, which appeared to embrace both an ethnic and an institutional identity.

[7] H. MacDougall, *Racial myth in English history* (Montreal and Hanover, NH, 1982), p. 46.
[8] Charles Davenant, *A discourse upon grants and resumptions*, in Davenant, *Political and commercial works* (ed. C. Whitworth, 5 vols., London, 1771), III, pp. 59–60. See also Davenant, *An essay upon the balance of power*, ibid., III, pp. 429.
[9] R. J. Smith, *The Gothic bequest* (Cambridge, 1987), pp. 40–1, 61–2; C. Gerrard, *The patriot opposition to Walpole* (Oxford, 1994), p. 112.
[10] Algernon Sidney, *Discourses concerning government* (ed. T. G. West, Indianapolis, 1990), pp. 204, 376, 477, 484.

Seventeenth- and eighteenth-century English Gothicists embraced both the national characters and institutions of the Continent as variants of their own culture. Englishness they celebrated more as an isomer of a common Gothic heritage than as a unique insular identity. Discerning Englishmen knew that it was not character but fortune which separated the English political experience from the normal run of things in the modern European despotisms. Although the famous 'peculiarities of the English' have some roots in the early modern period, these did not flower as a striking feature of the national culture until the nineteenth century. Instead there prevailed in eighteenth-century English discourse the notion that 'post-Roman Europe was originally unified by sharing Germanic freedoms'.[11]

However, the Gothicist interpretation of a family of peoples with crucial underlying resemblances did not usher in a crude vision of Europe as an ethnically homogeneous monolith. The contingencies of history, including a measure of acculturation with the different autochthonous groups encountered in the particular territories they conquered, as they operated on the slight variations in the original manners of the peoples who overran the Roman Empire, had resulted in a fascinating diversity of nations. Some historians argued that original variations within the primeval Gothic stock explained how the colonisation of Europe by this powerful ethnic strain had not resulted in a dull uniformity.[12] Others stressed that these various Gothic nations had retained many of their primeval family characteristics, but attributed the 'variety . . . observed in the constitutions of those northern nations that invaded the Roman Empire' to the attitudes the barbarian conquerors had towards the indigenous peoples they encountered throughout Europe.[13] Although scholars differed over the nature and degree of relationships within the family of Germanic nations, there was a general assumption that the English libertarian heritage was part of the broadly Gothic history of post-Roman Europe.

The European components of English Gothicism

Why was this European perspective so pronounced in seventeenth- and eighteenth-century English antiquarian culture? There were a number of factors which together assisted the formation of a Euro-Gothicist ident-

[11] J. Black, *Convergence or divergence? Britain and the Continent* (Houndmills, 1994), p. 146.
[12] James Ibbetson, *A dissertation on the judicial customs of the Saxon and Norman age* (London, 1780), p. 3.
[13] Sidney, *Discourses*, p. 204. For the English and European contexts of Sidney's Gothicism, see J. Scott, *Algernon Sidney and the Restoration crisis, 1677–1683* (Cambridge, 1991), pp. 245–6.

ity. It is important to highlight the long-term influence of the Gothic history (c. 550) compiled by Jordanes. This bequeathed early modern Gothicism two vivid images of ancient Scandza as the 'hive of races or womb of nations', whence the Goths poured forth under their king Berig to begin their wanderings.[14] These controlling metaphors of the hive and the womb were to shape antiquarian thought during the seventeenth and eighteenth centuries.[15] As a result, Gothicism became inseparable from this image of a teeming storehouse of nations, with its overt claim that the various Gothic nations, despite their later tribal and national subdivisions and divergent histories, shared a common origin and homeland. In the seventeenth century the idea of the kinship of the Gothic peoples was reinforced by the extension of the family tree back to the sons of Japhet. This Mosaic feature disappeared in the course of the early modern period, but the basic notion of a family remained, albeit shortened and secularised, within the powerful metaphor of the Gothic 'womb of nations'. The rediscovery of Tacitus in the second half of the fifteenth century was also of vital importance, given their wide appeal in early modern Europe. Peter Burke has argued convincingly that 'commentaries on Tacitus were to the seventeenth century what commentaries on Aristotle were to the later middle ages'.[16] The Goths tended to be conflated with the heroic libertarian Germans described by Tacitus in the *Germania*. The centrality of this text in the elaboration of the descendant Anglo-Saxon identity meant that English antiquarians could not disengage themselves from the ancient history of Europe.

English Gothicism emerged as part of a cosmopolitan conversation about the origins of Europe. So it is unsurprising that various foreign scholars should play a disproportionate role in the formation of England's Gothic identity. It was common for clerics and gentleman-antiquarians working on English history to have some experience of other fields, especially in patristics, the wider history of the church, and the classics. English history was written by scholars with a cosmopolitan hinterland. Camden and Sir Robert Cotton were at the centre of a web of scholarly correspondence which traversed north-west Europe.[17] As a consequence,

[14] P. Heather, *The Goths* (Oxford, 1996), pp. 9–12; S. Kliger, *The Goths in England* (Cambridge, MA, 1952), pp. 11–13, 112; T. J. Beck, *Northern antiquities in French learning and literature (1755–1855)* (New York, 1934), pp. 19, 45; F. L. Borchardt, *German antiquity in Renaissance myth* (Baltimore and London, 1971), p. 191.

[15] E.g. James Thomson, *Complete poetical works* (ed. J. Logie Robertson, 1908: repr. London, 1961), 'Liberty', pt III, pp. 354–5; pt IV, pp. 367–8; Blackstone, *Commentaries*, IV, p. 403.

[16] P. Burke, 'A survey of the popularity of ancient historians 1450–1700', *H+T* 5 (1966), 149; D. Kelley, '*Tacitus noster*: the *Germania* in the Renaissance and Reformation', in A. J. Woodman and T. J. Luce (eds.), *Tacitus and the Tacitean tradition* (Princeton, 1993), pp. 154, 164; Kliger, *Goths*, pp. 112–13.

English political discourse was receptive to external influences, especially given the importance of Latinity as a vehicle for political and historical writings. For example, the canon of English whig political thought embraced, with varying degrees of enthusiasm, a number of foreign texts, including François Hotman's *Franco-Gallia* and Juan de Mariana's history of Spain.[18] A wider Gothic perspective was also encouraged by an awareness of the common feudal laws and institutions which the English shared with the rest of Europe. Feudal jurisprudence rose to prominence as an intellectual discipline in seventeenth-century England when it began to displace the legend of England's immemorial law.[19] Feudalism was virtually tantamount to the history of Gothic institutions, a form of law common to all the kingdoms of Europe. There were widespread local variations in the feudal law, but it reinforced the notion that there was a basic Gothic unity underlying European diversity. Nobody disputed the existence of English feudalism: the big question was whether it had been imported from the Continent wholesale with the Normans, which reinforced the case for a Norman Conquest, or had been introduced earlier, perhaps under the Saxons, themselves drawing on continental influences.[20]

It should occasion little surprise, therefore, that various foreign scholars played a disproportionate role in the formation of England's Gothic identity. It is significant that English Gothicism should be if not of Anglo-Dutch parentage, at least indebted to Richard Verstegan's self-consciously continental midwifery. Verstegan, author of the foundational text of English Gothicism – *A restitution of decayed intelligence* (1605) – was an English Catholic exile of Dutch ancestry who changed his name from Rowlands to Verstegan on returning to the land of his forefathers. Later, he removed himself to Paris. Given Verstegan's origins and career it is hardly surprising that he advanced a broadly European interpretation of Gothic history, perhaps bringing some welcome coherence to his own mongrel heritage. The *Restitution* was a seminal work, going through five

[17] D. Woolf, *The idea of history in early Stuart England* (Toronto, 1990), pp. 116–19, 159, 170; K. Sharpe, *Sir Robert Cotton* (Oxford, 1979), esp. ch. 3; G. Parry, *The trophies of time* (Oxford, 1995), pp. 7–8. See also R. L. De Molen, 'The library of William Camden', *Proceedings of the American Philosophical Society* 128 (1984), 327–409.

[18] Sommerville, *Politics and ideology*, p. 78; J. H. M. Salmon, *The French religious wars in English political thought* (Oxford, 1959); François Hotman, *Franco-Gallia; or an account of the ancient free state of France, and most other parts of Europe before the loss of their liberties* (ed. Robert Molesworth, London, 1711); Juan de Mariana, *The general history of Spain* (1592–1605: trans. John Stevens, London, 1699); H. T. Colbourn, *The lamp of experience: whig history and the intellectual origins of the American revolution* (Chapel Hill, NC, 1965), Appendix II.

[19] J. G. A. Pocock, *The ancient constitution and the feudal law* (1957: reissue with retrospect, Cambridge, 1987), chs. 3, 5.   [20] *Ibid.*, ch. 8; Sommerville, *Politics and ideology*.

editions in the course of the seventeenth century.[21] Verstegan eschewed the narrowly insular, identifying Germany as the common womb of most of the leading nations of western Europe: 'many most warlike troops have gone out of Germany, and taken possession in all the best countries of Europe, where their offspring even to this day remaineth'.[22] Verstegan recounted the achievements of the various nations of the German stock. The kingdoms of Spain were founded by the Goths and Vandals, the Lombards had settled in northern Italy and there were various septentrional sprigs of the Germanic stem in Scandinavia. Above all, the Franks, a subdivision of the Sicambri, had established a kingdom in France under their leader Pharamond. The English nation – the Saxon branch of the ancient and noble race of Germans, supplemented by kindred Danes and Normans – were encouraged to take pride in their wider ancestry: 'Thus have we here seen the Germans leave places unto their posterity to inhabit in, in Italy, Spain, France, and Britain, where unto this day they remain, as the true witnesses of the great actions of their most victorious, and noble ancestors.'[23]

At this stage Holland, the University of Leiden in particular, was the home of Gothicist scholarship. Born in Heidelberg of a French father and Dutch mother, and brought up in Holland where his father was a professor at Leiden, Franciscus Junius (1589–1677) was to become one of the major pioneers in Anglo-Saxon studies. In England from 1620, Junius became librarian to the Earl of Arundel, but he also maintained contact with a wide network of philologists across Europe.[24] Saxon studies were later furthered by the assimilated Prussian David Wilkins (Wilke; 1685–1745). Best known for his *Concilia*, Wilkins also produced an edition of Anglo-Saxon laws.[25] Pierre Allix, a pastor of the French reformed church who fled to England after the revocation of Nantes, and later became a canon and treasurer of Salisbury Cathedral, brought to his adopted culture the Frankish Gothicism of Huguenot political thought. Allix reminded Englishmen that the assault on France's ancient constitution was largely a seventeenth-century phenomenon, and informed his new countrymen that the Frankish libertarian tradition was not yet defunct:

[21] Parry, *Trophies of time*, ch. 2; Kliger, *Goths*, p. 115; Woolf, *Idea of history*, p. 202.
[22] Richard Verstegan, *A restitution of decayed intelligence* (1605: London, 1634), p. 43.
[23] *Ibid.*, p. 45.
[24] Parry, *Trophies of time*, p. 8; S. Brough, *The Goths and the concept of Gothic in Germany from 1500 to 1750* (Frankfurt, 1985), pp. 91–2; E. N. Adams, *Old English scholarship in England from 1566 to 1800* (New Haven, 1917), pp. 70–1; D. Fairer, 'Anglo-Saxon Studies', in L. S. Sutherland and L. G. Mitchell (eds.), *The history of the University of Oxford*, vol. V, *The eighteenth century* (Oxford, 1986), p. 808.
[25] D. C. Douglas, *English scholars* (1939: London, 1943), p. 82; F. Powicke, 'Sir Henry Spelman and the *Concilia*', *Proceedings of the British Academy* 16 (1930), 367.

'let no body imagine that the ancient idea of the government of France, is quite effaced out of the spirit of the nation'.[26]

The 'classic exposition' of traditional English whig history was the work of an exiled Savoyard Huguenot, Paul de Rapin-Thoyras (1661–1725).[27] His *magnum opus* was translated into English by Nicholas Tindal (1687–1774) in fifteen volumes between 1725 and 1731, followed by a second edition in 1732–3, a third in 1743 and later versions which included Tindal's continuation. Rapin drew on the sixteenth-century French constitutional tradition associated with François Hotman, fusing it with native English shibboleths. Although the exceptional longevity of England's Gothic liberties constituted a central element in Rapin's story, he did not lose sight of the wider European perspective in which the preservation of England's ancient constitution ought to be viewed: 'Si on examine les histoires des autres royaumes fondez en Europe, par les Nations du Nord, on y trouvera de pareilles Assemblées, sous divers noms, comme de Diètes, de Champs de Mars, de Cortes, et autres.'[28]

The traditional whig shibboleths confirmed by Rapin were later challenged by the Swiss antiquarian Jean Louis De Lolme (1740–1805) in a major work on the English constitution. De Lolme reinforced England's much-vaunted libertarian identity while qualifying the wider identification with a Gothic Europe. The Swiss revisionist attributed the glories of English liberty to the Norman Conquest, 'the real foundation of the English constitution'. By a curious irony, the despotism established at the Conquest 'made England free'. The excessive power of the monarchy provoked in response a 'regulated resistance' and a 'spirit of union' between nobility and people. De Lolme acknowledged that the early Gothic nations of Europe, including the English, had shared similar institutional forms. However, the Saxon constitution appeared 'to have had little more affinity with the present constitution, than the general relation, common indeed to all the governments established by the northern nations, that of having a king and a body of nobility'.[29]

---

[26] Pierre Allix, *Reflections upon the opinions of some modern divines, concerning the nature of government in general, and that of England in particular* (London, 1689), p. 77; Kliger, *Goths*, pp. 188–9.

[27] H. R. Trevor-Roper, 'Our first whig historian: Paul de Rapin-Thoyras', in Trevor-Roper, *From Counter-Reformation to Glorious Revolution* (London, 1992), p. 262; J. Dedieu, *Montesquieu et la tradition politique anglaise en France* (Paris, 1909), pp. 84–99; D. Earl, 'Procrustean feudalism: an interpretative dilemma in English historical narration, 1700–1725', *HJ* 19 (1976), esp. 39 n.; D. Forbes, *Hume's philosophical politics* (Cambridge, 1975), pp. 233–40; P. Hicks, *Neoclassical history and English culture: from Clarendon to Hume* (Houndmills, 1996), pp. 146–50; K. O'Brien, *Narratives of Enlightenment: cosmopolitan history from Voltaire to Gibbon* (Cambridge, 1997), pp. 17–18. For an appreciation of Rapin's revisionism, see R. J. Smith, *Gothic bequest*, pp. 46–7.

[28] Paul de Rapin-Thoyras, *Histoire d'Angleterre* (10 vols., The Hague, 1724–7), I, pp. ix–x.

[29] Jean-Louis De Lolme, *The constitution of England* (1771: London, 1775), 8–9, 23.

English scholars were also attuned to the wider currents of continental Gothicist scholarship. In early modern Europe there were two main schools of interpretation concerning the origins of the Goths. Scandinavian scholars argued for the northern origins of the Goths in Scandia. Rival Danish and Swedish glosses on the Scandinavian interpretation of the origin of the Goths were deployed to advance these nations' ambitions in the Baltic (in particular their rival claims to Scania, today the southern area of Sweden, but, until 1658, under Danish rule), while German antiquarians drew on Tacitus's *Germania* to argue – against Scandinavian antiquaries – for an alternative origin in an unconquered German territory lying to the east of the Roman Empire.[30] There were also active links between English and Scandinavian scholarly communities, with English antiquaries taking considerable interest in many of the staple issues of Scandinavian Gothicism, such as runes, megaliths and bardic literature.[31] Verstegan incorporated into his *Restitution* the insights of Olaus Magnus (1490–1557), one of the founding fathers of Swedish Gothicism and author of the *Historia de gentibus septentrionalibus* (1555).[32] The Danish antiquarian and runologist Olaus Wormius (1588–1654) was a direct influence on many English antiquaries during the early seventeenth century, in particular Henry Spelman, and his work continued to shape the Gothicist scholarship of the Restoration era.[33] Later, in the seventeenth century, another renowned Suecomane, Georg Stiernhielm, was to become a Fellow of the Royal Society.[34] The proud Gothicist argument of Olaus Rudbeck's *Atlantica* was reproduced in brief in the transactions of the Royal Society.[35] However, the debate was not confined to the Swedes and the Germans, for scholars in a number of other European nations claimed descent from the Goths, and were deeply interested in questions which related to their ultimate ancestry. For example, Huet imported the Scandinavian hive thesis into French culture, and it remained an issue for eighteenth-century French historians: Montesquieu subscribed to the view that Scandinavia was the homeland of the Gothic peoples, while the Abbé Mably supported the alternative Germanist thesis.[36]

Just as French antiquarian culture constituted a secondary theatre of the scholarly conflict between Suecomanes and Germanists, so English historians took sides in the battle raging between these two main schools

---

[30] K. Skovgaard-Petersen, 'The literary feud between Denmark and Sweden in the sixteenth and seventeenth centuries and the development of Danish historical scholarship', in J. Brink and W. Gentrup (eds.), *Renaissance culture in context* (Aldershot, 1993); Brough, *Goths*.

[31] E. Seaton, *Literary relations of England and Scandinavia in the seventeenth century* (Oxford, 1935).   [32] *Ibid.*, p. 206.   [33] *Ibid.*, p. 137; Parry, *Trophies of time*, pp. 8, 284.

[34] Seaton, *Literary relations*, p. 189.   [35] *Ibid.*, p. 191; Beck, *Northern antiquities*, p. 51 n.

[36] Beck, *Northern antiquities*, pp. 22, 49, 78.

of European Gothicists. Robert Sheringham championed the insights of Suecomane Gothicism; his *De Anglorum origine* was 'saturated with the Uppsala spirit'.[37] James Tyrrell found the case advanced by Grotius and reiterated by Sheringham to be more compelling than the Germanist theories of Cluverius and Verstegan.[38] On the other hand, Edward Stillingfleet was critical of Rudbeck's Gothicist fantasy.[39] The issue rumbled on in English historiography well into the eighteenth century. Thomas Gray believed that the question was still 'undecided' whether the Goths had emerged from Scandinavia, were the descendants of Thracian Getae or had been 'a great colony of Scythians or Tartars'.[40] There were further echoes in English Gothicist discourse of the question debated by a number of prominent continental historians about whether the Getae had been a Germanic people or had become identified with the Goths only as a consequence of spurious etymologising.[41]

Philological concerns were central to this body of discourse. From the origins of English Saxonist philology in the English Reformation, its practitioners were keenly aware of the patriotic significance of their discipline, and of its repercussions on some of the most controversial issues in English political culture.[42] Nevertheless, by the early seventeenth century there was a powerful European orientation to what had become less of an English and more of a septentrional discipline. Nowell, Camden and Verstegan all identified the origins of the English tongue in a broader family of Germanic tongues.[43] Linguistics were neither narrowly Anglo-Saxon nor insular. Late seventeenth- and eighteenth-century English Saxonists were not preoccupied with the patriotic significance of their discipline to the exclusion of wider concerns. In his *English historical library*, which is largely a source manual and critical bibliography for the historian of England, William Nicolson urged the necessity of a cosmopolitan perspective for the student of Gothic antiquities: 'Our Saxon antiquary ought also to be skilled in the writings of those learned Germans, who have made collections of their old laws; or have written such glossaries, or other grammatical discourses, as may bring him acquainted with the many dialects of our ancestors and kinsmen in that part of the world.'[44] Elizabeth Elstob pronounced 'the ancient Francick' to be 'the

---

[37] *Ibid.*, p. 49; Seaton, *Literary relations*, p. 208.
[38] James Tyrrell, *The general history of England* (3 vols., London, 1697–1704), I, pt III, pp. 121–3.   [39] Seaton, *Literary relations*, p. 209.
[40] Thomas Gray, 'Gothi', in Gray, *Works* (ed. T. J. Mathias, 2 vols., London, 1814), II, pp. 104–5.
[41] Robert Sheringham, *De Anglorum gentis origine disceptatio* (Cambridge, 1670), ch. 9; Kliger, *Goths*, pp. 10–19.   [42] See above, ch. 5, n. 39.
[43] Pocock, *Ancient constitution*, p. 96.
[44] William Nicolson, *The English historical library* (3 vols., London, 1696–9), I, p. 128.

mother of the present German, and of near alliance with the Anglo-Saxon, all of them confessing their original from the Goths'.[45]

Philology interlocked with constitutional history. The gradual displacement of the immemorial common law as the basis of English identity with a more intensely Gothicist heritage was related to the discovery of broader English affinities with the legal and political institutions of the Continent. Feudal jurisprudence, which focused on Gothic legal institutions, had, from the early seventeenth century, helped to undermine the insular immemorialism of the English common law mind, and, by 1610, Selden was studying English feudal tenures in the light of continental history.[46] Moreover, according to John Pocock, Henry Spelman 'approached the English past as part of the history of Europe',[47] his feudalism pointing royalists in the direction of a non-insular interpretation of English constitutional history.[48] However, in the second half of the seventeenth century it was the fiercest opponents of absolute monarchy who were to adopt a European perspective, as republicans and defenders of England's traditional mixed constitutionalism painted a vivid and frightening picture of Europe's eroding Gothic liberties.[49]

The Commonwealth tradition

One of the most influential strains of late seventeenth-century Gothicism, the republican or commonwealth tradition of real whiggery, was linked to a historical sociology which stressed the role of a range of dynamic processes acting upon and transforming Europe's Gothic polities. As Caroline Robbins has shown, the Gothicism of the commonwealthmen was not wholly backward-looking, but an integral part of a sophisticated understanding of social and political change in early modern Europe. However, underlying this approach was an anxiety to control change in the hope of retaining traditional liberties and mixed constitutions. The commonwealthmen were aiming not so much to put the historical process into reverse gear as to 'observe and learn by it how best to circumvent the situations which over-ambitious monarch or indolent subject might create'.[50] In a sense the republican tradition validated the ethnic unity of Europe by emphasising the very recent changes which had thrown up a huge gulf between the constitutional liberties of the English and the

[45] Elizabeth Elstob, *The rudiments of grammar for the English–Saxon tongue* (1715: facsimile, Menston, 1968), 'Dedication'.
[46] Pocock, *Ancient constitution*, p. 286.   [47] *Ibid.*, p. 95.   [48] *Ibid.*, ch. 5.
[49] B. Worden, 'English republicanism', in J. H. Burns and M. Goldie (eds.), *The Cambridge history of political thought 1450–1700* (Cambridge, 1991), p. 470.
[50] Caroline Robbins, 'Introduction', in *Two English republican tracts* (Cambridge, 1969), pp. 55–6.

despotic yoke under which the peoples of the continental monarchies now suffered. Although there were those chauvinistic English writers who expressed such differences in terms of long-standing national characteristics, the more sophisticated sociological explanation advanced by the commonwealthmen was to enjoy a wide currency within the political and cultural elite.[51]

In his utopian masterpiece *Oceana* (1656) James Harrington analysed the collapse of Europe's mixed Gothic polities into monarchies and republics: 'Where are the estates, or the power of the people, in France? Blown up. Where is that of the people in Aragon, and the rest of the Spanish kingdoms? Blown up. On the other side, where is the king of Spain's power in Holland? Blown up.'[52] The solution to this crisis, Harrington suggested, was the construction of new institutions to secure civil and political stability. Stressing the opportunities as well as the risks presented by the decline of Gothic government, Harrington saw that the subversion of the traditional English polity in the Civil Wars offered the chance to remodel government and society in such a way as to overcome the flaws of the former Gothic system. Harrington was, indeed, a critic of feudalism, his views most pronounced in various remarks discussing the overbearing nobility of Marpesia (Scotland). The instability of the medieval era had arisen from a 'wrestling match' between monarchs and magnates, and now seventeenth-century England was reaping the whirlwind of a declining feudalism. Harrington drew attention both to the measures taken by Henry VII and Henry VIII against bastard-feudal retainers and to the redistribution of land among the gentry on the dissolution of the monasteries. Nevertheless, the republican machinery outlined by Harrington would enable England to transcend the difficulties created by a post-Gothic mismatch between the distribution of political power and the possession of land.[53]

The major intellects of the late seventeenth-century commonwealth tradition were receptive to the sociological and historical underpinnings of Harrington's analysis, but not to his basic prescription. The events of the Restoration and the apparently inexorable march of late Stuart government towards the familiar European destination of absolute monarchy

---

[51] J. G. A. Pocock, 'Machiavelli, Harrington and English political ideologies in the eighteenth century', in Pocock, *Politics, language and time* (1971: Chicago, 1989).

[52] James Harrington, *The commonwealth of Oceana* (and *A system of politics*; ed. J. G. A. Pocock, Cambridge, 1992), p. 144. For the common Gothic origins of Europe's feudal institutions (including those the 'Teutons' (Saxons) brought to Oceana (England)), see pp. 46–51.

[53] J. G. A. Pocock, *The Machiavellian moment* (Princeton, 1975), p. 388; Worden, 'English republicanism', pp. 451–4; Worden, 'James Harrington and *The commonwealth of Oceana*, 1656', in D. Wootton (ed.), *Republicanism, liberty and commercial society, 1649–1776* (Stanford, 1994).

prompted a reformulation of the Harringtonian tradition. The neo-Harringtonians saw the threat to the Gothic system, but wished to maintain
the medieval structures of the English constitution.[54] This mode of political analysis did reinforce a sense of English distinctiveness, though the
latter did not degenerate into an ethnocentric or hubristic triumphalism.
Quite the reverse. Several of the leading neo-Harringtonians, including
Sidney and Molesworth, were widely travelled figures. Sidney had served
on a diplomatic mission to Denmark in 1659 and had spent much of his
life in exile.[55] Molesworth's classic *An account of Denmark as it was in the
year 1692* was the product of missions to that land in 1689–90 and 1692.[56]
The cosmopolitan Molesworth confessed himself inspired by 'a sincere
desire of instructing the only possessors of true liberty in the world, what
right they have to that liberty, of how great a value it is, what misery
follows the loss of it, and how easily, if care be taken in time, it may be
preserved'.[57] The neo-Harringtonian interpretation of history drew upon
a pan-European domino theory, and there was considerable anxiety that
the Gothic constitutions of the British Isles would be the next to fall. It
was not so much as a badge of honour as grounds for paranoia that it was
'in England only that the ancient, generous, manly government of Europe
survives, and continues in its original lustre and perfection'.[58]

After the Glorious Revolution of 1688–9 had secured English liberties
from Stuart despotism, there was a strain of national triumphalism.
However, even within the broad ranks of whiggery a potent countercur-
rent of Gothicist republicanism called into question the differences between England and the Continent. Throughout the 1690s a mood of
anxiety predominated in the circles of the commonwealth whigs, over-
whelming any complacent drift into self-congratulation. The achievement of 1689 was seen as a holding operation, which had checked in the
British dominions the seemingly remorseless trend across Europe towards the subversion of parliaments, 'formerly so common, but lost
within this last age in all kingdoms but those of Poland, Great Britain and
Ireland'.[59] Molesworth had little truck with the complacent trumpeting of
the glories of England's recent Revolution, 'the effecting of which may be

[54] Pocock, *Machiavellian moment*, p. 416; Worden, 'Republicanism and the Restoration, 1660–1683', in Wootton, *Republicanism, liberty and commercial society*, esp. pp. 141–3; A. C. Houston, *Algernon Sidney and the republican heritage in England and America* (Princeton, 1991), ch. 5.

[55] J. Scott, *Algernon Sidney and the English republic, 1623–1677* (Cambridge, 1988), ch. 8.

[56] *Dictionary of national biography*.

[57] Molesworth, 'Preface', in Hotman, *Franco-Gallia*, p. ii.

[58] Thomas Rymer, *A general draught and prospect of government in Europe* (London, 1681), p. 66.

[59] Robert Molesworth, *An account of Denmark as it was in the year 1692* (London, 1694), p. 43. See Worden, 'Republicanism and the Restoration', p. 175.

called a piece of good luck, and that's the best can be said of it'.[60] At the heart of this influential branch of whig culture was the fear that the English were not so very different from their continental cousins. The inexorable rise since the Renaissance of the new monarchies was not the product of Counter-Reformation Catholicism, but of deeper social and institutional forces. After all, Protestant nations such as Denmark had succumbed to absolutism. There was no particular reason why, if the Lutheran and Gothic Danes had failed to withstand these trends, the English would escape unscathed. English liberties were perceived to be precarious precisely because the English were of the same ethnic stock as the enslaved nations of Europe. There were calls for the renovation of the English polity, the regeneration of the Saxon spirit, before England lapsed into a Williamite despotism. The anti-Williamite 'real whigs' Walter Moyle (1672–1721) and John Trenchard (1662–1723) argued during the standing army debate of the late 1690s that English exceptionalism had to be carefully defined.[61] There was no assumption of English superiority over those unfortunate Gothic nations on the Continent which had lost their traditional mixed institutions. Indeed, English liberties were commonly linked to the wider fate of the European balance of power, or the 'liberties of Europe'.[62]

Why had England so far escaped the common fate, when 'most nations in Europe [were] overrun with oppression and slavery'? Was it something in the English character? Or the peculiar virtues of England's ancient constitution? Moyle and Trenchard concluded that it was 'more owing to the accident of our situation, than to our wisdom, integrity or courage' that the English constitution survived the general crisis.[63] They advanced an explanation of this 'situation' very pertinent to England's current predicament: 'And if we enquire how these unhappy nations have lost that precious jewel liberty, and we as yet preserved it, we shall find their miseries and our unhappiness proceed from this, that their necessities or indiscretion have permitted a standing army to be kept among them.'[64] Thus far England had avoided such an impasse, but it was looming, for, as Moyle and Trenchard argued, it was part of the common European decline of the feudal militia. Peter Paxton, a London doctor and polymath (d. 1711), took a similar line, but added that it was dynastic unions which had first allowed princes to build up standing armies and eventual-

[60] Molesworth, *Account of Denmark*, 'Preface'.

[61] [Walter Moyle and John Trenchard], *An argument, shewing, that a standing army is inconsistent with a free government, and absolutely destructive to the constitution of the English monarchy* (London, 1697).

[62] E.g. Charles Davenant, *Essays upon I. the ballance of power II. the right of making war, peace and alliances III. universal monarchy* (London, 1701), esp. I.

[63] [Moyle and Trenchard], *Standing army*, p. 3.   [64] *Ibid.*, p. 4.

ly to destabilise the 'liberties of Europe'. Europe had formerly been a collection of weak Gothic principalities 'so constituted as befitted them to defend themselves, but not to ruin and oppress their neighbours; for the legislature and force were so admirably laid, and equally divided between the prince and people, that the first had authority enough to rule and assemble the last, for the preservation of themselves, but had not sovereignty enough to sport away their lives at his pleasure, for the conquering and enslaving others'.[65] The threat to English freedoms and European liberties came both from the rise of domestic absolutisms and also from the wider phenomenon in an unsettled states system of aspirations to universal dominion.

The eighteenth-century mainstream

In time this pan-European vision became an established feature of English political culture. At first a central plank of oppositional whiggism, it came to feature in establishment whiggism and in tory ideology of the early Hanoverian era. By the middle of the eighteenth century the English radical tradition was beginning to be more Anglocentric and assertively Anglo-Saxonist, and a narrowly parochial sense of the Gothic heritage was confined to these circles. On the other hand, the Euro-Gothicist perspective, devoid of its neo-Harringtonian gloss, helped shape the ideology of modern court whiggism. Through the cosmopolitan influence of the Scottish Enlightenment, the Eurocentric story of the rise and transformation of feudal institutions became one of the dominant refrains in British political culture.

Eighteenth-century English political culture resounded to the legend of Europe's shared Gothic origins. According to Squire the 'northern regions of Asia' constituted 'that vast hive from whose fruitful bosom were poured forth those mighty swarms of people which not only overspread the neighbouring countries of Scandinavia, or northern Europe, but by degrees covered all Germany, overwhelmed Spain and Gaul, and made themselves masters of the whole western empire'.[66] In a similar vein, Goldsmith described the Saxons as 'one branch of those Gothic nations, which, swarming from the northern hive, came down to give laws, manners and liberty to the rest of Europe'.[67] Whitaker considered that 'the

---

[65] Peter Paxton, *A scheme of union between England and Scotland with advantages to both kingdoms* (London and Edinburgh, 1705), p. 3; J. A. W. Gunn, 'The civil polity of Peter Paxton', *P+P* 40 (1968), 42–57. Gunn notes that as a modern anti-feudalist Paxton was sceptical of Gothicist claims.

[66] Samuel Squire, *An enquiry into the foundation of the English constitution; or, an historical essay upon the Anglo-Saxon government both in Germany and England* (London, 1745), pp. 5–7.

Longobards, Franks, Saxons, and Danes were all branches of that great tree of Germany, which in the fourth and succeeding centuries shot out her boughs into the south, and threw her shade over half the continent of Europe'.[68]

Even critics of Gothicism acknowledged the European scope of the myth. Josiah Tucker denounced as nonsense the notion that, because in France, Spain, Sweden and Denmark the traditional baronial liberty 'of doing mischief and of being a plague to each other, to their own vassals, and to all around them' had been eroded by the rise of absolute monarchies, this meant that these lands had 'lost their liberties'. For to Tucker 'true liberty' had been 'a stranger to every country, where the Gothic constitution was introduced'.[69] Like Hume, Tucker preferred the prospect of enjoying a degree of civil liberty in a modern civilised monarchy to fettered vassalage in a prized Gothic constitution. Nevertheless, his critique of Gothicism mirrored the European breadth of the ideology he was subverting.[70]

Eighteenth-century British historians celebrated Europe as a mosaic of Gothic polities, each state evolving through the vicissitudes of its own particular historical formation a variant on a basic institutional pattern. The dynamic individuality of the barbarian kingdoms which arose from the ashes of Rome was to be one of the central themes of Edward Gibbon's *Decline and fall of the Roman Empire*. Gibbon provides the classic, if atypical, example of an eighteenth-century English championship of a pan-European identity. As a cosmopolitan sceptic who combined the critical approach of Tucker, with a keen awareness of the genuine kernel of truth which lay beneath the more fantastic outer husk of the Gothic myth, he articulated for educated Englishmen the 'domestic' significance, albeit rigorously qualified, of the common Gothic heritage: 'the most civilized nations of modern Europe issued from the woods of Germany, and in the rude institutions of those barbarians we may still distinguish the original principles of our present laws and manners'. However, Gibbon subverted the pieties of a vulgar 'sentimental Gothicism'. Post-Roman Europe had endured the long sleep of dark-age barbarism, yet the 'Latin' West had been gradually reawakened through the

[67] Oliver Goldsmith, *The history of England* (4 vols., London, 1771), I, p. 34.

[68] John Whitaker, *The history of Manchester* (2 vols., London, 1771–5), II, p. 148.

[69] Josiah Tucker, *A treatise concerning civil government* (London, 1781), pp. 60–1. There were other ways of dissenting from the dominant Gothicist paradigm: the royalist Thomas Goddard, *Plato's demon: or the state-physician unmaskt; being a discourse in answer to a book call'd 'Plato Redivivus'* (London, 1684), p. 291, denied that the Goths had ever come to England.

[70] Tucker, *Treatise*, pp. 62, 65; Hume, 'Of refinement in the arts', in Hume, *Essays moral, political and literary* (ed. E. Miller, Indianapolis, 1987), p. 278.

slow acculturation of the Goths. The glory of European civilisation resided in the intricate and variant pattern of interaction between the legacy of Rome and the new customs imported by its barbarian successors. Gibbon's sceptical outlook also included a cosmopolitan distrust of English exceptionalism. The differences between England and the Continent were not massive, nor were such differences as did exist threatening. Instead, Gibbon celebrated the modest diversity of a Europe of 'twelve powerful though unequal kingdoms, three respectable commonwealths, and a variety of smaller though independent states' as a check on the sort of tyranny associated with monolithic empires.[71]

'Britons' and the European 'other'

As noted earlier, Linda Colley has argued that a growing sense of a shared Britishness in the eighteenth century was stimulated in part by a revulsion against a non-British otherness, with Francophobia, in particular, a vital unifying factor.[72] In a similar vein Gerald Newman has identified 'the field of anti-French conflict' as a 'mirror of British independence and might', noting that 'each major step in the consolidation of English rule in the British Isles – 1689, 1707, 1745, 1801 – was taken in the context of Anglo-French warfare'.[73] There is much to be said for this argument. However, it does need qualification, particularly as an explanation of the attitudes of the educated elites who contributed so much to the processes of integration. For the Euro-Gothic perspective so common in the works of patriotic English writers was also shared by Anglo-Irish and Scottish historians. Robert Molesworth imported this approach into Anglo-Irish political thought during the 1690s, and it was present as a vital rhetorical ingredient in the patriotism of William Molyneux.[74] It remained a familiar feature of Anglo-Irish historiography. Jonathan Swift argued that great councils were first introduced into England by the Saxons 'from the same original with the other Gothic forms of government in most parts of Europe'.[75] Henry Brooke, the Anglo-Irish antiquarian and patriot dramatist, declared of his *Gustavus Vasa* (1739) – a controversial and ambiguous celebration of a patriot king which was the first play to be banned in

---

[71] Gibbon, *DF*, I, p. 230; II, p. 513. I am indebted to the interpretation of Gibbon found in O'Brien, *Narratives of Enlightenment*, ch. 6.

[72] Colley, *Britons*; Colley, 'Britishness and otherness'.

[73] Newman, *Rise of English nationalism*, p. 75.

[74] Molesworth, *Account of Denmark*; William Molyneux, *The case of Ireland's being bound by acts of parliament in England, stated* (1698: n.p., 1706), p. 171. See also Henry Maxwell, *An essay towards the union of Ireland with England* (London, 1703), pp. 7, 12, 15.

[75] Jonathan Swift, 'An abstract and fragment of the history of England', in Swift, *Miscellaneous and autobiographical pieces, fragments and marginalia* (Oxford, 1969), p. 35.

London under the Stage Licensing Act of 1737 – that he took his material 'from the history of Sweden, one of those Gothic and glorious nations, from whom our form of government is derived, from whom Britain has inherited those unextinguishable sparks of liberty and patriotism, that were her light through the ages of ignorance and superstition'.[76] Francis Sullivan (1719–76), professor of law at Trinity College, Dublin, in the middle of the eighteenth century, lectured and wrote on the feudal jurisprudence of the broader Gothic family of nations, whose basic form of government had 'until these last three hundred years, prevailed universally through Europe'.[77]

The renowned Scottish patriot, Andrew Fletcher of Saltoun, was very much a commonwealthman, his works combining an abhorrence of continental absolutism with a cosmopolitan understanding of the crisis of Europe's Gothic institutions. France's despotic monarchy earned Fletcher's strident condemnation: there was 'not a freeman in France, because the king takes away any part of any man's property at his pleasure; and that, let him do what he will to any man, there is no remedy'.[78] But despotism and slavery were not innate in the French character; rather they were the product of an unfortunate set of circumstances which had plagued the various Gothic nations of Europe for the previous two centuries. Fletcher argued that there had been a common form of feudal government for about 1,100 years until 'the alteration of government which happened in most countries of Europe about the year 1500'.[79] Only the fortunate accident of geography had so far prevented the downfall of the Gothic constitutions of the British Isles. Island nations had no obvious need for the standing armies upon which absolute monarchies had risen. However, Fletcher was far from sanguine that the danger had passed, given prevailing pressures to measure up to a Continent of threatening leviathan-monarchies, which was already encouraging a dangerous drift towards the consolidation of British kingdoms into a more homogeneous and centralised unit. Indeed, in his *Account of a conversation for the right regulation of governments for the common good of mankind*, Fletcher argued that only a pan-European solution could secure an

---

[76] Henry Brooke, *Gustavus Vasa* (London, 1739), 'Prefatory dedication', p. iv; Gerrard, *Patriot opposition*, pp. 79, 114–16, 191–2, 242–3. However, for a more pessimistic view of a Europe fallen under the yoke of despotism, see Brooke, *An occasional letter from the Farmer to the free-men of Dublin* (Dublin, 1749), p. 5. For an Anglo-Scottish analogy, see William Paterson, *Arminius* (London, 1740).

[77] Francis Sullivan, *An historical treatise on the feudal law* (London, 1772: 2nd edn, Dublin, 1790), pp. 7, 19.

[78] Andrew Fletcher, *Second discourse of the affairs of Scotland* (1698), in *Andrew Fletcher: political works* (ed. J. Robertson, Cambridge, 1997), p. 61.

[79] Fletcher, *A discourse of government with relation to militias* (1698), in Fletcher, *Political works*, p. 2.

unambiguous freedom from despotism for the peoples of Britain, and particularly for the citizens of small and poor countries such as Scotland.[80]

Fletcher's sophisticated brand of anti-unionism was part of a wider Euro-Gothicist vision, a perspective which also helped to shape the eighteenth-century Scottish contribution to the construction of a united British identity. The Anglo-Scottish poet James Thomson engaged directly in his work with the construction of a British patriotism. His Britishness embraced a stock Francophobia[81] as well as a pan-European Gothicism, whose conventional praise for the 'northern nations' was qualified by a classicist's distaste for the barbarity of the dark ages. Thomson had a library which, as Christine Gerrard notes, contained not only accounts of England's historic liberties by the likes of Rapin and Nathaniel Bacon, but also the works of Tacitus, Olaus Magnus's *Compendious history of the Goths, Swedes and Vandals* and Molesworth's *Account of Denmark*.[82] It is hardly surprising that Thomson located 'the parent hive / Of the mixed kingdoms' of Europe at 'wintry Scandinavia's utmost bound'.[83] The Anglo-Saxons had brought to Britain a freedom which had once inspired 'the whole Scythian mass'.[84] Skirting round the constitutional implications of the Norman Conquest, the whiggish Thomson declaimed:

> Of Gothic nations this the final burst;
> And mixed the genius of these people all,
> Their virtues mixed in one exalted stream,
> Here the rich tide of English blood grew full.

As fellow Goths the English and Norman races were able to blend, despite political differences, into 'one fraternal nation' – the 'nation of the free'.[85]

The Scottish Enlightenment injected universalist and pan-European insights into the heart of British political culture.[86] The influential Edinburgh moral philosopher John Pringle devoted part of his lectures in ethics to surveying 'that form of government which took its rise from the irruption of the northern nations'.[87] The introductory volume of William Robertson's monumental *Charles V* (1769) was a panoramic pan-Gothi-

---

[80] Fletcher, *An account of a conversation for the right regulation of governments for the common good of mankind* (1704), in Fletcher, *Political works*.
[81] E.g. Thomson, *Poetical works*, 'Summer', p. 107; 'Liberty', pt IV, p. 388; pt V, pp. 401, 405, 410.   [82] Gerrard, *Patriot opposition*, p. 111.
[83] Thomson, *Poetical works*, 'Liberty', pt IV, p. 368.   [84] *Ibid.*, pt IV, p. 377.
[85] *Ibid.*, pt IV, pp. 378–9.
[86] K. O'Brien, 'Between Enlightenment and stadial history: William Robertson on the history of Europe', *BJECS* 16 (1993), 53–63.
[87] Quoted in R. Emerson, 'Scottish universities in the eighteenth century, 1690–1800', *SVEC* 167 (1977), 471–2.

cist survey of the progress of society in Europe from the subversion of the Roman Empire to the beginning of the sixteenth century.[88] Robertson's rival, Gilbert Stuart, also published a trilogy of libertarian histories which reflected concentric Gothicist loyalties.[89] Adam Smith lectured on the common transitions – allodial, feudal and modern – which underlay the history of post-Roman Europe.[90] John Millar distinguished two basic patterns in the formation of medieval Europe. When the Goths made conquests in the provinces of the former Roman Empire these areas became 'extensive rude kingdoms, in which the free people were all united in separate feudal dependencies'. On the other hand, those Goths outside the Empire in Sweden, Denmark and much of Germany were not 'induced by any prior union subsisting, through an extensive territory, to associate in very large communities', but remained clannish.[91] Sir John Dalrymple contended that the Germanic institutions of the feudal law constituted a decisive common pattern underlying Europe's diversity in other spheres: this Gothic 'system' had been 'established by every one of those nations, however different in their dialects, separated by seas and mountains, unconnected by alliances, and often at enmity with each other'.[92]

It is hard to disentangle the various strains of pan-European Gothicism, feudal jurisprudence and universalism, which together shaped the histories of post-Roman European development which were such a characteristic feature of the Scottish Enlightenment. Nevertheless, it is clear that they worked to dislodge chauvinistic values and to inspire concentric loyalties within the Scottish literati. North Britain was a province not only of Britain, but of the wider republics of European letters, and Gothic freedoms. Robertson saw no contradiction between glorying in the achievements of the Anglo-British constitution and acknowledging a

[88] William Robertson, *Works* (London, 1831 edn), pp. 333–432.
[89] Gilbert Stuart, *Observations concerning the public law and constitutional history of Scotland* (Edinburgh, 1779); Stuart, *An historical dissertation concerning the antiquity of the English constitution* (Edinburgh, 1768); Stuart, *A view of society in Europe in its progress from rudeness to refinement* (Edinburgh, 1778). See also W. Zachs, *Without regard to good manners: a biography of Gilbert Stuart* (Edinburgh, 1992); C. Kidd, *Subverting Scotland's past* (Cambridge, 1993), pp. 239–44.
[90] Adam Smith, *Lectures on jurisprudence* (ed. R. L. Meek et al., Oxford, 1978), 'Report of 1762–3' (hereafter *LJ (A)*); 'Report dated 1766' (hereafter *LJ (B)*).
[91] John Millar, *An historical view of the English government from the settlement of the Saxons* (1787: 4 vols., London, 1803), III, pp. 10–13.
[92] John Dalrymple, *An essay towards a general history of feudal property in Great Britain* (London, 1757), pp. 1–2. See also Andrew Macdouall, Lord Bankton, *An institute of the laws of Scotland in civil rights* (3 vols., Edinburgh, 1751–3), I, pp. 14 n., 18–19 n.; Alexander Wight, *An inquiry into the rise and progress of parliament chiefly in Scotland* (Edinburgh, 1784), pp. 18–19; James Beattie, *Dissertations moral and critical* (London, 1783), pp. 527–8, 533–4.

common European identity: 'The state of government, in all the nations of Europe, having been nearly the same during several ages, nothing can tend more to illustrate the progress of the English constitution, than a careful inquiry into the laws and customs of the kingdoms on the Continent.'[93] To some extent the remarkable achievement of the Scottish Enlightenment in reorientating English whig historiography has distorted our understanding of Anglo-Saxonism. The historians of the Scottish Enlightenment did challenge many of the shibboleths of vulgar English whiggery.[94] However, it would be wrong to make the assumption that before the Scottish Enlightenment the English historiography of liberty was resolutely 'solipsistic'[95] and detached from the broader development of political institutions in Europe. This was not the case. To a large extent English political culture was already integrated with the wider sweep of the Gothic origins of European institutions. What the Scottish Enlightenment did was to take this a stage further. The Scots argued that modern England was not as singular as commentators thought. Rather, there was a lot to be said for the achievement of a modern civilised absolute monarchy like France which maintained a large degree of civil liberty for its subjects.[96] The Scottish Enlightenment set the history of English liberty as a fortuitous story, but not dramatically so, within the broader picture of the rise of commercial civilisation in Europe. Yet, as we have seen, the pan-European identity promoted in the Scottish Enlightenment was not out of step with existing features of English political culture.

The limits of Francophobia

A strong sense of Gothic kinship with the Franks overlay and cut across the Francophobia which was such a defining feature of late seventeenth- and eighteenth-century English political identity. There is a powerful historical consensus that anti-French sentiments were at the heart of British political culture during the era of the 'Second Hundred Years' War'.[97] Michael Duffy has argued that 'a peak of Francophobia' was attained in late seventeenth- and eighteenth-century England. In every popular medium – prints and caricatures, literature and the theatre – he

[93] Robertson, *Charles V*, Note xlv, in Robertson, *Works*, p. 432.
[94] Forbes, *Hume's philosophical politics*, pp. 187, 311–12.
[95] D. Forbes, 'The European or cosmopolitan dimension in Hume's science of politics', *BJECS* 1 (1978), 57. See also Forbes, *Hume's philosophical politics*, pp. 142–50, 152 (where even Hume himself falls for the stereotype), and p. 299 (for the recognition that vulgar whiggism was based upon a wider European history of declining Gothic liberties).
[96] Hume, 'Of civil liberty' and 'Of the rise and progress of the arts and sciences', in Hume, *Essays*.
[97] M. Duffy, '"The noisie, empty, fluttring French": English images of the French, 1689–1815', *History Today* 32 (September 1982), 21.

detects a prevailing consensus that the French were quite 'alien', 'a monkey race', 'unnatural' and 'un-English'.[98] Francophobia, as Colin Haydon notes, also figured prominently in the anti-Catholicism of the first half of the eighteenth century, with English commentators critical not only of Popish–French militarism, arbitrary rule, poverty, superstition and slavishness, but also of the horrendous treatment meted out to the Huguenots, many of whom had since resettled in London (however, as Daniel Statt points out, the English response to Huguenot refugees was complex, fed not only by sympathy for Protestant co-religionists, but also fears about their Calvinism, anxieties over economic competition, stock Francophobia and – ironically – suspicions that some Huguenots might be crypto-Jesuits).[99] Jeremy Black has also established a general picture of mutual antagonism, though he concedes that the prevailing xenophobia was qualified by several countercurrents in English culture, including the recognition that French autocracy had a late medieval or even early modern provenance.[100] Duncan Forbes has identified 'chauvinistic Francophobia' as a central feature of vulgar whiggery.[101] A contemporary French observer, Fougeret de Montbron, held similar views of eighteenth-century English values: 'Before they learn there is a God to be worshipped', he expostulated, 'they learn there are Frenchmen to be detested.'[102]

There were indeed numerous critics of France among the ranks of historians and political pamphleteers. British culture abounded in clichéd comparisons between English freedoms and French tyranny, and between the plenty of roast beef and plum pudding enjoyed by the tenant farmers of England and the scrawniness of the impoverished clog-shod peasantry of France. Henry Care compared the arbitrary tyranny of the

[98] *Ibid.*, 21–6.

[99] C. Haydon, *Anti-Catholicism in eighteenth-century England* (Manchester, 1993), pp. 24–6, 47, 57, 127, 129, 136, 179, 253; D. Statt, *Foreigners and Englishmen: the controversy over immigration and population, 1660–1760* (Newark, DE, 1995), pp. 19–20, 168–72, 189–91, 193; G. Gibbs, 'The reception of the Huguenots in England and the Dutch republic, 1680–1690', in O. Grell, J. Israel and N. Tyacke (eds.), *From persecution to toleration: the Glorious Revolution and religion in England* (Oxford, 1991), esp. pp. 277–81.

[100] J. Black, *Natural and necessary enemies: Anglo-French relations in the eighteenth century* (London, 1986), esp. pp. 187, 192–3; Black, 'Ideology, history, xenophobia and the world of print in eighteenth-century England', in Black and J. Gregory (eds.), *Culture, politics and society in Britain 1660–1800* (Manchester, 1991), pp. 203–4.

[101] Forbes, *Hume's philosophical politics*, pp. 142–50, 312.

[102] Quoted in R. Porter, *English society in the eighteenth century* (Harmondsworth, 1982), p. 21. See also M. Duffy, *The Englishman and the foreigner* (Cambridge, 1985). But for a nuanced approach to the values of the elite, see P. Langford, *A polite and commercial people* (Oxford, 1989), p. 321. R. Gibson, *Best of enemies: Anglo-French relations since the Norman Conquest* (London, 1995), ch. 3, plausibly depicts the eighteenth century as an era of both 'cosmopolitanism and xenophobia'; but, as we shall see, Gallicanism and Gothicism further complicate this picture.

king of France to that of the grand Turk.[103] Anglo-French commercial, strategic and colonial rivalries found expression in hostile caricatures of the French, such as Hogarth's 'Calais Gate, or the Roast Beef of Old England'. It was a commonplace that contemporary French values were poisonous to the English. Social commentators such as the Reverend John Brown (1715–66) in his *Estimate of the manners and principles of the times* (1757) or John Andrews (1736–1809) in *A comparative view of the French and English nations, in their manners, politics, and literature* (1785) aroused fears about the effects of a foppish and effeminate Gallic contagion on the virtuous libertarian manners of the English people.[104] Francophobia even had a purchase on popular Gothicism. Colley can point to examples of Francophobic Gothicism, such as the Saxonist sermons delivered in the 1750s by John Free to the Society of Anti-Gallicans.[105] One poetaster declaimed that the French were 'by Nature design'd as a Foil / To the bright Saxon look, the great claim of our Isle'.[106]

Francophobia was a pronounced component of popular culture and a vital ingredient of national identity. However, while antagonism based on conflicting foreign policies, imperial ambitions, dynasticism and confessionalism was reinforced by popular xenophobia, the 'universal Francophobia of the media'[107] was mitigated within the political and cultural elite by a good measure of ambivalence. Popular anti-Gallicanism has to be set against the sophisticated Gothicist accounts of the history of liberty

---

[103] Henry Care, *English liberties: or, the free-born subject's inheritance* (London, 1680?), p. 1.

[104] Newman, *Rise of English nationalism*, esp. pp. 82–3; Colley, *Britons*, p. 88; K. Wilson, 'Empire of virtue: the imperial project and Hanoverian culture, c. 1720–1785', in L. Stone (ed.), *An imperial state at war* (London, 1994), p. 137. See also J. Sekora, *Luxury: the concept in western thought from Eden to Smollett* (Baltimore, 1977), ch. 2.

[105] L. Colley, 'Radical patriotism in eighteenth-century England', in R. Samuel (ed.), *Patriotism* (3 vols., London and New York, 1989), I, p. 173.

[106] 'The illustrious modern' (1718), quoted in H. Weinbrot, 'Politics, taste and national identity: some uses of Tacitism in eighteenth-century Britain', in Woodman and Luce, *Tacitus and the Tacitean tradition*, p. 177.

[107] Duffy, '"Noisie, empty, fluttring French"', 24. Despite this 'universal Francophobia', the Denmark of Molesworth remained a byword for rottenness: see *Northern revolutions: or, the principal causes of the declension and dissolution of several once flourishing Gothic constitutions in Europe* (London, 1757); Edward Wortley Montagu Jr, *Reflections on the rise and fall of the antient republicks, adapted to the present state of Great Britain* (London, 1759), pp. 363–6. For sceptical modern whigs such as Tucker, Poland with its stagnant Gothic constitution and untrammelled nobility was Europe's worst tyranny: Tucker, *Treatise*, pp. 62, 65, 165, 336; Gunn, 'Civil polity of Paxton', 57. For Turkey and Brandenburg as the blots on European political civilisation in the late eighteenth century, see E. Gould, 'American independence and Britain's counter-revolution', *P+P* 154 (1997), 128–9. For Russia as an oriental despotism lacking countervailing feudal institutions, see F. Venturi, 'From Scotland to Russia: an eighteenth-century debate on feudalism', in A. G. Cross, *Great Britain and Russia in the eighteenth century* (Newtonville, MA, 1979), esp. pp. 12–20.

commonly found in the higher echelons of English political culture from the middle of the seventeenth century onwards. Many eighteenth-century Englishmen recognised that national characters were not immutable, and were happy to acknowledge that their arch-enemies were not altogether different from themselves, the French having formerly enjoyed Gothic liberties.

The English critique of French despotism purveyed in historical treatises was quite specific, and did not extend to a blanket condemnation of the French people as a nation incapable of sustaining the burdens of freedom and self-government. Rather the French as the descendants of the Franks were considered a kindred people of the Anglo-Saxons, who had been unfortunate largely through the vicissitudes of late medieval and more recent European history – and not through any defect in their ethnic composition – to lose their Gothic birthright. There is a tone of elegy rather than hostility to most seventeenth- and eighteenth-century historical treatments of French constitutional history. Niggling concern about the fate of France shaded English hubris. John Oldmixon encouraged Englishmen to read widely in European history so that, by comparing 'the happiness of our constitution with the misery of other nations', they might become 'more tenacious in preserving it': 'France was once as happy as we are, if Mézeray, one of the best historians among the moderns, knew the history of his own country.'[108]

Anglo-French affinities did not rest solely upon the notion of a shared Gothic ancestry. Gothicism was supplemented by a perception of other shared values. Not only had the Franks and Anglo-Saxons been kindred liberty-loving peoples, so too were the aboriginal Gauls and Britons, closely related libertarian Celtic populations, upon whom they imposed themselves.[109] The British origins of the Church of England shared common features with the early Gallican church. 'We must search among the Gauls for the ecclesiastical polity of the ancient Britons', argued Ferdinando Warner in the midst of the eighteenth-century Anglo-French wars.[110] Both churches had subsequently been corrupted by medieval Catholicism. Having succeeded in restoring the historic *ecclesia anglicana*, the English Reformation provided a model for her wayward Gallican sister-church. In the late seventeenth century the estrangement of an assertively Gallican church from the papacy lent a degree of credibility to the hope that another historic church might yet be reclaimed from the clutches of Rome.[111] The anti-Catholicism which did so much to fuel

---

[108] John Oldmixon, *The critical history of England, ecclesiastical and civil* (2 vols., London, 1724–6), I, pp. 11–12.   [109] Rymer, *General draught*, pp. 13–15, 73.
[110] Ferdinando Warner, *Ecclesiastical history of England* (2 vols., London, 1756), I, p. 3.
[111] See William Cave, *A dissertation concerning the government of the ancient church, by bishops,*

English Francophobia was mitigated by Anglican–Gallican sympathies. Throughout the Second Hundred Years' War the English elite remained conscious of several threads which linked England, however tenuously at times, with the enemy.[112]

Even during the reign of Louis XIV, a period when Englishmen first began to worry seriously about the expansionist ambitions of the Bourbon monarchy, elements of the English elite displayed a keen awareness of a wider identity in which the French figured largely. It was clear that Louis wished to roll back the frontiers of the European Reformation. Some commentators feared that he wished also to establish a universal monarchy, a personal dominion over the whole of western Christendom. Andrew Marvell described Louis XIV as the 'presumptive monarch of Christendom'.[113] However, strategic concerns about the dangers of French expansionism did not extinguish all sense of those Gothic affinities shared by the English and the French. As we have seen already, Charles Davenant, a vigorous critic of French aspirations to universal monarchy, did not allow Francophobia to cloud his evaluation of France's legitimate place within the history of European liberties.[114]

Religious affinities reinforced the sense of a common Gothic heritage. Bruno Neveu notes that this era was a golden age of Anglo-Gallican reconciliation and intellectual cross-fertilisation.[115] On one side of the Channel, the works of William Wake and Wilkins on medieval *concilia* drew upon French learning, while on the other George Bull's *Defensio fidei Nicaenae* was warmly received by French clerics.[116] Similarly, French patristic scholarship, such as the work of Louis Ellies Du Pin (1657–1719), became an integral component of Anglican culture. Du Pin's *Nouvelle bibliothèque de tous les auteurs ecclésiastiques* was quickly translated into English (1696–1706) to become 'a staple work on the shelves of the

metropolitans and patriarchs (London, 1683), p. 219; John Inett, *Origines Anglicanae* (2 vols., London and Oxford, 1704–10), II, pp. vii–x. For the earlier appeal of Gallican jurisdictionalism to Laudians, see A. Milton, *Catholic and Reformed: the Roman and Protestant churches in English Protestant thought 1600–1640* (Cambridge, 1995), pp. 265–8.

[112] E.g. the patriotic anti-Catholicism of George Smith, *The Britons and Saxons not converted to Popery* (London, 1748), also comprehends, p. 265, praise for 'those learned assertors of the liberties of the Gallican church', carefully distinguished from Jesuits and 'high papalians'. In addition to the roles played by Gallicanism, enlightened cosmopolitanism and Gothicism, Francophobia was also mitigated by the widespread antiquarian acknowledgement of the shared customs and institutions of the ancient Gauls and Britons.

[113] Andrew Marvell, *An account of the growth of Popery and arbitrary government* (Amsterdam, 1677), p. 16. See also S. Pincus, 'From butterboxes to wooden shoes: the shift in English popular sentiment from anti-Dutch to anti-French in the 1670s', *HJ* 38 (1995), 333–61.

[114] Davenant, *Essays*.

[115] B. Neveu, 'Mabillon et l'historiographie Gallicane vers 1700', in Neveu, *Erudition et religion aux XVIIe et XVIIIe siècles* (Paris, 1994), pp. 223–4.   [116] *Ibid.*, p. 223.

more enlightened of the English clergy during the reign of Queen Anne'.[117]

The rise of Gallicanism drew attention to ominous cracks in the monolith of Counter-Reformation orthodoxy. The Four Gallican Articles of 1682 variously liberated sovereigns from the temporal claims of the papacy, reinforced the allegiance of the subject to the immediate sovereignty of the temporal monarch, highlighted the limitations on papal authority inherent both in General Councils of the Church and within the Gallican church, and emphasised that even in questions of faith the leading authority of the papacy was qualified by the consensus of the church. Anglican ecclesiology of the Restoration era drew on the work of Jean de Launoy, Etienne Baluze (1630–1718) and other Gallican apologists.[118] Du Pin's popularity in England owed something to the uncompromising Gallicanism of his *Dissertationes historicae de antiqua Ecclesiae disciplina* (1686), a treatise which found its way on to the *Index librorum prohibitorum* in 1688 where it joined other defences of Gallican liberties, such as the work of Jean Gerbais (1629–99), condemned by Innocent XI in 1680.[119] To a considerable extent, Anglicans and Gallicans shared a similar interpretation of the historic institutions of the early church. Anglicans and Gallicans both insisted on the primacy of the episcopacy in their respective ecclesiologies. Indeed, the argument for the historic autonomy of the Church of England from the patriarchal claims of Rome based on the sixth canon of the Council of Nicaea was also an important component of the case for the independent privileges of the Gallican church.[120]

French relations with the papacy became increasingly strained by Gallicanism, and by the issue of Jansenism, a strictly Augustinian approach to Catholic theology. The death of the orthodox – albeit pragmatically Gallican – Louis XIV opened a significant window of opportunity for Anglican–Gallican reconciliation. Negotiations began between lead-

---

[117] J. W. Thompson, *A history of historical writing* (2 vols., New York, 1942), II, p. 31.

[118] Joseph Bingham, *Origines ecclesiasticae* (1708–22: 2 vols., London, 1878), I, pp. 348–9.

[119] Neveu, *Erudition et religion*, p. 208. See also the Gallican exile, Oxford DD and client of Queen Caroline, Père Le Courayer, author of *Dissertation sur la validité des ordinations anglicanes* (1723) and of an English translation of Paolo Sarpi's *History of the Council of Trent* (1736): see R. Shackleton, *Montesquieu* (Oxford, 1961), pp. 132–3; S. Ollard, 'Reunion. 1. with the Roman church', in Ollard, G. Crosse and M. Bond (eds.), *A dictionary of English church history* (1912: 3rd edn, London, 1948), pp. 522–3. For the constitutionalism of Nicolas Le Gros, *Renversement des libertés de l'église gallicane* (1717), see D. Van Kley, 'The Jansenist constitutional legacy in the French prerevolution', in K. Baker (ed.), *The French Revolution and the creation of modern political culture*, vol. I, *The political culture of the Old Regime* (Oxford, 1987), pp. 173–4.

[120] Nicolson, *English historical library*, II, p. 20; Bingham, *Origines ecclesiasticae*, I, p. 348.

ing French ecclesiastics and Archbishop Wake about the possibility of an ecclesiastical union of the Anglican and Gallican churches. Nothing came of the project, but a residual sympathy for the 'learned assertors of the liberties of the Gallican church' remained a legitimate feature of Anglican churchmanship.[121]

The early Hanoverian era was characterised by a relaxation of British policy towards France, signalled by the Anglo-French alliance in 1716. A central strand of Walpolean foreign policy was an awareness that the Jacobite threat, despite its potential bridgehead in the Highlands of Scotland and the passive ideological and cultural support which it enjoyed throughout Britain, depended to a large extent on the patronage of members of the European states system disenchanted, for one reason or another, with Britain or Hanover. Thus, despite the scope for friction generated by Jacobitism, the first decades of the Hanoverian regime were remarkable for the relative lack of turbulence between the two powers.[122]

This rapprochement was paralleled by a good measure of fruitful intercourse between the respective political cultures of England and France. For eighteenth-century France, despite its code of censorship, was not an absolutist monolith. A broad school of revisionism led by Dale van Kley and Keith Baker, which vigorously eschews any suggestion of a teleological high road to the French Revolution, has demonstrated none the less the existence of a vigorous culture of 'political contestation' within the traditional contours of *ancien régime* France.[123] Ecclesiastical and theological disputes internal to Catholicism, in particular the controversies surrounding Gallicanism and Jansenism, were drawn into the temporal dimension of politics, becoming interwoven with the defence of the powers of the constitutional courts, the parlements. An embryonic public opinion developed over these issues, none of which posed a direct threat to the underpinnings of the *ancien régime* system.

The Gothic past was as much at the heart of eighteenth-century French political argument as it was across the Channel. Indeed, the debate over the continuity of the ancient English constitution that had flared up around 1680 in the battle over the Brady thesis was mirrored by a similar

---

[121] N. Sykes, *William Wake, Archbishop of Canterbury 1657–1737* (2 vols., Cambridge, 1957), I, pp. 252–314.

[122] Black, *Natural and necessary enemies*, ch. 1; D. Szechi, *The Jacobites: Britain and Europe 1688–1788* (Manchester, 1994).

[123] D. Van Kley, *The Jansenists and the expulsion of the Jesuits from France, 1757–1765* (New Haven, 1975); Van Kley, *The religious origins of the French Revolution* (New Haven, 1996); K. Baker, *Inventing the French Revolution* (Cambridge, 1990); J. Merrick, *The desacralisation of the French monarchy in the eighteenth century* (Baton Rouge, 1990), pp. 31–2, 50–2, 70, 76–7, 167.

conflagration in France around 1730.[124] The classic phase of the historiographical battle of the French Gothicists and Romanists began with the posthumous publication of the political writings of Henri de Boulainvilliers, comte de St Saire (1658–1722), which propagated the canonical version of the *thèse nobiliaire*.[125] This met a sharp rebuke from the Abbé Jean-Baptiste Dubos (1670–1742) in his *Histoire critique de l'establissement de la monarchie française* (1734). Dubos argued that the Franks had not come as conquerors, but as allies of the Romans. The powers of the emperor descended intact to the French monarchy in a story of continuity.[126]

France had two distinct traditions of Gothicist constitutionalism. Both parlements and Estates-General, their respective champions claimed, enjoyed a Gothic lineage. The Gothicist arguments made by Boulainvilliers and his ilk for the privileges of the *noblesse de race* and their institutions, were also to be appropriated by the parlementaires in their battle on behalf both of Jansenism and their own self-preservation.[127] According to Franklin Ford, 'by the eighteenth century, both the robe and the sword were committed to the Germanic theory of French history, to the notion of Frankish innovation as an element of cleavage with the heritage of Rome, and to the Champ de Mars as a cherished institutional ancestor'.[128] The usable past bequeathed by the Gothic Franks was to supply a major part of the 'ideological arsenal' of parlementaire ideology in the middle of the eighteenth century, most prominently in the work of Louis Adrien Lepaige.[129]

Anglomania was a prominent feature of eighteenth-century French discourse.[130] English country whiggism held some appeal for Jansenist constitutionalists, while the Abbé Mably, an admirer of Magna Carta, was to derive inspiration for his anti-feudal republicanism from Bolin-

---

[124] N. O. Keohane, *Philosophy and the state in France* (Princeton, 1980), pp. 346–50; F. L. Ford, *Robe and sword: the regrouping of the French aristocracy after Louis XIV* (Cambridge, MA, 1953), ch. 12; E. Carcassonne, *Montesquieu et le problème de la constitution française au XVIIIe siècle* (Paris, 1927), ch. 1. For the early eighteenth-century French Gothicist vision of 'a pre-Carolingian, quasi-democratic Germanic society', see T. Kaiser, 'The Abbé Dubos and the historical defence of monarchy in early eighteenth-century France', *SVEC* 267 (1989), 93.

[125] V. Buranelli, 'The historical and political thought of Boulainvilliers', *JHI* 18 (1957), 475–94; Carcassonne, *Montesquieu*, pp. 18–20; G. Chaussinand-Nogaret, *The French nobility in the eighteenth century* (1976: trans. W. Doyle, Cambridge, 1985), ch. 1; J. Q. C. Mackrell, *The attack on feudalism in eighteenth-century France* (London, 1973), pp. 20–4.

[126] Ford, *Robe and sword*, pp. 231–2; Mackrell, *Attack on feudalism*, pp. 26–7; Kaiser, 'Abbé Dubos', 77–102; Carcassonne, *Montesquieu*, pp. 42–4.

[127] Merrick, *Desacralisation*, pp. 84, 127.   [128] Ford, *Robe and sword*, pp. 228–9.

[129] Baker, *Inventing the French Revolution*, pt 1; Van Kley, *Religious origins*, pp. 203–10; Carcassonne, *Montesquieu*, ch. 6, pt 3; Merrick, *Desacralisation*, p. 85.

[130] Dedieu, *Montesquieu*, esp. ch. 3, for the early eighteenth century.

gbroke.[131] Most famously, Montesquieu, who travelled to England between November 1729 and the spring of 1731, devoted a chapter of *De l'esprit des lois* to an analysis of the workings of the English constitution, though this was, in some respects, misleading, and a qualified encomium. In spite of these drawbacks, Montesquieu became something of an honorary whig, not least for his pursuit of the misty origins of English liberties and institutions back to the customs which once prevailed in the ancient forests of Germany.[132] In *Lettres persanes* he had already appeared to endorse Revolution principles, glorifying limitations upon monarchy as 'le principe fondomental' of all the various historic kingdoms of Europe which the Goths established on the demise of the Roman Empire.[133]

Given the importance of Gothicism to the likes of Boulainvilliers and Montesquieu, it should occasion little surprise that the traffic between England and France during the first half of the eighteenth century was by no means all one way. Hostile criticisms of Bourbon despotism coexisted with a decidedly Frankish – if not quite Francophile – dimension to English political culture. Bolingbroke, who revamped English toryism by stealing whig clothes and constructing an anti-partisan patriotic ancient constitutionalism which distanced the tories from Jacobitism, began the process after returning from a decade's exile in France. Though he was a high-flying tory, the years in France had not infected him with absolutist notions; indeed, his journalistic vehicle, *The Craftsman*, expressed support for the parlementaire cause, and his historical writing was influenced by Rapin's Huguenot Gothicism. On the other hand, Bolingbroke was no uncritical admirer of the sort of aristocratic Frankish constitutionalism championed by Boulainvilliers. Though he recognised the common

---

[131] Baker, *Inventing the French Revolution*, pp. 90–3; Van Kley, *Religious origins*, pp. 216–17. Bolingbroke's political writings were known in France, influencing the parlementaire cause. There was a 1737 edition of *The Craftsman* as well as a translation of the *Dissertation upon parties* by Etienne de Silhouette in 1739 and further editions during the 1740s. See D. J. Fletcher, 'The fortunes of Bolingbroke in France in the eighteenth century', *SVEC* 47 (1966), 217–20; H. T. Dickinson, *Bolingbroke* (London, 1970), pp. 304–5.

[132] Shackleton, *Montesquieu*, pp. 117–45; Shackleton, 'Montesquieu, Bolingbroke, and the separation of powers', in Shackleton, *Essays on Montesquieu and on the Enlightenment* (ed. D. Gilson and M. Smith, Oxford, 1988); Dedieu, *Montesquieu*, ch. 5; J. Shklar, *Montesquieu* (Oxford, 1987), p. 21; Baker, *Inventing the French Revolution*, p. 173; I. Kramnick, *Bolingbroke and his circle* (1968: Ithaca, 1992), p. 150; M. Cranston, *Philosophers and pamphleteers* (Oxford, 1986), pp. 34–5. For the influence in Britain of Montesquieu's reflections on the English constitution, see F. T. H. Fletcher, *Montesquieu and English politics (1750–1800)* (London, 1939), esp. pp. 23–4, 30–1, 35–6, 116–28.

[133] Montesquieu, *Lettres persanes* (Paris, 1973), Lettre CXXXII, pp. 294–5. *The Spirit of the Laws* contributed to the Boulainvilliers–Dubos debate from a modified Germanist position: Carcassonne, *Montesquieu*, p. 673, notes that the *Spirit of the Laws* 'raffermit la thèse germaniste, gravement compromise par les exagérations de Boulainvilliers et par la critique de Dubos'.

libertarian characteristics of Europe's Gothic peoples, he believed that the Franks had from the very beginning introduced a democratic deficit into France's institutions, unlike the Visigoths of Spain whose Cortes 'may be more truly compared to a British parliament than the assembly of states of France could ever pretend to be'. However, complacent Englishmen should learn the same lesson from both the French and Spanish experiences: the common Gothic heritage of liberties was liable to erosion. Whereas the Franks, transformed into an aristocratic caste, lost their democratic Germanic values soon after the conquest of Gaul, the Castilians experienced a long slide into political corruption until losing their liberties in the first half of the sixteenth century.[134]

England was awash with translations of the French 'whig' classics. Molesworth translated Hotman's *Franco-Gallia*, while Charles Forman rendered the work of Boulainvilliers as *An historical account of the antient parliaments of France* (1739). Forman introduced Boulainvilliers to an English readership as an interpreter of an expiring French whiggery which once enjoyed a powerful institutional apparatus and the will to control the monarchy: 'That the French were once the freest nation in Europe, and perhaps in the world, the Count has put out of dispute . . . The Count shows the prodigious power of the ancient French parliaments, of which the present are not even a shadow; he shows them sitting in judgment, disposing of crowns, and passing sentences of deposition upon some kings, and of death upon others.'[135] The works of the Abbé Vertot on the revolutions of Europe and on Frankish questions were also widely translated into English in numerous editions.[136]

Anglo-French divergence was not assumed to be natural; at least there was very little discussion along such lines among the ranks of the educated who thought about such matters. Nevertheless, there were tensions within English culture between a keen sense of Anglo-French difference and a common heritage which historians acknowledged to have been shared by the various Gothic nations of Europe. Bolingbroke,

---

[134] Bolingbroke, *Dissertation on parties*, Letters XIV–XVI, in Bolingbroke, *Works* (5 vols., London, 1754), II; Black, *Natural and necessary enemies*, pp. 190–1; Kramnick, *Bolingbroke and his circle*, pp. 15–16, 253; B. Cottret, *Bolingbroke's political writings: the conservative Enlightenment* (Houndmills, 1997), pp. 39–42; Forbes, *Hume's philosophical politics*, pp. 240–1; O'Brien, *Narratives of Enlightenment*, p. 18.

[135] Charles Forman, 'Preface', in Boulainvilliers, *An historical account of the antient parliaments of France, or states-general of the kingdom* (trans. Forman, 2 vols., London, 1739), I, p. xxviii. See J. Barzun, *Race: a study in modern superstition* (London, 1938), p. 30.

[136] René Vertot, 'A dissertation, designed to trace the original of the French, by a parallel of their manners with those of the Germans', in *Vertot's miscellanies* (trans. John Henley, London, 1723); Vertot, 'An enquiry, whether the kingdom of France, from the establishment of that monarchy, has been an hereditary or elective state', in *Dissertations by the celebrated Abbots De Vertot and Anselm* (trans. M. Paschoud, London, 1726); Baker, *Inventing the French Revolution*, p. 208; Kaiser, 'Abbé Dubos', 93.

for example, subscribed to the view that there were deep and historic differences between English and French politics, though these did not diminish his respect for a common Gothicism: 'Both their ancestors and ours came out of Germany, and had probably much the same manners, the same customs and the same forms of government. But as they proceeded differently in the conquests they made, so did they in the establishments that followed.'[137] The French monarchy was founded on a more rapid conquest of Gaul and centralisation of the monarchy. Of course, Bolingbroke's interpretation of the differences between France and England was, like those of his contemporaries, institutional in focus, rather than ethnocentric. William Robertson acknowledged the great achievements of the Estates-General of 1355: 'spirited efforts were made in France long before the House of Commons in England acquired any considerable influence in the legislature'.[138] The subsequent decline of French representative institutions was mysterious: 'In England, almost all attempts to establish or to extend the liberty of the people have been successful; in France they have proved unfortunate. What were the accidental events, or political causes which occasioned this difference, it is not my business to enquire.'[139] Similarly perplexed by the vast gulf between the English constitution and the French monarchy, the Swiss antiquarian De Lolme set out to explain 'why, of two neighbouring nations, situated almost under the same climate, and having one common origin, the one has attained the summit of liberty, the other has gradually sunk under the most absolute monarchy'.[140] De Lolme noted that both had enjoyed similar feudal governments, but there was a major difference in the speed at which this form of government had consolidated: 'instead of being established by dint of arms and all at once, as in England, it had only been formed on the continent, and particularly in France, through a long series of slow successive events; a difference of circumstances this, from which consequences were in time to arise, as important as they were at first difficult to be foreseen'.[141] In his *Vindiciae Gallicae* (1791), James Mackintosh traced the decline of the French constitution from an 'infancy and youth' which was similar to that of the English and other Gothic governments to its early modern decrepitude. Why was its life cycle so different from the historical experience of the English body politic? In his answer Mackintosh revealed a profound debt to the Scottish Enlightenment: 'the downfall of the feudal aristocracy happening in France before commerce had elevated any other class of citizens into importance, its power devolved on the crown'.[142]

[137] Bolingbroke, *Dissertation on parties*, II, Letter XVI, p. 207.
[138] Robertson, *Charles V*, Note xix, in Robertson, *Works*, p. 403.   [139] *Ibid.*
[140] De Lolme, *Constitution of England*, pp. 17–18.   [141] *Ibid.*, p. 11.

Frankish analogies had an important place in English antiquarian culture.[143] The most sophisticated Saxonist antiquarianism remained European in the breadth of its interests, and, in some sense, identity. Rayner Heckford, for example, argued that from 'the ancient laws indeed of France, and other countries conquered by the Germans, much may be gathered for the better understanding of our Saxon laws'.[144] According to John Whitaker, the 'kindred nations' of Franks and Saxons had both been governed in the localities under systems of tythings, hundreds and counties.[145] English antiquarianism was reinforced by the theoretical insights of the Scottish Enlightenment on the evolution of feudal institutions. Adam Smith noticed basic similarities in the structures of government established by 'the Saxons in Britain, the Franks in Gaul, and the Burgundians and Wisigoths in the south of France'.[146] In his history of British feudalism, John Dalrymple noted that the basic distinction between allodial tenures and feudal benefices was common to the early medieval laws of both England and France: the Saxon division between allodial reve or folk land and feudal thane or boc land had been replicated in the Frankish categories of *alleux* and *féodaux*.[147] French comparisons were perhaps a natural complement to the insights of the vein of tory–royalist historiography inspired by Robert Brady, but such analogies were as often found within whiggish histories. During the Convocation controversy, for instance, proponents of the whig case drew on French constitutional analogies. Rightly sceptical of the reliability of the *Modus tenendi* – a fourteenth-century document relating the workings of the Anglo-Saxon parliament – as a foundation for his argument about the nature of England's ancient constitution, Wake turned instead to a Frankish analogy, noting that 'there was all along, in those days, a very near affinity, between the polity of France, and that of our own country, in its ecclesiastical as well as in its civil establishment'.[148]

What were perceived to be the basic differences between the English and the French nations? Were their basic national characters different? Temple argued that the Franks under Pharamond who established the

[142] James Mackintosh, *Vindiciae Gallicae* (1791: 4th edn, London, 1792), p. 18.
[143] See e.g. Thomas Madox, *Firma burgi* (London, 1726), 'Preface' and pp. 2–3; George St Amand, *An historical essay on the legislative power of England* (London, 1725), p. 30; Squire, *Enquiry into foundation*, p. 159 n.; James Ibbetson, *A dissertation on the national assemblies under the Saxon and Norman governments* (London, 1781), p. 3.
[144] Rayner Heckford, *A discourse on the bookland and folkland of the Saxons* (Cambridge, 1775), p. 8.   [145] Whitaker, *History of Manchester*, II, p. 113.
[146] Adam Smith, *LJ (A)*, p. 247.   [147] Dalrymple, *Feudal property*, pp. 10–12.
[148] William Wake, *The authority of Christian princes over their ecclesiastical synods asserted* (London, 1697), p. 154. See also Humphry Hody, *A history of English councils and convocations* (London, 1701), p. 377: 'A form of parliament very much resembling our ancient English parliaments, I find there was among our neighbours the French.'

kingdom of France and the Saxons of England were both branches of the same nation of Baltic Goths, the Suevi.[149] Had the French missed out on the sort of ancient mixed constitution enjoyed by the Anglo-Saxons? Rymer thought not. He described the limited constitution established by the Franks under Pharamond, noting that even Charlemagne had governed 'in the old parliamentary way'. However, the French constitution had gone into decline with the rise of a professional standing army. The revival of the defunct Estates-General now required 'a miracle like the Resurrection'.[150] This was a widely shared view. 'The whole polity of the old Franks and of our Anglo-Saxons is in every respect, as well regarding peace as war, so exactly similar', argued Samuel Squire.[151] Parliament was as much a component of the Frankish ancient constitution as it was of England's; Squire remarked that there was 'the greatest resemblance between the old Fields of March in France, and an Anglo-Saxon Witenagemot'.[152] Thornhaugh Gurdon subscribed to a similar view of the origins of parliaments: 'The original of the English government is much after the manner of that brought into Germany by the Saxons, by the Franks into Gaul, the Visigoths into Spain.'[153] Oldmixon mounted the argument that 'France was once as happy as we are.'[154] Revolution principles were as much part of the woof of French history as of English. 'Nor was it thus in England only', conceded Oldmixon; similar revolutions might be observed if one studied the historical operation of France's ancient constitution: 'Childeric was deposed by the assembly of the states in France, and Pepin was elected. Charles Duke of Lorraine was set aside and Hugh Capet chosen.'[155]

Even in the more markedly chauvinistic culture of the English Saxonist radicalism which emerged in the second half of the eighteenth century there lingered some sense of a Gothic affiliation to the French. James Burgh, for instance, noting that there 'was scarce an absolute prince in Europe, about the thirteenth century', found some comparisons between the Gothic histories of England and France; in 1355, for example, the French had 'made their King John sign a charter much like the Magna Charta of England'.[156]

[149] William Temple, *An introduction to the history of England*, in Temple, *Works* (4 vols., London, 1731), II, p. 537.   [150] Rymer, *General draught*, pp. 15, 23, 42–3, 66.
[151] Squire, *Enquiry into foundation*, p. 170 n.   [152] *Ibid.*, p. 190 n.
[153] Thornhaugh Gurdon, *The history of the high court of parliament, its antiquity, preheminence and authority* (2 vols., London, 1731), I, p. 22.
[154] Oldmixon, *Critical history*, I, p. 12.   [155] *Ibid.*, I, p. 23.
[156] James Burgh, *Political disquisitions* (3 vols., London, 1774–5), I, p. 21.

Gothick Asia

Just as the central Gothicist concept of 'the hive of nations' bridged some of the enmities between free-born Protestant England and the despotisms of Catholic Europe, so it also served to counteract the sense of difference between Europe and the Asiatic 'other'. In the eighteenth century Asia was a byword for barbaric practices, for luxury, for despotism and slavery, for stasis and for corruption. Its defining metaphor was the seraglio.[157] Nevertheless, Gothicism adds a complicating dimension to Edward Said's familiar thesis about the origins of orientalism. Broadly speaking, Said has argued that orientalism was a spurious body of knowledge which addressed not the real East but an Asiatic otherness conjured – by no means *always* unsympathetically – out of European prejudices and geopolitical dominance.[158]

Gothicism was, of course, yet another European prejudice whose champions constructed a fantastical northern Eurasia, but not an eastern otherness. Instead, the Eurasian focus of Gothicism implicated Asian manners and institutions *within* the history of European freedoms. However, it should be stressed from the outset that there were robust exceptions within British historiography to this broader affiliation. Rymer, for example, baldly contrasted the freedoms of Europe with an Eastern 'other' lacking in the parliamentary institutions – 'the government that always has obtained in Europe' – which defined the common European home.[159] Not all such contrasts were quite so sharp. Although Gibbon reported with some disdain the part played by oriental luxury in the corruption of Roman manliness, portrayed Byzantium as a lethargic oriental despotism and sneered at the successors of Kublai Khan who 'polluted' the court of China 'with a crowd of eunuchs, physicians, and astrologers, while thirteen millions of their subjects were consumed in the provinces by famine', he also celebrated the dynamism and vigour of various Asiatic peoples – including the Arabs, Mongols and Tartars – whose manners were similar to the barbarian Goths. The Tartars had enjoyed, he believed a Coroultai, or 'diet', and 'the rudiments of a feudal government', yet such customs and institutions were but the products of a common barbarity, which, beyond the peculiar circumstances of post-Roman Europe had all too often 'terminated' in corrupt, despotic empire. Ultimately, Gibbon remained a champion of European civilisation, expressing confidence that this citadel was now 'secure from any future irruption' of Asiatic barbarism.[160]

[157] For eighteenth-century British views of India as a land fit for despotism, see T. R. Metcalf, *Ideologies of the Raj* (Cambridge, 1995), pp. 6–9.

[158] E. Said, *Orientalism* (1978: Harmondsworth, 1985).

[159] Rymer, *General draught*, p. 9.

For many antiquaries, however, it was harder to separate the historical identities of Europe and the Orient. The shadowy Scythians of antiquity suggested a common parentage for the Goths of Europe and the peoples of northern and central Asia. Moreover, there was Biblical authority for such notions of Eurasian kinship. The *Universal history* (1736) traced the dispersal of Japhet's descendants not only throughout Europe, but also across northern Asia, Grand Tartary, Asia Minor, Media, Armenia and even India and China.[161] Thus, despite the emergence of the influential myth of oriental despotism, there were several commentators who traced profound links between the Goths of Europe and their brethren of the Asian steppes. Englishmen were informed by *A general history of the Turks, Moguls and Tatars* (1730) that 'we are no other than a colony of Tatars'.[162] The Saxonist James Ibbetson eagerly championed a wider Eurasian identity: 'The various tribes of barbarians that inhabited the northern regions of Europe and Asia were closely connected in their manners, customs and institutions, the circumstances in which they disagreed were minute, the great outlines were the same.' In tracing the similarities in manners and customs of 'the Scythian and German nations', Ibbetson insisted that 'the Saxon on the shores of the Baltic was not to be distinguished from the Hun on the banks of the Araxes'. There were, however, crucial differences in social evolution. The emergence of the feudal system, according to Ibbetson, had occurred among the western peoples – the Visigoths, Lombards, Franks and Saxons – from the sixth to the ninth century, but 'by their Asiatic brethren at a much later period in the remotest parts of the East'.[163]

The Scottish orientalist John Richardson, on the other hand, subscribed to the view that feudalism was 'an exotic plant' which had been transmitted to Europe by Tartars, in whose Asiatic homeland feudalism was 'indigenous, universal and immemorial'.[164] Richardson was not alone in detecting the existence of feudal institutions in the Ottoman Empire, India and Persia. A long tradition of Scottish feudalist scholars from Thomas Craig of Riccarton through to John Millar had speculated about the feudal nature of oriental zaims and timariots.[165] According to

[160] E.g. Gibbon, *DF*, I, p. 1032; II, p. 514; III, p. 806; J. Burrow, *Gibbon* (Oxford, 1985), pp. 49–50, 74–9.

[161] *An universal history, from the earliest account of time to the present* (7 vols., London, 1736–44), I, pp. 117–18.

[162] Quoted in P. J. Marshall and G. Williams, *The great map of mankind: British perceptions of the world in the age of Enlightenment* (London, 1982), p. 88. See also R. J. Smith, *Gothic bequest*, p. 40 n.

[163] James Ibbetson, *A dissertation on the folclande and boclande of the Saxons* (London, 1777), pp. 3–6.

[164] John Richardson, *A dissertation on the languages, literature, and manners of eastern nations* (1777: 2nd edn, Oxford, 1778), p. 153.

Richardson, Temujin, the leader of the Mongols who would win renown and notoriety as Genghis Khan, had been a feudal monarch, limited in his powers by a parliamentary institution, the Kouriltai (Gibbon's Coroultai): 'Those general meetings, called Kouriltai, bear so near a resemblance to the diets of the Gothic nations, that a strong additional argument may thence be drawn to support the hypothesis of the early Tartar establishments in Germany and Scandinavia.'[166] He also detected military vassalage, juries and other familiar aspects of the Gothic–feudal heritage in the history of the Tartars. Indeed, the succession to Genghis Khan of his youngest son, Olug Nuvin, in preference to the latter's elder brothers, reminded Richardson of feudal forms found much nearer to home: 'the situation of Olug Nuvin is a curious instance of a singular custom, long prevalent in Tartary, as well as among the northern nations; and even to be found in our old Saxon tenures, under the description of Borough English'.[167] However outrageous Richardson's comparison, his Eurasianism was not as eccentric as it seems. Adam Smith, for instance, argued that the constitutions of Gothic Europe took their 'rise from the same Tartarian species of government'. There were only minor differences between the Tartar and Gothic systems, and these were largely the result of the Goths' 'knowledge of agriculture and of property in land', which were unknown to the nomadic Tartars.[168]

At the turn of the nineteenth century, despite the advent of a more strident Anglo-Saxonism, some historians still adhered to the wider European perspectives of traditional Gothicist antiquarianism. Henry Hallam (1777–1859), for example, in his *View of the state of Europe* (1818) recognised the ancient Gothic constitutions of France and Spain.[169] Institutional divergence remained the keynote of Anglo-French contrast. Archibald Alison began his *History of Europe during the French Revolution* with an exploration of the common Gothic institutions of Europe, followed by a survey of the 'Comparative progress of freedom in France and England'.[170] Even Thomas Macaulay, who believed that, 'from a very

---

[165] John Millar, *The origins of the distinction of ranks* (1771: Basel, 1793 edn), pp. 206–10; P. Burke, 'Scottish historians and the feudal system: the conceptualisation of social change', *SVEC* 191 (1980), 537–9; Kidd, *Subverting*, p. 112 n. Russia was something of an exception to this picture; see the work of the Scot William Richardson outlined in Venturi, 'From Scotland to Russia', pp. 16–20.

[166] Richardson, *Dissertation on eastern nations*, pp. 159–61.   [167] *Ibid.*, p. 162.

[168] Adam Smith, *LJ (A)*, p. 244. See also *LJ (B)*, p. 416. However, the Scottish Enlightenment had no immunity from stereotypes of oriental despotism: see John Logan, *Dissertation on the government, manners and spirit of Asia* (1787), in Logan, *Elements of the philosophy of history* (1781: ed. R. Sher, Bristol, 1995).

[169] R. J. Smith, *Gothic bequest*, pp. 141–2.

[170] Archibald Alison, *History of Europe during the French Revolution* (10 vols., London, 1833–42), I, ch. 1.

early age, the English had enjoyed a far larger share of liberty than had fallen to the lot of any neighbouring people', upheld a traditional Gothicist line on the recent early modern crisis of parliaments:

The constitution of England was only one of a large family. In all the monarchies of Western Europe, during the middle ages, there existed restraints on the royal authority, fundamental laws, and representative assemblies. In the fifteenth century, the government of Castile seems to have been as free as that of our own country. That of Aragon was beyond all question more so.[171]

In France, where the monarch was 'more absolute', the Estates-General and later the parlement of Paris had exercised constitutional functions. Early modern England had avoided the sorry fate of the nation's continental kin: 'but she escaped very narrowly'.[172] In the next generation Bishop Stubbs (1825–1901) relocated the decline of the French constitution to the seventh century, making the bulk of French history a saga of authoritarianism arising from the illiberal nature of the original Frankish conquest: from its origins the Frankish polity had been a perversion of Gothic liberties, and the French character was burdened with an unfortunate legacy of centralised autocracy.[173]

Racial categories were also shifting. John Stuart Mill regarded the French as 'essentially a southern people' who lacked the vigorous characteristics of the 'self-helping and struggling Anglo-Saxons'.[174] The broad continental vision of traditional Gothicism was narrowing into a Nordic Teutonism, which, while never exclusively drawn from physical anthropology, tended to exclude the southern peoples of Europe.[175] Given the obvious caveat that nineteenth-century English racialism was no monolith of prejudice or single-issue determinism, its effect was nevertheless to vulgarise an older form of Gothicism organised around a history of institutional variations. A long-standing awareness of a common European home vanished from national consciousness, displaced by Teutonism and the saga of an island race.

[171] Thomas Babington Macaulay, *Essays and lays of ancient Rome* (London, 1886), 'Hallam' (1828), pp. 69–71; 'Hampden' (1831), p. 193; 'Mahon' (1833), p. 240.
[172] *Ibid.*, 'Hallam', pp. 69, 71; J. Burrow, 'Political science and the lessons of history', in S. Collini, D. Winch and Burrow, *That noble science of politics* (Cambridge, 1983), pp. 195–6.
[173] J. Burrow, *A liberal descent* (Cambridge, 1981), p. 142; Burrow, 'Political science', pp. 200–1; S. Collini, *Public moralists* (Oxford, 1991), p. 351.
[174] Quoted in Metcalf, *Ideologies of the Raj*, p. 32. See Collini, *Public moralists*, pp. 107–8.
[175] B. Melman, 'Claiming the nation's past: the invention of the Anglo-Saxon tradition', *Journal of Contemporary History* 26 (1991), 575–95; G. Stocking, *Victorian anthropology* (1987: New York pbk, 1991), p. 62; C. Parker, 'The failure of liberal racialism: the racial ideas of E. A. Freeman', *HJ* 24 (1981), 825–46. However, note the limits of English racialism. See E. Hobsbawm, *Nations and nationalism since 1780* (Cambridge, 1990), p. 108.

10   The varieties of Gothicism in the British Atlantic world, 1689–1800

The familiar association of Gothicism with English nationhood tends to obscure the importance of Gothic identities for other political communities in the British world. Although absorption in the Saxon past constituted one of the principal foundations of an assertive English nationhood, the significance of Gothicism was polymorphous and far from straightforward, especially in the eighteenth century. As well as defining the English core-nation, the rhetoric of Gothicism was also a salient feature of political culture in the various dominions of the eighteenth-century British monarchy. The Anglo-Irish political nation, the British colonists in North America and, from the middle of the eighteenth century, the people of Scotland celebrated a Gothic heritage of liberty, laws and institutions as a major component of their respective political identities.

Gothic identity was a vital ingredient of eighteenth-century British nationhood. The extension throughout the British Atlantic world of the cult of English libertarianism, including the view that England was the source of most of the freedoms enjoyed by the various British peoples, suggested a vital imaginative connection to the motherland. Moreover, the notion of an imagined Gothic community also reinforced the bonds of a common British identity. Yet Gothicism was no monolith. The sense of a shared ethnic history with England was not in itself a guarantee of an easy provincial relationship with the English core. As well as strengthening the process of British integration, the rhetoric of Gothicism also had the capacity to inject into political discourse a powerful solvent of imperial unity. Far from being an unambiguous glue of British integration which promoted provincial adherence to the English core, pride in the Gothic heritage could at crucial moments exacerbate Anglophobic anti-metropolitan resentments.

The widely divergent contexts of colonial America, Protestant Ireland and Enlightenment Scotland saw the emergence of different dialects of this common political language. The Irish Protestant nation exploited the protean associations of the Gothic past as a means of holding in equilibrium divergent allegiances to Irish constitutionalism and an English libertarian inheritance. In the American colonies an enthusiastic provincial emulation of England's political identity proved capable of fostering peripheral nationalism. The widespread reception of an oppositional-whig reading of English constitutional history led to disenchantment with the perceived corruptions of contemporary English government. Independence derived much more from a frustrated colonial Saxonism than it did from any sense of 'American' identity. In Scotland in the middle of the eighteenth century, by contrast, the substitution of an enlightened Gothicism for a discredited Gaelic historical mythology assisted Anglo-Scottish integration.

The Gothic identities of the Protestant Irish nation

The identity of the eighteenth-century 'Anglo-Irish' political nation and the terminology which the historian should use to describe it remain thorny historiographical issues. Historians of eighteenth-century Irish political culture have been perplexed by the lack of any perceived incompatibility between the true Hibernian patriot and the proud heir of England's libertarian heritage. Both were, it seems, familiar aspects of the same Anglo-Irish self-image. The usefulness of the term 'Anglo-Irish' as a description of this dual identity is self-evident; yet, J. C. Beckett has noted that the epithet gained widespread currency only in the late nineteenth century.[1] Thomas Bartlett notes the complex feelings of a Protestant Irish community which felt the need to 'define itself against two "Others", the inhabitants of the mother country and the native Irish'. Given this tension it is unsurprising that eighteenth-century 'Protestant nationalism', in the words of Bartlett, was 'ambiguous, conditional and flawed'; a 'short-lasting' phenomenon, it evolved between the 1690s and the constitutional revolution of 1782, only to collapse suddenly during the 1790s.[2] The origins of this 'Protestant nationalism' have also been called into question. Toby Barnard has shown that in the second half of the seventeenth century Protestant Irishmen identified both with the parliament of the motherland and Ireland's own ancient constitution, without being committed to either a 'full-blooded unionism' or a 'proto-nationalism'.[3]

---

[1] J. C. Beckett, *The Anglo-Irish tradition* (London, 1976), p. 10.

[2] T. Bartlett, 'Protestant nationalism in eighteenth-century Ireland', *SVEC* 335 (1995), 79; Bartlett, '"A people made rather for copies than originals": the Anglo-Irish, 1760–1800', *International History Review* 12 (1990), 11–25; Bartlett, *The fall and rise of the Irish nation: the Catholic question 1690–1830* (Dublin, 1992), p. 38.

[3] T. Barnard, 'The Protestant interest, 1641–1660', and Barnard, 'Conclusion. Settling and unsettling Ireland: the Cromwellian and Williamite revolutions', both in J. Ohlmeyer (ed.), *Ireland from independence to occupation, 1641–1660* (Cambridge, 1995), pp. 237, 239, 288–9.

This scepticism is shared in other quarters. Jim Smyth believes that too much emphasis has been placed on the Irishness of the Anglo-Irish community in the early years after the Revolution: the Protestant community was driven into Irishness by an English reluctance to admit their overseas kindred to the benefits of union.[4] There were a variety of staging posts between the poles of Englishness and Protestant Irishness. David Hayton warns the student of Anglo-Irish identity to be aware of the different shades of emphasis which could result from the variety of biographical experiences and family backgrounds to be found in the Protestant nation. Some Anglo-Irish were descended from recent settlers, others from more established Irish lineage; some resided exclusively in Ireland, while others flitted between Ireland and the mother country.[5] Another of the central points of contention is whether, as J. G. Simms and others have argued, the eighteenth-century Anglo-Irish were 'colonial nationalists',[6] or, as D. G. Boyce has countered, their identity was regnal.[7] This line has recently received some powerful support from Sean Connolly, who has undermined the colonial paradigm by reintegrating eighteenth-century Ireland into *ancien régime* Europe as a confessional state allied to an Anglican Church of Ireland which discriminated against presbyterian colonists as well as an indigenous Roman Catholic population.[8] Other categories have also been applied to the problem. In particular, Joep Leerssen suggests that the language of nationhood is inappropriate when discussing an eighteenth-century Enlightenment patriotism couched in terms of universalism and philanthropy.[9]

The enigma of eighteenth-century Anglo-Irish identity is not reducible to a single solution. Religion, ethnicity, colonialism and legitimate identification with the parliamentary institutions of both Dublin and Westminster together contributed to the multiplication of possible permutations of Protestant Irish self-expression. In addition, the Gothic identity of the

---

[4] J. Smyth, '"Like amphibious animals": Irish Protestants, ancient Britons, 1691–1707', *HJ* 36 (1993), 785–97.

[5] D. Hayton, 'Anglo-Irish attitudes: changing perceptions of national identity among the Protestant Ascendancy in Ireland, ca. 1690–1750', *Studies in Eighteenth-Century Culture* 17 (1987), 145–57.

[6] See the essays by J. G. Simms, J. L. McCracken and R. B. McDowell in T. W. Moody and W. E. Vaughan (eds.), *A new history of Ireland*, vol. IV, *Eighteenth-century Ireland 1691–1800* (Oxford, 1986).

[7] D. G. Boyce, *Nationalism in Ireland* (1982: 2nd edn, London, 1991), pp. 102–7. See also Bartlett, '"A people made rather for copies than originals"', 14, for the idea of sister kingdoms.

[8] S. J. Connolly, *Religion, law, and power: the making of Protestant Ireland 1660–1760* (1992: Oxford pbk, 1995).

[9] J. Leerssen, 'Anglo-Irish patriotism and its European context', *ECI* 3 (1988), 7–24. William Molyneux, *The case of Ireland's being bound by acts of parliament in England, stated* (1698: n.p., 1706), p. 3, upheld 'the cause of the whole race of Adam'.

Protestant political nation was an important complicating factor in the formation of a multifaceted identity. The various strands within the Gothic history of the Anglo-Irish community – English and Norman–Irish, ethnic and regnalist – created the potential for a coherent set of concentric loyalties. Without resolving Anglo-Irish ambiguities into a seamless whole, an analysis of Irish uses of the Gothic past indicates the broad parameters within which a consistent identity was sustained.

The ambiguities of Anglo-Irish Gothicism arose, in large part, from the appropriation by the emerging Irish Protestant nation of the late seventeenth century of the history of their 'Gothic' precursors, the twelfth-century settlers, and of the constitution they established. Ireland's Protestant political nation was predominantly composed of the New English settlers of the late sixteenth and seventeenth centuries, but also included other groups such as Old English families who had embraced Protestantism, and a small number of Protestant Old Irish. The processes of fusion and appropriation were reflected in the reformulation of the Irish 'Gothicist' tradition, whose champions flaunted both its indigenous and metropolitan components. The institutional heritage of the Old English community was grafted on to a colonialist remembrance of the rightful inheritance bequeathed to all Englishmen. The Anglo-Irish nation defined itself as English, the descendants of the various English settlers in Ireland from the time of Henry II, and also as the upholders of the free institutions, ancient limited constitution and political autonomy of the medieval Irish kingdom. The largely spurious adoption by the New English of the heritage of medieval Irish constitutional achievement was not accompanied by a corresponding renunciation of the libertarian inheritance bequeathed to modern Englishmen by their medieval ancestors. The Irish Protestant community contrived to blur the difference between the legacies of English and Irish constitutional history. Initially, this shared commitment to Ireland's parliamentary heritage and English liberties had been the common heritage of Old English Catholics and New English settlers. As late as the 1640s representatives of both groups, the New Englishman Audley Mervyn and the Old English lawyer Patrick Darcy, could speak similar hybrid languages of common law immemorialism and Irish parliamentarism. From the Restoration era this became more of an exclusively Protestant identity.[10]

From the Williamite war to the middle of the eighteenth century there was a period of strong Anglocentric consciousness, which included an

[10] A. Clarke, 'Colonial constitutional attitudes in Ireland, 1640–1660', *Proceedings of the Royal Irish Academy* 90 (sect. C) (1990), 357–75; Beckett, *Anglo-Irish tradition*, pp. 32–3, 36–7; N. L. York, *Neither kingdom, nor nation: the Irish quest for constitutional rights, 1698–1800* (Washington, DC, 1994), ch. 1.

aspiration for Anglo-Irish incorporating union. However, the English parliament snubbed Irish overtures in preference for an incorporating union with the Scots in 1707.[11] This provoked Jonathan Swift's classic allegory of jilted love, *The story of the injured lady* (written 1707, but not published until 1746), which played on the common bonds shared by the English and the Protestant Irish.[12] The perceived exclusion of the Irish from the benefits of incorporating union appeared to confirm the helot status of the Irish. An insensitive motherland had been trampling underfoot the interests of her progeny: a number of mercantilist measures had emanated from the English parliament during the late seventeenth century, such as the Woollen Act (1699), which restricted Irish trade.[13] The result in the case of 'Annesley v. Sherlock', decided on appeal to the Lords at Westminster, who overturned an earlier appellate decision of the Irish House of Lords, and the subsequent Declaratory Act of 1720, which also asserted the right of the British parliament to make statutes binding upon Ireland, did much to confirm Irish Protestant anxieties. This was quickly followed by the ultimate indignity – and tangible economic grievance – of Wood's Halfpence, the ill-considered grant of a minting patent to one William Wood who imposed upon the Irish a debauched currency.[14] The Anglo-Irish were embarrassed and outraged to be treated as second-class Englishmen. In 1726 Swift complained of the travesty that 'all persons born in Ireland are called and treated as Irishmen, although their fathers and grandfathers were born in England': the Anglo-Irish ought rather to have been 'on as good a foot as any subjects of Britain'.[15] Ironically, this heightened sense of an Englishness deprived led in turn led to concern for the regnal privileges of the Irish kingdom. It was but a short step from Anglo-Irish unionism to a defiant patriotism, and both positions depended, in good part, on the language of Gothicism.

The fluid polyvalent qualities of its Gothic heritage helped to resolve

[11] J. C. Beckett, *The making of modern Ireland 1603–1923* (1966: London, 1981), p. 157; Smyth, '"Like amphibious animals"', 795–6; J. Hill, 'Ireland without union: Molyneux and his legacy', in J. Robertson (ed.), *A union for empire* (Cambridge, 1995), pp. 287–9.
[12] Jonathan Swift, *The story of the injured lady*, in J. McMinn (ed.), *Swift's Irish pamphlets* (Gerrard's Cross, 1991), pp. 23–8. For the anti-presbyterian impetus of Irish tory unionism, see J. Smyth, 'The communities of Ireland and the British state, 1660–1714', in B. Bradshaw and J. Morrill (eds.), *The British problem, c. 1534–1707* (Houndmills, 1996), p. 254.
[13] L. Cullen, *An economic history of modern Ireland since 1660* (2nd edn, London, 1987), p. 34; I. Hont, 'Free trade and the economic limits to national politics', in J. Dunn (ed.), *The economic limits to modern politics* (Cambridge, 1990), pp. 78–89.
[14] M. Flaherty, 'The empire strikes back: "Annesley v. Sherlock" and the triumph of imperial parliamentary supremacy', *Columbia Law Review* 87 (1987), 593–622; Cullen, *Economic history of modern Ireland*, p. 36.
[15] Swift to the Earl of Peterborough, April 28, 1726, in F. Elrington Ball (ed.), *The correspondence of Jonathan Swift* (6 vols., London, 1910–14), III, p. 309.

certain problems which dogged the Irish Protestant nation. These ethnic and historical ambiguities enabled the Anglo-Irish nation to mobilise alternative rhetorical strategies as it struggled to cope with the vicissitudes of its relationship with the mother-nation. The sense of a shared Gothic ancestry with the English also meant that Anglo-Irish patriots were less than wholehearted in their commitment to the institutions of the Irish kingdom. At any rate, late seventeenth- and early eighteenth-century Anglo-Irish patriotism fell far short of nationalism. The controversial polemicist William Molyneux, the author of the classic text of Anglo-Irish political thought, *The case of Ireland's being bound by acts of parliament in England, stated* (1698), which denied the authority of the English parliament to legislate for Ireland, was not a nationalist.[16] Anglo-Irish patriots celebrated their colonial heritage of English liberties, but denied that Ireland was a colony. Molyneux furiously rejected any equivalence between Ireland's constitutional status and that of Virginia, New England or Maryland.[17] England and Ireland were separate and distinct kingdoms but the historic rights of the English nation had been transferred to and were replicated in the English nation in Ireland. However, although he defended Ireland as 'a complete kingdom within itself',[18] Molyneux also welcomed the prospect of English parliamentary authority over Ireland, if that meant Irish representation in a united parliament. Parliamentary union with England was for Molyneux 'an happiness we can hardly hope for'.[19] In 1703, a resolution of the Irish House of Commons called for the restoration to the Irish political nation of its full constitutional rights, but conceded that 'a more firm and strict union' with England would be an acceptable alternative route to the desired end of untrammelled parliamentary self-government.[20] The Gothicist tradition permitted two sets of symbolic reference. The Anglo-Irish took pride in such English shibboleths as Magna Carta as their own, while also celebrating peculiarly Irish totems. For example, the privileges and procedures of their own historic constitution were laid out in the *Modus tenendi parliamenta in Hibernia*, an edition of which was published in 1692 by Molyneux's brother-in-law Bishop Anthony Dopping.[21]

The language of Gothicism could be deployed effectively and without embarrassment to answer various demands in the different spheres of

---

[16] Hill, 'Ireland without union'.   [17] Molyneux, *Case of Ireland*, p. 145.
[18] *Ibid.*, p. 144.   [19] *Ibid.*, p. 94.
[20] J. G. Simms, *William Molyneux of Dublin* (ed. P. H. Kelly, Dublin, 1982), p. 115; York, *Neither kingdom, nor nation*, p. 32. For Anglo-Irish unionism, see C. Robbins, *The eighteenth-century commonwealthman* (Cambridge, MA, 1959), pp. 147–9; J. Smyth, 'Anglo-Irish unionist discourse, c. 1656–1707', *Bullán* 2 (1995), 17–34.
[21] Simms, *Molyneux*, p. 92; Robbins, *Commonwealthman*, pp. 138, 140; York, *Neither kingdom, nor nation*, pp. 19–20 n., 26.

Anglo-Irish discourse. Within Ireland, Gothicism answered the needs both of exclusivism and comprehension. Aspects of the Gothic past might be used as a foil with which to contrast the noble and spirited ethnic heritage of Ireland's ruling Protestant caste with the inferior character of the Gaelic Irish.[22] On the other hand, Gothicism was one of the vital preconditions of the emergence of a more latitudinarian Anglo-Irish identity. A common commitment to Ireland's Gothic parliamentary heritage assisted the formation of an Anglo-Irish identity which, while predominantly New English, also embraced a significant minority of Protestant Old English.[23]

The malleability of the Gothic inheritance also allowed the Anglo-Irish to flirt with different ideological defences of their historic liberties. Though Irish institutions had a curious dual identity both as essential components of the Gothic heritage of that portion of the English nation which had settled in Ireland, and as flowers of the constitution of the Gothic kingdom of Ireland, these were easily accommodated. Gothicism reinforced Anglo-Irish aspirations to full self-government in the face of English assertions of Irish 'dependence': Ireland's political nation was able to claim government by consent as a fundamental part of its Gothic libertarian inheritance.[24] However, the English Gothic heritage also functioned, particularly in the early eighteenth century, as a vehicle for unionist aspiration.[25] For instance, during the constitutional debates generated by Molyneux's assertion of Irish regnal autonomy, Henry Maxwell (1669–1730) was able to concede the case of Ireland's dependence on England without rejecting the fundamental principles of patriot ideology. Maxwell wanted the Protestant English community to enjoy to the full their legitimate freedoms as Englishmen through incorporation with the political institutions of England. In particular, Maxwell utilised Gothicist kinship to the full in his argument for union. His argument for an Anglo-Irish union played on the common ethnicity – 'blood' – of the English and Irish political nations:

it was more difficult to unite Wales, than it is now to unite Ireland. For at the time of the Union the language, custom and laws of Wales, were very different from those of England; whereas in Ireland they are all the same. And Ireland has

---

[22] J. Hill, *From patriots to unionists* (Oxford, 1997), pp. 10–11; C. Leighton, *Catholicism in a Protestant kingdom* (Houndmills, 1994), pp. 36–7. See also the distinction drawn from colonial America between Ireland's landholding 'whites' and Catholic 'blacks', in Hill, 'Ireland without union', p. 293.

[23] Beckett, *Anglo-Irish tradition*, pp. 40, 52; F. G. James, *Lords of the Ascendancy* (Dublin, 1995), pp. 52, 99–100; Bartlett, *Fall and rise*, p. 23. See also Clarke, 'Colonial constitutional attitudes', and the precedent related in Hill, 'Ireland without union', pp. 280–1. Moreover, for a revisionist Catholic identification from the middle of the eighteenth century with the coming of the 'Strongbonian race', see Leighton, *Catholicism in a Protestant kingdom*, p. 123.   [24] Hill, *Patriots to unionists*, pp. 87–9.

[25] Henry Maxwell, *An essay towards an union of Ireland with England* (London, 1703), p. 18.

already for some ages been acquainted with the English government . . . the people of Ireland are naturally the offspring of England, the Welsh are not; and therefore the Irish have a better claim to the portion of a child.[26]

Maxwell would have been happy to see an Ireland incorporated 'into the nature of a county of England'.[27] Later, when Irish unionists had clearly been spurned by the motherland, Gothicism reinforced the sense of genuine hurt and grievance at Anglo-Irish exclusion from what they claimed was rightfully theirs. The protean character of their Gothic identity helped to break down Anglo-Irish inhibition about such mercurial revisions of their attitudes to the relationship with England.

Despite their Gothic commitments, the Anglo-Irish were not confined to a particular version of Englishness. There was a strong Norman component to Irish Gothicism, but this did not preclude a commitment to an Anglo-Saxon identity. Hayton has aptly described as 'Anglo-Norman constitutionalism' the language used by patriots such as Molyneux to defend the interests of the Irish Protestant nation.[28] This discourse constituted the multifaceted core of Anglo-Irish identity. It associated the Anglo-Irish nation not only with England's Gothic tradition of mixed constitutionalism, but also with the imported version established in Ireland. Moreover, while it had been only in the twelfth century that the Norman freebooters had settled in Ireland, the Anglo-Irish, on occasions, delved back beyond this era of English history, to the ancient Anglo-Saxon constitution, which they celebrated as part of their ethnic and institutional heritage. The Anglo-Saxon past was as much a standard shibboleth of the Anglo-Irish community as of mainland English identity. The Dublin radical of the middle of the eighteenth century, Charles Lucas (1713–71), spoke the language of Anglo-Saxon constitutionalism. Like Molyneux, Lucas denied that Ireland had been conquered by the English crown, but he placed greater emphasis upon the Saxon component of the Anglo-Norman patriot tradition, celebrating the allodial tenures of Anglo-Saxon England, the antiquity of the witenagemot and the restoration through Magna Carta of the ancient constitution in post-Conquest England. However, Lucas exploited to the full the ambiguities in the Irish Gothicist tradition. He spoke both of 'our forefathers, in this kingdom' – the Anglo-Normans – and of 'our Saxon ancestors'. There was even a hint of immemorialism in his radicalism. According to Lucas, juries were 'not unknown to the ancient Britons . . . practised by the Saxons and confirmed since the invasion of the Normans, by Magna Carta'.[29]

---

[26] *Ibid.*, p. 19.   [27] *Ibid.*, p. 56.   [28] Hayton, 'Anglo-Irish attitudes', 153.
[29] Charles Lucas, *The political constitutions of Great-Britain and Ireland, asserted and vindicated* (London, 1751), pp. 28, 66, 171; Hill, *Patriots to unionists*, pp. 86–90. For tensions in Lucas's position on 'conquest', see Leighton, *Catholicism in a Protestant kingdom*, pp. 78–9.

Their Gothic identity enabled the Anglo-Irish to identify both with the English nation and with the wider family of Gothic peoples across Europe. Anglo-Irish historians made a significant contribution to the history of English liberty. Temple, Swift, Goldsmith and Burke all embarked on histories of England.[30] On the other hand, Molesworth produced an edition of the classic French Gothicist treatise of ancient constitutional liberties, Hotman's *Franco-Gallia* (1573).[31] The wider history of the Goths in Europe was also a concern, as we saw in an earlier chapter, of Henry Brooke and Francis Sullivan.[32] These twin English and European aspects of their Gothic inheritance enabled the Anglo-Irish nation to press for their full inheritance of rights as Englishmen, and, when these were not forthcoming, to assert the privileges of the kingdom of Ireland's historic twelfth-century Gothic constitution. The accepted discourse of legitimation by descent could be exploited in both Anglocentric and regnalist directions without internal contradiction. Gothicism exerted a unionist pull, but also allowed the Anglo-Irish to protect themselves as one of medieval Europe's Gothic kingdoms from excessive English ministerial interference in their constitutional arrangements.

In particular, the Anglo-Irish felt themselves to belong to the shrinking and largely British body of survivors of the Gothic family of nations. Sullivan argued in his treatise on the feudal law how important its study was 'for the understanding the nature of the Gothic forms of government, which, until these last three hundred years, prevailed universally through Europe'.[33] This European perspective contributed to the emergence of an Irish patriotism in which there was an assimilation of Ireland's particularistic privileges with the wider cause of the traditional Gothic liberties to those of the sort which were being eroded all across Europe. The Irish were keenly aware of the decline of the Gothic mixed constitutions, and – from the middle of the eighteenth century in particular – of the peculiar threat to their own institutions posed by the Poynings' Law procedure,[34] by the sharp practices adopted by the English administration to control the Irish parliament and by the claim of the English parliament to legislate for Ireland. Unsurprisingly, Gothicist anxiety took on a special flavour in Anglo-Irish political culture. The classic version of the Gothicist domino

---

[30] William Temple, *An introduction to the history of England*, in Temple, *Works* (2 vols., London, 1731); Jonathan Swift, 'An abstract and fragment of the history of England', in Swift, *Miscellaneous and autobiographical pieces, fragments and marginalia* (Oxford, 1969); Oliver Goldsmith, *The history of England* (4 vols., London, 1771); Edmund Burke, *An essay towards an abridgement of English history*, in Burke, *Works* (16 vols., London, 1803–27), X.

[31] François Hotman, *Franco-Gallia* (trans. Robert Molesworth, London, 1711).

[32] Henry Brooke, *Gustavus Vasa* (London, 1739); Francis Sullivan, *An historical treatise on the feudal law* (London, 1772). See above, ch. 9.

[33] Sullivan, *Historical treatise*, p. 19.   [34] Hill, 'Ireland without union', p. 290.

theory was the work of an Irish commentator: Molesworth made a significant and highly influential contribution to the analysis of the apparently relentless corruption and decline of the mixed Gothic constitutions of Europe in his *Account of Denmark* (1694).[35] Moreover, Molyneux's resounding conclusion to *The case of Ireland* drew on the perception of a Europe-wide decline of limited Gothic institutions to highlight the need for the English parliament to show some sensitivity to the privileges and claims to autonomy of the Protestant Irish nation:

> The rights of parliament should be preserved sacred and inviolable, wherever they are found. This kind of government, once so universal all over Europe, is now almost vanished from amongst the nations thereof. Our king's dominions are the only supporters of this noble Gothic constitution, save what little remains may be found thereof in Poland. We should not therefore make so light of that sort of legislature and as it were abolish in one kingdom of the three wherein it appears, but rather cherish and encourage it whenever we meet it.[36]

Maxwell, arguing in 1703 for an Anglo-Irish incorporating union, warned Englishmen that if, instead of governing the Irish by consent within a united body politic, England attempted to rule Ireland by force, then the Anglo-Irish relationship might threaten England's Gothic constitution. According to Maxwell, the creation and perpetuation of standing armies had foreshadowed the fall of 'all the free monarchies that were lately in Europe'.[37] Later, during the Wood's Halfpence controversy of the 1720s, Swift was, somewhat pointedly, to declare a keen interest in 'the several Gothic institutions in Europe; and by what incidents and events they came to be destroyed'.[38]

This intensely felt interest in the fate of Europe's Gothic polities lapsed over the course of the eighteenth century.[39] Unionism was another victim of changes in political culture, a casualty in particular of the new version of Anglo-Irish patriotism which emerged in the middle of the eighteenth century. From the late 1760s there was a growing desire for reform and autonomy, often still couched in terms of the rights of Englishmen, but no longer hitched to unionism.[40] Moreover, this was also a period when, as well as upholding their strong Gothic identity, a section of the Anglo-Irish

---

[35] See above, ch. 9.   [36] Molyneux, *Case of Ireland*, p. 174.

[37] Maxwell, *Essay towards an union*, p. 12.

[38] Jonathan Swift, *A letter to the right honourable the lord viscount Molesworth* (1724), in McMinn, *Swift's Irish pamphlets*, p. 96.

[39] However, for an exception, see [The ghost of Trenchard], *Northern revolutions* (London, 1757), which explored the English metropolitan threat to Ireland's Gothic liberties by way of discussing the treatment by Denmark of its Norwegian province. See Robbins, *Commonwealthman*, p. 155, who establishes the Irish context.

[40] J. Kelly, 'The origins of the Act of Union: an examination of unionist opinion in Britain and Ireland, 1650–1800', *IHS* 25 (1987), 236–63.

elite began to dabble in Gaelic cultural pursuits, and to identify with some of the aspirations of the more enlightened cultural leaders of Ireland's Catholic community.[41] Nevertheless, the Irish patriot revolution of 1780–2 owed nothing to the antiquarian discovery of the Gaelic past or to a renewed sense of ethnic or national distinctiveness. Indeed, in the late eighteenth century, critics of Gaelic Ireland's Milesian legends, such as Edward Ledwich, endowed ancient Ireland with a Gothic history, arguing that the pre-Milesian colonists, the Tuatha-Dé-Danaan, had been Danish, and that a later wave of Goths in the twelfth century had contributed enormously to civilising Ireland's Gaelic barbarians.[42]

Revisionist historians such as Gerry O'Brien have become increasingly sceptical of the motivations of the Irish patriots of the late eighteenth century. The totemic figures of colonial nationalism, Flood and Grattan, have become victims of Namierite iconoclasm. The decision by Townshend as viceroy to dispense with the system of parliamentary management by the 'undertakers' and the factions under their control created a situation whereby ambitious men of talent lost the opportunity to ascend the ladder of office through enlistment in a connection; instead, there was a recourse to parliamentary rhetoric and making a such a nuisance of oneself that one had to be bought off with office. O'Brien shows how this amendment to the rules of the high political game contributed substantially to the escalation of political grievance in the post-1767 Irish parliament.[43] Nevertheless, the historian of political ideas and identities can still learn a great deal from the rhetoric deployed by ostensible 'patriots' as they ascended the greasy pole.

The reformed constitutional settlement of 1780–2 included the amendment of Poynings' Law, the repeal of the Declaratory Act and important measures securing the independence of the judiciary and limiting the duration of the mutiny act.[44] This patriot revolution consisted largely of an attempt to replicate the full portfolio of English liberties in an Irish setting. Patriotism was a compelling mélange of excluded Englishness, natural rights and Gothicist particularism, the latter focused on Ireland's historic parliamentary privileges.[45] The patriots were inspired

---

[41] J. T. Leerssen, *Mere Irish and Fíor-Ghael* (1986: 2nd edn, Cork, 1996), pp. 361–73.
[42] R. B. McDowell, *Ireland in the age of imperialism and revolution 1760–1801* (Oxford, 1979), pp. 150–1; C. O'Halloran, 'Golden ages and barbarous nations: antiquarian debate on the Celtic past in Ireland and Scotland in the eighteenth century' (University of Cambridge Ph.D thesis, 1991), pp. 126–35, 248–9. The argument for the Danish provenance of the round towers had been around since Thomas Molyneux's *Discourse concerning the Danish mounts, forts and towers in Ireland* (1726).
[43] G. O'Brien, *Anglo-Irish politics in the age of Grattan and Pitt* (Dublin, 1987).
[44] McDowell, *Ireland in the age of imperialism and revolution*, ch. 6.
[45] F. G. James, 'Historiography and the Irish constitutional revolution of 1782', *Eire-Ireland* 18 (1983), 8.

above all by the potent rhetoric of an English liberty which embodied the natural rights of man. Although by this stage a desire for union was no longer a prominent aspect of Anglo-Irish political culture, the strong sense of Irishness manifested during the Revolution stemmed from a spurned unionism and the failure of the English nation to allow their overseas cousinry to enjoy their ancestral English liberties to the full. Grattan captured the continuing importance of an English inheritance to the emergence of the Anglophobic assertiveness of late eighteenth-century Irish patriotism: 'we are too near the British nation, we are too conversant with her history, we are too much fired by her example, to be any thing less than her equal; any thing less, we should be her bitterest enemies – an enemy to that power which smote us with her mace, and to that constitution from whose blessings we were excluded'.[46] Yet these blessings were a legitimate part of Ireland's Gothic inheritance: 'The same laws, the same charters, communicate to both kingdoms, Great Britain and Ireland, the same rights and privileges; and one privilege above them all is, that communicated by Magna Charta, by the 25th of Edward III, and by a multitude of other statutes, "not to be bound by any act except made with the archbishops, bishops, earls, barons and freemen of the commonalty", viz. of the parliament of the realm.'[47]

Nevertheless, there was a major departure from the earlier phases of Anglo-Irish patriotism. The 1782 republication of Molyneux's *Case of Ireland* omitted the pro-unionist aspiration, which had been a widely desired alternative to autonomous self-government for the Anglo-Irish political nation.[48] By the 1780s the Anglo-Irish nation had lost much of its desire for a union, but retained its ethnic and historical links with the English nation and its past. Only a minority of the Protestant Irish elite indulged itself in Celtic rediscovery. Nevertheless, Gothic kinship was no guarantee of any warmth on the part of cadet branches towards the main line of the English ethnie. As the Anglo-Irish asserted their historic Gothic liberties in defiance of the mother country, colonial Americans were taking the defence of their proud Anglo-Saxon heritage a crucial stage further.

Defending Saxon America

By the middle of the eighteenth century British North America already comprised a rich ethnic mixture of English, Scots-Irish and Germans, with smatterings of Scots, Welsh, Dutch, Swedes and other Europeans.

---

[46] Henry Grattan, 'Speech moving a Declaration of Irish rights, 19th April, 1780', in *The speeches of the Right Honourable Henry Grattan in the Irish, and in the imperial parliament* (4 vols., London, 1822), I, p. 51.   [47] *Ibid.*, I, p. 50.   [48] Simms, *Molyneux*, p. 118.

In addition, many of these groups exploited the labour of a large under-caste of African slaves. It was not uncommon for these nationalities to retain aspects of their Old World identities. Indeed, in recent years revisionist research on religious revivalism in this period has steadily diminished the notion that the Great Awakening was a peculiarly American religion of the frontier which invigorated healthily democratic and vital New World Christianity in opposition to the tired and complacent religiosity of Europe. Rather, historians are beginning to rediscover the transatlantic basis of American revivalism, its roots in European religious phenomena and developments, such as the Scots and Scots-Irish communion season or the rise of German pietism, and the ways in which experimental religion could stimulate Old World vernaculars and reinforce non-American nativism.[49] Nevertheless, in spite of this hybridity, the predominant and hegemonic ethnic identity of the various colonial political cultures was English and Gothicist.[50] This was not only a consequence of English predominance in the political arena. The importance of the common law, for instance, led to the wider inculcation of an English identity among non-English settlers. A prominent example is the Scottish immigrant James Wilson (1742–98) whose initiation into the Anglo-Saxonist tradition occurred as a result of his immersion in the classical texts of the common law when apprenticed to the Philadelphia legal practice of John Dickinson (1732–1808).[51] The influence of journals, pamphlets and histories sent from England and, occasionally, recycled in the colonies contributed to a wider dissemination of Gothicist perspectives.[52] The careful researches of Trevor Colbourn into college and personal libraries, booksellers' catalogues and colonial reprints have demonstrated the accumulating potential of Gothicist ideas in colonial society.[53] Eventually, Gothicism was to prove one of the few ideas capable of binding the various colonies together in an intercolonial opposition to the British government during the 1760s and 1770s. The Gothic heritage was not in itself the driving force of Revolutionary ideology, but it played

---

[49] N. Landsman, 'Revivalism and nativism in the middle colonies: the Great Awakening and the Scots community in east New Jersey', *American Quarterly* 34 (1982), 149–64; M. Westerkamp, *Triumph of the laity: Scots-Irish piety and the Great Awakening, 1625–1760* (Oxford, 1988); L. Schmidt, *Holy fairs: Scottish communions and American revivals in the early modern period* (Princeton, 1989); J. Frantz, 'The awakening of religion among the German settlers in the middle colonies', *WMQ* 3rd ser. 33 (1976), 266–88.

[50] H. T. Colbourn, *The lamp of experience: whig history and the intellectual origins of the American revolution* (Chapel Hill, NC, 1965); R. Middlekauff, *The glorious cause: the American revolution, 1763–1789* (1982: Oxford pbk edn, 1985), p. 120.

[51] Colbourn, *Lamp of experience*, p. 119.

[52] *Ibid.*; B. Bailyn, *The ideological origins of the American revolution* (Cambridge, MA, 1967), chs. 2–3; Bailyn, *The origins of American politics* (New York, 1968), ch. 1.

[53] Colbourn, *Lamp of experience*, Appendix II.

a significant role in the two major trends in eighteenth-century colonial identity formation: Anglicisation and the final transformation of English-ness into a nascent American nationhood.[54]

There is now a consensus among American historians that eighteenth-century Americanisation was an ironic side effect of Anglicisation. From the Glorious Revolution until 1763 the principal dynamic of colonial development was Anglicisation. The effect of Anglicisation, or more properly, re-anglicisation, was to erode the strong particularist identities of the seventeenth-century colonies. Localism had been stimulated by the significant impulse often given by sectarianism or by confessional differences to settlement in North America, and by the importance of its peculiar charter privileges to the emerging identity of each individual colony. Only in the eighteenth century did a process of Anglicising homogenisation impose on this particularist mosaic a new pattern suggestive of intercolonial community and the shared interests of Englishmen in America. Anglicisation contained the necessary rudiments of a common enterprise of American nation-building.[55]

In the economic sphere the colonies became progressively drawn within the ambit of British commercial activity. On the demand side, the experience of America's Tidewater consumers was analogous to that of the burghers of English provincial towns such as Norwich or Bristol: they were keen to follow where London led. The colonies became, in a sense, the outer reach of an increasingly integrated English economy. As the consumers of English ports and county towns developed a growing taste for London designs and fashions, they became more uniform in their material life. At a further remove, this was the experience of eighteenth-century colonials. As Norwich became more like Bristol, so Boston became more like Philadelphia.[56]

Anglicisation of the cultural sphere took different forms in New England from the rest of the colonies. In New England, where the Puritans had nurtured their own colleges, beginning with Harvard in 1636, an indigenous cultural leadership receptive to English ideas and publications, in particular the remodulated theology of the English latitudinarians and the new concepts of refinement and polite conversation

---

[54] See J. P. Greene, *Peripheries and center: constitutional development in the extended polities of the British Empire and the United States 1607–1788* (1986: New York, 1990); T. H. Breen, 'An empire of goods: the Anglicization of colonial America, 1690–1776', *Journal of British Studies* 25 (1986), 467–99; Breen, '"Baubles of Britain": the American and consumer revolutions of the eighteenth century', *P+P* 119 (1988), 73–104.

[55] J. Murrin, 'A roof without walls: the dilemma of American national identity', in R. Beeman, S. Botein and E. C. Carter II (eds.), *Beyond confederation: origins of the Constitution and American national identity* (Chapel Hill, NC, 1987).

[56] Breen, 'Empire of goods'; Breen, '"Baubles of Britain"'.

associated with *The Spectator* and similar journals, began to dilute the strong sense of a separate New England Puritan way. Soon, the cultural elite of Harvard College was producing its own versions of the Addisonian journal. In other colonies, including Virginia, which were slower to develop their own educational institutions, cultural leaders tended to be imported directly from the motherland.[57]

Economic and cultural Anglophilia were not compromised in the first half of the century by any festering sense of 'political Anglophobia'. Emulation and Anglicisation were also facets of political culture. 'The central cultural impulse among the colonists was', according to Jack Greene, 'not to identify and find ways to express and to celebrate what was distinctively American about themselves and their societies but, insofar as possible, to eliminate those distinctions so that they might – with more credibility – think of themselves and their societies – and be thought of by people in Britain itself – as demonstrably British.'[58] However, this process was double-edged. The growing realisation that the metropolitan nation was dismissive of the pretensions of the colonists to the full enjoyment of the rights of Englishmen triggered a reaction whereby the sense of grievance fostered by exclusion was transformed into a growing sense of American difference from the mother-nation.[59] Gothicism was an important factor in this critical realignment. For Saxon libertarianism was both an identity shared with the metropolis and one of the foundations upon which a new American nationalism was to be built.

For most of the seventeenth century, political culture in New England had been based almost exclusively around Puritan concepts.[60] The distinctive scriptural politics of the region were adulterated by the secular English idiom of liberty and property during the political crisis of the 1680s. As the mother country endured a spate of government-inspired quo warranto proceedings and borough remodelling in the aftermath of the Exclusion crisis, so the Lords of Trade contemplated the reorganisation of undesirable aspects of colonial governance. In 1684 the Massachusetts charter was abrogated, and in 1686 Sir Edmund Andros became the first governor of the enlarged and imperial Dominion of New England. Andros questioned existing land titles, and introduced quitrents. When news of the Revolution in England reached the Dominion of New England in 1689, Andros and his cronies were imprisoned and the old constitutional forms were reinstated. According to T. H. Breen there

[57] N. Fiering, 'The transatlantic republic of letters: a note on the circulation of learned periodicals to eighteenth-century America', *WMQ* 3rd ser. 33 (1976), 642; Murrin, 'Roof without walls', p. 337.

[58] J. P. Greene, *Pursuits of happiness* (Chapel Hill, NC, 1988), p. 175.

[59] Greene, *Peripheries*, pp. 129–44, 162–9.

[60] H. Stout, *The New England soul* (Oxford, 1986), pts I and II.

was an important transition in the political discourse of New England. The region's traditional Scripture politics were jettisoned for the language of historic English liberties. Breen suggests that what may have been intended as a 'rhetorical stance' to win support from the Williamite establishment in the mother country for the reinstitution of the charter privileges of Massachusetts became in time 'an expression of a sincere belief'. Through resisting attempts by the Lords of Trade 'to make the Puritans more English', the colonists had come to adopt the political identity of free-born Englishmen. Henceforth, while New England retained a sense of its own peculiar heritage, its own distinctive brand of institutions and public rituals, and a powerful filiopietism towards its seventeenth-century founders, this was overlaid with the transatlantic language of English Gothicism. Whereas in the seventeenth century Old Testament Scripture politics had been the exclusive vehicle of public discourse in New England, in the eighteenth century it was joined, and, to an extent displaced, by ancient Anglo-Saxon constitutionalism, pride in Magna Carta and assertions of the rights of Englishmen to trial by jury and rule by consent.[61]

English constitutionalism became the dominant language of political debate throughout the eighteenth-century colonies. It was never to swamp completely the various discourses of proprietary, ethnic and religious issues in Pennsylvania, or the distinctive Erastian Anglicanism of Virginia gentry politics, but it was to be the pole star of colonial political identity.[62] In the eighteenth century the sense of a common historical experience of the Revolution of 1688–9 and of warfare against Roman Catholic France created a stronger identification both with the motherland and as an intercolonial community.[63] The strong colonial identity of the seventeenth century was eroded. Increased communications too played their part in the creation of an intercolonial political culture responsive to an Anglo-Saxon identity found in histories, pamphlets and journals.

The eighteenth-century colonies imported the staples of English whig historiography. Colonial pamphlets and newspapers sang the old songs of

---

[61] T. H. Breen, *The character of the good ruler* (New Haven and London, 1970), esp. pp. 136–8, 143–4, 151–67, 182–4, 247, 254, 259–60, 263–4.

[62] For the Gothicism of William Penn, see *England's present interest discovered* (n.p., 1675), pp. 7–15; J. R. Pole, *Political representation in England and the origins of the American republic* (New York and London, 1966), pp. 80–1, 404; S. Kliger, *The Goths in England* (Cambridge, MA, 1952), pp. 81–2. However, for the distinctiveness of local political cultures, see e.g. P. Bonomi, *Under the cope of heaven: religion, society, and politics in colonial America* (New York, 1986), esp. pp. 168–81; R. Isaac, *The transformation of Virginia, 1740–1790* (Chapel Hill, NC, 1982).

[63] R. Bloch, *Visionary republic: millennial themes in American thought, 1756–1800* (Cambridge, 1985).

Anglo-Saxonism, the common law, the glories of Magna Carta (which was held to have restored Saxon liberties) and the vicissitudes of the English libertarian heritage.[64] The landscape of colonial political culture did not, however, replicate exactly the contours of metropolitan whiggery. In particular, the commonwealth tradition which embodied the radical whig critique of the failings, omissions and compromises of establishment whiggery was more prominent in the colonies than at home.[65] The mainstream of colonial political culture took on an oppositional hue. One of the most popular and definitive texts in the imported canon of colonial whiggery was the work of John Trenchard and Thomas Gordon, *Cato's letters*. Trenchard and Gordon were dissatisfied with the limited achievements of the Glorious Revolution of 1688, a damp squib which had failed to restore the ancient liberties of Englishmen. *Cato's letters* indoctrinated many Americans into a radical critique of English whig complacency.[66] As Gordon Wood has argued, a selective absorption of English oppositional ideology 'implicated the Americans in a peculiar conception of English history . . . and in an extraordinarily radical perspective on the English constitution they were so fervently defending'.[67] An enthusiastic commitment to a historic English identity initiated the process of divergence from the motherland.

In addition to receiving a heavy dose of Anglo-Saxonism from the mother country, American political culture was also heavily indebted to the wider European perspective of the decline of Gothic constitutions, a prominent feature of commonwealth ideology. Such works as Molesworth's *Account of Denmark* were part of the canon of historiographical works widely read in the colonies.[68] This perspective allowed colonists to read into any attack on their local legislatures not a remodelling of the loose structure of British overseas governance, but the thin end of an absolutist anti-parliamentarian wedge – as an assault on the Gothic privilege of parliamentary self-government.[69]

Although the existence of a distinctive American Gothicist identity

[64] Bailyn, *Ideological origins*, pp. 80–2; L. H. Leder, *Liberty and authority: early American political ideology, 1689–1763* (Chicago, 1968), p. 121.

[65] Bailyn, *Ideological origins*, pp. 34–54.

[66] D. Jacobson, 'Introduction', in Jacobson (ed.), *The English libertarian heritage from the writings of John Trenchard and Thomas Gordon in 'The independent whig' and 'Cato's letters'* (Indianapolis, 1965), pp. xxxi, liii; Bailyn, *Origins of American politics*, ch. 1, esp. pp. 54–5; R. Hamowy, 'Introduction', in *Cato's letters* (ed. Hamowy, 2 vols., Indianapolis, 1995), p. xxxvi; Middlekauff, *Glorious cause*, p. 133; Colbourn, *Lamp of experience*, pp. 49–51; Colbourn, 'John Dickinson, historical revolutionary', *Pennsylvania Magazine of History and Biography* 83 (1959), 282–3; D. Lutz, *A preface to American political theory* (Lawrence, KS, 1992), p. 136.

[67] G. Wood, *The creation of the American republic, 1776–1787* (1969: New York, 1972), p. 14.   [68] Bailyn, *Ideological origins*, pp. 39, 65–6.

[69] Greene, *Peripheries*, pp. 127, 133–4.

long predated the crises of the 1760s and 1770s, it was the excitable political debate of these critical decades which introduced Americans to a significant new phase of Anglo-Saxonism that contributed to widening the ideological distance between colonies and motherland. From the accession of George III English radicalism became more assertively Saxonist, and overtly critical of the failures of eighteenth-century whig parliamentarians to restore the ancient democratic freedoms of the Saxon constitution, such as annual parliaments and a general freeman franchise. According to Colbourn, Saxonism 'became a basic revolutionary doctrine in America in the 1760s'.[70] Gerald Newman in his study of the rise of English nationalism in the middle of the eighteenth century has described the effects of the wave of English Saxonist radicalism of the 1760s and 1770s on American political culture as 'the American Saxon Revolution'.[71]

Saxonism became one of the most salient features of American political culture, contributing to its stridently oppositional character. *An historical essay on the English constitution* (1771), a work attributed to Obadiah Hulme, has been described by Bernard Bailyn as 'a book both determinative and representative of the historical understanding that lay behind the emerging American constitutionalism' of the Revolutionary period.[72] *The genuine principles of the ancient Saxon, or English constitution* (1776), a patriot pamphlet published in Philadelphia which included the text of the Declaration of Independence, drew heavily upon Hulme's Saxonist treatise.[73] James Burgh's *Political disquisitions*, published in 1774, which told the history of England as a saga of declension from a democratic Saxon constitution, was an immediate sensation in the colonies, and was reprinted in Philadelphia the next year.[74] James Otis (1725–83) argued: 'Liberty was better understood and more fully enjoyed by our ancestors before the coming in of the first Norman tyrants than ever after, till it was found necessary for the salvation of the kingdom to combat the arbitrary and wicked proceedings of the Stuarts.'[75] This picture was reinforced by Catherine Macaulay, whose history was a canonical feature of patriot

---

[70] Colbourn, *Lamp of experience*, p. 31.
[71] G. Newman, *The rise of English nationalism: a cultural history 1740–1830* (London, 1987), p. 191.
[72] Bailyn, *Ideological origins*, p. 184; Colbourn, *Lamp of experience*, pp. 63, 65, 170–1.
[73] Colbourn, *Lamp of experience*, pp. 190–1; Wood, *Creation of the American republic*, p. 227.
[74] O. Handlin and M. Handlin, 'James Burgh and American Revolutionary theory', *Proceedings of the Massachusetts Historical Society* 73 (1961), 38–57; Colbourn, 'Dickinson', 285–6.
[75] James Otis, *The rights of the British colonies asserted and proved* (Boston, 1764), in B. Bailyn (ed.), *Pamphlets of the American revolution 1750–1776*, vol. I, *1750–1765* (Cambridge, MA, 1965), p. 441.

political culture.[76] The Norman Yoke thesis appeared too in one of the most influential pamphlets of 1776, Tom Paine's *Common sense*, which was scathing in its denigration of the Conquest: 'A French bastard landing with an armed banditti, and establishing himself king of England against the consent of the natives, is in plain terms a very paltry rascally original.'[77]

Americans were not all subscribers to the Norman Yoke thesis. However, there appears to have been a widespread view that English constitutional history since the Saxon golden age had been, for one reason or another, a story of decline and corruption. The Virginian politician Richard Bland (1710–76), writing in 1766 against the taxation of the colonies by the metropolis, claimed that it was the legislation of the reign of Henry VI restricting the county franchise to forty-shilling freeholders which had fatally undermined the ancient freeholding democracy of the Anglo-Saxon constitution.[78]

Anglo-Saxonism was a fundamental component of the republican ideology of corruption which has been shown to be the dominant ideological motivation behind the Revolution. Gothicism added a vivid emotive ethnocentric dimension to the revolutionary language of civic humanism. The Anglo-Saxons with their local tithings and hundreds embodied the republican ideal of participatory self-governance, while in their simplicity of lifestyle they represented something of a native English Sparta. In this way the dependence of liberty on virtuous manners came to be illustrated not only by classical exempla but also with reference to the familiar course of English history. English freedom had been at its most vigorous, unrestrained and democratical in an era while the Saxon race of independent sturdy plain-living yeomen had yet to taste the fruits of luxury. Thus the history of England blended with the message of commonwealth ideology and the ideals of the non-importationist 'homespun' movement championed by American patriots.[79]

Saxonist primitivism was an important ingredient in the commonwealth idiom identified by Bailyn as the crucial ideological configuration of American patriots.[80] Worried colonists used the ready-made code of

---

[76] Colbourn, 'Dickinson', 278; Colbourn, *Lamp of experience*, pp. 153, 159; Colbourn, 'Thomas Jefferson's use of the past', *WMQ* 3rd ser. 15 (1958), 64.

[77] Thomas Paine, *Common sense* (1776), in Paine, *Political writings* (ed. B. Kuklick, Cambridge, 1989), p. 13.

[78] Richard Bland, *An inquiry into the rights of the British colonies* (Williamsburg, 1766), in C. Hyneman and D. Lutz (eds.), *American political writing during the founding era 1760–1805* (2 vols., Indianapolis, 1983), I, pp. 70–1; Pole, *Political representation*, pp. 436–8, for Plantagenet liberties and the suffrage restriction of 1430.

[79] E. Morgan, 'The Puritan ethic and the American revolution', *WMQ* 3rd ser. 24 (1967), 3–43. For New England, see G. Nash, *The urban crucible* (Cambridge, MA, 1979), p. 345.

oppositional whiggery to read between the lines of contemporary fiscal reforms. Anxiety about tory conspiracies found confirmation in the larger picture of English constitutional degeneration. Although Saxonism was only one contributing factor to the escalation of hostile posturing, and to the raising of the ideological temperature of political debate, it was none the less a vital one which gave Americans a powerful imaginative and compelling sense of the values for which they were struggling. Moreover, it persuaded conservative colonists that it was the mother country, not the colonists, which was innovating and perverting accepted historic ways. Thus the eventual break towards independence could be presented less as a novel bid for separatism, and more as an attempt to construct a cordon sanitaire between an enervated motherland whose corrupt people, sunk in luxury and effeminacy, had forgotten their ancient libertarian manners, and the vigorous, virtuous and, as yet, uncorrupted colonists of North America who were striving to preserve their ancestral freedoms.[81]

The American version of the English Gothic heritage was prelapsarian. It was the desire to recover a lost Englishness in a new Eden which transformed a heightened admiration for the English libertarian heritage into a drive for independence from the beloved mother country. American independence was part of a project of restoration – restoring to the descendants of the free Anglo-Saxons an ancient constitution which had been progressively corrupted in England itself. Americanisation was part of an attempt to realise an idealised Englishness, to recover a golden age.[82]

Colonial political culture had nurtured a Gothic fantasy of England which the motherland could not sustain. In the process of disenchantment, Americans began to perceive the English nation as alien to the authentic values of English nationhood as preserved in the North American colonies. Independence became, in a sense, the only viable option for the maintenance and repair of the moth-eaten fabric of Anglo-Saxon liberty.

The strategy of imperial reform and retrenchment which followed the Seven Years' War appeared to endanger the loose arrangements under which the colonies had developed assemblies, modelled on the mother parliament, which had the customary right to control taxation. Grenville's plans threatened the rights of overseas Englishmen to withhold consent from taxation through their own parliamentary institutions.[83] American fears were compounded by the legacy of the Revolutions of

---

[80] Wood, *Creation of American republic*, p. 31.

[81] Bailyn, *Ideological origins*; Wood, *Creation of the American republic*, p. 36; J. G. A. Pocock, *The Machiavellian moment* (Princeton, 1975), pp. 507–8.

[82] F. McDonald, *Novus ordo seclorum* (Lawrence, KS, 1985), p. 76.

[83] Middlekauff, *Glorious cause*, pp. 126–7.

1689 when the colonists had, on word of the Glorious Revolution in England, rebelled in their respective colonies against the existing regimes.[84] The association of these colonial revolts against imperial reform with what was perceived as a revolution to preserve the ancient constitution in the motherland created an ideological framework through which to view the events of the 1760s and 1770s. It seemed natural to connect a new batch of imperial reforms with further threats at home to England's traditional constitution and liberties.

Moreover, the threat to the existing privileges of the colonial assemblies coincided with the appearance of the new strain of Saxonism in English radical polemic. The reception of this radical Gothicism among the frightened colonists enabled patriot pamphleteers to exacerbate anxieties about fiscal measures by tracing their provenance to the wider corruption of the English constitution. Saxonist history helped both to reinforce this picture of a degenerate, oppressive Normanist England, which had fallen prey to the forces of tyranny, and to point up the contrast with the free 'Saxon' colonies of America.

American patriots challenged parliamentary sovereignty only when it threatened their customary rights and the status of their colonial assemblies, but they did not reject English identity outright. According to John Murrin, the colonists demanded the common rights of Englishmen, 'not unique privileges for Americans'.[85] They insisted that they were as English as metropolitan Englishmen, and feared that their location on the margins of the English world might result in exclusion from their full heritage of entitlements. William Hickes wrote: 'As a colonist my most ambitious views extend no further than the rights of a British subject. I cannot comprehend how my being born in America should divest me of this . . . If we are entitled to the liberties of British subjects we ought to enjoy them unlimited and unrestrained.'[86]

This assertive English 'provincialism' coincided with the reception of the full-blown interpretation of English constitutional corruption. Transatlantic distance reinforced a misreading of English politics: the rhetorical strategies of ousted Old Corps whigs, which included a flirtation with oppositional ideology, were accepted as gospel. The myth of a revived neo-toryism under George III and his favourite, the unfortunately surnamed John Stuart, Lord Bute, heightened the sense that the threatened Englishness of the North American peripheries was the authentic Anglo-Saxon libertarian tradition, unlike the bastardised tory Normanism of George III's England. As well as dramatising the – technical and negoti-

[84] D. Lovejoy, *The Glorious Revolution in America* (New York, 1972).
[85] Murrin, 'Roof without walls', p. 340.
[86] William Hicks, *The nature and extent of parliamentary power* (Philadelphia, 1768), p. xi.

able – differences with Westminster, Gothicism also salved consciences in America about breaking allegiance. Patriots contended that the mother country which had changed, but not America, which remained true to historic English values. Hence, as Wood points out, the break from England did not entail a departure from the principles of the ancient English constitution, only from their supposed perversion under a debased regime.[87]

The events of 1776 were a revolt in defence of existing privileges, not a movement to liberate an oppressed nationhood. There was no American national consciousness, and even the sense of an American national interest was embryonic: as late as 1754 the colonists had proved indifferent to the Albany Plan of Union, a scheme for intercolonial co-operation in the interests of imperial defence against the French.[88] Given the lack of a distinctive 'American' identity, the transition from colonial loyalism in 1763 to 'American' independence in 1776 is hard to explain. The Calvinist resistance theories held by the Congregationalists of New England and the presbyterians of the middle colonies go some way towards accounting for rebellion,[89] but not for the escalation towards nationalism. The same proviso holds true for natural rights, which obviously enjoyed a wide currency during the 1770s. Indeed, natural rights – to enjoy trial by jury, to be governed by consent and to be taxed through one's own parliamentary bodies – were scarcely distinguishable from English liberties, and often yoked together.[90] Although the language of natural rights was not limited in its appeal to any one constituency within the colonies, it lacked the emotive force of other – more particular – ideological formations, whether ethnic or confessional.[91] It seems unlikely that natural rights

---

[87] Wood, *Creation of the American republic*, pp. 32–3, 200–2.

[88] Greene, *Peripheries*, pp. 157–8; R. Merritt, *Symbols of American community, 1735–1775* (New Haven, 1966); A. G. Olson, 'The British government and the colonial union, 1754', *WMQ* 3rd ser. 17 (1960), 22–34; J. Bumsted, '"Things in the womb of time": ideas of American independence, 1633 to 1763', *WMQ* 3rd ser. 31 (1974), 533–64; E. Marienstras, 'Nationality and citizenship', in J. P. Greene and J. R. Pole (eds.), *Blackwell encyclopedia of the American revolution* (Cambridge, MA, and Oxford, 1991), pp. 669–72.

[89] A. Baldwin, *The New England clergy and the American revolution* (Durham, NC, 1928); B. Bailyn, 'Religion and revolution: three biographical studies', *Perspectives in American History* 4 (1970), 85–169; J. C. D. Clark, *The language of liberty 1660–1832* (Cambridge, 1994), pp. 122–3, 264–6, 276.

[90] For a historiographically sophisticated refurbishment of natural rights 'liberalism', see T. H. Breen, 'Ideology and nationalism on the eve of the American revolution', *Journal of American History* 84 (1997), 13–39, which quotes the *Newport Mercury*, 14 September 1767: 'To enjoy our natural rights and the liberties of English subjects, is the supreme felicity of mankind . . . Natural rights, and the liberty of English subjects undoubtedly belong to Americans' (38).

[91] See Bonomi, *Under the cope of heaven*, which presents a convincing case of emotional mobilisation drawing upon existing tensions arising out of the Great Awakening.

alone were used to construct the imaginative platform which bridged the distance between the negative rhetoric of grievance and the visionary rhetoric of nation-building.

There was no single route across this bridge. The New England errand into the wilderness, the millennialist message of struggle with such forces of evil as the papacy and the corrupt monarchy of George III and the history of Saxon freedom together provided complementary myths of America's situation capable of subverting traditional allegiances. Millennialism contributed to the emergence of the dispute between the colonies and the government of the mother country as a clash between virtuous freedom and a dark tyranny.[92] To some extent the glorious providential history of New England was able to provide an identity for Americans struggling for independence from the mother country. Until the middle of the seventeenth century, New England identity had been orientated towards the reformation of England. The Restoration led to a reorientation of New England identity as an overseas refuge from a fallen England. Henceforth, New England provided a model for the rejection of Englishness.[93] However, the New England tradition had little resonance in the middle and southern colonies. Saxonism, on the other hand, was not limited geographically in its influence.

Gothicism featured prominently within the political thought of the leading patriots both in New England and in Virginia. In Massachusetts John Adams (1735–1826) spoke the language of Gothicist radicalism and used it to anchor his sense of identity: in his view, Hengist and Horsa were 'the Saxon chiefs from whom we claim the honour of being descended, and whose political principles and form of government we have assumed'.[94] One of Adams's principal works of polemic, and his earliest claim to 'patriot' fame, was a series of essays entitled 'Dissertation on the

Bonomi's nuanced study of the ways in which conflicts between Old Lights and New Lights (including Old and New Side presbyterians) created an intercolonial culture of public contestation provides a more convincing link between the Great Awakening and the Revolution than the pioneering work of A. Heimert, *Religion and the American mind from the Great Awakening to the Revolution* (Cambridge, MA, 1966). For the role of anti-episcopal campaigns in mobilising patriot opinion, see C. Bridenbaugh, *Mitre and sceptre* (New York, 1962); W. Hogue, 'The religious conspiracy theory of the American revolution', *Church History* 45 (1976), 277–92.

[92] See e.g. J. Berens, *Providence and patriotism in early America, 1640–1815* (Charlottesville, VA, 1978); C. Beam, 'Millennialism and American nationalism, 1740–1800', *Journal of Presbyterian History* 54 (1976), 182–99; Bloch, *Visionary republic*; M. Lowance Jr, 'Typology and millennial eschatology in early New England', in E. Miner (ed.), *Literary uses of typology from the late middle ages to the present* (Princeton, 1977); S. Bercovitch, *The Puritan origins of the American self* (New Haven, 1975). However, for a corrective, see M. Endy, 'Just war, holy war and millennialism in revolutionary America', *WMQ* 3rd ser. 42 (1985), 3–25. For the convergence of republican and millennialist discourse, see N. Hatch, *The sacred cause of liberty: republican thought and the millennium in Revolutionary New England* (New Haven, 1977).   [93] Stout, *New England soul*, ch. 3.

[94] Quoted in Colbourn, *Lamp of experience*, p. 171.

canon or feudal law'. Adams was an anti-feudalist, though he fell short of the full-blown commitment to allodial tenures found in the writings of Thomas Jefferson (1743–1826). Concerning the English settlers in America, Adams wrote:

> To have holden their lands allodially, or for every man to have been the sovereign lord and proprietor of the ground he occupied, would have constituted a government too nearly like a commonwealth. They were contented, therefore, to hold their lands of their king, as their sovereign lord; and to him they were willing to render homage, but to no mesne or subordinate lords; nor were they willing to submit to any of the baser services. In all this they were so strenuous, that they have even transmitted to their posterity a very general contempt and detestation of holding by quitrents.[95]

It was this approach to the feudal corruptions of England which inspired in Adams a sense of American difference from the motherland: 'The canon and feudal systems, though greatly mutilated in England, are not yet destroyed. Like the temples and palaces in which the great contrivers of them once worshipped, they exist in ruins; and much of the domineering spirit of them still remains.'[96]

In Virginia Jefferson articulated a similar strain of radical Gothicism. Jefferson's lifelong obsession with the English Saxon past began through his connection with George Wythe, in whose practice he began his legal training in 1762.[97] The history of the common law was for Jefferson, as for so many other colonial patriots, the foundation of their Anglo-Saxonism, though for Jefferson his fascination with Anglo-Saxon culture was to extend far beyond the obvious terrain of legal shibboleths into the more obscure areas of ecclesiastical antiquities and Saxon philology.[98] His Saxonism remained a vital aspect of Jefferson's political personality, and was significant not only in stirring his patriotic opposition to Westminster, but also in determining the radical version of American politics which he espoused, and which he transmitted to posterity as the Jeffersonian tradition.

In his important Revolutionary pamphlet, *A summary view of the rights of British America* (1774), Jefferson posited a direct parallel between the migrant German peoples who crossed the North Sea to settle in dark-age England, and their descendants who had left England to establish overseas colonies in North America:

---

[95] Adams, 'A dissertation on the canon and feudal law', in Adams, *Works* (Boston, 1865), III, p. 455.

[96] Adams, 'Dissertation on the canon and feudal law', III, p. 464.

[97] S. R. Hauer, 'Thomas Jefferson and the Anglo-Saxon language', *PMLA* 98 (1983), 879; M. Peterson, *The Jefferson image in the American mind* (New York, 1960), p. 415.

[98] E.g. Hauer, 'Jefferson and the Anglo-Saxon language'; R. Mott, 'Sources of Jefferson's ecclesiastical views', *Church History* 3 (1934), 267–84.

Our ancestors, before their emigration to America, were the free inhabitants of the British dominions in Europe, and possessed a right which nature has given to all men, of departing from the country in which chance, not choice, has placed them; of going in quest of new habitations, and of there establishing new societies, under such laws and regulations as to them shall seem most likely to promote public happiness. That their Saxon ancestors had, under this universal law, in like manner left their native wilds and woods in the north of Europe; had possessed themselves of the island of Britain, then less charged with inhabitants, and had established there that system of laws which has so long been the glory and protection of that country. Nor was ever any claim of superiority or dependence asserted over them by that mother country from which they had migrated.[99]

Unsurprisingly, a couple of years later when independence had been declared, Jefferson wanted Hengist and Horsa – according to tradition the leaders of the Saxons who had first landed on the shores of Kent – to adorn the seal of the new nation.[100] Hengist and Horsa were more than totems. Jefferson's Saxonist identity rested on twin pillars, with the analogy in the situations (and freedoms) of Saxon and American settlers bolstering identity from the claim of direct ethnic descent. For Jefferson, the parallel reinforced his radical anti-feudalist and anti-clerical vision of what American society could and should be.

Jefferson believed that America should be free of many of the engines of oppression which had disfigured the old world, including post-Norman England: 'America was not conquered by William the Norman, nor its lands surrendered to him, or any of his successors. Possessions there were undoubtedly of the allodial nature.'[101] The anti-feudalist reform of Virginia society began straight away in 1776, when the Virginia assembly passed Jefferson's bill abolishing entails.[102] Such reforms were predicated on Jefferson's defintion of the authentic Gothic heritage. He wrote to Edmund Pendleton: 'Has not every restitution of the ancient Saxon laws had happy effects? Is it not better now that we return at once into that happy system of our ancestors, the wisest and most perfect ever yet devised by the wit of man, as it stood before the eighth century?'[103]

The Saxon past was also central to Jefferson's intensely felt critique of encroachments on man's natural liberty of conscience. Jefferson's theology was in essence a commitment to the pure simple system of morality espoused by Jesus, and complementing this core a critique of the corrup-

---

[99] Thomas Jefferson, *Summary view of the rights of British America* (1774: London, 1774 edn), pp. 7–8. See J. Ellis, *American sphinx* (New York, 1997), pp. 31–4, for the Saxonist theory of expatriation.

[100] M. D. Peterson, *Thomas Jefferson and the new nation* (New York, 1970), p. 98.

[101] Jefferson, *Summary view*, p. 37.

[102] Peterson, *Jefferson and the new nation*, pp. 60, 113–14; C. Ray Klein, 'Primogeniture and entail in colonial Virginia', *WMQ* 3rd ser. 25 (1968), 545–86.

[103] D. Wilson, 'Jefferson vs. Hume', *WMQ* 3rd ser. 46 (1989), 58–9.

tions, both doctrinal and institutional, of the basic Christian message.[104] Jefferson denied the divinity of Christ, arguing that such a belief was part of the corruption of a moral doctrine into a superstitious Christology. Paul and Athanasius had both injected pagan philosophy into the simple way of Jesus. These primitive and patristic corruptions of the message of Jesus had been followed by the institutional iniquity of the rise of priest-craft – 'an engine for enslaving mankind' – and prelacy, including tithes and other ecclesiastical taxes, and the machinery of persecution.[105] In the case of England, Jefferson argued that a designing clergy had begun under the Saxons to adulterate its free Gothic institutions. In defiance of the received juridical wisdom found in Hale and Blackstone, Jefferson argued that Christianity was not part of the common law, and did not enjoy its protection. For the common law was that body of custom inaugurated by the Saxons on their settlement in England in the fifth century; but the conversion of the first Saxon king took place only about 598, and the last about 686:

> Here, then, was a space of two hundred years, during which the common law was in existence, and Christianity no part of it . . . If therefore from the settlement of the Saxons to the introduction of Christianity among them that system of religion could not be a part of the common law, because they were not yet Christians, and if, having their laws from that period to the close of the common law, we are able to find among them no such act of adoption, we may safely affirm (though contradicted by all the judges and writers on earth) that Christianity neither is nor ever was a part of the common law.[106]

Jefferson was not so much Anglophobic as driven by an uncompromis-ing form of Anglophilia – anti-Normanism. Norman corruptions disgust-ed him, but he remained attached as a Saxonist patriot to the true libertarian spirit of the motherland. However, such feelings were compli-cated by Jefferson's logic. His personal brand of Gothicism granted him an oddly detached view of England. For Jefferson believed that the roots of his Gothic ethnie lay in Germany. England was the scene of the first great migration, America the second.[107] Perpetuating the libertarian values of the racial stock mattered more than any temporary territorial allegiance.

Despite the winning of independence, American nationhood remained

---

[104] A. Koch, *The philosophy of Thomas Jefferson* (New York, 1943), ch. 4; E. Sheridan, 'Introduction', in D. W. Adams (ed.), *Jefferson's extracts from the Gospels* (The Papers of Thomas Jefferson, 2nd ser., Princeton, 1983), for the variations in Jefferson's theory of Christian corruption over the course of his long intellectual career.

[105] Mott, 'Sources of Jefferson's ecclesiastical views'.

[106] Thomas Jefferson, 'Inquiry whether Christianity is a part of the common law' (1768?), in M. DeWolfe Howe (ed.), *Cases on church and state in the United States* (Cambridge, MA, 1952), p. 11.   [107] Jefferson, *Summary view*, pp. 7–8.

to be constructed.[108] The federal Constitution reflected the continuing strength of colonial particularisms and a reluctance to submerge local corporate identities in an undifferentiated national republic. Moreover, the framers of the Constitution, although anxious to construct a mechanism capable of resolving the problems incident to a continental republic, retained considerable admiration for the English constitution.[109] Even as it was superseded by their efforts, the English constitution remained a cynosure of the American founding generation. In spite of a growing self-consciousness about the 'new nation' and of American difference, Saxonism continued to enjoy some currency.

The English heritage continued to exercise American political culture. There was, quite naturally, considerable ambivalence about the ideological significance of America's English heritage. Outside the ranks of the Hamiltonian Federalists, modern England was vilified as a wen of corruption and social decay.[110] Historic Englishness was less controversial, though there was considerable debate – and doubt – about the extent to which American law was founded on the historic precedents of the English common law.[111] The Anglo-Saxon era would remain a usable past for an independent America.[112]

During the 1790s the vexing question of Anglicisation was prominent in the agenda of American political, economic and social debate. The Hamiltonian strategy for economic growth seemed to involve replicating the British financial revolution in the new republic. Republican opposition to the Hamiltonian system drew heavily on the anti-Walpolean critique of the Robinarchy which had been such a prominent feature of English political culture in the 1730s. Jeffersonians envisaged modern England as a corrupt commercial nation weighed down by legions of stock-jobbers. The eighteenth-century British fiscal-military state was a leech which had drained the vital spirit of liberty out of the formerly vigorous English nation. England was now experiencing the rapid onset of national decrepitude. Jeffersonians revived the English politics of nostalgia which contributed to an agrarian ideology which was, ironically, Anglophobic in its anxiety to avoid the fate of contemporary English society. Moreover, among Jeffersonian republicans, the tradition of Fran-

---

[108] Murrin, 'Roof without walls'.
[109] McDonald, *Novus ordo seclorum*, ch. 2.
[110] D. McCoy, *The elusive republic* (1980: New York, 1982).
[111] B. Mann, 'Legal reform and the revolution', in Greene and Pole, *Blackwell encyclopedia of the American revolution*, pp. 438–9; Jefferson to Randolph, 18 August 1799, in *The portable Thomas Jefferson* (ed. M. Peterson, 1975: Harmondsworth, 1977), pp. 479–82.
[112] D. W. Howe, *The political culture of the American Whigs* (Chicago, 1979), p. 39; Kliger, *Goths*, pp. 106–10; Kliger, 'Emerson and the usable Anglo-Saxon past', *JHI* 16 (1955), 476–93; T. F. Gossett, *Race: the history of an idea in America* (Dallas, 1963), ch. 5.

cophilia, which dated back to the crucial support received from the French monarchy during the War of Independence, was enhanced by the advent of the French Revolution. Yet this Jeffersonian compound of Francophilia, a critique of English debilitation and an anxiety lest the United States become corrupted by an imitation of English models continued to coexist with Anglo-Saxonism. Indeed the myth of Anglo-Saxon simplicity, both social and institutional, complemented the Jeffersonian ideals of agrarianism and minimal government.[113]

Jefferson himself remained a radical whig Saxonist long after the winning of independence. Merrill Peterson has noted that, 'even after the ultimate appeal to nature in 1776, the shadow of the English heritage, hovered over Jefferson's mind'.[114] According to Craig Walton, English whig historiography supplied the 'historical precedent for republicanism and for popular sovereignty'.[115] Jefferson was delighted by the appearance in 1796 of John Baxter's *A new and impartial history of England* which was essentially Hume's text with the offending tory (as it seemed to Jefferson) passages removed. Jefferson praised Baxter's work as 'Hume's History republicanized'.[116] Even towards the end of his life Jefferson continued to be exercised by the central debates of English whig historiography. Writing in 1824 to the English Saxonist radical Major John Cartwright, Jefferson remained obsessed with his Saxonist interpretation of English history and with Hume's critique of whig historiography. Hume, 'the great apostle of toryism' was denounced as an apologist for Norman usurpation. Jefferson remained committed to a vivid ethnic interpretation of the course of English constitutional history: 'It has ever appeared to me, that the difference between the whig and the tory of England is, that the whig deduces his rights from the Anglo-Saxon source, and the tory from the Norman.'[117] It was not simply that Jefferson remained a radical whig in his politics: it was also an ethnic allegiance to Saxonism. Jefferson had long studied Anglo-Saxon philology, probably from the 1760s, yet as vice-president of the new independent nation in the late 1790s he still found time to compose an essay on Anglo-Saxon grammar. Moreover, thanks to Jefferson's inspiration and pressure, the University of Virginia included Anglo-Saxon in its curriculum when it opened in 1825.[118] He

---

[113] L. Banning, *The Jeffersonian persuasion* (Ithaca and London, 1978).

[114] Peterson, *Jefferson and the new nation*, p. 57.

[115] C. Walton, 'Hume and Jefferson on the uses of history', in D. W. Livingston and J. T. King (eds.), *Hume: a re-evaluation* (New York, 1976), p. 390.

[116] Colbourn, 'Jefferson's use of the past', 69; Walton, 'Hume and Jefferson', 389–93; Wilson, 'Jefferson vs. Hume', 65–8.

[117] Jefferson to John Cartwright, 5 June 1824, in *The portable Thomas Jefferson*, pp. 577–82; Pole, *Political representation*, p. 438.

[118] Hauer, 'Jefferson and the Anglo-Saxon language', 880, 883, 891; Wilson, 'Jefferson vs. Hume', 57.

did not intend Old English language study to be narrowly philological in its influence, but to be of wider social significance, in particular for an understanding of the American legal heritage. Jefferson remained convinced of the importance of a full knowledge of the Anglo-Saxon heritage to the formation of the American republican citizen.

Saxonism played an even more central role in the political thought of James Wilson, who was, after James Madison, the most sophisticated and influential political philosopher among the ranks of America's founding fathers. It was Wilson who solved the problem of locating sovereignty in the system of separated executive, legislative and judicial branches in the new American Constitution, by positing the subordination of the machinery of government to the ultimate, though notional, authority of the American people.[119] Thus Wilson was in a sense the creator of a full-fledged doctrine of American democratic nationalism. Yet he did not understand the founding generation to be forging American nationhood *de novo*; rather, he conceived American republicanism to be restorative of the ancient Anglo-Saxon constitution. Throughout his 'Lectures on law', delivered at the College of Philadelphia in 1790–1, Wilson took pride in the ways in which both the United States and the Commonwealth of Pennsylvania had in their constitutions restored fundamental elements of Anglo-Saxon law and government, which had been lost or corrupted in the mother country. In his own special sphere of jurisprudence, Wilson proclaimed: 'The common law, as now received in America, bears, in its principles, and in many of its more minute particulars, a stronger and fairer resemblance to the common law as it was improved under the Saxon, than to that law, as it was disfigured under the Norman government.'[120]

Wilson viewed the spirit of American republicanism as a direct renewal of Anglo-Saxon principles, a Saxonist phoenix arising from the ashes of the English libertarian tradition, not as a modern invention: according to Wilson under the early Anglo-Saxons there had been no hereditary offices and dignities, only an open meritocratic system of office-holding in which respect was paid to the office rather than to persons. Even the apparently novel machinery of the federal constitution had a Gothicist pedigree. Wilson perceived the Saxon heptarchy as a confederacy, and discovered the same forms among the ancient Germanic peoples described by Tacitus, such as the Suevi.[121] Indeed, the principle of confederacy was part of the 'genius' of the Germanic stock. Wilson had reimagined himself, an

---

[119] Wood, *Creation of the American republic*, pp. 530–1.
[120] James Wilson, 'Lectures on law delivered in the College of Philadelphia' (1790–1), in *The works of James Wilson* (ed. R. G. McCloskey, 2 vols., Cambridge, MA, 1967), I, pp. 348, 420.   [121] *Ibid.*, I, pp. 252–3, 433–4; II, p. 576.

independent American, as a political heir of the Anglo-Saxons, and the new American republic as a Gothic community – though he himself was born in Scotland,[122] a nation which until the early eighteenth century had enjoyed a predominantly Gaelic identity.

The Scottish Enlightenment and the rediscovery of a Gothic North Britain

A mild form of Gothicism was a vestigial presence in the political culture of early modern Scotland, largely confined to the sphere of feudal juris-prudence. Traditionally, Scottish identity found expression in the much-vaunted continuity of Scotland's monarchy back to the ancient Gaelic kingdom of Dalriada in the west Highlands.[123] However, from the middle of the eighteenth century the Scottish political nation rejected the ancient constitutional myth of an elective monarchy in its Gaelic past, and in its stead Scots adopted a Gothicised identity. By this, I mean that Scots recognised the ancient Celtic origins of their nation, but acknowledged that Scotland's historic institutional forms were largely accounted for by the reception of feudal influences during the middle ages. In particular, the new sociological whig historians of the Scottish Enlightenment em-phasised the discontinuity in Scotland's history between its primitive Celtic antiquity, and the Gothicisation of Scottish manners, institutions and laws which had occurred during the eleventh and twelfth centuries.

In the later middle ages there had been some appreciation of the non-Celtic dimension of Scottish nationhood, but it had never been adopted as a central feature of the nation's public identity. From the fourteenth century Scottish Lowland commentators had begun to distin-guish between the 'Teutons' of Lowland Scotland, and the Gaels of the Highlands, most famously in a section of John of Fordun's chronicle.[124] Nevertheless, the ideological imperatives of the continuing struggle to fend off English claims to suzerainty over Scotland enjoined adherence to a Gaelic origin myth. The early modern period witnessed the ultimate embellishment of Scotland's Gaelic identity in the polished Latinity of George Buchanan's *Rerum Scoticarum historia* (1582). Buchanan's achievement clipped some of the more outrageous elements from the national origin myth, but ensured the continued vitality of the central thesis until the eighteenth century.[125] The only major proponent of a Gothic alternative to Scotland's Gaelic identity before the Revolution of

---

[122] Colbourn, *Lamp of experience*, p. 119.   [123] See above, ch. 6.
[124] John of Fordun, *Chronica gentis Scotorum* (ed. W. F. Skene, Edinburgh, 1871, with companion transln, 1872), ch. 9.
[125] C. Kidd, *Subverting Scotland's past* (Cambridge, 1993), chs. 2–5.

1689 was the feudal jurist Thomas Craig of Riccarton. Craig's *Ius feudale*, compiled in the early seventeenth century, but first published in 1655, was the seminal text of a tradition of Scottish feudal jurisprudence which was implicitly Gothicist. Craig's treatment of Scottish institutions side-stepped the ancient constitution of Dalriada, as if to suggest that the nation's vague Celtic myth of origins had little to say about the practical-ities of early modern Scottish law and administration. By contrast, Craig drew attention to the place of Scottish institutions within an evolving pan-European system of feudal law. Nevertheless, there was no overt insistence on this Gothic identity.[126]

The transition from a predominantly Gaelic to a Gothic political ident-ity coincided with the appearance of a powerful wave of anti-feudalist polemic in Scottish political culture inaugurated by the commonwealth-man Andrew Fletcher of Saltoun, who was keenly aware of the decline of Gothic governments throughout Europe and of the ever-present threat to the liberties of the British dominions whether from outright absolutism via standing armies or insidiously via centralisation.[127] Of all the neo-Harringtonians of the late seventeenth century, Fletcher probably preser-ved most of Harrington's original anti-feudalist vision. A qualified Gothi-cist, Fletcher criticised Scottish feudalism and was concerned to establish a fabric of civil and political liberty more attuned to the needs of the commons than had been the case in Gothic Europe. Anti-feudalism and an awareness of the progressive dynamic of European history were to be defining features of the Scottish Gothicist tradition, characteristics which were certainly lacking in American political culture, and peripheral to the Irish Gothicist vision. However, the real watershed here came only in 1729 with the publication of Innes's *Critical essay*, which demolished the Fergusian regnal lists upon which Scotland's traditional Dalriadic ident-ity depended.[128] The language of the ancient Dalriadic constitution did linger on in political debate, but from the middle of the eighteenth century enlightened Scots literati came to adopt a variant of the Gothic identity which flourished in England. Within a few decades of the Union of 1707 Scots acquired the language of English Gothicist constitutional-ism. Scots pamphleteers quickly picked up the grammar – unfamiliar to a nation whose parliamentary institutions had been unicameral – of triadic mixed constitutionalism.[129]

Moreover, in the middle of the eighteenth century pioneering Scottish

---

[126] Thomas Craig, *Ius feudale* (ed. and trans. J. A. Clyde, 2 vols., Edinburgh and London, 1934), I, pp. 49–70.

[127] Fletcher, *A discourse of government with relation to militias*, in *Andrew Fletcher: political works* (ed. J. Robertson, Cambridge, 1997), p. 3.

[128] See above, ch. 6.

[129] C. Kidd, 'North Britishness and the nature of eighteenth-century British patriotisms', *HJ* 39 (1996), 370–2.

jurists such as Lord Kames and Sir John Dalrymple of Cranstoun drew attention to the shared contours of Anglo-Scottish constitutional history since the eleventh century.[130] Kames argued that since the Norman era the common 'Gothic' family characteristics of English and Scottish institutions had accustomed Scots to borrowing many of their laws and customs from south of the border. According to Kames, 'the whole island originally was governed by the same law'. Scottish and English law had 'such resemblance, as to bear a comparison almost in every branch'. There was a basic affinity between Anglo- and Scoto-Norman laws:

When one dives into the antiquities of Scotland and England, it will appear that we borrowed all our laws and customs from the English. No sooner is a statute enacted in England, but, upon the first opportunity, it is introduced into Scotland; so that our oldest statutes are mere copies of theirs. Let the Magna Charta be put into the hands of any Scotsman, without giving its history, and he will have no doubt that he is reading a collection of Scots statutes or regulations.[131]

Dalrymple, a disciple of Montesquieu, approached constitutional and legal history from a similarly Anglo-Scottish perspective in his *Essay towards a general history of feudal property in Great Britain* (1757): 'The progress of these laws, however little attended to, is in both countries uniform and regular, advances by the same steps, goes in almost the same direction, and when the laws separate from each other, there is a degree of similarity in the very separations.'[132] Building on this approach, John Millar treated Scottish history as a subsection of the history of England, noting that Lowland Scotland 'had received a number of Anglo-Saxon inhabitants, who contributed to propagate those constitutions and customs which prevailed in England'.[133] The sceptical antiquarian demythologiser, Sir David Dalrymple, Lord Hailes (1726–92), traced the origins of Scottish feudal institutions and tenures to the demands of Gothic migrants to Scotland for written charters guaranteeing security of possession, adding that feudalism had proved so convenient that the Celtic natives had soon adopted it in place of their traditional tanistry.[134] There was considerable evidence for the existence in the medieval pasts of

---

[130] R. J. Smith, *The Gothic bequest* (Cambridge, 1987), pp. 71–80; Kidd, *Subverting*, pp. 161–2.

[131] Kames, *Essays upon several subjects concerning British antiquities* (Edinburgh, 1747), pp. 4–5. See also Alexander Wight, *An inquiry into the rise and progress of parliament chiefly in Scotland* (Edinburgh, 1784), pp. 18–19, 41.

[132] John Dalrymple, *An essay towards a general history of feudal property in Great Britain* (London, 1757), p. v.

[133] John Millar, *An historical view of the English government from the settlement of the Saxons* (1787: 4 vols., London, 1803), III, pp. 13–14. See Robert Heron, *A new general history of Scotland* (5 vols., Perth and Edinburgh, 1794–9), I, pp. 144–5, for the statement that the Anglo-Saxons were 'the most considerable stock of our ancestors'.

[134] Hailes, *Annals of Scotland from the accession of Malcolm III* (1776, 1779: 3rd edn, 3 vols., Edinburgh, 1819), I, pp. 32–4.

England and Scotland of an era of shared Norman jurisprudence. For example, the ancient Scots law text, the *Regiam Majestatem*, bore marked similarities to the English juridical handbook associated with the twelfth-century English justiciar Ranulph de Glanville.[135] The jurist Walter Ross contended that 'both in principles and practice' the legal systems of Scotland and England 'were originally the same'.[136]

There was an influential version of Scottish legal history, propagated most succinctly by Patrick Swinton, which saw the College of Justice, established in 1532 on a French model, as an alien and absolutist intrusion into the Scots common law.[137] Its significance for this school of interpretation was as a national calamity, not as a matter of patriotic pride; it was, according to Nicholas Phillipson, tantamount to a Scottish 'Norman Yoke'.[138] However, by the same token, the recovery of an indigenous legal tradition from beneath this continental system might best be achieved by assimilation to English legal forms. Not only had England avoided such continental perversions, but it had retained features, such as the civil jury, which had once been the common inheritance of the English and the uncorrupted Scottish legal systems of the medieval era. Thus, attempts to import the English civil jury into Scotland were, largely, initiated by Scots jurists, who saw in this measure of assimilation the restoration of a vital component of Scotland's ancient Gothic constitution.[139] Anglophilia and indigenous patriotism were not necessarily inconsistent. A pertinent example of this is revealed by the response to the proposed Judges' Bill of 1785 which proposed a reduction in the size of the Court of Session. Five of the nine county head courts which opposed this measure called, instead, for the introduction of the English civil jury trial into the Scottish courts.[140] Some Scots argued that civil jury was part of the ancient Gothic constitution of Scotland which had been corrupted during the later middle ages.[141] Others saw the liberating potential of innovation and Anglicisation. Yet, despite the different historical twists, both sides saw the practical benefits involved. Anglicisation held out the

---

[135] Kidd, *Subverting*, pp. 148–50; H. MacQueen, '*Regiam majestatem*, Scots law, and national identity', *SHR* 74 (1995), 19–23.

[136] Walter Ross, *Lectures on the practice of the law of Scotland* (2 vols., Edinburgh, 1792), II, p. 4.

[137] Patrick Swinton, *Considerations concerning a proposal for dividing the court of session into classes or chambers* (Edinburgh, 1789), pp. 11, 15–16; James Boswell, *A letter to the people of Scotland on the alarming attempt to infringe the articles of the union, and introduce a most pernicious innovation by diminishing the number of the Lords of Session* (London, 1785), p. 4.

[138] N. T. Phillipson, *The Scottish whigs and the reform of the Court of Session, 1785–1830* (Stair Society 37, Edinburgh, 1990), p. 91.   [139] Kidd, *Subverting*, p. 164.

[140] N. T. Phillipson, 'Nationalism and ideology', in J. N. Wolfe (ed.), *Government and nationalism in Scotland* (Edinburgh, 1969), pp. 170–5.

[141] Swinton, *Considerations*, p. 10.

prospect of a return to the ancient Gothic freedom once enjoyed by earlier generations of Scots, but which had evaporated with the Romanist corruptions involved in the establishment of the French-inspired College of Justice. If the history of Scots and English laws was essentially a saga of divergence from shared libertarian institutions, then assimilation within a united British state suggested a happy ending, a reconvergence whose basic principles entailed a reinvigoration of Scotland's original Gothic jurisprudence.

It was precisely because they did not invest heavily in such myths of Englishness as the ancient Anglo-Saxon constitution that Scots remained wedded to union. They did not have unrealistic fantasies about the heritage of English Gothic liberties. Rather, they held a very sensible pragmatic view of the benefits of Anglicisation. To eighteenth-century North Britons Anglicisation entailed incorporation within a liberal world of civilised, post-feudal modernity.[142] Scottish Gothicism was both pan-European and Anglo-British in its outlook. The broader pan-European perspective simultaneously helped to moderate enthusiasm for the glories of English constitutionalism and to illuminate the substance of the English libertarian achievement. England's much-vaunted constitution was not a unique expression of the English national character from time immemorial, yet it was none the less exceptional in a Europe where the Gothic monarchies which had once been limited by powerful nobilities tended, in general, to become despotisms rather than to develop, except in one lone case, mixed institutions with a more pronounced democratic component. Indeed, the Scottish Enlightenment was both Gothicist (in its rejection of Scotland's traditional myth of Gaelic origins) and anti-Gothicist in the way it cut the English Gothic myth down to size.[143] Many North Britons, including Robertson, were tireless critics of the oppressions meted on the people by Scotland's turbulent Gothic nobility.[144] For Scotland's intellectual elite the Gothic heritage was both a badge of some pride and a butt of an intense domestic anti-feudalism.

Nevertheless, some Scots radicals did adopt unreservedly the language of Anglo-Saxonism. However, Scottish Anglo-Saxonism was very different from that found in the colonies. It displaced indigenous ethnocentric radicalism from an unchallenged dominance in Scottish radical culture, and may well have defused the explosive potential of the Covenanting tradition to support a Scottish Jacobin nationalism. Moreover, since

[142] Kidd, 'North Britishness'.
[143] E.g. Millar, *English government*, II, pp. 74–80, on the narrowly aristocratic achievement – at first – of Magna Carta.
[144] Kidd, *Subverting*, pp. 165–84; Kidd, 'The ideological significance of Robertson's *History of Scotland*', in S. J. Brown (ed.), *William Robertson and the expansion of empire* (Cambridge, 1997).

Anglo-Saxon liberties were the fortuitous heritage of Scots by incorporating union, rather than their entitlement by descent, its radical significance was muffled: Scots could not, unlike the Americans, argue that throwing off the rule of a corrupt England would restore their prized ancient Saxon liberties. Scots radicals too had absorbed the rhetoric of anti-feudalist propaganda directed specifically at Scotland's native noble caste. Thus Saxonism and anti-feudalism coexisted in Scottish radical culture without inciting widespread demands for national liberation from England's Norman Yoke.[145]

Outside the ranks of the radical movement, Scots were not taken in by the myth of an Anglo-Saxon golden age. For the historians of the Scottish Enlightenment, authentic civil liberty was part of the tissue of modernity, a beneficent side effect of the general European processes of civilisation and refinement. The English were right to take pride in their heritage of Anglo-Saxon constitutionalism, but were warned not to mistake limitations on monarchical government for personal freedom and security of property which prevailed within a defeudalised society.[146]

Scottish Gothicism was different from both the Anglo-Irish and American versions in its intellectual origins. In Scotland Gothicism was very much a product of the debunking of an earlier chauvinistic myth. As a result there were in-built sceptical, sociological and cosmopolitan dimensions to Scotland's Gothic identity. Scotland did not have a deep-rooted Gothic identity; to some extent this explains why Scottish Gothicism was not deployed, as in Ireland and America, in defence of threatened particularisms. The lukewarm Gothicism of the Scottish Enlightenment was founded on the notion that Scots had borrowed – rather than inherited – Gothic manners and institutional forms.[147]

These case studies illuminate the artifice and contingency which lurk behind supposedly primordial and natural identities. The language of Gothic liberty took different forms throughout the eighteenth-century British world. Sometimes it acted to unite the empire, at others to dissolve allegiance. In general, Gothicism was a crucial bulwark of British integration. Hanoverian loyalism was complicated by the problem of Hanover itself, a dynastic possession whose defence was not in the British national interest. Moreover, until the personal tribulations of George III in 1788, Hanoverian dynasticism lacked emotional appeal.[148] Frayed by confes-

---

[145] J. Brims, 'The Scottish "Jacobins", Scottish nationalism and the British union', in R. A. Mason (ed.), *Scotland and England 1286–1815* (Edinburgh, 1987).

[146] Kidd, *Subverting*, ch. 9.   [147] Kidd, 'North Britishness', 382.

[148] L. Colley, 'The apotheosis of George III: loyalty, royalty and the British nation 1760–1820', *P+P* 102 (1984), 94–129.

sional differences, the British Protestant cause operated less successfully as a positive rallying cry than as a vehicle for anti-Catholic prejudice.[149] To a greater extent than Hanoverian loyalism or anti-Catholicism, Gothicist rhetoric had the potential to create an emotive and fulfilling identification with an imagined community of Britons. It combined the vividness of an ancient ethnic and historical heritage with a direct appeal to self-interest: the practical benefits conferred by Gothic descent or incorporation included freedom, democracy, the rule of law and limitations on the ability of the state to encroach on the property of the subject without his consent.

Moreover, the adaptability of Gothicism enabled Scottish and Anglo-Irish historians to enrich the formation of English identity. The fertility and durability of the English whig tradition depended on its remaining permeable. Scottish intellectual influences merging with the modern whiggery of the Walpolean historians fostered the rise of a comprehensive evolutionary tradition largely resistant to deconstruction. The Scottish Enlightenment reinvigorated English Gothicism in its own image. The modified Gothicism of the Scottish Enlightenment accorded with the dominant trend in English whig historiography of the middle of the eighteenth century, which led away from a prescriptive ancient constitutionalism towards an evolutionary account of the consolidation of English liberties culminating in the Glorious Revolution of 1688.[150] In the non-radical mainstream of British political culture Scots and English historians together reconstructed a stronger whig tradition which rejected some of the excesses of Gothicism.[151]

Each provincial community imparted a different spin to the ethnic bias of the British Gothicist tradition. The colonial Americans were almost exclusively Saxonist in their identity; the Anglo-Irish understandably put great stress on the Norman component of their political heritage; while, outside the radical fringes of Scottish culture, North Britons had little enthusiasm for an explicitly ethnic Saxonism, preferring instead to focus on the institutional achievements of the Scoto-Norman era and the recent recovery of this shared British heritage. Of course, these differences sprang in part from the particular constitutional and political relationships of the province to the mother country.

However, the fundamental difference may stem from attitudes to feudalism. Was the feudal law a legitimate part of the Gothic libertarian

---

[149] L. Colley, *Britons: forging the nation 1707–1837* (New Haven and London, 1992).
[150] I. Kramnick, 'Augustan politics and English historiography: the debate on the English past, 1730–1735', *H+T* 6 (1967), 33–56.
[151] J. G. A. Pocock, 'The varieties of whiggism from exclusion to reform', in Pocock, *Virtue, commerce and history* (Cambridge, 1985).

heritage? In the Scottish tradition, feudalism was a fundamental part of the liberation process, but to many American commentators it was by definition antithetical to liberty. The modern whiggism of the middle and late eighteenth century comprehended the importance of the evolution of the Gothic system away from strict feudalism and the wider social developments which mitigated and alleviated restrictions on civil liberty. By contrast, in the American colonies as well as in English radical circles, the ancient Gothic constitution was prized in itself. In Britain feudalism was regarded as part of the process of social evolution towards a better form of civil liberty as it modified in response to new socioeconomic conditions, most notably the rise of towns and commerce. The most valued liberty was post-feudal. In America the most valued form of liberty was pre-feudal, and feudalism was regarded as an unmitigated evil which had corrupted a Saxon golden age.

Anglophobia was the downside of a culture of high expectations associated with the Gothic heritage, which, except in Scotland, tended to end in disappointment and disenchantment. Gothicism fuelled discontent with the mundane realities and compromises of government finance and trading regulations. The practicalities of empire-building could not live up to the Gothic fantasy of an Englishman's freedoms. A blurring of natural rights with the historic privileges enjoyed by the Saxon peoples suggested that the rights of Englishmen were, in a sense, natural rights. Herein lay the force of Englishness – an identity both ethnic and universal. Yet the obverse of this was an Englishness easily reducible to natural rights, and, in this form, capable of sustaining a movement for self-determination.

11   Conclusion

To be misunderstood – at least in part – is the inevitable fate of all
authors, a prospect which looms very large in the present case. This
project has *not* been about the importance of ethnic identity in the
discourse of the British world during the seventeenth and eighteenth
centuries: rather, it has involved an attempt to demonstrate its secondary
place in political argument. Our real subjects have been the mainstays of
the early modern world view – respect for the authority of the Bible, one's
confession and the established institutions of church and state. These
have been approached obliquely through the ways in which the inescapable, but ill-defined, facts of 'ethnicity' were shaped by the gravitational
pull of these first-order determinants of public debate.

While ethnic consciousness played a relatively minor role in politics,
pedigrees – of families, peoples, nations, institutions, church practices
and doctrines – clearly mattered a great deal. Furthermore, given the
narrow confines of a 6,000–year-old world, it was far from impossible to
trace such lineages back to their ultimate origin, though few had the
assurance of the Scots antiquary Sir Thomas Urquhart of Cromarty who
traced his family line back to Adam 'surnamed the protoplast'.[1] There is,
however, a serious point here: provenance was the keystone of legitimacy,
whether Biblical, confessional or institutional. As we have seen, this
applied equally to the roots of racial diversity, which had to be accommodated to Biblical monogenesis; to the origins of 'ethnic' idolatry which
had to be explained in such a way as not to challenge the unique authority
of Christian revelation; to the rise of differing Christian confessions
whose legitimacy was determined by conformity to Scripture, to the best
and purest antiquity and – in some cases – to the original polity of the
national church in question; and to the beginnings of states and their
prescriptive 'ancient constitutions'. Lineage was inextricably interwoven into the various discourses of legitimacy which dominated the

[1] Thomas Urquhart, *Pantochronochanon* (1652), in Urquhart, *Works* (Maitland Club, Glasgow, 1834), p. 155. Cf. G. H. Jenkins, *The foundations of modern Wales, 1642–1780* (1987:
Oxford, 1993), pp. 240–1.

tradition-bound world of the British *ancien régime*.[2]

Nevertheless, it is far from easy to tease out unambiguous conclusions about the precise status of 'ethnicity' in this milieu. On the other hand, I have tried to highlight the very ambiguities which surround the uses of ethnic identity in various sorts of argument. Here, we see clearly how historical contexts expose the limitations of the naked ahistorical models proposed by social scientists. Boundary relationships and binary oppositions take us only so far in understanding ethnic identities; but we should not forget the fabric of inherited stuff out of which particular ethnic histories were clothed. Mythmakers fashioned ethnic descents out of the jumble of the available historical materials. These were not the arbitrary products of free association. Rather there was a subtle interplay of accepted history, political necessity and ideological resourcefulness. The past – and distant antiquity in particular – was supple, but could be massaged only within the limits of historical plausibility. Having stated this caveat, however, I believe that ethnic ficticity was an important adjunct of the politics of legitimacy throughout the early modern period. Just as antiquarians milked the past to justify the present, subordinating historiography to ideological necessity, so they peopled their usable pasts with equally usable ethnic groups. Far from being a rigorously entailed inheritance, an ethnic origin myth had to be calibrated against other ideological priorities.

The familiar staples of early modern political discourse – ancient constitutions, conquest theory, regnal status within composite states and ecclesiastical polity – exerted an enormous influence on the expression of identity. Thus, although ethnic identities were not absent from the early modern world, the form they took rendered them vulnerable to colonisation by other ideological types, the most common parasites being arguments for the prescriptive legitimacy of institutions. Hence, 'regnalism', a term used by the medievalist Susan Reynolds, seems more appropriate as a description of pre-modern national identities than 'ethnocentrism'. After all, the focus of early modern political discourse was on the institutions of the *regnum*, not upon the 'ethnie'.[3]

Despite my reservations about advancing any tight definition of ethnicity – which would, I fear, be overly reductive – certain patterns do emerge from this study. Most obviously, the correspondence between ethnicity

---

[2] J. C. D. Clark, *English society 1688–1832* (Cambridge, 1985); S. Connolly, *Religion, law, and power: the making of Protestant Ireland 1660–1760* (1992: Oxford pbk, 1995); C. Leighton, *Catholicism in a Protestant kingdom* (Houndmills, 1994).

[3] S. Reynolds, *Kingdoms and communities in western Europe 900–1300* (1984: Oxford, 1986), ch. 8, 'The community of the realm', esp. pp. 252 n., 254. Ethnicity was of course a dimension of regnalism: see Reynolds, 'Medieval *origines gentium* and the community of the realm', *History* 68 (1983), 375–90, for the part played by myths of communal descent in cementing regnal solidarity among hybrid populations.

and nationhood was far from straightforward. Take the case of Gothicism which, as well as contributing towards the libertarian self-image of the English, provided a counterweight to Francophobia, reinforced British integration and also helped to heighten an awareness among colonial patriots of exclusion from their inherited rights as Englishmen. Alternatively, consider the Irish Protestant nation who identified themselves not only with two distinct waves of colonisation, the Old English in the twelfth century and the New English in the sixteenth and seventeenth, but also exploited the ancient Gaelic past and even the history of the pre-Milesian Fir-Bolg; on occasions, they also identified themselves as the English nation in Ireland.

We have also gained some insight into the different – but similarly chequered – relationship between ethnicity and race. Here the historical evidence failed to support current preoccupations of scholars in a variety of disciplines with the issue of 'otherness'.[4] First and foremost, racial, linguistic and cultural diversity presented a series of theological problems. How could one account for such a range of differences from a common origin within the orthodox timespan of roughly 6,000 years, and without placing too much explanatory strain on the curse of Ham or the confusion of languages at Babel? Beneath the superficial variety of mankind early modern literati sought a hypothesised and Biblically authorised unity.

Westerners did, as critics have alleged, construct an exotic image of the Orient, which tended to emphasise its noxious, alien features, as in the cliché of 'oriental despotism'. However, as we have seen, Britons did not view the East simply as a scene of otherness, but also manufactured it in the image of Christian Europe and its divisions. The disservice done to Asian civilisations lay not in an uncomprehending rejection of their alien features, but in an all-too-confident assumption of an underlying familiarity, whether derived from Platonic notions of the *prisca theologia*, euhemerist-diffusionism or the twofold philosophy. The quest for Noachic origins, concealed monotheism and encoded Trinitarianism hampered appreciation of the authenticity and genuine distinctiveness of non-Judaeo-Christian cultures.[5] India, in particular, was seen by several eighteenth-century British scholars as a civilisation of immense richness in whose antiquities and Hindu theology decisive evidence might be found for the underlying unity of mankind and the dispersal of the patriarchal religion by the descendants of Noah.[6] Nor was it surprising, given the belief that northern Eurasia had been peopled by the stock of Japhet, to

---

[4] E.g. E. Said, *Orientalism* (1978: Harmondsworth, 1985); M. Chapman, *The Celts: the construction of a myth* (Houndmills, 1992).   [5] See above, chs. 2–3.

[6] See above, ch. 3. For the traditional early modern line that wisdom and knowledge had their origins in the East, see J. Levine, 'Deists and Anglicans: the ancient wisdom and the idea of progress', in R. Lund (ed.), *The margins of orthodoxy* (Cambridge, 1995), pp. 219–20.

find common features between the manners and customs of the Goths and the Tartars.[7] Even Islam, viewed as an imposture by the orthodox, nevertheless had its champions among radical proponents of a unitarian natural religion,[8] and fared little worse than Roman Catholicism in a Protestant demonology which associated the latter's rites with pagan superstition and its hagiolatry with polytheism.[9]

The undoubted practice – and justification – of imperialism, white colonialism, racial subordination, cultural extirpation and enslavement should not obscure the logic of ethnic theology.[10] The orthodox scholarly elites of the early modern British world did not think in essentialist terms of innate ethnic *difference*, but historically in terms of processes of *differentiation* from a common stock. History explained – and diminished – such variations. Exposure to certain climates over a long period had, for

---

[7] See above, chs. 2–3, 9. This idea was still respectable in 1792 when Sir William Jones delivered his ninth anniversary discourse to the Asiatick Society in Calcutta, 'On the origin and families of nations', in Jones, *Discourses delivered at the Asiatick Society 1785–1792* (reprint, with intro. by R. Harris, London, 1993), pp. 194, 201.

[8] See P. Harrison, *'Religion' and the religions in the English Enlightenment* (Cambridge, 1990), pp. 9, 111, 166–7, 174, for the construction of 'other' religions through the 'projection of Christian disunity onto the world'; J. Champion, *The pillars of priestcraft shaken* (Cambridge, 1992), ch. 4; R. Porter, *Gibbon* (London, 1988), pp. 130–1.

[9] For the critique of 'pagano-papism', see Harrison, *'Religion' and the religions*, pp. 9, 49, 110, 144–6; M. T. Hodgen, *Early anthropology in the sixteenth and seventeenth centuries* (Philadelphia, 1964), pp. 328–9. For an anti-Christian Islam, but an identification of the papacy as the real Antichrist, see A. Milton, *Catholic and Reformed: the Roman and Protestant churches in English Protestant thought 1600–1640* (Cambridge, 1995), pp. 114–15.

[10] I endorse the position outlined by B. Braude, 'The sons of Noah and the construction of ethnic and geographical identities in the medieval and early modern periods', *WMQ* 3rd ser. 54 (1997), 104–5: 'it should be acknowledged that belief in common Noachic descent gave no guarantee of human compassion, let alone mere indifferent acceptance. On the contrary, the treatment of Jews, blacks, and Indians in the early modern world arose despite, not because of, theological acceptance of a shared genealogy. No matter how destructive European behavior was, it would have been even worse had the many conflicting visions of human origins – pre-Adamic, polygenetic, diabolic, or animal ancestry, for example – gained general acceptance.' Braude rightly stresses the 'interconnectedness' of self and other within the Mosaic paradigm. This does not, however, invalidate the argument, found in I. Hannaford, *Race: the history of an idea in the west* (Baltimore, 1996), pp. 133–4, 148, that the curse of Ham and the confusion of Babel also contributed to notions of racial differentiation. Nor is my position inconsistent with the arguments found in A. Hastings, *The construction of nationhood* (Cambridge, 1997), esp. chs. 1 and 8, that (1) Old Testament Israel constituted the principal model of nationhood for medieval and early modern Europe, that (2) Christian conceptions of community, torn between the ideal of Christendom and the paradigm of the chosen people with a special divine mission, appear ambivalent on the subject of universalism by comparison with the Islamic vision of the *umma*, and that (3) the modern nation-state owes a great deal to Biblical culture, especially to the translation of the Scriptures into the vernacular. Nevertheless, notions of differentiation were mediated through Christianity, while Biblical orthodoxy and confessional adherence also relegated ethnicity and nationhood in the scale of collective values.

example, resulted in a measure of racial diversity. Despite unquestioned assumptions of a normative white European dominance, ethnic theology emphasised racial kinship, however distant the degree of cousinage, rather than hierarchy.

Closer to home, there were also questions of institutional legitimacy to be resolved. As we saw above, the strategies of Lowland Scots to extirpate the Gaelic culture of the Highlands did nothing to shake the adherence of Lowland Scots to an ancient Gaelic constitution in church and state. Nor should we forget other points of contact. When educated Englishmen looked across the Channel, they did not see a race of Frenchmen who were slaves by nature, but fellow Goths who had – through the accidents of history and continental geopolitics – lost liberties and institutions broadly similar to those which the English had, by a contrasting chain of contingencies and providences, preserved and enlarged.

These conclusions must remain tentative and provisional. Moreover, historians can never rest complacent with the historicity of their own analytic categories. Beneath the soft argument that 'ethnic identities' were of only second-order importance in the political discourse of the seventeenth and eighteenth centuries, there lurks an – as yet – un-articulated sense that in a world structured around concepts of jurisdiction and allegiance, rank and order, gentility and dependence, dynasty and church, the very notion of 'identity' (as opposed to loyalty, station, degree, honour, connection, orthodoxy and conformity) might itself be anachronistic.[11]

---

[11] See the view that early modern national consciousness was 'overladen with religious and constitutional presuppositions' in O. Ranum, 'Introduction', in Ranum (ed.), *National consciousness, history, and political culture in early modern Europe* (Baltimore and London, 1975), p. 12, and the 'legal and religious conceptual structure' identified in J. C. D. Clark, *The language of liberty 1660–1832* (Cambridge, 1994), p. 46; Hannaford, *Race*, pp. 147–8, 173, 184. For jurisdictional notions of subjecthood, such as the French category of *regnicole*, which preceded the rise of territorial nationality, see P. Sahlins, *Boundaries: the making of France and Spain in the Pyrenees* (Berkeley and Los Angeles, 1989), esp. pp. 28–9, 54–9, 93, 113. For the importance of corporate privileges in the 'retrograde patriotism' of eighteenth-century elites, see Leighton, *Catholicism in a Protestant kingdom*, pp. 26–7.

Index